Development Naivety and Emergent Insecurities in a Monopolised World:
The Politics and Sociology of Development in Contemporary Africa

Edited by
Munyaradzi Mawere

Langaa Research & Publishing CIG
Mankon, Bamenda

Publisher:
Langaa RPCIG
Langaa Research & Publishing Common Initiative Group
P.O. Box 902 Mankon
Bamenda
North West Region
Cameroon
Langaagrp@gmail.com
www.langaa-rpcig.net

Distributed in and outside N. America by African Books Collective
orders@africanbookscollective.com
www.africanbookscollective.com

ISBN-10: 9956-550-98-1

ISBN-13: 978-9956-550-98-2

© Munyaradzi Mawere 2018

Authors' Biography

Munyaradzi Mawere is a Professor in the Simon Muzenda School of Arts, Culture and Heritage Studies at Great Zimbabwe University in Zimbabwe. He holds a Ph. D in Social Anthropology, Master's Degree in Social Anthropology, Master's Degree in Development Studies, Master's Degree in Philosophy and, a B. A (Hons) Degree in Philosophy. Before joining this university, Professor Mawere was a lecturer at the University of Zimbabwe and at Universidade Pedagogica, Mozambique, where he has worked in different capacities as a senior lecturer, assistant research director, postgraduate co-ordinator, and professor. He is an author of more than 50 books and over 230 academic publications with a focus on Africa straddling the following areas: poverty and development, African philosophy, society and culture, democracy, politics of food production, humanitarianism and civil society organisations, urban anthropology, existential anthropology, cultural philosophy, area studies, experimental philosophy, environmental anthropology, society and politics, decoloniality and African studies. Some of his bestselling books are: *Humans, Other Beings and the Environment: Harurwa (Edible stinkbugs) and Environmental Conservation in South-eastern Zimbabwe* (2015); *Theory, Knowledge, Development and Politics: What Role for the Academy in the Sustainability of Africa?* (2016); *Democracy, Good Governance and Development in Africa: A Search for Sustainable Democracy and Development,* (2015); *Culture, Indigenous Knowledge and Development in Africa: Reviving Interconnections for Sustainable Development* (2014); *Myths of Peace and Democracy? Towards Building Pillars of Hope, Unity and Transformation in Africa* (2016); *Harnessing Cultural Capital for Sustainability: A Pan Africanist Perspective* (2015); *Divining the Future of Africa: Healing the Wounds, Restoring Dignity and Fostering Development,* (2014); *African Cultures, Memory and Space: Living the Past Presence in Zimbabwean Heritage* (2014); *Violence, Politics and Conflict Management in Africa: Envisioning Transformation, Peace and Unity in the Twenty-First Century* (2016); *African Philosophy and Thought Systems: A Search for a Culture and Philosophy of Belonging* (2016); *Africa at the Crossroads: Theorising Fundamentalisms in the 21st Century* (2017); *Colonial Heritage, Memory and Sustainability in Africa: Challenges, Opportunities and Prospects*

(2016); *Underdevelopment, Development and the Future of Africa* (2017), and *Theorising Development in Africa: Towards Building an African Framework of Development* (2017); *African Studies in the Academy: The Cornucopia of Theory, Praxis and Transformation in Africa?* (2017); *GMOs, Consumerism and the Global Politics of Biotechnology: Rethinking Food, Bodies and Identities in Africa's 21ˢᵗ Century* (2017); *Human Trafficking and Trauma in the Digital Era: The Ongoing Tragedy of the Trade in Refugees from Eritrea* (2017); *The Political Economy of Poverty, Vulnerability & Disaster Risk Management: Building Bridges of Resilience, Entrepreneurship and Development in Africa's 21ˢᵗ Century* (2018); and *Jostling Between "Mere Talk" and Blame Game? Beyond Africa's Poverty and Underdevelopment Game Talk* (2018).

Nkwazi Mhango is author of *Saa ya Ukombozi, Nyuma ya Pazia, Souls on Sale, Born with Voice, Africa Reunite or Perish, Africa's Best and Worst Presidents: How Imperialism Maintained Venal Regimes in Africa, Psalm of the Oppressed, Perpetual Search, Dependency: Can Africa Still Turn Things Around for the Better?* and *'Is It Global War on Terrorism' or Global War over Terra Africana?: The Ruse Imperial Powers Use to Occupy Africa Militarily for Economic Gains;* member of Writers' Association of Newfoundland and Labrador (WANL) St. John's NL Canada and is an alumnus of Universities of Dar es Salaam (Tanzania) Winnipeg and Manitoba (Canada) majoring in Conflict Resolution and Peace and Conflict Studies and Law. Also, Mhango has contributed many chapters in various academic books.

Fidelis Peter Thomas Duri is a Senior Lecturer of History in the Department of Archaeology, Culture and Heritage, History and Development Studies at Great Zimbabwe University. He is a holder of a PhD in History from the University of the Witwatersrand in Johannesburg, South Africa. He has published a number of books and articles which focus on environmental history, socio-cultural dynamics, subaltern struggles, African border studies, and Zimbabwe's socio-political landscape during the colonial and post-colonial periods. In addition to reviewing a number of scholarly articles, he has also edited books such as *Resilience Amid Adversity: Informal Coping Mechanisms to the Zimbabwean Crisis during the New Millennium* (2016) and *Contested Spaces, Restrictive Mechanisms and Corridors of Opportunity: A Social History of Zimbabwean Borderlands and*

Beyond since the Colonial Period (2017). He is also a member of the editorial boards of international journals which include the *Zimbabwe Journal of Historical Studies* and the *International Journal of Developing Societies.*

Solomon Mutambara is a holder of a PhD in Environmental Science from the University of Botswana. He also holds a Master of Science in Safety Health and Environmental Management from Midlands State University in Zimbabwe, a Master of Science in Human Resources Management from the University of Zimbabwe and a B. A (Hons.) Geography from the Group Buckinghamshire University, United Kingdom as well as a Diploma in Project Management for Development Professionals. He has worked as a Consortium Team Leader for the Enhancing Community Resilience and Sustainability Programme Education/Training from July 2013 – October 2015. Currently, he is a team leader at Care International in the Zimbabwe Resilience Building Fund's ECRAS (Enhancing Community Resilience and Sustainability) project aiming at building the resilient livelihoods for the rural communities, where he is responsible for the overall management in project planning, project implementation, research, monitoring and evaluation, stakeholder coordination, project reporting and staff supervision for the consortium of 3 International Non-Governmental Organisations. His research interest is on livelihoods resilience, sustainable agricultural/rural development, policy and capacity building of development agencies.

Odeigah, Theresa Nfam is a holder of a PhD in History; B.A Degree in History; M.A. (History), and Post Graduate Diploma in Education. She is a lecturer in the Department of History and International Studies at the University of Ilorin, Kwara State, Nigeria. She is an Economic Historian specialising in the Niger Delta Region of Nigeria. She has published widely in scholarly journals in the area of economic history.

Joseph Muroiwa is a Marketing Specialist with CARE International in Zimbabwe under the Zimbabwe Resilience Building Fund (ZRBF) supported Enhancing Community Resilience and Sustainability

(ECRAS) project. His roles and responsibilities involve identifying pro-poor value chains suitable for improving incomes for the marginalised rural communities as well as linking the farmers to inputs and output markets. He holds a Masters Degree in Strategic Management (Chinhoyi University of Technology) and a Bachelors Degree in Agricultural Economics from the University of Zimbabwe. Joseph is currently studying for a Doctor of Philosophy Degree in Agricultural Economics with the University of Fort Hare, South Africa. He has worked in Zimbabwe's agricultural private sector for more than 10 years as an Operations Manager responsible for implementing contract farming arrangements for smallholder farmers.

Andile Mayekiso holds a PhD in Social Anthropology obtained from the University of Cape Town. His thesis title: *'Ukuba yindoda kwelixesha'* ('To be a man in these times'): Fatherhood, marginality and forms of life among young men in Gugulethu, Cape Town. His thesis examines how young, marginalised men in Gugulethu, a poor township in Cape Town, formulate their conceptions of fatherhood and fathering, and understand their roles and involvement with their children. Andile worked as a project manager for a very large cohort study of an intervention in neighbourhoods of Khayelitsha and Mfuleni townships (Cape Town). This large randomized control trial focused on HIV & drug abuse prevention for South African men. Currently, Mayekiso is a lecturer at the University of Johannesburg in the department of Anthropology and Development Studies. He worked closely with researchers from the University of California, Los Angeles (UCLA). In 2008, he joined the Children's Institute of UCT as a researcher to conduct ethnographic fieldwork of infants' born to HIV-positive mothers in Gugulethu Township.

Golden Maunganidze is a holds a Master of Arts Degree in Media and Society Studies from the Midlands State University (MSU) and several midcareer journalism courses from Germany. He is Edward R. Murrow fellow (2011) as well as 2016 Mandela Washington fellow and has won several awards in the past, which include The child reporter of the year from National Journalistic and Media Awards (NJAMA) in 2009 and National Integrity Award from Transparency

International Zimbabwe (TIZ). He has over ten years' experience working in the Zimbabwean media industry. He currently lectures in the Department of English and Media Studies at Great Zimbabwe University (GZU), where he teaches practical journalism courses. Before joining GZU, Maunganidze worked as a journalist and editor for various community newspapers in Masvingo, Zimbabwe.

Joseph Mupinga is currently researching for a PhD in Development Studies. He holds a Master's Degree in Educational Administration, Planning and Policy Studies from the Zimbabwe Open University. He also holds a Postgraduate Diploma in Education and a BSc (Hons) Degree in Politics and Administration from the University of Zimbabwe as well as several development related diplomas and certificates. He is the incumbent Provincial Head for Masvingo Province under the Ministry of Women Affairs, Gender and Community Development since 2006. He directs formulation, implementation, monitoring and monitoring and evaluation of government policies, programmes and projects for women empowerment, gender equality and community development. His research interests are but not limited to poverty, energy studies, women and poverty.

Kilibone Choeni is a lecturer in the Department of African Languages and Literature at Great Zimbabwe University. She is a holder of a Master's Degree in Tshivenda from the University of Venda and a Post-Graduate Diploma in Education from the Great Zimbabwe University. Her research interests are but not limited to culture, literature and onomastics.

Simeon Maravanyika is a holder of a PhD in African Environmental History from the University of Pretoria in South Africa. He is currently a lecturer in the Department of History, Archaeology and Development Studies, Simon Muzenda School of Arts, Culture and Heritage Studies, Great Zimbabwe University. His main research focus is commodity history, aspects natural resources management praxis, climate change and adaptation in Africa and soil conservation on white farms in the colonial period.

Silibaziso Mulea is a Temporary Full-Time lecturer of Tshivenda in the Department of African Languages and Literature at Great Zimbabwe University. She holds a Master's Degree in Tshivenda from the University of Venda as well as a Diploma in Education from United College of Education. She is currently a registered PhD candidate with the University of South Africa. Her research interests include but not limited to culture, Indigenous Knowledge Systems and onomastics.

Henry Chiwaura is currently a PhD Candidate in Culture and Heritage Tourism with the University of KwaZulu-Natal, South Africa. He obtained his MA in Heritage Studies from the University of Zimbabwe. Chiwaura is an incumbent Lecturer in Archaeology, Museums and Heritage Studies at Great Zimbabwe University, Zimbabwe. His research interests include, but not limited to, heritage management, museology and public archaeology.

Last Alfandika is a PhD Candidate in Media Studies at the University of the Witwatersrand, South Africa. His research interests are Media policy; media activism; alternative media; digital media studies and Cultural studies.

Tobias Marevesa is a New Testament lecturer in the Department of Philosophy and Religious Studies, under the Joshua Nkomo School of Arts and Humanities at the Great Zimbabwe University where he teaches New Testament Studies and New Testament Greek. He is pursuing doctoral studies at the University of Pretoria in South Africa. His areas of interest are Bible and politics, Pentecostal expressions in Zimbabwean Christianity, culture, human rights, and gender-based violence. He has also published in the area of Bible and conflict-resolution in the Zimbabwean political landscape. He has attended and presented a number of papers in both regional and international conferences and has published articles in reputable international journals. He is a member of Reading Association of Nigeria (RAN), Association for the Study of Religion in Southern Africa (ASRSA), African Consortium for Law and Religion Studies (ACLARS), and International Consortium for Law and Religion Studies (ICLARS). He is serving as an External Examiner in a few Teachers' Colleges in Zimbabwe.

Prosper Hellen Tlou received her Master of Arts with Bachelor of Arts Honours from the University of Venda (UNIVEN), Bachelor of Arts Degree at Great Zimbabwe University and is teaching Tshivenda language at Great Zimbabwe University. She currently serves as a Tshivenda coordinator in the Department of African languages and literature. Her research interest focuses on linguistics, onomastic and Sociolinguistics

Table of Contents

Chapter 1

The (In)securities and Futures of Development in Africa

Munyaradzi Mawere

"Development without security is like a running away horse"
(Mawere 2018)

Introduction

While there is growing scholarly fascination in Africa about what is emergent in the field of development both in terms of theory and practice, it is hardly noticed that there are emergent insecurities which threaten real development on the continent. These insecurities and threats warrant nothing closer to celebration but pretermit and resistance by the African front to ensure long living development. One may wonder where the emergent insecurities hide if ever there are any.

Though not visible to the "common eye", I note that there are emergent insecurities spawned by those that hide behind the discourses about development theories and models; the emergent insecurities arising from those hiding behind discourses around democracy and liberalism; and emergent insecurities originating from those behind discourses on post-development and postnation [African] state. These emergent insecurities are a truth that need to be unearthed and told to the world.

In spite of increasing number of theories and models on development in Africa, the continent of Africa is yet to see light to ensure "real" development that is both community/people-centred and context-based. This is chiefly because up until today, Africa is failing to promote the knowledge building of local culture, local contemporary concerns and local skills that lay the crucial foundation for the acquisition of a clear development framework that aims to improve people's lives. Worse still, Africa has not seen improved security in all its variations, whether in terms of social security, human security, state security, religious security, political security, cultural security, national security and government security, yet security is critical for any meaningful development. The different forms of insecurity have actually remained steadily growing on a continent that remains threatened by global politics where, as it has been before, Africa continue being threatened by Euro-American dominance and subjugation whims. From trans-Atlantic slave trade through colonialism to contemporary gestures of neocolonialism by the Global North, it is crystal clear that the latter remains determined to rule the world at any cost. For the Global North, there is no need to look beyond its own tenure or to envision any visionary leader of the world besides itself be it in politics or in the field of knowledge. This is why the Global North has never make any provisions for genuine democracy and global leadership renewal in Africa so to speak. Every aspect of global politics, be it in terms of knowledge production, democracy and governance, development and global economic management, or environmental management, remain centred around the Global North, and the Global North alone! This is quite disturbing in a world where democracy is preached in high voices.

Critical questions arise for Africa – in fact for the ordinary African and not the elite Africans most of whom have turned themselves oppressors of their own people – to digest in view of this obtaining situation: "Is it possible for Africa to achieve real development in a world where the Global North dictates the rules of development? Is it possible for Africa to achieve real democracy where democracy is preached to them in high voices and autocracy practiced instead? Is it possible for the world to achieve real diversity in the sphere of development where the Global North demands religious allegiance for its development theories and models without giving room for Africa to plan for itself? How can African contributions to global development and to the study of Africa in its interconnections with the rest of the world be accorded prominence beyond tokenism, especially in a world where the Global North dominates and dictates the pace of development? And, how can Africa stir its own imagination and contribute to the cultural and socio-economic development at a global level?"

In view of the foregoing discussion and questioning, I argue that for a long time now the Global North has demonstrated politics of immaturity and self-conceited egomaniacism where it believes that it alone knows everything and what it believes in (even when it is the most disastrous thing ever as was the case of SAPs) and says is law. Can then the Global North entrusted to keep the lead? I note that a genuine and true leader does not take offence to criticism, alternative ways of knowing or doing things, and diversity, but values all this as an avenue for improvement. This virtue has always lacked in the Global North's leadership chemistry to the extent that all other countries of the world especially those in the Global South such as Africa have never been free from insecurity of whatever scale and name. What is even more worrying is that many of the African leaders have adopted and deployed the very leadership style of the Global North they blame for their woes such that the African ordinary feels all the insecurities as they descend upon them right from the far horizons.

Having exposed the various forms of insecurity that Africa has been subjected to throughout history right from the moment of its contact with the Global North, this chapter and indeed the whole book interrogates the genuineness of development models, theories, technologies, modes of politics, epistemologies, and economics that have been either imposed on Africa by the North or adopted by Africa over the years as a template for development. The chapter as with the book as a whole questions if in the presence of such insecurities Africa can ever achieve any genuine development.

Agency and the quest for human dignity and secure sustainable development

So long emergent insecurities linger around the clock of development, no real development will take place. This seem frightening and intimidatory, but that's the truth every concerned citizen of the world should grapple with. The question that concerned citizens should raise is: How can Africa and the world beyond achieve secure and sustainable development?

To answer this question, there is need to critically and meticulously interrogate and understand the hope and aspirations of people as they negotiate their space in the ongoing process of becoming. At this point, we recognise that all humanity aspire to be recognised as such and never otherwise, and that humanity develop new modes of agency as they progress along the path of becoming. All these are in turn better understood in terms of coloniality and decoloniality. Coloniality as described by Mignolo (2011: 2) is "the underlying logic of the foundation and unfolding of Western civilisation from the Renaissance to today – a logic that was the basis of historical colonialisms". It is the endurance of the effects of slavery, colonialism, racism and apartheid long after the formal overthrow of slavery and the demise of colonialism in the Global South. Coloniality is often contrasted with decoloniality (or decolonialism), which has been described as analytic and practical options confronting and delinking from the colonial matrix of power (or coloniality) (Ibid: xxvii). In this sense, decoloniality has been described by other scholars as "a kind of thinking in radical exteriority" (Vallega 2015: x) in the sense that it questions (or problematises) the histories and dynamics of power emerging from the Global North. It is the resistance and antithesis of coloniality in so far as it is an extension of liberation. It is for this reason that other scholars such as Quijano (2007: 68) understand decoloniality as "a response to the relation of direct, political, social, economic and cultural domination established by Europeans". Decoloniality thus, is both "a political and epistemic project" (Mignolo 2011: xxiv-xxiv) that seeks to undo and reverse the logic of Western civilisation, particularly coloniality and modernity. It seeks to correct and eliminate the misconception that Western modes of thinking are universal. This means that decoloniality is not postcolonialism, which in itself is "the oppositional practice by people of colour, Third World intellectuals or ethnic groups" (Mignolo 2000: 87) which confines itself in the academy. Decoloniality thus moves beyond postcolonialism in so far as it seeks transformation both in the academy and beyond. Neither is decoloniality decolonisation, which in itself is political and historical, marking the end of the period of territorial domination of land in Global South by Europe.

It is important to note that while formal and explicit colonisation ended during the 19th century in the [Latin] Americas and in the 20th century in much of the Global South (and Africa in particular), its successors, particularly globalisation, modernity, and Western imperialism perpetuate inequalities and social discriminations started by colonialism. Racial, ethnic, epistemological, religious, social, and economic inequalities persist. Such centres of power continue lingering in all spheres of the African life – a clear testimony that coloniality has never gone anywhere far and the decolonialism from the 19th century to the present has not done much to reverse the gains and momentum of coloniality. Coloniality therefore did not disappear with decolonisation – the 19th century in Latin America and the 20th century in Africa and Asia. In fact decolonisation did not eliminate coloniality but "merely transformed its outer form" (Quijano & Wallerstein 1992: 550). There is no doubt that the founders and architects of coloniality have always make attempts to usurp or hijack the decolonial project so as to effectively neutralise and toning it down from being a revolutionary philosophy to a reformist philosophy. Attempts have been made by both Europe and America to silence African histories, cultures and philosophies. This realisation calls for the need for what I call "radical decolonialism" or what Mignolo (2011: 52) refers to as a "new humanity" or "social liberation from all power organised as inequality, discrimination, exploitation and domination" (Quijano 2007: 178).

Radical decolonialism means interrogating the remnants of coloniality (globalisation, modernity, genocide, racism, ethnocide, and westernisation), and the objectives and achievements of decoloniality since it started in the 16th century, with a view to improve planetary human relations and achieve planetary justice and peace. It is a spirited search for generative liberation and complete humanisation of both the oppressor and the oppressed. In the sphere of development, radical decolonialism entails interrogating Western models, ways of knowing, ideas and theories of development that have been either explicitly or implicitly imposed on Africa in the [false] name of development and globalisation. Without this interrogation, development in Africa continue hitting a brick wall, bouncing and tumbling without a clear path, logic or framework. This

5

critical interrogation is necessary because any meaningful development should be people-centred. Besides, it should be context-based so that it responds directly to the needs, hopes, and aspirations of the people.

Chapter outline

Chapter 2 by Nkwazi Mhango creatively deploy African philosophy of Maendeleo, particularly the one that focuses on the drive for an individual (or society) to develop himself (or itself) as it revolves around humanity and Ubuntu, to demonstrate how development is not a new concept in contexts such as Africa. More particularly, Mhango uses Maendeleo's philosophy to show how development in Africa should always be people-centred as opposed to the Western model and philosophy of development which follows the top-bottom approach. For Mhango, the people-centred development makes [African] society "better than Western whose application has failed to pull Africa out of Western-defined development". Mhango, thus, urges African developmentalists to ponder over what, how, for whom, and for what end development in Africa is being initiated and practised, when dealing with development of and for the continent.

Fidelis Duri's Chapter 3 critically focuses on the National Youth Service Training Programme, which dates back to the Robert Mugabe era. In particular, Duri looks at the 'security' institution, launched by the ZANU-PF government in 2001, whose graduates have popularly come to be known as 'Green Bombers' – a nickname they received because of "the colour of their military-style uniforms and for their reputation for violence" (Meldrum, 19 February 2003: 1). The argument advanced by Duri is that ZANU-PF 'security' institutions such as the infamous National Youth Service Training Programme constituted "a major source of gross human rights abuses and various insecurities for many Zimbabwean citizens during the period 2001-2009". For Duri, the National Youth Service Training Programme also constituted institutionalisation of violence in the Zimbabwe state as the ZANU-PF institution monopolised political space in a way that either derailed or shattered development of the Zimbabwean society. Duri concludes that the institutionalisation of violence, as has been the case in Zimbabwe since the turn of the millennium is never health for any meaningful development in society.

Chapter 4 by Joseph Muroiwa, Solomon Mutambara and Munyaradzi Mawere deeply dissects into and exposes the insecurities and vulnerabilities rampant in many rural communities of Africa such as Zimbabwe. In particular, the chapter critically examines how value chain approach can be used to help build resilience in a manner that promote [positive] development in Africa's rural communities. The trio's major argument is that pro-poor value chain developmental approaches to resilience building is critical to improving livelihoods for the poor marginalised communities of Africa as they promote active participation in markets while improving people's standards of living. In view of development challenges encountered by marginalised communities in rural Africa, the trio submit that value chain approach is critical to building community resilience and to act as development bridges for rural communities.

In Chapter 5, Tobias Marevesa and Prosper Hellen Tlou prompt a meticulous rethinking of land redistribution, justice and development in Africa. To make their case stronger and more appealing, Marevesa and Tlou make reference to Zimbabwe's redistribution exercise between 1985 and 2017 by way of surveying the successes and failures of the exercise from the rare perspective of religion and culture. While acknowledging the fact that land redistribution in Africa and Zimbabwe in particular have been examined from different perspectives, Marevesa and Tlou, offer a unique contribution to the land redistribution exercise in Zimbabwe – from a religious and cultural heritage perspective. On that note, Marevesa and Tlou advance the argument that "although the land redistribution process in Zimbabwe had its own shortfalls, it generally brought a lot of positive development in the country where many Zimbabweans have become successful commercial farmers". The chapter thus, offers a fresh perspective to the often hotly debated land redistribution programme in Zimbabwe. It concludes that even though land redistribution process brought in some positives on the development front of the indigenous people of

Zimbabwe, there was tremendous injustice on the part of traditional leadership (such as the herdsmen and chiefs), some of who were 'badly' treated in the resettlement and land redistribution process thereby chocking community development.

Chapter 6 by Andile Mayekiso and Munyaradzi Mawere uses the case study of Cape Town (in South Africa) to explore the security issues and ethical dilemmas generally encountered by male researchers as they gather data for their researches from female participants in the field of sexuality and sensitive health matters such as experiences of giving birth and struggles of living with HIV in highly stigmatised communities. Mayekiso and Mawere's chapter thus, exposes the ethical dilemmas generally encountered during fieldwork, with a view to provide insights on how such dilemmas can be professionally and ethically handled. The chapter concludes that experiences involving men studying women participants are always complex and multifarious especially when one has to research with women in their houses with their male partners absent, but all the same the issues that arise should always be handled carefully and with the highest degrees of professionalism and ethics possible.

In Chapter 7, Last Alfandika draws our attention to often neglected insecurities surrounding media policy in Zimbabwe. More specifically, Alfandika critically makes an appraisal of the media policy and regulation trajectory right from the inception of print and broadcasting media in Rhodesia (colonial Zimbabwe) to the present day Zimbabwe. He argues that the contextual background and the historical emergence and development of media policy right from the built up of media and security laws continue to characterise the media sphere even in the post-colonial Zimbabwe. This is evidenced by the promulgation of inconsistent and ambivalent media and security laws in post-colonial Zimbabwe such as the Broadcasting Service Act (BSA) (2000), Access to Information and Privacy Protection Act (AIPPA) (2002), Public Order and Security Act (POSA) (2002) and Interception of Communications Act (ICA) (2007). For Alfandika, this obtaining situation poses security threats to both the media practitioners and the development of the ordinary citizens in general.

Gloden Maunganidze's Chapter 8 reflects on the laws that govern the operations of social media and cyber communications in

Zimbabwe. On this note, the chapter takes a deep analysis of both the contemporary laws as well as proposed laws that are likely going to be part of Zimbabwe's legislations in the near future. Maunganidze notes that although all pieces of legislations have dark sides, it is apparent that some of the laws passed by governments in Africa are crafted to quash descending voices that criticise sitting governments. To illustrate this point, Maunganidze makes reference to the period in Zimbabwe since 2000, which saw the government of Zimbabwe coming with draconian laws such as the Information and Protection of Privacy Act (AIPPA), Interception of Communications Act (ICA), Censorship and Entertainment Controls Act (CECA), and Criminal Law Codification Reform Act, among others. For Maunganidze, it is because of the insecurities generated by these laws that civic society in Zimbabwe especially organisations such as Media Institute of Southern Africa (MISA- Zimbabwe), Voluntary Media Council of Zimbabwe (VMCZ) and the Zimbabwe Union of Journalists (ZUJ) 'have been on record accusing the Zimbabwean government for passing draconian media laws that restrict the free flow of information'.

In Chapter 9, Henry Chiwaura and Munyaradzi Mawere makes a critical appraisal of the regulatory framework for aquaculture. As such, the chapter explores, exposes and underlines deficiencies rampant in Zimbabwe's aquaculture legislative and policy issues. The duo argue that these legislative inefficiencies should be addressed in a manner that promote nuanced understanding of environmentalities and ontologies, especially of relationships, social interconnectedness and interdependence between social 'actors' in the cosmos if Zimbabwe is to attain sanity and an effective legal and policy framework for aquaculture industry.

Chapter 10 by Solomon Mutambara audaciously grapples with extractive engagement of key value chain actors, particularly how these always act as a major barrier to resilient livelihoods and economic growth for farmers in rural Zimbabwe. On this note, Mutambara exposes different ways in which rural farmers are trapped in the chasms of vulnerability by different value chain players including the government, wholesalers, retailers, formal traders, and the private sector. In view of these revelations, Mutambara advances the need for rural farmers to promote positive attitude towards livelihood strategies that can potentially build resilience and bridges of development.

In Chapter 11, Odeigah Theresa Nfam and Munyaradzi Mawere reflectively look at the relationship obtaining between herdsmen and farmers in the Niger Delta Region of Nigeria and how that relationship has degenerated to become a security threat to the whole region. Given that the problems in the Niger Delta Region are historical, the duo argue that the conflicts, the resulting violence and criminality that have always been associated with the relationship between herdsmen, farmers and the generality of the people of the Niger Delta Region are security problems that require a historic-structural and multidisciplinary approaches to disentangle and resolve. The duo conclude that as long as the Nigerian government ignores the historic-structural and multidisciplinary approaches in its bid to resolve the problems in the region, these problems will remain perennial and a threat to both human security and development of the entire region.

Chapter 12 by Simeon Maravanyika interrogates 'the establishment of an ambitious agricultural and resource conservation programme in the colony's settler farming districts, then termed the "Intensive Conservation Areas" (ICAs) Programme' from as early as the 1940s. As Maravanyika argues, the programme proved to be a major driving force of the colonial agricultural sector, and for that major reason, the majority of ICAs continued to function after Zimbabwe's attainment of independence, without much government support. What is worrying for Maravanyika is that the story of colonial conservation on settler farms as well as the legacy of ICAs is often not given prominence by economic historians, yet there is a lot – negatives and positives – that can be learnt from these. On this note, Maravanyika explicates the success of settler agriculture in the colony and why the then Southern Rhodesia's farmers largely succeeded while their counterparts in colonial Zambia and Malawi were only relatively successful. As such, Maravanyika concludes that "the literature on the colonial settler agricultural sector, which is timely in an era where Zimbabwe's new post-Mugabe government has fingered the agricultural sector as a low-hanging fruit that can act as a springboard for catapulting the country out of its decades-long economic malaise". Thus, lessons and insights should be drawn from the past to help nurture the present and project the future.

Joseph Mupinga and Munyaradzi Mawere's Chapter 13 grapples with the interplay between the marginalised (such as women), energy poverty and development as initiated by the global elites. For review of literature and other such findings, the chapter demonstrates how the provision of energy services to rural population, and rural women in particular, is a prerequisite for sustained socio-economic growth and development intervention for people living in poverty rural Africa. Thus, besides unveiling development naivety and emergent insecurities surrounding the marginalised in rural Africa, Mupinga and Mawere conclude that as long as energy poverty and development insecurities continue lingering around the so-called marginalised, economic growth and development in general will remain a tantalising reality to many people living in the rural communities.

In Chapter 14, Fidelis Duri uses Zimbabwe's situation during Robert Mugabe's rule, particularly from 2000, to illustrate how statist machinations are often unsustainable and monocultural in nature to the extent that they stifle economic diversity and expose the ordinary people to socio-economic insecurity. He argues that "elitist mechanisms to spur economic development through a dissonant and contradictory combination of populism, centralisation/statism and coercion, often fail to achieve the desired results for reasons that seem very apparent". For him, the deployment of force, for instance, is never an effective instrument to motivate people to work and produce. For this reason, Duri submits that the Zimbabwean state's "centralisation of production and marketing processes is a disastrous top-to-bottom approach" that mirrors Western-biased approaches imposed directly or otherwise in many African societies. That top-to-bottom approach, for Duri, demotivates producers as it kills off the spirit of competition.

The last and 15th Chapter by Kilibone Choeni, Silibaziso Mulea and Munyaradzi Mawere tackles head-on the sensitive issue of indigenous contraceptives. Making reference to the Vhavenda culture in Zimbabwe and other such African communities, the trio argue that "the pejorative labelling of traditional family planning methods of the indigenous people of Africa as a result of globalisation and westernisation is not only nefarious but a crime against the people of Africa and the Vhavenda in particular". Basing from their findings from the field, Choeni, Mulea and Mawere argue that these traditional family planning methods are effective, safe, cost effective and have passed the test of time. As such, there is need for serious reconsideration, restoration and effective use of traditional family planning methods on the premise that the practices are not only indigenous but less costly, mostly safe to use and promote human development.

This is a must-read volume for students and practitioners of Development Studies, Security Studies, African Studies, Sociology, Political Science, and Area Studies.

References

Mignolo, W. (2000) (Post)Occidentalism, (post)coloniality, and (post)subaltern rationality', In: Afzal-Khan, F. & Seshadri-Crooks, K. (eds). *The pre-occupation of postcolonial studies*, Duke PU: Durham.

Mignolo, W. (2007) Delinking, *Cultural Studies* 21 (2-3): 449-514.

Mignolo, W. (2011) *The darker side of modernity: Global futures, decolonial options*, Duke UP: Durham.

Quijano, A. (2007) Coloniality and modernity/rationality, *Cultural Studies* 21 (2-3): 168-178.

Quijano, A. & Wallerstein, I. (1992) Americanity as concept: Or the Americas in the modern world system, *International Social Science Journal* 131: 549-557.

Vallega, A. A. (2015) *Latin American philosophy: From identity to radical exteriority*, Indiana University Press: USA.

Chapter 2

Development without the People? What has Always Missed in Development Paradigms "Imposed" on Africa?

Nkwazi Mhango

Introduction

> *A country, or village cannot be developed, it can only develop itself....If real development means growth of people...If real development is to take place people must be involved....Knowledge does not only come out of books....We would be fools if we allowed the development of our economies to destroy human and social values which African societies have built up for centuries* (Nyerere 1968, in Swantz 2009: 29).

If anything, development is one of the most researched concepts in the contemporary world. This is because all human beings need development in order to live well. However, this has not been the case universally. Looking into the above quote, whatever type of development in whatever aspect, must revolve around the people. It [development] must be people-centred, people-intended and people-oriented for it to make sense. In the current capitalistic and monopolistic world geared by apathies, greed, disregard of others, and, above all, stinking individualism, all enhanced by endemic and systemic bad governance, corruption and thievery, development seems to be cartelised by a few countries in the West instead of being globally unitive (O'fallon 2012) seeking to do justice to all members of the society by pulling people out of manmade poverty that can be attributed to greed and selfishness. This is why Nelson Mandela (2014) had this to say: "overcoming poverty is not a gesture of charity. It is an act of justice. It is the protection of a fundamental human right, the right to dignity and a decent life. While poverty persists, there is no true freedom" (p. 130). So, too, in Africa, development is monopolised by the ruling class as opposed to African developmental heritage in which such a process would be unitive seeking to create and maintain societal benefits, harmony, interests and unity. In both cases, what is ongoing *vis-à-vis* development is nothing but blatant injustice and the violation of human rights. To understand what this means, try to ask yourself as to why, for example, Africans who sit on immense resources of value, are poor as opposed to the Europeans and others who illegally benefit from Africa's resources simply because they are monopolised by a clique of thieves in power.

Using African philosophies of Maendeleo, or the drive for an individual or society to develop himself or itself as it revolves around humanity and Ubuntu, this chapter seeks to shed light on how development is not a new concept. In addressing this aspect, I am trying to show how the two philosophy centre development on people instead of things which is opposite to the Western model and philosophy of development. The insistence of the two philosophies on humanity but not materiality makes them better than Western whose application has failed to pull Africa out of Western-defined development. Thus, the discussion on the concept of development will kick off by seeking to educate ourselves about the concept before delving deep into it. In so doing, the question that one must ponder on is development in what, how and for whom and for what ends?

Development or Maendeleo and Swahili philosophy

This chapter addresses naivety and insecurities in Africa which emanate from the monopolisation of power by the Global North as a precursor of underdevelopment. The chapter explores African conceptualisation and utilisation of development based on maendeleo model of development. Looking at the major underpinnings of African or Swahili conceptualisation of development, who is now scrutinising national and international development models that are at work globally today? Swahili has their way of defining development which means maendeleo in Swahili emphasising that development has the duty in continuing or improving in a certain aspect, degree economically, politically or socially without necessarily harming anybody or avoiding public scrutiny (Smith 2008). In this chapter, I examine maendeleo development as a process revolving around improvement of somebody's situation. Some of the undergirding underpinnings will be borrowed from three famous persons namely the philosopher president Julius Nyerere, Tanzania's first president, former South African president Nelson Mandela, a peacemaker and former Uruguayan president Jose Mujica, a disciplinary, frugal and pragmatic figure that left the world gapped when it comes to serving the people as opposed to self-service that has recently characterised leadership in the world.

Further, Harrison (2008) notes that Maendeleo or development is "the ability to 'bring development' to one's home area provided a way of shoring up legitimacy…" (p. 177). In other words, the African philosophy of development espoused must be a responsible one based on the consent and needs of its stakeholders but not their rulers or leaders as it currently is.

Nevertheless, it must be underscored that development or maendeleo can also denote the continuation of something without necessarily being linear and perpendicular. For example, if somebody continues in cascading in alcoholism or anything negative, in Swahili, the word used will be "endelea" or proceeds in or develops into something. So, too, maendeleo or development means different things to different people (Dean 2012). This is basically why the perception of development between collective and individualistic societies may differ not to mention the manner and styles through which development can be actualised and realised. For example, for colonial and neocolonial Europe, enslaving and colonising others were acceptable in bringing about the development that Europe enjoys today (Mhango forthcoming) while in Africa, development means improving the condition and situation of the society. Additionally, development can be top-down or vice versa, depending on who seeks the said development. While development can be brought about by enslaving or colonising others as was the case of Europe, for Africa, development is emancipatory and transformational as it aims at making those attaining self-reliance from the village to the national level (Nyerere 1968: 248 cited in Lal 2012). For development to make sense, it must emanate from those it aims at but not imported or superimposed as it currently is in the case of Africa. Nyerere cited in Major and Mulvihill (2009) notes that:

People cannot be developed; they can only develop themselves. For, while it is possible for an outsider to build a man's house, an outsider cannot give man pride of self-confidence in him as a human-being. Those things man has to create in himself by his own actions. He develops himself by what he does, he develops himself by making his own decisions, by increasing his understanding of what he is doing and why; by increasing his own knowledge and ability and by his full participation as an equal in the life of the community he lives in (p. 17).

Nyerere puts more emphasis on a couple of things such as human dignity, inclusivity at a societal level, the increase of knowledge, people, society, power, and self-confidence in deciding how development should be realised. This approach is very important due to the fact that maendeleo or development that excludes people does not make any sense; and is undesirable. Likewise, development that is superimposed on people does not belong to them. Therefore, the will not value it. This is why many projects in some African countries are sabotaged by the people either because of poverty, ignorance or seeking to revenge for what it negatively caused to them. This means that it is very important to address power dynamics when dealing with development to make sure that those involved in the process know exactly their location in the process.

Balanced and centralised power as a tool for development

Borrowing from Nyerere's assertion in the beginning of the chapter, development can be easily attained if power is balanced; and the only way to balance power is through decentralisation of power. The decentralisation of power is the only tool for empowerment through creating a practical network of power. For example, if an individual is developed he or she will develop the family that will develop the village that way up to the national level. For, if power is decentralised, everybody will be able to know the scale and scope of his or her power. As well, such decentralised power can be used as checks-and-balance tool among the development partners due to the fact that every stakeholder will use the decentralised power to defend his or her constituency according to the power division.

I argue that power-decentralisation approach is able to bring accountability, openness and, as a result, cut down malpractices such as corruption in community and national developmental projects. For, experience shows that government officials use their power to create and execute bogus development projects as a guise of making quick money (Ahlin and Pang 2008). This is currently a practice in many countries, mainly poor ones that allow their economies to be taken advantage of by Western countries through the International Financial Institutions (IFIs) led by the International Monetary Fund (IMF) which interfere in many countries without any improvement since this imperialistic drive started under various tags such as Structural Adjustment Programmes (SAPS) that sap the said economies to end up becoming experimental objects. The SAPs destabilised many economies in poor countries after coaxing them to introduce painful austerity measures in order to secure loans (Brautigam 2009). Thanks to the SAPs, many African countries saw many people a retrenchment of government subsidies and social expenditure which negatively affected many people so as to increase the number of poor and unemployed people (Cohen 2006) in Africa. Instead of ushering in sustainable development, the SAPs have locked development in many countries. This has been ongoing simply because "the currently dominant view is that institutions are the ultimate determinants of economic performance (Chang 2011: 476). Due to this controversial view, the IFIs, as the champions of neoliberal policies as espoused by imperial powers, many countries are in big debts resulting from such experimental and exploitative policies and programs that, in many instances, go unchecked. The situation is worse globally however with antithetic results wherein rich countries benefit and poor countries lose. It takes two to tango. Egger and Winner (2005: 949) cited in Aidt (2009) draw a conclusion after exploring 73 developed and less developed countries; and found that corruption is a stimulus for FDI. What would happen if a common citizen through decentralised power is able to task the government? What would happen if poor countries would use this decentralised power to task rich countries to repatriate their riches looted during the slave era and colonialism? For, any development to make sense, it must allow everybody to be able to locate or relocate where he/she is in the process. Likewise, stakeholders need to locate their interests either as an individual or a group to see to it that they stand for them. It is from such understanding that part of the speech of José Mujica (April 21, 2016, cited in Cafezeiro, Viterbo, da Costa, Salgado, Rocha and Monteiro, 2017) notes that "[...] we are social. No one can live alone. We need a cardiologist, a mechanic, a teacher, *a lawyer, a nurse, and so on* for our *children*. We need someone to drive the bus, someone who supports us in life, a midwife at birth and a gravedigger when we die" (p. 136). Therefore, everyone counts and needs the very development in order to efficiently contribute to the society or human family.

Further, Nyerere (1968) argue that people and land which include all resources as well as good policies and good leadership are the prerequisites of meaningful development. Ironically, Africa has all such ingredients on its development menu save for good governance or leadership. Globally, all ingredients are present save the lack of equity and justice. Again, accountable, creative and responsible leadership is hard to get under neoliberal policies which in themselves are not safe for the "weak" and vulnerable societies of the world. For, the leadership that is lacking human elements is the one that is ready to practically sacrifice (Obo and Adejumo 2014) for the development of others as it was for president Mujica of Uruguay whom many like to refer to a poor president. Such leaders can only be moulded by ethical and moral philosophy such as Maendeleo and Ubuntu, an African philosophy that looks at things cyclically. Ubuntu revolves around the philosophy that you are because I am. Therefore, if you think about exploiting me, you practically are exploiting yourself.

Apart from Swahili which is a language with many speakers in Africa, other languages such as Shona, Tswana, Kinyarwanda, Kiganda and many others have their natural words for the concept to indicate that development is not a new concept to Africa. For example, Zimbabwe's most popular language, Shona, calls development "Budiriro" (Murisa 2010) while Tsonga which is spoken in Mozambique, South Africa, Swaziland and Zimbabwe, the word for development is "nhluvuko" (Hlungwani 2012). Of course many African languages have their terms for development, which shows that the concept is not something new to Africa. By having the words to denote the concept it means such languages must have their epistemological underpinnings of the concept. In the two examples provided, development as a concept is relative; similarly, as it is the case for Western concept of development.

Ironically, despite espousing straightjacket if not one-size-fits-all development model, those doing so have never bothered to seek the consent and inputs of those they say they want to bring development to. How can the stakeholders know the whole concept without defining it so that those targeted can analyse, understand and ponder on it so as to decide if they want or do not want the intended development? Almost in all African culture, humanity is connected to the environment. Sadly though, this approach was felled soon after Africa's colonisation. To resuscitate it, Ngara cited in Nashon, Anderson and Wright (2008) notes that the enhancement of development in Africa will be possible only through introducing the pedagogy of liberation in order to restore dignity and self-efficacy. This is because; African ways of knowing constitute invaluable aspects of African heritage that harmonises Africa's past broken story of development with its modern realities of globalisation. This stance resonates with many aspects of poor Africans whose actualisation and realisation of true development has remained a pipedream if not a mere drama. Because the elites naively define and monopolise everything societal for the detriment of those excluded simply because their legality and powers are maintained by an exploitative international systems that gyrate around capitalistic and neoliberal policies.

Ubuntu philosophy of Development

To see how African interconnectivity of almost everything is unbreakable including development, we can examine the philosophy of Ubuntu on development. Under Ubuntu, all things are interconnected in a cyclical manner which seeks to create coexistence, harmony, equity, justice, interdependence and all-encompassing development and livelihood. Essentially, Ubuntu is about being harmonious with each other including nature (Shumba 2011) all aimed at achieving human sustainable development, interdependence and mutual coexistence. Moreover, there is a different approach between Western conceptualisation of development and Ubuntu. For Ubuntu, development is only meaningful when it collectively revolves around dignified humanity but not individually as it is in the Western society where development is centred on individuals. This African understanding of development should not be misconstrued as Ubuntu's refusal to admit personal enrichment. Mandela and Modise (2006) cited in Hosking (2015) notes that a traveller through a country would stop at a village without necessarily asking for food or for water simply because when he or she arrives, the people give him food, entertain him or her. Mandela goes on to note that this is one aspect of Ubuntu that can be experienced in various aspects. Further, Mandela posits that Ubuntu does not mean that people should not enrich themselves due to the fact that the question that needs to be asked is: Are you going to do so in order to enable the community around you to be able to improve?

Further, while many Western concepts including development divorce morality from their ethos, Ubuntu dictates that development only makes sense when it revolves around ethic underpinnings to the whole community. However, Western genre of development has been abusively over-glorified and over-romanticised so as to become dominant globally not to mention how this has tricked African countries to allow themselves to be subject to developmental experiments conducted by the IFIs led by the Bretton woods and exploitative neoliberal policies. This is totally different from African application and conceptualisation of development as a continuum. This way, everybody fends for everybody as humans. This needs to be the guiding mechanism of development. For, development cannot occur in a vacuum without people. When we discuss development, we must put in mind that this development must be people centred, people-driven and people oriented.

As Mandela cited in Hosking (*Ibid*) succinctly puts it, one of the tools to thwart poverty is development; and ushering development is not a charity but a human duty and right, especially by averting greed and selfishness. If you look at the number of billionaires the world has today and how much they have monopolised compared to the whole human family, you will understand how global poverty is a manmade phenomenon. If every human can understand that s/he needs the basics of life, there would not be such humungous gaps between individuals and countries that have more than they deserve except for their megalomaniac ignorance. Jose Mujica (2013) cited in Briganti (2016) defines poor people as the ones who describe him as a poor person simply because he does not have too much. For Mujica who is frugal, living with little while freedom revolves around having time to live the way one likes based on his frugal philosophy.

Essentially, what Mujica wants to harmer in is nothing but stressing the importance of equity, ethics frugality and justice among nations and people in perceiving development. Taking it from Mujica's understanding, I advance that the development that revolves around materials in order to benefit a certain class or group of people at the detriment of the majority is harm if not negative development. For example, you do not need to be a geek to know that the invention of internet has easily globalised the world in order for irresponsible use and unaccountable corporate to own and later destroy the world. As stated in African Ubuntu philosophy or defined in Swahili, development must have collective responsibility as well as human centrality undergirding the concept as opposed to material centrality. However, Schumpeter (1934) cited in Lawal (2007) defines development as a multifaceted process that revolves around increasing the skill and ability for maximum freedom that goes in tandem with accountability and responsibility. Thanks to invention of the internet, interpersonal connection is shifting from the one a person knows to the virtue world. Ethics is a little bit eroded wherein cons and hackers are now threatening the harmony of the world. Importantly, in defining development, we must define people in order to avoid letting a few people or nations as it currently is to dominate and monopolise development for the peril of many. The development that allows some nations to dupe and exploit other nations is harmful to society. Development that burdens or overexploits resources knowingly these resources are finite in the world is harmful. Development that produces harmful tools such as poisonous food and chemicals and weapons is harmful and negative.

Unethical development is harmful; and does not deserve to occur or being supported.

Harmful development and environment

As for the current development under a monopolistic world, ecological and environmental considerations are lacking. It is worse to note that even African countries that were supposed to teach others environmental awareness and vitality have fallen in the trap of careless and immoral development defined by greed and individualism and personal or national selfishness. Mujica cited in Ganis (2015) warns that rich countries are only interested in their own economic development even if it results in alienating other groups from their cultures and resources. This is why countries like Angola and the Democratic Republic of Congo (DRC) are relatively poor while those who colonised or are now exploiting them become immensely rich even when their own countries are with no resources (Mhango 2015, 2017). Mhango questions the rationale behind small countries such as Belgium, Portugal, Netherlands and Spain, *inter alia*, to be richer than the two countries mentioned above. Due to blindly and greedily subscribing to such harmful neoliberal policies, many countries, mainly in Africa, are now blindly and greedily courting trouble under the banner and pretexts of development. Interestingly, when such projects are created, leaders do not fully involve their people. This is not only different from African philosophy of development that insists that whatever is done must first assure the people of communal benefit (Malunga 2006) but it is also against it. Many dams, roads, and other infrastructure are under construction in order to bring about desired change and development for particular countries; thus to their people. Again, if you ask if the beneficiaries were fully involved and their inputs incorporated and valued, you get different answers. For example, one can argue that the dam or road will benefit the public. There are a couple of questions we need to answer before wholesomely buying into this communality of benefit. For example, who engineered the project and why? Is a dam or road what people want first based on their priorities and informed decision? These and others are important questions to ponder on before simply stating that the dam or road is going to bring development without necessarily knowing how those targeted intend to use it to do so. I am saying this after evidencing many areas with resources of value such as water, hydroelectric sources, minerals, wildlife and many more left out of the intended development nationally and globally. Simple example to substantiate this point can be drawn from urban-rural exploitation in Africa in which urban areas are more developed and have many more amenities than rural ones despite the fact that Africa is still an agriculture-based continent; for much produces are produced in the rural areas.

Essentially, under the core-periphery rural-urban setting (Woltjer 2014)–which is a typical replica of the setting between rich and poor countries–rural Africa has been deprived of development and services since many African countries acquired their independence. However, the situation is totally different in Western countries where all amenities and services available in urban areas are also found in rural areas. Since independence, in many African countries, development projects, thanks to governmental monopoly, urban-development projects, displaced–still do–many people, mainly in rural areas; and nothing is done internationally. Wudineh (2006, cited in Yntiso 2008) provides an example of Ethiopia wherein the Lease Board of Addis Ababa City Administration awarded Sheraton Addis 37.7 ha for development project, which is expected to displace 12,585 people living in 2, 797 homes, 604 of which are privately owned without equitably compensating them fairly. The number of victims is bigger. However, if it is compared to millions (Agrawal and Redford 2009) who have already been affected, the phenomenon seems to grow bigger and bigger shall anything not be done to address it decisively. This material-oriented development started many years in Africa. For example, the post-colonial governments in various African countries displaced thousands of their citizens simply because they were embarking on aped development from Europe that does not consider humanity as it is in Maendeleo and Ubuntu philosophies. Stanley (2004) provides some statistics noting that Ghana and Zambia displaced 80,000 and 57,000 people respectively when they constructed their Dam projects of Akosombo and Kariba respectively soon after acquiring their independence. Sometimes, countries involved in such antidevelopment projects tend to not see the underdevelopment such projects cause. For example, if you ask the governments of Ethiopia, Ghana and Zambia if they studied the socio-economic ramifications such projects caused, I do not think you can get right answers. If the true concepts of Ubuntu and Maendeleo would be accommodated, such displacements would be avoided not to mention finding acceptable, logical and well-balanced solutions to the problems. Ironically, while Africa is needlessly destroying its people under the guise of bringing material oriented development, Stanley observes that the situation is different in developed countries where laws protect private property so as to offer property owners the right to accept or reject the amount of money offered them compensation.

Arguably, the aim of this chapter is not to act as an anti-development epistemology. This is because; all humans deserve and need development conditionally that such development should address their aspirations, expectations and problems as a people. Further, this development should not be imposed on the people it targets. Therefore, to do away with negative displacements resulting from development, there must be positive or voluntary resettlement wherein the victims should be listened to so that they can contribute their inputs about how the process should look like and be carried out. Schmidt-Soltau and Brockington (2007) cites the example of Korup National Park in Cameroon wherein agreed to be resettled based on informed consent. The major aim of such a setting is to avoid blind or imbalanced development wherein some stakeholders are excluded in policymaking. However in many cases, if the project is financed through loans they are the ones that will pay in future.

Consumerism as a harbinger to development

Another face of imbalanced development resulting from development-induced tendencies can be seen on how many innocent people in various African countries have already been displaced to give room for the so-called "development". Whose development that has neither their consent nor inputs of the stakeholders is? Again, who is considering the costs and ramification of the said development to mother earth? Under Swahili view of the concept, development can be either positive or negative. This is because the act of continuing can occur both positively or negatively. For example, the world has recently evidenced unpresented leapfrog in consumerism thanks to the belief that it creates money (Pupavac 2010); and thus, catalyses development without necessarily considering the ramifications of such development. For example, when the prophets of consumerism propped this theory, they did not consider that the material they were encouraging people to consume carelessly and greedily are naturally finite. This monolithic way of looking at development has recently led to conflict resulting from scarcity and resource control, principally if we consider that "consumerism, is the internationalisation of production including: foreign direct investment, international technology licensing, international subcontracting, leasing, management agreements and so on" (Westra 2006: 15) wherein a few technologically and scientifically developed countries tend to benefit on the expenses of their antithesis. There cannot be any meaningful and true development for all in the development that results in mindless consumerism that turns humans into consuming machines for the peril of the world. Essentially, this is what neoliberal mass-consumption leads to; shall it not be stopped and replaced by going back to ethical consumption. Former Uruguayan president Jose Mujica cited in Hernandez (2012) addresses this question succinctly. He notes that:

But what are we thinking? Do we want the model of development and consumption of the rich countries? I ask you now: what would happen to this planet if Indians would have the same proportion of cars per household than Germans? How much oxygen would we have left? Does this planet have enough resources so seven or eight billion can have the same level of consumption and waste that today is seen in rich societies? It is this level of hyper-consumption that is harming our planet (p. 15).

Due to cozy language of development, consumerism has evaded scrutiny as far as the depreciation of resources is concerned. Consumerism as development itself becomes harmful due to the fact that it lacks a united strategy in actualising and realising development. There cannot be any desirable development wherein players have either different or opposing goals, interests and strategies as it currently is in the neoliberal brand of development in which rich countries drum the agenda of perpetually exploiting poor countries and turn them into surplus-dumping grounds if not the dumping for counterfeit and harmful goods as China and India are doing in Africa currently (Goredema 2013; Osinibi 2013; and Shaw 2017). This is because "counterfeit drug manufacturing is fast becoming a profitable business in China and India" (Bollampally and Dzever 2015: 186) whose major market is currently Africa. While Africa is turning a blind eye thanks to being ruled by corrupt and inept rulers who have pauperised their people so as to be forced to buy cheap but dangerous goods, others have already taken stern measures to curb this development. Idris (2007) cited in Agubamah (2014) notes that "in 2006, in the US the NAFDAC banned pharmaceutical imports from some Chinese and Indian companies" (p. 67) simply because such goods were not only hurting the consumers but also the economies of recipient countries whose people are not only fed hazardous stuff but also robbed of their money. Under the drive to attract investment for development, Africa has recently allowed China and India to flood its countries with substandard goods ranging from drugs, food and textile. Despite wrestling with a huge population to feed, China currently exports sea foods to some African countries such as Kenya and Tanzania while they sit on Lakes such as Nyanza, Tanzania and the Indian Ocean. Ironically, Smith, Roheim, Crowder, Halpern, Turnipseed, Anderson, Asche, Bourillón, Guttormsen, Khan and Liguori (2010) disclose that "at the global scale, regions with low undernourishment are net importers of seafood from regions with high undernourishment" (p. 784).

Despite the menace of counterfeit goods, mainly drugs, there are substantial tonnes of literatures on ethical consuming and zillions of tonnes of literature on the importance of consumerism wherein production and consumption are linked to see if it benefits consumers and producers equally and equitably (Garcia Martinez and Poole 2009). Again, where are the tens of tonnes of literature about imminent dangers such counterfeit goods cause to consumers in

Africa for example? Where are literatures about strict resource limitability in the world? However, in addressing the deprivation of resources as a sequel of greedy and needless consumerism, there is one important question that needs to be asked in order to avoid naivety if the phenomenon. How enduringly sustainable consumerism is? Are the profits consumerism brings more important than the menaces it causes? Who is going to be responsible shall anything go wrong as it has already indicated? As we try to answer such important questions, we will be able to see the naivety and emergent dangers the monopolistic world suffers from. Higgins-Desbiolles (2010) notes that "climate change, despite the warnings that the ecological system is giving us that the resources we consume and the pollutions we emit in sustaining consumerism are taking us to the finite limits of the Earth ' s capacity" (p. 125). Although almost all policymakers globally know how finite resources are, they pretend to serve present interests as they ignore the future ones. It becomes even surreal to note that greed resulting from capitalistic individualism and selfish has blinded the world so as to stop talking about the future generations. The current generation is disserving the past and future generations. For, the past generations left what we are now devouring so that the current generation would build on where they left for the benefit of the coming generations. If neoliberal development had some moral underpinnings, the first question development advocates and gurus were supposed to ask is: How would I feel had the past generations decimated resources the way I am doing today?

Globally, in the name of development, many countries are pushing the envelope *vis-à-vis* consumerism and development. An ideal can be drawn from the U.S after President Donald Trump assumed office. His predecessor, Barack Obama had embarked on purposeful drive to invest in clean and renewable energy by harnessing the powers of wind, sun and science in general. Again, after Trump came to office, he revised everything. He sent back the U.S to the old age of depending on biofuels and coal. To cap it all, Trump pulled out the U.S of the 2015 Paris Agreement (Ikenberry 2017; Santos 2017; and Tollefson 2017) and there is a lacuna internationally on how to stop such self-destroying injustice and naivety despite the fact that scientists have already warned that the Paris Agreement is the only available last chance of preventing a global catastrophe (Chirico 2017). Greed and ignorance seem to be driving forces in this self-destruction. Had they not been, Trump's slogan of 'making America Great Again' would not have taken precedence over the drive to make the world a safe place for all.

Conclusion

After exploring development, its relativity, and practicability, I can conclude this chapter noting that for development in Africa to make sense, it must be inclusive, collective and none-exploitive in that all stakeholders must have some inputs on how development is to be brought. More importantly, in defining and pondering on development, people at all levels should come first before anything. As argued hereinabove, development that excludes community centrality does not make sense. As cited in Nyerere hereinabove, nobody can develop anybody. Instead, somebody can help somebody to develop if this development is geared and enhanced by the targeted person. Everybody is responsible for his or her development. Likewise, the so-called underdeveloped countries cannot be developed by the so-called developed countries whose intervention has always aimed at exploiting poor countries, making them even poorer as experience say it all when it comes to Africa.

I have therefore advanced that when we ponder development, apart from seeking accurate definition fitting our interests and environment, we must seek to decentralise the understanding, theories and practices of development that are currently exploitative, imperial and unequitable. Major questions we need to address are, *inter alia:* How should development look like? Who owns the process? How development should be actualised? Who dictate the process? To do so, the current model of development needs to incorporate other models from various societies especially when intended development is carried out in such areas. This will help the stakeholder not only to conceptualise the process but also to feel that they are part and parcel of it. Once such an approach has been embarked upon chances for the stakeholders to generate inputs and defend the process are high. By incorporating other models of development suitable to certain localities, we will not only be decolonising development but also enriching the process due to the fact that it will have more inputs. This is because every people have the duty and right to bring about their development through inclusivity based on an informed decision to contribute to and participate in the process.

In a nutshell, although development is one of a highly researched and contested concept, much still needs to be done to address the failure of developmental policies, models and theories that have already been experimented on poor countries and came a cropper. This means, there is something wrong with how development is understood and dealt with. One of such anomaly of dealing with development is the fact that rich countries control, define and manipulate everything to see to it that their interests are served.

Abbreviations

DRC	Democratic Republic of Congo
NAFDAC	National Agency for Food and Drug Administration and Control
IFIs	International Financial Institutions
US	United States
FDI	Foreign Direct Investment
IMF	International Monetary Fund

References

Agrawal, A. & Redford, K. (2009) Conservation and displacement: an overview, *Conservation and society*, 7(1): 1.

Agubamah, E. (2014) Bilateral relations: periscoping Nigeria and China relations. *European Scientific Journal, ESJ*, 10(14).

Ahlin, C., & Pang, J. (2008) Are financial development and corruption control substitutes in promoting growth? *Journal of Development Economics*, 86 (2): 414-433.

Aidt, T. S. (2009) Corruption, institutions, and economic development. Oxford Review of Economic Policy, 25(2): 271-291.

Bollampally, K., & Dzever, S. (2015) The impact of RFID on pharmaceutical supply chains: India, China and Europe compared. *Indian Journal of Science and Technology*, 8(S4), 176-188.

Brautigam, D. (2009) *The dragon's gift: the real story of China in Africa.* Oxford University Press.

Briganti, A. (2016) Creating a Unified Foundation for Generative Sustainable Development: Research, Practice and Education: the Perspective of a Development Economist and Practitioner. *European Journal of Sustainable Development*, 5(4): 79.

Cafezeiro, I., Viterbo, J., da Costa, L. C., Salgado, L., Rocha, M., & Monteiro, R. S. (2017) Strengthening of the Sociotechnical Approach in Information Systems Research. *I GranDSI-BR*, 133.

Chang, H. J. (2011) Institutions and economic development: theory, policy and history. *Journal of Institutional Economics*, 7(4): 473-498.

Chirico, F. (2017) The challenges of climate change, migration and conflict in pursuit of the Sustainable Development Goals: A call to responsible and responsive policy makers. *J Health Soc Sci*, 2(2): 137-142.

Cohen, B. (2006) Urbanisation in developing countries: Current trends, future projections, and key challenges for sustainability. *Technology in society*, 28(1-2): 63-80.

Dean, E. (2012). The paradox of power: connection, inequality, and energy development on Tumbatu Island, Zanzibar. *Ethnology: An International Journal of Cultural and Social Anthropology*, 49(3), 185-206.

Ganis, A. (2015) Josè Mujica's Speech at the UN: a Post-colonial Look at a Neo-colonial Issue, *UN Conference*, USA.

Garcia Martinez, M., & Poole, N. (2009) Fresh Perspectives 4—Ethical consumerism: development of a global trend and its impact on development.

Marizane, A. S. (2016) Religious change in the trans-frontier Nyungwe-speaking region of the middle Zambezi, c. 1890-c. 1970, *Doctoral dissertation*, SOAS University of London.

Harrison, G. (2008) From the global to the local? Governance and development at the local level: reflections from Tanzania. The Journal of Modern African Studies, 46(2), 169-189.

Hernandez, V. (2012) Jose Mujica: The world's 'poorest' president. BBC News Magazine, 14.

Higgins-Desbiolles, F. (2010). The elusiveness of sustainability in tourism: The culture-ideology of consumerism and its implications. Tourism and Hospitality Research, 10(2), 116-129.

Hlungwani, M. C. (2012) Deverbal nominals in Xitsonga, *Doctoral dissertation,* Stellenbosch: Stellenbosch University).

Hosking, E. N. (2015) *Fostering new spaces: Celebrating and growing a diverse economy in Cape Town,* South Africa.

Ikenberry, G. J. (2017) The Plot against American Foreign Policy: Can the Liberal Order Survive. *Foreign Aff.,* 96, 2.

Kamuzora, F. (2010) Nyerere's vision of economic development. Africa's Liberation, 93.

Lal, P. (2012) Self-reliance and the state: the multiple meanings of development in early post-colonial Tanzania. *Africa,* 82(2): 212-234.

Lawal, G. (2007) Corruption and development in Africa: challenges for political and economic change. Humanity and Social Sciences Journal, 2(1): 1-7.

Major, T. and Mulvihill, T. M. (2009) Julius Nyerere (1922–1999), an African philosopher, re-envisions teacher education to escape colonialism. *New proposals: Journal of Marxism and interdisciplinary inquiry,* 3(1): 15-22.

Malunga, C. (2006) Learning leadership development from African cultures: A personal perspective. *INTRAC Praxis* Note, 25, pp.1-13.

Mandela, N. and Speech, T. S. (2014) 8 Reflecting on global childhood poverty. Developing as a Reflective Early Years Professional: A Thematic Approach, p.130.

Mhango, N. N. (2015) *Africa Reunite or Perish,* Langaa RPCIG: Bamenda.

Mhango, N. N. (2017) *Africa's Dependency Syndrome: Can Africa Still Turn Things around for the Better?* Langaa RPCIG: Bamenda.

Murisa, T. (2010) *Livelihoods after Land Reform in Zimbabwe.* PLAAS. University of the Western Cape.

Nashon, S., Anderson, D. and Wright, H. (2008) African ways of knowing, worldviews and pedagogy. *Journal of Contemporary Issues in Education,* 2(2).

O'fallon, S. (2012) Nelson Mandela and unitive leadership. *Integral Leadership Review,* 12(4), pp.1-20.

Obo, U. B. & Adejumo, T.O. (2014) Uruguay's Jose Mujica And Nigerian Rulers: Selfless and Exemplary Leadership Versus Prebendal and Ruinous Rulership, *Review of History And Political Science,* 2(1).

Osinibi, O. M. (2013) *The Political Economy of Development and Underdevelopment in Africa,* Langaa RPCIG: Bamenda.

Pupavac, V. (2010) The consumerism-development-security nexus. *Security Dialogue,* 41(6): 691-713.

Santos, G. (2017) Road transport and CO2 emissions: What are the challenges? *Transport Policy,* 59, pp.71-74.

Schmidt-Soltau, K. & Brockington, D. (2007) Protected areas and resettlement: What scope for voluntary relocation? *World Development,* 35(12): 2182-2202.

Shaw, M. (2017) Africa's changing place in the global criminal economy, *Institute for Security Studies Papers,* pp.1-40.

Shumba, O. (2011) Commons thinking, ecological intelligence and the ethical and moral framework of Ubuntu: An imperative for sustainable development, *Journal of Media and Communication Studies,* 3(3): 84-96.

Smith, J. H. (2008) *Bewitching Development: witchcraft and the reinvention of development in neoliberal Kenya.* University of Chicago Press.

Smith, M.D., Roheim, C.A., Crowder, L.B., Halpern, B.S., Turnipseed, M., Anderson, J.L., Asche, F., Bourillón, L., Guttormsen, A.G., Khan, A. and Liguori, L. A. (2010) Sustainability and global seafood, *Science,* 327(5967): 784-786.

Stanley, J. (2004) *Development-induced displacement and resettlement: Forced Migration Online Research Guide,* Refugee Studies Centre, University of Oxford.

Swantz, M. L. (2009) What is development? Perspectives to global social development, p.29.

Tollefson, J. (2017) Trump say no to climate pact. *Nature*, 546, p.198.

Westra, R. (2006) The capitalist stage of consumerism and South Korean development, *Journal of Contemporary Asia*, 36(1): 3-25.

Woltjer, J. (2014). A global review on peri-urban development and planning, *Journal Perencanaan Wilayah dan Kota*, 25(1): 1-16.

Yntiso, G. (2008) Urban development and displacement in Addis Ababa: The impact of resettlement projects on low-income households, *Eastern Africa Social Science Research Review*, 24(2): 53-77.

Chapter 3

'Green Bombers,' Torture and Terror: Political Security and the Nazi Legacy in Zimbabwe, 2001-2009

Fidelis Peter Thomas Duri

Introduction

During the period 2001-2009, the majority of Zimbabweans suffered from a plethora of socio-economic and political insecurities which were largely caused by the ruling Zimbabwe African National Union Patriotic Front (ZANU-PF) government, under the leadership of President Robert Mugabe, which prioritised political survival at the expense of the livelihoods of most ordinary people. The ruling party's popularity nose-dived from the early 1990s largely because of its implementation of austerity measures that had been recommended by the World Bank and the International Monetary Fund (Bond and Manyanya, 2001). The formation of the opposition Movement for Democratic Change (MDC) in September 1999, under the leadership of Morgan Tsvangirai, with considerable funding from commercial white farmers, posed further challenges to ZANU-PF's legitimacy (Ibid; Hill, 2003; Meredith, 2002). This was proved by the February 2000 referendum in which a new constitution proposed by ZANU-PF was rejected by 55% of the electorate, most of who had been mobilised by the MDC and local civil groups (Bond and Manyanya, 2001; Meredith, 2002; Raftopoulos, 2003).

The referendum defeat was a bitter pill to swallow for ZANU-PF, a party that had ruled Zimbabwe since independence in 1980 (Raftopoulos, 2003). In an attempt to regain its popularity, the ruling party sanctioned the invasion of commercial farms, mostly white owned, from February 2000, with the intention of redistributing them to landless indigenous Zimbabweans (Ibid). This was a multi-pronged strategy to win the vote of many ordinary Zimbabweans by allocating them land and at the same time pauperise commercial white farmers in order to cut off any financial support they could give to the MDC (Alexander, 2003; Raftopoulos, 2003). These political shenanigans resulted in a broad range of socio-economic and political insecurities for many Zimbabweans.

The farm invasions, for example, caused a multiplicity of insecurities for the majority of citizens. The country became food insecure as many farms were either unutilised or underutilised by their new owners, most of who did not have the technical knowhow and other resources to engage in commercial farming (*Reuters Alert*, 20 March 2007; Richardson, 2005). Thousands of farm workers lost their jobs and became destitute (Chambati and Moyo, 2004). The farm grabs constituted a gross violation of property rights and investor confidence waned (Richardson, 2005). The country increasingly ran out of foreign currency owing to investor flight, deindustrialisation, the drastic decline in export crops and international isolation (Raftopoulos, 2003; Richardson, 2005). The government increasingly became bankrupt to the extent of being incapacitated to provide basic services to its citizens, the majority of who were unemployed, famished and languishing in profound poverty (Richardson, 2005). Hyperinflation set in as the government printed paper money (Berger, 9 October 2008; Fuller, May 2012; *Sokwanele*, 20 July 2007; *Thomson Reuters Foundation*, 13 July 2014; Watson, 1 March 2003; Wines, 2 May 2006). Persistent droughts also ravaged the country (*Reuters Alert*, 20 March 2007). These livelihood insecurities were aggravated by orgies of violence meted out by ZANU-PF on its political opponents (Raftopoulos, 2003).

While it is quite apparent that most of the socio-economic and political insecurities and uncertainties experienced by many Zimbabweans can largely be blamed on ZANU-PF's political expediency, the ruling party in turn scapegoated Western powers, particularly Britain and the United States. It indeed became routine for the then President, Robert Mugabe, and several ZANU-PF officials to blame Western powers for Zimbabwe's socio-economic challenges and insecurities such as drought (*BBC News*, 28 June 2005), hunger (*NBC News*, 3 June 2008), cholera outbreaks (*BBC News*, 12 December 2008; *Telegraph*, 12 December 2008); corruption (*Financial Gazette*, 11 December 2014; *Zimbabwe Situation*, 22 February 2014),

Civil Service salary delays (*Nehanda Radio*, 9 July 2016) and civil protests (*City Press*, 18 August 2016).

In addition, the ruling ZANU-PF party inexorably reminded Zimbabweans to be on guard against the invasion of the country by Western powers, especially Britain and the United States. While opening the ZANU-PF annual conference in December 2002, Mugabe, for example, warned that Western powers were a serious threat to Zimbabwe's internal security (*Irish Times*, 13 December 2002). During the Tenth Conference of the Committee of Intelligence and Security Services in Africa (CISSA), an organ of the African Union, held in Harare in early May 2013, Mugabe blamed Western powers for fuelling political conflicts and insecurity in Africa (Shoko, 7 May 2013). The paranoid Mugabe and many ZANU-PF officials often vilified opposition parties such as the MDC for being puppets and accomplices of Western powers in the mission to destabilise the country (Ncube, 19 February 2016).

Since 2000, the then President Robert Mugabe used the rhetoric of Western threats to Zimbabwe's internal stability to justify the setting up various 'security' institutions in the country. In October 2007, for example, Mugabe launched an intelligence academy named after him, claiming that it would train officers who could counter security threats posed by Western powers (*Reuters*, 26 October 2007). The academy, which is located near Harare, is called Robert Mugabe School of Intelligence (Ibid). On 14 September 2012, Mugabe also officially opened the National Defence College, north of Harare, arguing that it would produce manpower to fend off any future invasion of the country by Western powers (*News 24 Archives*, 15 September 2012). The college was built from a US$98 million loan sourced from China (Ibid).

That said, this chapter focuses on the National Youth Service Training Programme, one such 'security' institution, launched by the ZANU-PF government in 2001, whose youthful graduates are popularly known as 'Green Bombers' (Solidarity Peace Trust, 5 September 2003). They earned this nickname because of "the colour of their military-style uniforms and for their reputation for violence" (Meldrum, 19 February 2003: 1). The National Youth Service training centres were forced to close in 2006 owing to financial and other resource constraints. The last recruitment of the youths for training was done in 2005 (Manyukwe, 12 May 2006). In 2009, the programme was officially terminated (National Youth Development Trust, 1 July 2011). Since its inception in 2001, the programme managed to train 80 230 youths (*Southern Daily*, 12 September 2015).

According to the government, the scheme was necessary for purposes of safeguarding Zimbabwe's internal security (Solidarity Peace Trust, 5 September 2003). It should be noted, however, that the Green Bombers gained notoriety in Zimbabwe, particularly during the period 2001-2009, for terrorising opposition supporters and officials, and causing political, social and economic insecurities which resulted in untold misery (Ibid) as well as derailing or even shattering all hopes for development for and by many ordinary Zimbabweans.

Since the onset of the new millennium, Mugabe often claimed that Zimbabwe had its own political traditions and that Western powers were not qualified to lecture to Zimbabweans on issues of human rights, governance and internal security (Mutenheri, 2009). It is fascinatingly ironic that the instrumentalisation of the youths for political expediency is derived from Western philosophical traditions in countries such as Nazi Germany, where Hitler employed youth brigades to brutalise political rivals and entrench his power position.

Similarly, in Zimbabwe during the period 2001-2009, the Green Bombers were virtually a ZANU-PF para-military force meant to harass political rivals (Chinaka, 19 March 2008; *New Zimbabwe*, 1 March 2015). They were also widely referred to as the 'youth militia' or the 'ZANU-PF militia' (Immigration and Refugee Board of Canada, 2006). As in Nazi Germany, the graduates constituted a youth militia that was notorious for beating up, torturing, dispersing and killing opposition supporters (*Los Angeles Times*, 24 July 2008). In the words of Elias Mugwade (10 April 2008: 1), the Green Bombers are "the President's (Mugabe's) storm troopers deployed to enforce ZANU-PF rule and to intimidate anyone viewed as an enemy of the ruling party." In the words of Catherine Philp (25 June 2008: 1), they were "Mugabe's thugs" and "ZANU-PF's shock troops." These sentiments were reiterated by *The Scotsman* (11 December 2001: 1) which remarked that, "They are Mr. Mugabe's personal storm troopers." Their horrendous brutalities on political rivals also earned them the nickname 'Taliban Force,' after the global terrorist organisation known as the Taliban (Smith, 1 March 2005).

This chapter argues that ZANU-PF 'security' institutions such as the infamous National Youth Service Training Programme and its graduates, the Green Bombers, constituted a major source of gross human rights abuses and various insecurities besides being a source of socio-economic insecurity for many Zimbabwean citizens during the period 2001-2009 and even beyond. In fact, such institutions are ZANU-PF instruments of monopolising political space by unleashing terror on its opponents and terrorising the generality of the population into submission, and whose economic consequences have brought serious socio-economic crises to the Zimbabwean state.

Conceptualising [in]security

The 1994 United Nations Development Programme (UNDP) report offered useful insights into the global debate on [in]security. The report argued that the conceptualisation of [in]security was narrowly focused on nation states as political units at the expense of the livelihood concerns of ordinary people (UNDP, 1994). The report also identified the accessibility of basic material needs, the absence of threats to one's survival (freedom from want), and a dignified and violence-free existence (freedom from fear) as critical elements of human security (Ibid; Thomas and Wilkin, 1999).

In 2000, Kofi Annan, the then United Nations (UN) Secretary-General, reiterated the need to broaden the definition of security from concentrating solely on the defence of a given country from external threats, but to also encompass the general wellbeing of individuals, communities and societies (Annan, 2000). He argued:

> Human security, in its broader sense, embraces far more than the absence of violent conflict. It encompasses human rights, good governance, access to educational and health care and ensuring that each individual has opportunities and choices to fulfil his or her potential. Every step in this direction is also a step towards reducing

poverty, achieving economic growth and preventing conflict. Freedom from want, freedom from fear...are the interrelated building blocks of human- and therefore national- security (Ibid: 1).

Beland (2007) expressed similar sentiments by defining insecurity as the state of fear or anxiety within individuals, sections of the population or even a whole society that stems from a concrete or alleged lack of protection.

Vulnerability, as Suhrke (1999) noted, is the core of human insecurity. The vulnerable people are usually those who are exposed to physical threats to life and deprived of livelihood-sustaining resources. In April 2001, while presenting the UN Millennium Report, Kofi Annan, the then UN Secretary-General, concurred that the exposure of individuals and communities to a broad range of socio-economic vulnerabilities and internal violence are the chief sources of insecurity in many countries (UN, 22 April 2001).

The ruling ZANU-PF party in Zimbabwe deliberately turned a deaf ear to the new dimensions proffered to global security discourses by the 1994 UNDP report and subsequent contributions from various quarters. As noted earlier on in this chapter, the Zimbabwean government was inexorably paranoid about the threat of a military invasion by Western powers, particularly from the onset of the new millennium, instead of addressing the internal socio-economic and other insecurities such as fear and political violence, most of which it had caused, that were being experienced by many Zimbabweans.

In seeking to mitigate such challenges, Thomas and Wilkin (1999) advised that human security cannot be achieved by individuals or groups at the expense of others. As will be noted later on in this chapter, the attempts by the ZANU-PF government to address the imagined threat of a Western military invasion, supposedly backed by local opposition political parties, by, among other things, creating a paramilitary force known derisively as the Green Bombers, actually generated a multiplicity of internal insecurities for the majority of Zimbabweans. ZANU-PF took an egocentric approach to the perceived security threat by, among other strategies, using the Green Bombers to chastise and harass some sections of the population such as the whites and opposition supporters thereby creating a highly volatile socio-political dispensation.

The fact of the matter, however, is that ZANU-PF was politically insecure owing to its waning legitimacy within the country and the rising popularity of the MDC (Alexander, 2003; Hill, 2003; Raftopoulos, 2003). This largely explains the emergence of the Green Bombers as a paramilitary force whose major preoccupation was to orchestrate terror on opposition apologists so as to guarantee ZANU-PF's perennial stay in power. These measures created insecurities within the general public. Such a situation was deliberately created by ZANU-PF to instil what Corey Robin (2004) termed 'repressive fear' among Zimbabweans in order to resuscitate its political fortunes. This illustrates beyond doubt that security in many spheres of life cannot be attained by certain constituencies at the expense of others.

As was the case in Nazi Germany, the activities of the Green Bombers in Zimbabwe illuminate how a government desperate to cling to power at any cost can largely contribute in jeopardising the socio-economic and political security of its citizens. It is, therefore, prudent to begin by exploring such practices in Nazi Germany from the 1930s to the 1940s in order to historically contextualise the activities of the Green Bombers in Zimbabwe.

The rise and institutionalisation of the 'Hitler Youth' in Nazi Germany

Hitler was the leader of the National Socialist German Workers' Party (Nazi) that ruled Germany during the period 1933-1945 (Kershaw, 2008). During his rise to power, Hitler mobilised the youth and drafted them into paramilitary units for his party. In 1922, he formed the *Jungsturm Adolf Hitler*, a youth wing for boys that was based in Bavaria, with the aim of training future members of the *Sturmabteilung* (SA) or Storm Regiment/ Troopers, an adult paramilitary wing of the Nazi Party, which was popularly known as the Brown Shirts, from the colour of the shirts of their uniforms (Campbell, 1998; McNab, 2009). In Munich, during the same year, Hitler also launched the *Jugendbund* (Youth Wing) as the official Nazi

41

Party youth organisation. This unit recruited boys aged between 14 and 18 years. In 1926, the *Jugendbund* was renamed *Hitler-Jugendbund Deutsher Arbeiterjugend* (Hitler Youth, League of German Worker Youth). It was, however, commonly referred to as *Hitler Jugend* or Hitler Youth (Campbell, 1998; Koch, 2000; Lauridsen, 2004). By 1930, the Hitler Youth had more than 25 000 boys aged 14 years and above. It also had a junior unit (*Deutshes Jangvolk*) for boys aged between 10 and 14 years (Butler, 1986; Koch, 2000).

In 1926, Hitler formed the *Schwesterschaften*, a youth wing for girls, which was renamed *Bund Deutscher Madel* (League of German Girls) in 1930 (Koch, 2000; Lauridsen, 2004). This unit was made up of girls aged between 10 and 18 years (Sandor, 2012). In 1932, the female wing was reorganised into two units: one for girls in the 10-14-year age group and the other for those aged between 14 and 21 years (Ibid).

Both the male and female youth wings came to be collectively referred to as 'Hitler Youth.' Having been fully established, the entire youth organisation was made up of four wings, two for males and two for females. The male units were *Deutsche Jungvolk* (German Young People) for boys aged between 10 and 13 years, and *Hitler Jugend* for those in the 14-18-year age group. The female wings were *Jungmadelbund* (League of Young Girls) for those aged between 10 and 14 years, and *Deutsche Maidel* (League of German Girls) for the 14-21-year age group (*History Learning Site*, 9 March 2015; Koch, 2000; Lauridsen, 2004).

In October 1932, the membership of the Hitler Youth totalled 107 000 (*Storm Front*, 20 September 2007). By the end of 1932, the Hitler Youth had more than 108 000 boys and girls (Lauridsen, 2004). The figure rose to 2.3 million in 1933, 3.6 million in 1934, and 3.9 million in 1935 (Ibid). In early 1935, an estimated 60% of Germany's young people were members of the Hitler Youth (*Storm Front*, 20 September 2007). The membership skyrocketed to 5.4 million in 1936, 5.8 million in 1937, 7 million in 1938 and 8.7 million in 1939 (Lauridsen, 2004). In early 1939, approximately 87% of the eligible boys and girls in Germany belonged to the Hitler Youth (*Storm Front*, 20 September 2007). In 1939, a law was passed which made it mandatory for all German male children to become part of the Hitler

Youth (Koch, 2000; Lauridsen, 2004). Those children who had not undergone training in the youth camps were denied jobs and entry into universities (Evans, 2005).

The boys wore brown-shirted uniforms, similar to those of the SA (Koch, 2000). Girls put on schoolgirl-like uniforms comprising skirts, blouses and army boots (*History Place*, 1999). Up to 1934, all the male and female youth wings were under the command of the SA (Campbell, 1998; McNab, 2009). From 1934, Hitler began downsizing the SA and assigned the *Schutzstaffell* (SS), the elite squadron of the Nazi Party, to take command of the youth wings (McNab, 2009). As will be noted later in this chapter, Zimbabwe's National Youth Service Training Programme recruits were also young boys and girls who came to constitute the core of ZANU-PF's paramilitary unit.

The youth wings underwent training in Country Service Camps (*Landjahr*). In 1941, these camps had more than 26 000 girls (Sandor, 2012). The curriculum in the camps was largely derived from Hitler's autobiography, *Mein Kampf* (My Struggle), which outlined Nazi ideological frameworks such as the leadership cult, nationalism, Aryan racial supremacy, anti-Semitism, anti-communism and the one-party state (Evans, 2005; Kershaw, 2008). Even in the contemporary world, as Ross (2011) aptly observed, the *Mein Kampf* is read by politicians in search of ideas to enhance their political fortunes and monopolise political space. This chapter will demonstrate that Zimbabwe's National Youth Service Programme and the subsequent instrumentalisation of its youthful graduates for political expediency by the elite were largely derived from Hitler's political philosophy as articulated in his autobiography.

Propaganda was a central aspect of the training programme. In addition to inculcating the values of German nationalism and national pride, History lessons in both the public education system and within the training camps were designed in a way that extolled the personality cult of Hitler. All lessons emphasised Hitler's life and rise to power (*History Place*, 1999). The young recruits were brainwashed to appreciate that Hitler had liberated Germany from Jewish and Communist conspiracy (*History Place*, 1999). The youths were also taught the history of Nazi heroes (Hakim, 1995; Von

Shirach, 10 November 2016). They were told that the Nazi Party would rule for 1 000 years. The trainees were instructed to be intolerant to opposition parties such as the Communists through the slogan: "All opposition must be stamped to the ground!" (Mitcham, 1996: 139). They were obliged to be loyal to Hitler and the Nazi Party (Hakim, 1995; Von Shirach, 10 November 2016). The children were instructed to exercise blind obedience to Hitler to the extent of even spying on, and denouncing, their parents if they did not support the Nazi Party (Hofman, 21 June 2014; Ross, 2011). To this end, the youths were indoctrinated to prepare themselves for "heroic death" in defence of Hitler and the Nazi Party (Figiel, 2014: 123). As Eric Ross (2011: 1) noted:

> Hitler was more than Father to these brainwashed delinquents; he was God. They were encouraged by the massive propagandist apparatus of the state to rebel against their fathers and to worship Hitler, who replaced family and human love with a glorified, high-minded idea of Death for German Fatherland.

The curriculum also propagated racial hatred among the youths. The trainees were indoctrinated to hate the Jews and the Romans, and to regard the Aryan Germans as a superior race (Koch, 2000; Lauridsen, 2004; Von Shirach, 10 November 2016). Racial indoctrination also involved "teaching young children how to spot a Jew by describing the physical traits which Nazis believed were associated with inferior people" (*History Place*, 1999: 2). The trainees were also taught anti-Semitic songs, one of which went: "Yes, when the Jewish blood splashes from the knives, things will go twice as well" (*History Place*, 1999: 2).

Both boys and girls underwent physical education and military training in the camps in an attempt to create "fearless, brutal and domineering" youths (*Storm Front*, 20 September 2007: 20). In the *Mein Kampf*, Hitler had emphasised the importance of physical training for the youths: "...A less well-educated, but physically healthy individual with a sound, firm character, full of determination and willpower, is more valuable to the *Volkish* community than an intellectual weakling" (*Storm Front*, 20 September 2007: 12). In one of his later speeches, Hitler further elaborated:

> My rules are hard. Weakness must be crushed. In the fortified bastions of my order, there will grow young people who will terrify the world. I want strong, imperious, undaunted, cruel youths. This is the youth I want. They must bear the pain. They must not have anything weak and fragile. They must have free, commanding, wild beast in their eyes… (Miller, 1999: 157).

Upon joining the training camps, the boys underwent a period of induction in physical training during which they were expected to run 60 metres in 12 seconds, and do cross-country hiking lasting for a day and a half (*History Place*, 1999). In addition, the recruits were engaged in a courage test which involved jumping from a first or second storey platform into a large canvas on the ground (Ibid). From then on, the boys spent 15% of their time on physical education (Von Shirach, 10 November 2016).

Military training for boys involved, among other things, athletics, marching, bayonet drills, grenade throwing, trench digging, map reading, gas defence, pistol shooting (*History Learning Site*, 9 March 2015), camping trips, terrain exercises, glider flying (Lauridsen, 2004) and assault sessions (Koch, 2000). They were also engaged in hide-and-seek games known as 'Trapper and Indian.' The boys also participated in war games during which they were organised into platoons that would train to hunt each other like enemies (*History Place*, 1999; *Storm Front*, 20 September 2007). Boxing was also an important part of physical training in order to nurture belligerence within the youths (*Storm Front*, 20 September 2007). During the period of training, every boy was given a performance booklet where he recorded his progress in athletics and other physical and military exercises (*History Place*, 1999).

For girls, the military training included running 60 metres in 14 seconds, throwing a ball for 12 metres, undergoing an hour's march and swimming for 100 meters. The training programme for girls, however, largely involved preparing them for motherhood.

Motherhood training encompassed various domestic chores such as home hygiene and making a bed (*History Learning Site*, 9 March 2015).

It can be noted that, in addition to the military training, the curriculum in the camps was basically a political crusade that was intended to reorient young people to cherish the Nazi ideology which included, among other things, one-partyism, leadership personality cult, racism and violence. They were taught a falsified and one-sided genre of history that starved the past of critical analysis and brainwashed them to romanticise, celebrate and glorify the Nazi party and its heroes, particularly Hitler, and denigrating and brutalising opposition parties. Having been indoctrinated in this way, most German youths were beholden to Hitler and his regime for many years to come. Similarly, the Zimbabwean Green Bombers underwent intensive military training during which they were indoctrinated to glorify ZANU-PF and the then President, Robert Mugabe, and to demonise and terrorise other constituencies such as opposition supporters, commercial white farmers and Western apologists.

Instrumentalisation of the Hitler Youth as a Nazi militia in Germany and abroad

After graduating from the training camps, the youths were used as a militia to ensure Nazi dominance in Germany and abroad. During Hitler's rise to power, uniformed Hitler Youth and the brown-shirted SA roamed the streets in various parts of Germany campaigning for Hitler and the Nazi Party (*Storm Front*, 20 September 2007). The campaigns were often bloody as the youths clashed with the Communists using fists, sticks and firearms (Ibid). During the period 1931-1933, for example, 23 Hitler Youth, including a 12-year-old boy, were killed during such clashes (Ibid).

The graduates subjected Nazi opponents to incessant orgies of terror. They gained notoriety for torturing, intimidating and executing political rivals, and disrupting the rallies of opposition parties. Some of the youths were enlisted as Junior *Gestapo* (Secret Police) agents whose function was to operate as an internal Nazi police force, ensure security and order at meetings, spy on disloyal people and denounce those who did not support Hitler; even their own parents (Kershaw, 2008; *Storm Front*, 20 September 2007). They also killed many Jews, Romans, Communists and trade unionists in Germany (Koch, 2000; McNab, 2011).

In addition, many Hitler Youth were often deployed to various parts of Germany to instil Nazi 'discipline.' From the late 1930s, for example, more than 50 000 youth militia patrolled the streets in the country's urban centres on a mission to enforce Nazi 'ethics.' During the patrols, the militia forcibly cut short the hair of fellow youths and harassed girls who used cosmetics, among other things (Hofman, 21 June 2014).

Many Hitler Youth joined the *SS Totenkopfverbande*, the Death Head Brigade, which tortured and executed inmates in *Konzentrationslager* or concentration camps (*Storm Front*, 20 September 2007). Together with the SA, SS and the *Gestapo*, the youth wings often rounded up political opponents, trade unionists and prisoners of war and detained them, in most cases illegally, in concentration camps during the period 1933-1945. Examples of the major Nazi concentration camps that were set up within Germany include Dachau, established in 1933, Sachsenhausen (1936), Buchenwauld (1937), Flossenburg (1938), and Mauthausen (1938). Ravensburg, which accommodated female inmates, was opened in 1939 (United States Holocaust Memorial Museum, 2 July 2016). In 1939, the number of people detained in the camps stood at 21 000 (Evans, 2005). The figure rose to 715 000 in January 1945 (Evans 2008). Between 1933 and 1945, more than 3.5 million Germans were detained in the camps for varying periods of time (Almond, 1946; Clay, 1994; Mitchell, 1988).

Inside the concentration camps, the detainees were subjected to a broad range of gross human rights abuses. They were forced to work on various SS projects such as building and renovating concentration camps, crushing rocks for stone quarry, coal mining and road construction (United States Holocaust Memorial Museum, 2 July 2016). In addition, they were often tortured, starved and murdered (Almond, 1946; Clay, 1994; Mitchell, 1988). The Hitler Youth participated in the Nazi Holocaust in which more than six million Jews were killed, with most of the atrocities being committed within the concentration camps (Hofman, 21 June 2014).

Many members of the Hitler Youth fought in defence of Nazi Germany during the Second World War and most of them were killed since they had not been adequately trained for the battlefront (Butler, 1986; Koch, 2000; Lauridsen, 2004). At the height of the Second World War in 1943, for example, boys as young as 17 years were sent to the battlefront to fight. In May 1944, the average age of boys recruited into the army was 16 years and seven months. Most of the boy-child soldiers served as anti-aircraft assistants in the air defence units. By 1945, there were an estimated 200 000 young air force and naval assistants in the German army that was fighting in the Second World War (Hofman, 21 June 2014). During the last encounters of the war, some 5 000 Hitler Youth wearing "man-sized uniforms, several times too big, and helmets that flopped around their heads" confronted the Soviet army and after battling for five days, "4 500 had been killed or wounded…Many committed suicide rather than be taken alive by the Red Army" (*Storm Front*, 20 September 2007: 22).

Girls who had graduated from the Hitler Youth were also recruited into the army to perform various tasks within Germany during the Second World War. In 1945, there were about 500 000 women and girls aged between 16 and 26 years serving in the German army. Their tasks included collecting, knitting and sewing army uniforms (Hofman, 21 June 2014), nursing wounded soldiers in health institutions, and stationing themselves along railway lines to offer encouragement and refreshments to soldiers leaving for the battlefront (*Storm Front*, 20 September 2007).

This section demonstrated how the militarisation of the youths by Hitler's Nazi Party in its efforts to monopolise political space made many German civilians and some youthful graduates themselves to become insecure in various spheres of life. As fear gripped the nation, societies became polarised along political lines while families were torn apart as some indoctrinated children turned against their parents. As will be noted later in this chapter, a similar dispensation of government-induced insecurity also prevailed in Zimbabwe after the launching of the National Youth Service

Training Programme in 2001 and the subsequent reign of terror waged by its graduates, the Green Bombers.

Zimbabwe's National Youth Service Training Programme and the emergence of the Green Bombers

In Zimbabwe, the National Youth Service Training Programme originated during the last year of colonial rule when the National Service Act of 1979 was passed (Shumba, 2006). The programme was, however, shelved in 1980 when Zimbabwe became independent (National Youth Development Trust, 1 July 2011). After independence, the National Youth Service Act of 1999 called for the creation of a National Youth Service Training Programme as "an important component in youth development" (Ibid: 1). This was in fact the re-emergence of the 1979 National Youth Service Training Programme which originated during the last year of colonial rule when the National Service Act was passed.

In 2000, the Zimbabwe Government unveiled the National Youth Policy "to underline the importance of the National Youth Service as a developmental platform for youths" (Ibid, p.1). In 2001, the National Youth Service Training Programme was launched, largely through the efforts of Border Gezi, the then Minister of Youth, Gender and Employment Creation (Solidarity Peace Trust, 5 September 2003). The programme's first training camp was set up in the Mount Darwin District in August 2001. This institution was named Border Gezi Training Centre, after its founder. It was for this reason that the graduates of the programme were also popularly referred to as 'Border Gezis' by the general public (Zimbabwe Human Rights Non-Governmental Organisation Forum, 2002). The Border Gezi Training Centre began with 1 000 recruits (Smith, 1 March 2005; *Zimbabwe Independent*, 2 August 2001).

From 2001, many other such centres were established in various parts of the country (*New Zimbabwe*, 1 March 2015). These included 21 Barracks in Mashonaland Central Province, Mhangura Mine in Mashonaland West Province, Dadaya Barracks in the Midlands Province, Guyu in Matabeleland South Province, Kamativi Mine in Matabeleland North Province, Mushagashe in Masvingo Province, and Inyati Mine in Manicaland Province (*Chronicle*, 26 April 2001). The scheme targeted youths aged between 10 and 30 years of age (Solidarity Peace Trust, 5 September 2003). Initially, the training period for each group of recruits lasted for six months but was later reduced to 120 days (*Irin News*, 8 September 2003; Meldrum, 19 February 2003).

By December 2002, approximately 9 000 boys and girls had been formally trained at the major camps while 10 000-20 000 had received less formal training at district centres (*Irin News*, 8 September 2003; Solidarity Peace Trust, 5 September 2003). By the end of 2004, about 22 000 boys and girls had undergone training at the major centres (*Daily News*, 14 December 2004). In April 2008, more than 50 000 youths had graduated from the training camps (Mugwade, 10 April 2008).

The then President of Zimbabwe, Robert Mugabe, and ZANU-PF officials argued that the National Youth Service Training Programme was meant to instil patriotism and national pride in Zimbabwean youths (*New Zimbabwe*, 1 March 2015). According to Border Gezi, the programme was meant to create 'politically conscious youth' who upheld the values of citizenship, national duty, patriotism and responsibility. He also asserted that the scheme was intended to train youths to uphold their cultural values and develop in them, vocational and other developmental skills (Madondo, 2006; Solidarity Peace Trust, 5 September 2003).

Despite these official pronouncements, it is without doubt that the programme was launched with the major aim of resuscitating ZANU-PF's waning political fortunes. In August 2001, for example, Absalom Sikhosana, the then Secretary for Youth in the ZANU-PF Politburo, praised the National Youth Service Programme for alerting the youths to be wary of the machinations of opposition parties and Western countries: "Youths have discovered the opposition for what it is; that it has nothing to offer a black person...White men are deceitful...We have managed to expose all the trickery of the white man" (*Chronicle*, 27 August 2001: 2). These sentiments were echoed by Elliot Manyika, the then ZANU-PF Chairperson for Mashonaland Central Province, who stated that the scheme would inform the youths that "they must change their mindset … and not aspire to be a servant of the white man. Whites are going where they came from" (Ibid, p.2). Ironically, though, the very idea of a youth militia to terrorise political opponents and non-indigenous populations such as the Jews had its origins in Western countries such as Nazi Germany under Hitler. Thus, ZANU-PF leaders were knowingly perpetuating a Nazi legacy of violence, fear and insecurity among many citizens which they professed to be bitterly opposed to.

Some Zimbabwean youths voluntarily joined the National Youth Service Training Programme with the hope of finding employment after graduating (*Los Angeles Times*, 24 July 2008). In fact, the National Youth Service Certificate of Attendance became "a pre-requisite for joining the army or police or for enrolling in government vocational training institutions" (Madondo, 2006: 1). By the beginning of March 2005, for example, about 16 600 graduates from the National Youth Service Programme had reportedly secured employment in government security institutions such as the army, police and the intelligence (Smith, 1 March 2005). Thus, as their 20th century Nazi predecessors, some Zimbabwean political elites of the new millennium often capitalised on the prevailing socio-economic insecurities such as chronic hunger, unemployment and widespread poverty to enlist vulnerable youths and use them as "tools to fight battles for sustenance of power" (Marongwe and Makaye, 2016: 184) instead of being tools to fight underdevelopment and socio-economic insecurity.

The curriculum of the programme was largely intended to brainwash and indoctrinate the youths to venerate Mugabe and regard him as infallible. Besides being urged to cherish 'unity' and patriotism, the youths were indoctrinated to demonise Western countries, to support ZANU-PF and Robert Mugabe, and to uphold one-party state politics (*Los Angeles Times*, 24 July 2008; Mugwade, 10 April 2008). The youths were oriented to characterise ZANU-PF heroes and Robert Mugabe in saintly and messianic ways to the extent of unleashing terror and causing untold suffering on political opponents and the general population. According to the Immigration and Refugee Board of Canada (2006: 2):

The youths are taught Mugabe's own version of history. The manual they learn from is written by the President himself. The lesson is simple and racist. Mugabe and his party, ZANU, are the heroes of the blacks. The opposition party, the MDC, is backed by the whites and is bad. Questioning this is forbidden.

George Ayittey (1998: 158) rightly noted that the cultivation of a leadership personality cult is a characteristic feature of most dictatorial regimes in post-colonial Africa: "Most African political systems have exhibited various shades of the 'Big Man' patrimonial rule." Chazan, Mortimer, Ravenhill and Rothchild (1992: 162) further elaborated:

> The political style fostered is consequently autocratic: Leaders of this sort choose to dominate rather than compromise, to dictate rather than to reconcile. Charismatic leaders in Africa therefore bore the external trappings of omnipotence…to the point of endowing the leader with godlike attributes.

As was the case with Hitler's *Mein Kampf*, the curriculum of the Zimbabwean National Youth Service Programme was derived from one source, *Inside the Third Chimurenga*, reportedly authored by Robert Mugabe in 2001 (Ranger, 2004; Tendi, 2009). In fact, the book is an anthology of speeches delivered by Mugabe since 2000. Most of the speeches in the manual chastise opposition parties, particularly the MDC, and the whites, and glorify the ZANU-PF party and its heroes (Ibid). In one of his tirades against opposition parties and their Western sympathisers recorded in *Inside the Third Chimurenga*, Mugabe (2001: 88) said:

> …The MDC…is immovably and implacably moored in the colonial yesteryear and embraces wittingly or unwittingly the repulsive ideology of a return to white settler colonial rule. MDC is as old and as strong as the forces that control it; that converge on it and control it; that drive and direct; indeed sponsor and spot it. It is a counter-revolutionary Trojan horse contrived and nurtured by the very inimical forces that enslaved and oppressed our people yesterday.

The inexorable chanting of ZANU-PF slogans was an essential aspect of ideological training within the camps (Smith, 9 March 2003). Every lesson on patriotism started "by raising of fists in the ZANU-PF salute and the chanting of slogans in praise of Mugabe, ending with denunciation of [the then] British premier, Tony Blair" (Mugwade, 10 April 2008: 1). It becomes apparent that the Green Bombers were a ZANU-PF militia or private army that was trained primarily to harass political opponents and ensure Mugabe and the ruling party's stranglehold in power. Thus, in July 2002, Welshman Ncube, the then MDC Secretary General, castigated the National Youth Service Training Camps as "…indoctrination centres" where "young children will have ZANU-PF garbage forced down their throats" (*Daily News*, 3 July 2002: 2). These sentiments were reiterated in December 2015 by Obert Gutu, the then spokesperson for the opposition MDC-T party, who characterised the Green Bombers as ZANU-PF's "storm troopers in any election period. They are a grouping of brainwashed young political thugs who are fed on a regular diet of ZANU-PF propaganda" (Chidza, 30 December 2015: 2).

The white community in Zimbabwe became vulnerable to various forms of insecurity given the racist curriculum in the National Youth Service Camps. As Mhango (2016: 138) noted, "racial politics" is often employed as a divide-and-rule strategy by dictatorial regimes in Africa. In 2003, at Tsholotsho Camp, for example, the instructors told the recruits to "beat white people because the MDC wants to give the country back to the whites" (Smith, 9 March 2003: 1). It should be noted that in any given country, security in all spheres of life cannot be attained in the absence of unity and patriotism among citizens. Instead of instilling such values in the youths, the National Youth Service Programme propagated racial hatred and political intolerance. In this way, the programme produced many misguided graduates with a belligerently intolerant disposition towards other sections of the population such as the whites and opposition supporters.

The fact that militarism was another important aspect of the National Youth Service curriculum clearly demonstrates that the Green Bombers were a ZANU-PF private army. In addition to being indoctrinated to glorify ZANU-PF and its leadership, the recruits underwent military drills. This was a clear indication that the Green Bombers were a ZANU-PF militia trained to terrorise opposition supporters as was the case with the Hitler Youth in Nazi Germany. The programme's instructors were military personnel such as war veterans and retired army officers (Madondo, 2006). The military training involved, among other things, morning runs and marching (National Youth Development Trust, 1 July 2011). At Border Gezi Camp, for example, the training included toy-toying throughout the night and running from 5am to 8am (Smith, 9 March 2003). At another camp in north-eastern Zimbabwe, the recruits were trained to run 10 kilometres within 45 minutes and those who made it were promised jobs in the Zimbabwe National Army (Mugwade, 10 April 2008). In January 2004, one senior instructor at Mushagashe Training Camp in Masvingo Province commented on the rigorous nature of the military exercises: "It is only those who would have proved to be too weak who spread lies about our training programme. We test recruits for endurance, and anyone who thinks he is coming here for a picnic should forget it" (*Irin News*, 23 January 2004: 1).

By July 2003, the recruits were being trained to handle weapons (Madondo, 2006). The youths were also well-trained in torture techniques which they would inflict on their victims (Meldrum, 19 February 2003). In February 2003, a National Youth Service graduate confirmed: "They teach political orientation and history of the liberation struggle. They do teach some skills, like carpentry, but we did lots of military training and physical exercise. We learned songs. In military training, we learned methods to interrogate and beat people" (Ibid: 1).

In March 2003, two youths who had graduated from the National Youth Service Programme revealed that they had been taught to murder people in "ways that would be quick and silent and (leaving) no evidence" (Smith, 9 March 2003: 1). They elaborated on some of the lynching techniques they had been taught at Border Gezi Training Centre: "Maybe, two of us would approach you like we were lost. One would grab you on the front of the neck and the others would push you down and hold you so that you do not have a chance to scream before you die" (Ibid, p.1). It can be noted that, as was the case with the Hitler Youth in Nazi Germany, Zimbabwe's National Youth Service Programme acted as "a pot of breeding child/ youth soldiers as evidenced by the pseudo-military style of training that was aligned to the principles of the Zimbabwe African National Union Patriotic Front" (National Youth Development Trust, 1 July 2011: 2).

Many opposition supporters and some sections of the general public, therefore, did not view the National Youth Service graduates as guarantors of internal security but as threats to political freedom, peace and development. In 2002, Nelson Chamisa, the then MDC National Youth Chairperson, for example, noted that the ZANU-PF government sought to militarise the youths after "its realisation that it has lost its support amongst the youths. It reminds one of the despotic and desperate regimes such as that of Kamuzu Banda and Adolf Hitler. It is an exercise in political dishonesty" (Solidarity Peace Trust, 5 September 2003: 16). These sentiments were echoed in January 2004 by David Chimhini, a human rights activist and Chairperson of the Civic Education Trust (ZIMCET), who castigated the National Youth Service Training Centres as "quasi-military camps" that were set up to produce a violent militia to "ensure the survival of ZANU-PF...(and) terrorise perceived enemies and members of the political opposition..." (*Irin News*, 23 January 2004: 1).

It is lamentable that the National Youth Service Programme also rendered many of its recruits and graduates vulnerable in socio-economic terms. The scheme concentrated much on political indoctrination and military training instead of equipping the youths with socio-economic skills necessary for their sustenance and upliftment. This tragedy was succinctly captured by the Solidarity Peace Trust (5 September 2003: 5) when it lamented:

> It takes great wickedness for those in power to be prepared to sacrifice a whole generation, the youths of the nation, in order to maintain their own hold on power. But that is precisely... wickedness... The youths of Zimbabwe are being used, and abused, in a most cynical and calculating way by the very people entrusted with responsibility for their welfare. Behind the mask of a programme

bearing the innocuous title 'National Youth Service Training' lurks a pernicious evil that threatens not only to destroy the nation's youths but also to subvert many of the core Christian values upon which the nation was built. It is the great merit of this report that it tears off this mask and exposes to full view the inner workings of this scheme...The National Youth Service Training Programme masquerades as a youth training scheme that imparts useful skills and patriotic values...Nothing could be further from the truth. The reality is a paramilitary training programme for Zimbabwe's youths with the clear aim of inculcating blatantly antidemocratic, racist and xenophobic attitudes. The youth militias so created are used as instruments of the ruling party, to maintain their hold on power by whatever means necessary, including torture, rape, murder and arson. Having been thoroughly brainwashed, the youth militias are deployed to carry out whatever instructions they receive from their political commissars, on the understanding that they will never be called to account by this regime for any of their deeds...Those responsible for instigating this vile system have introduced into the body politic, a cancer, which now spreads through the nation unchecked and leaves destruction in its wake. The nation's youths are being deliberately corrupted and brutalised, and then deployed to wreak havoc among the people, for no other purpose but to carry forward ZANU- PF's political agenda. The moral, spiritual and physical well-being of a whole generation of Zimbabweans is being sacrificed for the short-term political advantage of those in power, with incalculable long-term effects upon the very fabric of the nation.

Indeed, Prosper Izaya, one of the founder commanders of the National Youth Service Programme, told the United States Embassy officials in Zimbabwe in March 2012 that the scheme was introduced to indoctrinate the youths to support ZANU-PF and destroy opposition parties. Izaya revealed that he deserted the programme in 2005 because he was opposed to the widespread political violence and insecurity that was being perpetrated by the youth militia across the country (*Insider Zimbabwe*, 29 March 2012).

It should be underlined that the ideological training in the National Youth Service Camps was primarily meant to indoctrinate young boys and girls to become ardent supporters of ZANU-PF, just as the Hitler Youth had been brainwashed to be prepared to die for the Nazi party. It therefore becomes apparent that the physical and military training that the Green Bombers underwent was intended to groom them to become future combatants who would defend ZANU-PF at any cost, in the same manner as the Hitler Youth did for the Nazi Party in Germany. As the next section will demonstrate, the activities of the Green Bombers endangered the lives of opposition supporters and the general public in various ways as they sought to ensure that ZANU-PF monopolised political space in Zimbabwe.

The Nazi-style reign of terror by the Green Bombers in Zimbabwe

Political violence is one of the major sources of internal insecurity in many African states. In Zimbabwean politics, as was the case in Nazi Germany, violence has always been "an alternative tool of mobilisation" (Marongwe and Makaye, 2016: 179). The instrumentalisation of youth militias to terrorise political rivals was a Nazi strategy that is often adopted in various parts of post-colonial Africa by despotic regimes on the continent. In Ghana, for example, Kwame Nkrumah formed the Young Pioneers to harass political rivals - a strategy that was also employed by President Hastings Kamuzu Banda in Malawi when he set up the red-shirted Youth League - a paramilitary force of the ruling Malawi Congress Party (Ayittey, 1998). Similar youth vigilantes were the Committees for the Defence of the Revolution in Ghana under the leadership of Jerry Rawlings, and the *Interahamwe* in Rwanda (Ibid).

In Zimbabwe, the Green Bombers were often deployed by ZANU-PF in various parts of the country as "campaign tools and machinery of violence in communities" (National Youth Development Trust, 1 July 2011: 2) and "political guns...to coerce people and force them to support it" (Jakes, 31 January 2016: 1). During the three months preceding the Presidential election of 9-11 March 2002, for instance, gangs of marauding youth militia and war veterans descended on opposition supporters and subjected them to a multiplicity of abuses which included beatings, arson, torture, intimidation, displacement, murder and mounting roadblocks where commuters without ZANU-PF membership cards were victimised. The assailants used any weapons they could lay their hands on such as logs, iron and wooden bars, axes, knives, barbed wire, chains, whips and screwdrivers (Zimbabwe Human Rights Non-Governmental Organisation Forum, 2002). During the run-up to the Presidential election of March 2002, ZANU-PF youth militias allegedly assaulted 6 085 MDC supporters and displaced a further 7 728 from their homes (Physicians for Human Rights, 2002). In its report to the Southern African Development Community (SADC), Amnesty International (January 2002) indicated that seven MDC supporters had been killed by the 'Green Bombers' under the leadership of war veterans during the period stretching from 20 December 2001 to 1 January 2002 (Smith, 9 March 2003).

During election periods in 2000 and 2002, the Green Bombers, war veterans and some soldiers from the Zimbabwean National Army reportedly conducted terror campaigns against civilians suspected of supporting opposition parties. There were numerous reports of people being forced to disembark from buses, after being identified as opposition supporters, and being assaulted with clubs and machetes. Reports abound of the militia disrupting opposition rallies and killing those opposed (or perceived as opposed) to the ZANU-PF party (Chinaka, 19 March 2008). On 31 December 2002, for example, more than 100 youths who had graduated from Border Gezi Training Camp descended on Harare's suburbs of Kuwadzana and Mabvuku where they beat up several people after accusing them of supporting the MDC (*US-Africa Online*, December 2002). By the end of 2002, the Green Bombers had become "a common but fearsome sight" across the country due to "their propensity for violence" (*Irin News*, 18 December 2002: 1). Their reign of terror became "so endemic that the daily ritual of violence no longer shocked Zimbabweans" (Hart, 3 March 2002: 1).

In August 2003, one youth militia testified during an interview that: "We are ZANU-PF's 'B' team. The army is the 'A' team and we do the things the government does not want the 'A' team to do," while another confessed that: "It was about vandalism... We were used to do the things the State does not want to do themselves. Then they can just say it was just the youths, not us" (Solidarity Peace Trust, 5 September 2003: 4). Thus, as was the case in Nazi Germany, the Green Bombers were "the storm troopers in the regime's military-style campaign to kill and disperse opposition supporters, and to force people to vote for Mugabe…" (*Los Angeles Times*, 24 July 2008: 1). Indeed, they were "nothing but a ZANU-PF tool of coercion" (Dzamara, 8 April 2005). Vokal Da Poet (5 January 2016: 1) reiterated:

> Green Bombers make sure that people of the community know the road of the ZANU-PF party. They make sure that people go to rallies so that big people are not embarrassed when they come to do a rally and too few people come. They go door to door and make people go to the rally. At elections, Green Bombers make sure people are voting for the right person, putting the X on the right place, and not the puppets of the West who want regime change. And they discipline other young people who support 'funny' parties by beating them up. After election they can go to work for ministers and Members of Parliament and other big people for free. Just give them food and a place to sleep and beer.

When Zimbabwe experienced severe drought and chronic food shortages in 2002 and 2003, the youth militia was unleashed by the government to attack overcharging retailers, apprehend people found with scarce consumer goods, and seize commodities that were being sold on the parallel market (Madondo, 2006). In many cases, the youths barred opposition supporters from accessing food aid from the state-controlled Grain Marketing Board (Physicians for Human Rights, 20 November 2002). In March 2003, a former Green Bomber confessed: "We were not paid. They gave us pap (sadza) only. We sold mealie-meal in the shops to those with ZANU-PF cards. If MDC people came, we chased them away. We were very rough" (Smith, 9 March 2003: 1).

During election periods, torture camps manned by the Green Bombers and war veterans were set up in various parts of the country to intimidate and harass opposition supporters. On 1 March 2002, for example, these terror camps reportedly accommodated an estimated 20 000 to 50 000 youth militia countrywide (Solidarity Peace Trust, 5 September 2003). The ruling ZANU-PF Party also sought to influence the outcome of elections in its favour by locating some polling stations within the reach of the Green Bombers. During the run-up to the March 2002 Presidential election, for instance, the youths were deployed at 146 National Youth Service Training Centres and terror camps throughout the country, very close to, and at times within, polling stations (Solidarity Peace Trust, 5 September 2003). In the town of Marondera, 12 out of 43 polling stations were located within militia camps. In a few districts in the provinces of Mashonaland, 42 polling stations were located within or close to training camps (Ibid).

Following the March 2002 Presidential election which was won by Robert Mugabe amid controversy, the youth militia embarked on an orgy of retribution against people suspected to have voted for Morgan Tsvangirai, the then MDC leader. Within a few weeks, six MDC polling agents had been murdered while more than 18 000 opposition supporters were displaced from their homes (Zimbabwe Human Rights Non-Governmental Organisation Forum, 2002). In addition, 22 people were tortured while 100 others were detained at youth terror camps (Amnesty International Press Release, 18 March 2002). In April 2002, about 1 000 women, mostly MDC supporters, were still detained in the camps where most of them were subjected to sexual abuses by the militia (Amnesty International Press Release, 5 April 2002).

In January 2003 alone, the Human Rights Forum reported 30 cases of brutality by the 'Green Bombers' on civilians, mostly MDC supporters, in Harare's Kuwadzana Suburb (Meldrum, 19 February 2003). Jameson Gadzirai, a 23-year-old political activist and member of a residents association in Kuwadzana Suburb, narrated how he was brutalised by the youth militia:

> They were Green Bombers. I could tell from the uniforms. They started beating us. They suspended us in the air and whipped our backs and our backsides. They beat the soles of our feet. They were organised, very systematic. And they kept asking us questions: "Who did we work

for?" "Who was paying us?" "Who were we spying for?" They seized our cell phones and when they found the numbers of lawyers and (Harare's MDC) Mayor Elias Mudzuri, they said that proved we were spies (Ibid, p.1).

In 2008, the ZANU-PF government set up military bases across the country where opposition supporters were savaged by the Green Bombers (*Los Angeles Times*, 24 July 2008). On 18 June 2008, for example, ZANU-PF militia were reportedly involved in the murder of Nyoka Chokuse, the MDC Buhera South District Chairman (*Nehanda Radio*, 6 March 2010). They were also accused of committing various crimes such as rape and destroying people's property (Manyukwe, 12 May 2006). Themba Ndlovu, a 22-year-old former Green Bomber, revealed some of the brutalities they inflicted upon political opponents and the general public, which included gang rape on a 12-year-old girl and savage beatings:

> I beat people with crowbars, sticks and whips. I did not mind if they screamed because the police were on our side. Afterwards, we had many beers and we make a party. Our leaders brought a young lady, a white person, and we raped her. We were four raping her. We kept her hostage in our camp (*Scotland on Sunday*, 24 August 2003: 1).

Besides targeting political rivals, the Green Bombers also attacked white Zimbabwean communities, whom they accused of supporting opposition parties and conspiring to recolonise the country. This prompted some analysts to draw comparisons between the Mugabe's Green Bombers and Hitler's Brown Shirts who waged a horrendous racial war against the Jews in Germany (Mugwade, 10 April 2008). In April 2008, for example, a white Zimbabwean woman narrated how she was stopped in her car by the youth militia in Mutorashanga, 90 kilometres north of Harare:

> They had crowbars and they demanded to see a ZANU-PF card. When I said I didn't (have) one, they made me chant: "Forward with Osama Bin Laden; Forward with Robert Gabriel Mugabe; Down with

whites." It was terrifying. There was a police Land Rover there, but the police just sat and watched (Mugwade, 10 April 2008: 1).

By the end of 2008, political insecurity had become the order of the day as the Green Bombers were actively involved in coercing Zimbabweans to support ZANU-PF. As Catherine Philp (25 June 2008: 1), a *New York Post* journalist, observed in Harare: "Fear has made it hard to tell a real ZANU-PF supporter these days. One man said he was terrified of getting a beating because he did not have a ZANU-PF T-shirt; the party office had run out."

This section has illuminated how, as was the case in Nazi Germany, many Zimbabweans were traumatised by being subjected to a broad range of insecurities by the terror campaigns of the Green Bombers. The political freedom of many citizens was violated as they were terrorised to support ZANU-PF. In addition, others became critically vulnerable in socio-economic terms due to displacement and torture which disrupted their subsistence and income-generating activities. Some even lost their lives. These developments made the general population to live in perpetual fear.

Tasting their own medicine: Backlash against the Green Bombers

Despite causing severe hardships on many sections of the population, the Green Bombers also created numerous insecurities for themselves. Their activities antagonised some Zimbabweans who came to view them as social outcasts. In some cases, some victims organised themselves to repulse their offensives. For many of them, their career prospects of becoming useful participants and partners in the development of the country were ruined by their induction into unproductive lives of intolerance, hate and belligerence which ostracised them from their communities. In addition, some of them experienced psychosocial problems after murdering people.

Many Green Bombers lived in fear of reprisals from victims who had survived their brutal campaigns. This irony of the effects of violence on victims and perpetrators was aptly captured by *The Los Angeles Times* (24 July 2008: 1) which noted that "the fearsome

Zimbabwe militias are also afraid." In July 2008, for example, a 25-year-old former Green Bomber from Harare confirmed during an interview that he was "afraid to walk alone in his neighbourhood because an angry mob might rise up and kill him for what he had done in Mugabe's name" (Ibid, p.1).

During terror operations, the safety of marauding Green Bombers was not guaranteed because many of their victims did not give up without a fight. Some sections of the civilian population actually organised themselves to retaliate against the marauding assailants. In December 2002, for example, some residents of St Mary's Suburb in the City of Chitungwiza set up vigilante groups to repel offensives by the ZANU-PF militia (*Irin News*, 18 December 2002). Job Sikhala, the then MDC Member of Parliament for St Mary's Constituency, said, "In my constituency, there is a watertight mechanism to counter the Green Bombers. I have a security team of young men and women who have managed to chase the militias away as soon as they are reported in the constituency" (Ibid, p.1).

For many youthful assailants, their future prospects of taking part in the socio-economic development of the country and themselves were shattered as they were trained to hate and kill opponents. In the context of development, many youths who graduated from the National Youth Service Programme constitute "Zimbabwe's lost generation" (Peta, 7 January 2010: 1). As Bagenda-Sssemugooma, quoted by Madondo (2006: 1), noted:

> ...Each dictator uses young people. Hitler had them too and we have heard of the KANU Youth wingers in Kenya as well. The problem is that they are not educated through committing atrocities. This has to stop. How can we allow Mugabe to destroy yet another future generation for his personal gains? The young people should be told that they are Zimbabweans; what they do is not right and it will have a long term effect on their lives even after Mugabe has left.

It was emotionally disorienting on the part of many Green Bombers to be unleashed against their family members and relatives. As noted earlier in this chapter, Hitler obliged the youth to spy on, and even kill, their parents and relatives if they did not support the

Nazi party. In Zimbabwe, family unions also became insecure as similar instructions were sometimes given to the youth militia by ZANU-PF officials. In March 2003, for example, two National Youth Service graduates fled to South Africa in protest after they had been ordered by ZANU-PF officials to kill their close relatives for supporting the MDC (Smith, 9 March 2003). One of the youths revealed that he had been instructed to murder his uncle while the other had been ordered to do the same to his father (Ibid). A Green Bomber who also deserted in protest in May 2003, said, "For me, it got too bad. There was too much beating – old people, young people, our own aunts and uncles. I had to run away" (Hentoff, 6 May 2003: 1). These events authenticated the comments that had been made in December 2002 by Nelson Chamisa, an MDC official, on the political intentions of the National Youth Service Programme: "It has become apparent that this so-called National Youth Training Service is in fact a ZANU-PF party service where the murderous ZANU-PF is recruiting children to terrorise their parents" (*US-Africa Online*, December 2002: 1).

The future of many youths was also ruined by their induction into a life of drugs which they were usually given before undertaking terror campaigns. The youth assailants were often drugged with alcohol and dagga by ZANU-PF officials before being sent on a mission to kill on the slogan that "you feel nothing for anyone" (Smith, 9 March 2003: 1). This strategy had also been employed by Charles Taylor in Liberia during the 1990s when he intoxicated child-warriors with "marijuana, cocaine, and a mixture of cane juice and gunpowder, which can cause brain damage" (Ayittey, 1998: 59). Nkosinathi Sibanda, a 17-year-old young man who joined the National Youth Service Programme in November 2002, recalled that they were given marijuana and alcohol before being deployed on terror campaigns "to numb their consciences" so that "you never mind, you just fight" (*Scotland on Sunday*, 24 August 2003: 1). As a result, he became unscrupulous and went on to beat up nearly 500 people and vandalise 20 farms during his three months as a Green Bomber (Ibid).

The perpetrators of violence also suffered from psychosocial insecurities related to the indigenous African beliefs in the existence of avenging spirits of deceased persons that haunt the living (Eppel, 2006; McLaughlin *et al*, 2003; Mutekwa, 2010; Muwati *et al*, 2006; Nhemachena, 2014). In Zimbabwe, the avenging spirits are known as *ngozi* by the Shona and *uzimu* by the Ndebele (Bourdillon, 1982). According to Benyera (2014: 21), *ngozi/uzimu* is "a traditional justice system...in which the deceased person returns in spirit to haunt his/her murderer's family until the members admit to committing the crime. This leads to their subsequent payment of compensation to the deceased's family, usually in the form of cattle and money."

In early 2010, for example, hundreds of ZANU-PF militia who had murdered MDC activists across the country were reportedly "being haunted by avenging spirits (*ngozi*) of the deceased. Some have grown sugarcane on their heads while others have gone mad as the spirit of those they murdered continue to haunt them" (*Nehanda Radio*, 6 March 2010: 1). Naison Nemadziva, the then Buhera South Member of Parliament, confirmed these developments:

> The stories might sound unreal but it is true. Most of these perpetrators have fled their homes. I can confirm three reports of avenging spirits in Buhera South, that of Chokuse, Chibamba and Chokuda who have been haunting...those responsible for their deaths asking them why they killed them (Ibid, p.1).

This account was corroborated by Bodias Nendanga, the then Buhera Ward 24 Councillor, who said: "It is now common knowledge that the murderers are no longer enjoying the comfort of their homes. Their victims knock on their homes during the night and some actually see them" (Ibid, p.1). Phathisa Nyathi, a Zimbabwean historian, weighed in and added that it was inevitable that ZANU-PF assailants who had been involved in the murder of political opponents would be haunted by avenging spirits in accordance with indigenous African jurisprudence:

> It should be a lesson to other people. It shows that if you allow yourself to be used, it does not affect the person who gave the order, but it affects you the murderer. The sender is very safe, and the one who spilt blood suffers...When such things happen in our culture,

what is important is to re-establish the lost equilibrium, the lost harmony, and the injured social relations. The Shona have the best solution to this; the operation of *ngozi* where the murderer has to pay (Dube, 30 October 2010: 1).

Even though the African indigenous beliefs in *ngozi* may be dismissed as superstitious by Eurocentric critics and 'modern' scientists, it should be noted that the fear of avenging spirits of their deceased victims is a lived reality for many Green Bombers who murdered political opponents. In mid-2008, for example, a 25-year-old former Green Bomber, confirmed that he lived in fear as he believed that "the spirits of those he killed will come and take vengeance" (*Los Angeles Times*, 24 July 2008: 1).

Some youths who were averse to a life of drugs, hate and violence deserted National Youth Service training camps and ZANU-PF terror campaigns. Those who abandoned the National Youth Service Training Programme and terror campaigns became targets of Zimbabwe's secret police who tormented them on charges of desertion (*Scotland on Sunday*, 24 August 2003).

This section has illustrated the various insecurities that came to besiege many Green Bombers who had been used as tools of violence by ZANU-PF. Indeed, the desertion of some youths from ZANU-PF terror campaigns and their subsequent confessions clearly show that they were ever cognisant, or later realised, that a violent disposition, besides being anti-social, does not secure a productive and prosperous future.

Conclusion

It is abundantly clear that many insecurities plaguing ordinary people in the contemporary world, particularly Africa, are largely caused by the machinations of power-hungry political elites rather than Western governments. This chapter has shown how the ZANU-PF government systematically increased collective insecurities through violence to create an atmosphere of fear and terror in order to guarantee its self-perpetuation in power. Among other things, private militias comprising the youths were indoctrinated, instrumentalised and transformed into political apparatus and merchants of violence to harass opposition supporters and other sections of the population. As the chapter has noted, the terror campaigns waged by the Green Bombers bifurcated the society and subjected the generality of Zimbabweans to a broad range of socio-economic and political insecurities.

Despite being the perpetrators of violence, the Green Bombers were themselves not secure, both socio-economically and politically. In fact, the chapter has illuminated how power mongers abuse the youths by inducting them into a career of intolerance and thuggery instead of nurturing them to dispense their energies in a positive, moral and diligent manner in order to develop themselves and their communities. The chapter has exposed how power-hungry politicians such as Hitler and his 21st century ZANU-PF disciples patronised the youths and turned them into hooligans and pawns in political contestations. It is, therefore, lamentable that dictators often play "a subversive role" (Peta, 7 January 2010: 1) by mobilising and manipulating young people into becoming "cannon fodder in political games" (Fay Chung quoted by Peta, 7 January 2010: 1) instead of engaging them in meaningful development projects. Thus, this chapter has articulated how the Nazi legacy of political repression caused various insecurities on both the perpetrators and victims of violence in Zimbabwe during the period 2001-2009.

References

Alexander, J. (2003) 'Squatters, veterans and the state in Zimbabwe,' in: B. Raftopoulos, A. Hammar and S. Jensen (eds.) *Zimbabwe's unfinished business: Rethinking land, state and nation in the context of crisis*, Harare: Weaver Press, pp.83-117.

Almond, G. (1946) 'The German Resistance Movement,' in: *Current History*, Volume 10, pp.409-527.

Amnesty International (January 2002) *Memorandum to the Southern African Development Community on the deteriorating human rights situation in Zimbabwe*, London: Amnesty International.

Amnesty International Press Release (18 March 2002) 'Zimbabwe: Citizens' rights not politics must set the agenda,' London: Amnesty International.

Amnesty International Press Release (5 April 2002) 'Zimbabwe: Assault and sexual violence by militia,' London: Amnesty International.

Annan, K. (2000) 'Secretary-General salutes International Workshop on Human Security in Mongolia,' Available at: www.un.org/News/Press, Accessed 20 October 2017.

Ayittey, G.B.N. (1998) *Africa in chaos*, New York: St Martin's Press.

BBC News (28 June 2005) 'UK, US caused Zimbabwe droughts,' Available at: www.news.bbc.co.uk, Accessed 18 October 2017.

BBC News (12 December 2008) 'UK caused cholera, says Zimbabwe,' Available at: www.news.bbc.co.uk, Accessed 18 October 2017.

Berger, S. (9 October 2008) 'Zimbabwe inflation hits 231%,' Available at: www.telegraph.co.uk, Accessed 17 July 2015.

Beland, D. (2007) 'Insecurity and politics: A framework,' in: *Canadian Journal of Sociology*, Volume 32, Number 3, pp.317-340.

Benyera, E. (2014) 'Debating the efficacy of transitional justice mechanisms: the case of national healing in Zimbabwe, 1980-2011,' D.Phil. Thesis, University of South Africa.

Bond, P. and Manyanya, M. (2001) *Zimbabwe's plunge: Exhausted nationalism, neoliberalism and the search for social justice*, Asmara: Africa World Press.

Bourdillon, M.F.C. (1982) *The Shona peoples: An ethnography of the contemporary Shona, with special reference to their religion*, Gweru: Mambo Press.

Bradford, P. (19 July 2013) 'African experiences of youth political violence: Reflections on Zimbabwe,' Available at: www.beyondthehague.com, Accessed 24 November 2016.

Butler, R. (1996) *Hitler's young tigers: The chilling true story of the Hitler Youth*, London: Arrow Books.

Campbell, B. (1998) *The SA generals and the rise of Nazism*, Kentucky: University Press of Kentucky.

Chambati, W. and Moyo, S. (2004) *Impacts of land reform on farm workers and farm labour processes,* Harare: African Institute for Agrarian Studies.

Chazan, N. Mortimer, R. Ravenhill, J. and Rothchild, D. (1992) *Politics and society in contemporary Africa,* Boulder: Lynne Reiner Publishers.

Chidza, R. (30 December 2015) 'ZANU-PF recruits 80 000 Green Bombers,' in: *Newsday,* Harare: Zimbabwe.

Chinaka, C. (19 March 2008) 'Mugabe's iron fist - War veterans, green bombers,' Available at: http://www.reuters.com/article/us-zimbabwe-election-mugabe-idUSL1813904020080320, Accessed 8 October 2016.

Chronicle (26 April 2001) 'National service to instil patriotism among youths,' Bulawayo: Zimbabwe.

Chronicle (27 August 2001) 'Party woos back youths,' Bulawayo: Zimbabwe.

City Press (18 August 2016) 'Mugabe blames the West for protests,' Available at: www.city-press.news24.com/news, Accessed 18 October 2017.

Clay, D. (1994) *Contending with Hitler: Varieties of German resistance in the Third Reich,* Cambridge: Cambridge University Press.

Da Poet, V. (5 January 2016) 'Green Bomber militia return,' in: *Village Idiot Diaries,* Available at: http: //ilizwi263.com/2016/green-bomber-militia-return-village-idiot-diaries, Accessed 8 October 2016.

Daily News (3 July 2002) 'National service plans slammed,' Harare: Zimbabwe.

Daily News (14 December 2004) 'Youth militia creep into security services,' Harare: Zimbabwe.

Dube, J. (30 October 2010) 'Chokuda case: Avenging spirits exact justice?' Available at: www.thestandard.co.zw, Accessed 23 October 2017.

Dzamara, I. (8 April 2005) 'Green Bombers to run council elections,' in: *Zimbabwe Independent,* Harare: Zimbabwe.

Eppel, S. (2006) 'Healing the dead: Exhumations and reburials as a truth-telling and peace-building activity in rural Zimbabwe,' in:

T. Borer (ed.) *Truth-telling and peace-building in post-conflict societies*, Notre Dame: University of Notre Dame Press, pp.1-23.

Evans, R.J. (2005) *The Third Reich in power*, New York: Penguin Group.

Evans, R.J. (2008) *The Third Reich at war*, New York: Penguin Group.

Figiel, D. (2014) 'The experience of the Hitler Youth,' in: *Journal of Education, Culture and Society*, Number 2, pp.112-125.

Financial Gazette (11 December 2014) 'British firms underplay Zimbabwe corruption,' in: *The Financial Gazette*, Harare: Zimbabwe.

Fuller, A. (May 2012) 'Breaking the silence: Oppression, fear and courage in Zimbabwe,' In: *The National Geographic Magazine*, pp.4-6.

Hakim, J. (1995) *A history of us: War, peace and all that jazz*, New York: Oxford University Press.

Hart, P. (3 March 2002) 'One last throw of the dice,' Available at: www.telegraph.co.uk/news, Accessed 23 October 2017.

Hentoff, N. (6 May 2003) 'Mugabe's victims: Mostly black,' Available at: www.villagevoice.com, Accessed 23 October 2017.

Hill, G. (2003) *The battle for Zimbabwe: The final countdown*, Cape Town: Zebra Press.

History Learning Site (9 March 2015) 'Hitler youth movement,' Available at: www.historylearningsite.co.uk, Accessed 10 November 2016.

History Place (1999) 'Hitler Youth: Prelude to war, 1933-1938,' Available at: www.historyplace.com, Accessed 17 November 2016.

Hofman, S.J. (21 June 2014) 'When we were 17: Youth at the crossroads 1945: A youth in ruins,' Available at: http://www.dw.com/en, Accessed 17 November 2016.

Immigration and Refugee Board of Canada (2006) 'Zimbabwe: The Green Bombers or the youth militia; whether it is still operating; its leadership; whether it commits human rights abuses and if so, whether the militia's abuses have been reported to the police and police response; whether it targets MDC supporters (2001-2006),' Available at: http://www.refworld.org, Accessed 9 October 2016.

Insider Zimbabwe (29 March 2012) 'Founder of Green Bombers spills the beans,' Available at: www.insiderzim.com, Accessed 16 November 2016.

Irin News (18 December 2002) 'Backlash against ZANU-PF militia,' Available at: www.irinnews.org/fr/node, Accessed 23 October 2017.

Irin News (8 September 2003) 'Report accuses youth militias of systematic violence,' Available at: www.irinnews.org, Accessed 24 November 2016.

Irin News (23 January 2004) 'Green Bombers deserting poor conditions in camps,' Available at: www.irinnews.org, Accessed 16 November 2016.

Irish Times (13 December 2002) 'Western hostility means whites suffer – Mugabe,' Available at: www.irishtimes.com/news, Accessed 18 October 2017.

Jakes, S. (31 January 2016) 'Youths used as political guns in Zimbabwe,' Available at: www.bulawayo24.com, Accessed 24 November 2016.

Kershaw, I. (2008) *Hitler: A biography*, New York: W.W. Norton and Company.

Koch, H.W. (2000) *The Hitler Youth: Origins and development, 1922-1945*, New York: Cooper Square Press.

Lauridsen, J. T. (2004) 'Hitler Youth,' in: P.S. Fass (ed.) *Encyclopedia of Children and Childhood in History and Society, Volume 2: World History in Context*, pp.430-431, Available at: www.ic.galegroup.com, Accessed 10 November 2016.

Littlejohn, D. (1990) *Sturmabteilung: Hitler's Storm Troopers, 1921-1945*, London: Osprey Publishing.

Los Angeles Times (24 July 2008) 'Fearsome Zimbabwe militias are also afraid,' Available at: http://latimes.com/2008, Accessed 8 October 2016.

Madondo, O. R. (2006) 'The problem of youth in Mugabe's Zimbabwe,' Available at: http://www.africafiles.org/article.asp?ID=6498, Accessed 8 October 2016.

Manyukwe, C. (12 May 2006) 'Youth training centres closed,' in: *Zimbabwe Independent* Harare: Zimbabwe.

Marongwe, N. and Makaye, P. (2016) 'Violence and the politics of the Movement for Democratic Change- Tsvangirai's (MDC-T) mobilisation and continued survival, 1999-2014,' in: M. Mawere and N. Marongwe (eds.) *Myths of peace and democracy? Towards building pillars of hope, unity and transformation in Africa*, Bamenda: Langaa Research and Publishing Common Initiative Group, pp.167-194.

McLaughlin, E. Fergusson, R. and Hughes, G. (2003) 'Introduction: Justice in the round: Contextualising restorative justice,' in: McLaughlin, E. Fergusson, R. Hughes, G. and Westmorland, L. (eds.) *Restorative justice: Critical issues*, London: Sage, pp 1-19.

McNab, C. (2009) *The SS: 1923-1945*, Stroud: Amber Books Limited.

McNab, C. (2011) *Hitler's master plan: The essential facts and figures for Hitler's Third Reich*, Stroud: Amber Books Limited.

McNab, C. (2013) *Hitler's elite: The SS, 1933-1945*, London: Osprey Publishing.

Meldrum, A. (19 February 2003) 'Living in fear of Mugabe's green bombers,' Available at: https://www.theguardian.com/world, Accessed 8 October 2016.

Meredith, M. (2002) *Mugabe: Power and plunder in Zimbabwe*, New York: Public Affairs.

Mhango, H.I. (2016) 'Violence, power, politics and (anti-)development in Africa,' in M. Mawere and N. Marongwe (eds.) *Violence, politics and conflict management in Africa: Envisioning transformation, peace and unity in the twenty-first century*, Bamenda: Langaa Research and Publishing Common Initiative Group, pp.117-150.

Miller, A. (1999) *Prisoners of childhood*, Poznan: Media Rodzina.

Mitcham, S. W. (1996) *Why Hitler?* Westport: Praeger Publishers.

Mitchell, O. C. (1988) *Hitler's Nazi state: The years of dictatorial rule, 1934-1945*, New York.

Mugabe, R. G. (2001) *Inside the Third Chimurenga*, Harare: Department of Information and Publicity.

Mugwade, E. (10 April 2008) 'Youth coerced into regime militia,' Available at: https://iwpr.net, Accessed 16 November 2016.

Mutekwa, A. (2010) 'The avenging spirit: Mapping an ambivalent spirituality in Zimbabwean literature in English,' in: *African Studies*, Volume 69, Number 1, pp.161-176.

Mutenheri, F. (2009) 'Human rights record and democracy in Zimbabwe since independence: An overview,' in: *Journal of Sustainable Development in Africa*, Volume 11, Number 3, pp.206-216.

Muwati, I. Gambahaya, Z. and Mangena, F. (2006) 'Echoing Silences as a paradigm for restorative justice in post-conflict Zimbabwe: A philosophical discourse,' in: *Zambezia*, Volume XXXIII, Number i/ii, pp.1-18.

NBC News (3 June 2008) 'Mugabe blames West for Zimbabwe hunger,' Available at: www.nbcnews.com/id, Accessed 18 October 2017.

National Youth Development Trust (1 July 2011) 'National youth service: Its feasibility and efficiency in the current dispensation: A position paper by the National Youth Development Trust,' Available at: www.wordpress.com/2011/07/01, Accessed 10 October 2016.

Ncube, M. (19 February 2016) 'The last days: Hunger stalks Zimbabwe as Mugabe clings on,' Available at: www.theweek.co.uk, Accessed 18 October 2017.

Nehanda Radio (6 March 2010) '*Ngozi* haunts ZANU-PF killers,' Available at: www.nehandaradio.com, Accessed 23 October 2017.

Nehanda Radio (9 July 2016) 'Mugabe blames salary delays on sanctions by the West,' Available at: www.nehandaradio.com, Accessed 18 October 2017.

New Zimbabwe (1 March 2015) 'Green Bomber training for all youths, Mugabe,' Available at: www.newzimbabwe.com/news, Accessed 8 October 2016.

News 24 Archives (15 September 2012) 'Mugabe turns to China for military defence,' Available at: www.news24.com/Africa, Accessed 18 October 2017.

Nhemachena, A. (2014) 'Knowledge, *chivanhu* and struggles for survival in conflict-torn Manicaland, Zimbabwe, D.Phil. Thesis, University of Cape Town.

Peta, B. (7 January 2010) 'Independent appeal: Rescuing Zimbabwe's lost generation,' Available at: www.independent.co.uk, Accessed 24 November 2016.

Philp, C. (25 June 2008) 'Mugabe's thugs "reeducate" opponents at Camp Hell,' Available at: www.nypost.com, Accessed 23 October 2017.

Physicians for Human Rights: Denmark (20 November 2002) *Vote ZANU-PF or starve: Zimbabwe, August to October 2002*, Johannesburg: Physicians for Human Rights: Denmark.

Physicians for Human Rights: Denmark (2002) *Zimbabwe: Post-Presidential election- March to May 2002*, Copenhagen: Physicians for Human Rights, Denmark.

Raftopoulos, B. (2003) 'The state in crisis: Authoritarian nationalism, selective citizenship and distortions of democracy in Zimbabwe,' in: A. Hammar, B. Raftopoulos and S. Jensen (eds.) *Zimbabwe's unfinished business: Rethinking land, state and nation in the context of crisis*, Harare: Weaver Press, pp.217-41.

Ranger, T. (2004) 'Historiography, patriotic history and the history of the nation: The struggle over the past in Zimbabwe,' in: *Journal of Southern African Studies*, Volume 30, Issue 2, pp.215-234.

Reuters (26 October 2007) 'Mugabe launches Robert Mugabe Intelligence Academy,' Available at: www.reuters.com/article, Accessed 18 October 2017.

Reuters Alert (20 March 2007) 'Zimbabwe says drought will worsen food shortages,' Available at: www.alertnet.org, Accessed 16 February 2017.

Richardson, C.J. (2005) 'The loss of property rights and the collapse of Zimbabwe,' in: *Cato Journal*, Volume 25, Number 3, pp.541-565.

Robin, C. (2004) *Fear: The history of political idea*, New York: Oxford University Press.

Ross, E. (2011) 'Hitler Youth: Hitler's secret weapon,' Available at: www.logos-publishing.com, Accessed 17 November 2016.

Sandor, C. (2012) *Through innocent eyes: The chosen girls of the Hitler Youth*, Bloomington: Balboa Press.

Scotland on Sunday (24 August 2003) 'Zimbabwe's deserters tell of terror gang and rape,' Available at:

www.scotlandonsunday.com/international.cfm?id, Accessed 23 October 2017.

Scotsman (11 December 2008) 'Elliot Manyika,' Available at: www.scotsman.com, Accessed 16 November 2016.

Shoko, J. (7 May 2013) 'Mugabe slams West over Africa's conflicts at security meeting,' Available at: www.theafricareport.com, Accessed 18 October 2017.

Shumba, R. (2006) 'National identities in the National Youth Service of Zimbabwe,' Unpublished Dissertation, South Africa: University of Johannesburg.

Smith, C. (9 March 2003) 'I was ordered to kill my father,' Available at: www.iol.co.za/news, Accessed 16 November 2016.

Smith, R. (1 March 2005) 'Fear, terror and the spoils of power: Youth militias in Zimbabwe,' Centre for the Study of Violence and Reconciliation, Available at: www.csw.org.za, Accessed 16 November 2016.

Sokwanele (20 July 2007) 'Zimbabwean refugees suffer in Botswana and South Africa,' Available at: www.sokwanele.co.zw, Accessed 2 April 2015.

Solidarity Peace Trust (5 September 2003) *National Youth Service Training- 'Shaping youths in a truly Zimbabwean manner': An overview of youth militia training and activities in Zimbabwe, October 2000-August 2003,* Johannesburg: Solidarity Peace Trust.

Southern Daily (12 September 2015) 'Youth militia returns? ZANU-PF reintroduces Green Bombers,' Available at: http://thesoutherndaily.co.zw/2015/09/12/youth-militia-returns-zanu-pf-reintroduces-green-bombers/, Accessed 8 October 2016.

Storm Front (20 September 2007) 'Hitler and the youth,' Available at: https://www.stormfront.org/forum/t42220/, Accessed 17 November 2016.

Suhrke, A. (1999) 'Human security and interest and security of states,' in: *Security Dialogue*, Volume 30, Number 3, pp.265-276.

Telegraph (12 December 2008) 'Mugabe claims cholera was released by the British,' Available at: www.telegraph.co.uk, Accessed 18 October 2017.

Tendi, M. (2009) *Becoming Zimbabwe: Teaching history in context in Zimbabwe*, Wynberg: Institute for Justice and Reconciliation.

Thomas, C. and Wilkin, P. (1999) *Globalisation, human security and the African experience*, London: Lynne Reiner Publishers.

Thomson Reuters Foundation (13 July 2014) 'Zimbabwe crisis,' Available at: www.trust.org, Accessed 2 June 2015.

UN (22 April 2001) 'UN Secretary-General Millennium Report, Chapter 2,' Available at: www.un.org.millennium/sg/report, Accessed 20 October 2017.

UNDP (1994) *Human development report: New dimensions of human security*, New York: Oxford University Press.

United States-Africa Online (December 2002) 'Zimbabwe militants reported on terror run,' Available at: www.usafricaonline, Accessed 24 November 2016.

United States Holocaust Memorial Museum (2 July 2016) 'Concentration camps, 1933-1939,' Available at: www.ushmm.org, Accessed 15 November 2016.

Von Shirach, B. (10 November 2016) 'Youth in Nazi Germany,' Available at: www.123helpme.com, Accessed 10 November 2016.

Watson, F. (1 March 2003) 'Understanding the food crisis in Zimbabwe,' Available at: www.ennonline.net/fex, Accessed 21 June 2015.

Wines, M. (2 May 2006) 'How bad is inflation in Zimbabwe?' Available at: www.nytimes.com, Accessed 7 July 2015.

Zimbabwe Human Rights Non-Governmental Organisation Forum (2002) *Are they accountable? Examining alleged violators and their violations, pre- and post- the Presidential election of March 2002*, Harare: Zimbabwe Human Rights Non-Governmental Organisation Forum.

Zimbabwe Independent (2 August 2001) 'War veterans to take charge of national youth training,' Harare: Zimbabwe.

Zimbabwe Situation (22 February 2014) 'Mugabe blames corruption on the British,' Available at: www.zimbabwesituation.com/news, Accessed 18 October 2017.

Chapter 4

Building Development Bridges and Resilience for Africa's Marginalised Communities: The 'Magics' of Value Chain Approach in Resilience building and Development Pragmatics

Joseph Muroiwa, Solomon Mutambara & Munyaradzi Mawere

Introduction

Resilience building is becoming popular with modern developmental work, yet it falls short in real development practices in many African communities where vulnerability and underdevelopment continue defying the logics of development. Building resilience seeks to improve people's lives and reduce the need for recurring humanitarian assistance to the disadvantaged communities. In 2011, 13.3million people were affected by the worst drought in the horn of Africa with other millions in the Sahel Region suffering from drought, conflicts and other pressures (USAID, 2008). During the 2015/16 agricultural season, Southern African countries such as Zimbabwe, Mozambique, South Africa, Zambia, Namibia, Malawi and Botswana plunged into the El Nino induced drought which resulted in losses of crops and livestock. This shock resulted in declining incomes and livelihoods for the marginalised and vulnerable rural communities. The consequential outcomes of the El Nino shock led the World Food Programme (WFP) to declare level 3 emergence in Lesotho, Madagascar, Mozambique, Swaziland, Zambia and Zimbabwe (WFP, 2016). Zimbabwe alone faced a cereal deficit of 650 000mt during the 2015/16 season with a record of over 25 000 cattle poverty deaths (GOZ, 2016). Although the donor community is trying its level best to mobilise food aid, the ever-increasing need for humanitarian assistance in [Southern] Africa as a result of unpredictable natural calamities makes it difficult to meet the needs of the disadvantaged communities.

While it may not be possible to control natural shocks and stresses, it remains imperative to assist [rustic] communities to safeguard their developmental gains through building their absorptive, adaptive and transformative capacities. Without efforts to build bridges of both resilience and development transformationals among rural communities, there is no doubt that Africa will remain trapped on the seabed of poverty and underdevelopment.

This chapter exposes the insecurities and vulnerabilities rampant in many rural communities of Africa. It further examines how value chain approach can be used to help build resilience while promoting [positive] development in the communities. We argue that the main objective of developing pro-poor value chain developmental approaches to resilience building is critical to improve the livelihoods and standards of living of the poor marginalised communities through their active participation in markets. In view of the highlighted challenges, we propose the need to build community resilience and develop bridges of development using the value chain approach.

The operationalisation of value chains in resilience

While a plethora of definitions for resilience has been conjured so far, USAID's interpretation seems enjoying wide appreciation. USAID (2008) defines resilience as the ability of people, households, communities, countries and systems to mitigate, adapt to, recover from shocks and stresses in a manner that reduces chronic vulnerability and facilitate inclusive growth. Resilience is the capacity of communities (or individuals) to bounce back (Paton & Johnson, 2001), recover from or adjust easily to a misfortune or stress (Brown & Kilig, 1996) without a large amount of assistance from outside the community (Millet, 1999). All these interpretations are in tandem with FAO's (2016), which considers resilience as the ability to prevent disasters and crises as well as to absorb, accommodate or recover from them in a timely, efficient and sustainable manner.

On the other hand, the value chain concept is a full range of activities which are required to produce a good or service from the beginning through the different stages of production and delivery to final users (Kaplinsky & Morris, 2001). The value chain developmental approach has been adopted by governments, donors and NGO to reduce poverty over the past decades. (Stoin *et al.*, 2012). The value chain approach is useful in identifying key stakeholders in the value chain, their level of interaction and functions in adding value to commodities on market. More importantly, the value chain approach strengthens the mutual beneficial linkages among value chain stakeholders so that they work together to take advantages of market opportunities and also building trust among value chain participants (Webber & Labaste, 2010). Joshi *et al* (2016) reverberate that the value chain development approach enables the farmers and development workers to understand the entire market system and identify leverage points along the chain. This connotes that value chain approach affords opportunities for farmers to improve market linkages and increase their share of benefits and income. The stronger the win-win nature of the value chain relationship, the more likely it is going to endure over time (Stoin *et al.*, 2012).

The key stakeholders in pro-poor value chain developmental approach include producers, processors, consumers, government, business and knowledge and research institutions. In the ensuing section, we elaborate on these stakeholders for a clear grasp of how each of them operates:

Producers
In value chains, the producers perform the production function, grading as well as aggregating the commodities to be marketed. The producers ensure that the commodities produced are of the highest quality possible as is expected or required by the ultimate consumers.

Processors
Processors are responsible for transformation of raw materials into usable products by the consumers. They add more value to the raw materials besides making sure that they [raw materials] are usable by consumers.

Consumers

The consumers are the final end users of commodities and services in the value chain. They encourage the producers to produce more and the processors to realise profits for their processing services. Without consumers, processors are not motivated to engage in processing; no wonder in business they say 'customer is king'.

Government

The role of the government is to provide conducive environment – both in terms of the law and market – for the operations of value chains to take place. Government creates policies that enable dialogue platforms and the macro environment under which value chains operate.

NGOs

These usually assume intermediary roles in value chains. In other words, NGOs provide overall insight of value chain activities. They act as quality assurance overseers on the roles and services provided by the government and other value chain stakeholders.

Knowledge and Research Institutions

These include colleges, universities and research centres whose functions include raising critical questions for development, carrying out research and development functions as well as disseminating the information to the value chain stakeholders. Knowledge and research institutions also provide networks for innovation as well as developing the capacities for local and global institutions.

When the pro-poor value chain developmental programmes are successfully implemented in resilience building and development bridging, the communities will benefit immensely through improved income levels, access to markets, creation of jobs, and improved standards of living. The business community will benefit through improved market share and profits, while the private sector benefits in that it will find it easier to do business due to improved relations with regulatory authorities such as the local authorities and government (GIZ, 2013). The government as a stakeholder will not be left out in this whole win-win game. It will also benefit from improved revenues from taxes and improved business climate.

More importantly, the value chain approach is crucial in identifying bottlenecks preventing progress and the required institutional support (Baker, 2006). It assists in addressing constraints such as poor market access and lack of farmer bargaining power (Saarelainen & Sievers, 2011). Understanding the value chain in full is therefore critical as it facilitates the identification of constraints to development. The value chains operate within markets that are interlinked and interdependent. The linkages within the value chains can impinge on one another (Mutambara *et al.*, 2015). The impediments to performance of value chains could be lying within the system or the environment in which the value chain will be operating, hence these inter-linkages and interdependence should be recognised (Mutambara *et al.*, 2015). It is worth noting however that developmental partners may not have the capacity to address the constraints but the ability to identify the challenges may enable positive results to be realised in the process. To close this gap, the value chain approach emphasises value creation at each and every stage of the chain; a characteristic which makes it different from supply chain.

In order to ensure full participation of all stakeholders in value chain development, consulting all actors in early stages of priority sector identification is important. Early engagement ensures stakeholder by-in to the proposed intervention. Also, stakeholder engagement is critical as it helps create trust, address common challenges, and strengthening the identified value chains. In the Dominican Republic, a study carried out by USAID (2008) on the adoption of value chain methodologies that benefit small and very small firms, revealed that the exclusion of key government representatives led to serious problems like crime and trash collection.

Limited participation of some stakeholders or lack of it thereof always backfires. It normally results in conflicts, poor performance of businesses and low production. Studies conducted by Saarelainen & Sievers (2011) revealed that improved dialogue between fish breeders, paddy farmers and local administrative authorities in Sri-

Lanka assisted in resolving conflicts regarding water usage following the blocking of water by fish breeders. The setting up of a local dialogue platform in the province resulted in the solving of the water conflicts and enabled the development of the fish value chain. Similarly, research conducted by Boudi *et al.*, (2016) to analyse the performance of the olive oil value chain in Algeria revealed that poor agricultural practices, institutional environment, lack of market transparency, market uncertainties, lack of quality control, absence of traceability monitoring systems, lack of certification and labelling as well as limited access to effective extension services were the major bottlenecks affecting the value chain. This resonates with Woodhill's (2012) findings that the use of multi-stakeholder approaches such as innovation platforms and functional producer groups result[ed] in improvement in oil seed production by smallholder farmers in Uganda. This has also been complimented by financial support from institutions such as Stanbic and donor support from SNV and the Netherlands Development Organisation.

Having elaborated on the operationalisation of value chain approach in bridging and promoting development, there is need to understand the underpinnings of the same when it comes to forging resilience. This is critical as more often than not resilience feeds into long-term development.

Why the value-chain approach in resilience building?

As in paving way for development indicators in general, value chain can also enliven resilience. The value chain approach allows value chain actors to improve on resilience building as it promotes collaborative approaches to development, which in itself has long-term benefits to any development endeavour. As they enjoy collaboration, chain actors are afforded the capacity to recover quickly from shocks and other adversities. The USAID (2008) says it all when it urges, in view of value chain, that producers, distributors and buyers must always cooperate to ensure that products produced meet consumer expectations and that the goods get from producers to customers. To ensure that the interests of the poor and the marginalised groups are catered for, the value chains should be able to benefit the disadvantaged members of the communities in a sustainable way. The value chains approach enables the decision makers to map up strategies that can be used to incorporate the targeted groups at different stages of the chain as producers, service providers or as traders and assist them to rise above situations and to higher levels of the chain.

For sustainable development of agricultural value chains, the value chain approach assists in compelling stakeholders to be always focused on delivering value to each other and identifying areas that need to be improved. The core rents and barriers to participate in the value chain are easily identified including those benefiting from production (Mitchell *et al.*, 2009). In a value chain, the major objective is to deliver maximum value to the end users for the least possible total cost (Reddy, 2013) over an extended period of time. A value chain analysis provides ways of understanding the relationships that always exist between value chain stakeholders.

As part of the resilience building game involves open communication, the value chain approach promotes smooth flow of information and open communication along the value chain. Value chains become more effective, inclusive and more resilient when there is smooth flow of information and knowledge (Saarelainen & Sievers, 2011). Sharing of information along the value chain encourages the value chain stakeholders to build long-term stable and collaborative relationships based on mutual trust and commitment. Forms of institutional failure such as opportunistic behaviour, rent seeking and free riding which have been noted to be major constraints in the development of sustainable value chains are eliminated when there is free flow of information (Mutambara *et al*, 2015). In most value chains, lack of trust among stakeholders, weak flow of information and incompetent leadership has resulted in lack of collaboration along the value chains (Webber & Labaste, 2010). The value chain approach recognises that the poor people's participation in the market as welfare-recipients provides a poor basis for lasting or sustainable development, but should be based on mutual trade exchanges (Ferrand *et al.*, 2004).

The Value Chain Developmental (VCD) approach can be complimented with other approaches such as the Local Economic

Development (LED) platforms where main private and public stakeholders in a particular area jointly design and implement common developmental strategies and utilise locally available resources (Canzanelli, 2001).

This can be done through participatory approaches such as innovation platforms. According to (Homann-Kee Tui *et al.*, 2013), innovation platforms are meant to bring together different stakeholders to identify solutions to common problems. The platform consists of groups of individuals with different interests and objectives. Stakeholders include communities, farmers, government, NGOs, research, and private sector who come together and share common vision and objectives (Pali & Swaan, 2013). The players collectively discuss possible ways of achieving the set goals and objectives. By bringing the stakeholders together, skills, experiences, opinions and resources are shared in pursuit of solving common problems affecting them.

It is also crucial for the value chain stakeholders to consider the institutional arrangements comprising of local culture of the community, norms, values and other factors affecting value chain development. Other external environmental factors include understanding the market systems, demand and supply considerations as well as the quality requirements.

The farmers need to be organised into formal groups to make their voices more audible. The farmer groups or associations are critical in addressing common challenges and strengths in the value chain. Smallholder farmers usually have less bargaining power due to their lack of organisation and are usually forced to accept prices and product requirements given by the buyers (Saarelainen & Sievers, 2011). Tollens (2006) echoed that most smallholder farmers do not have information about where their products are most wanted and as a result, their bargaining power is weakened.

In order to strengthen the role of and trust of value chain players, the ECRAS project, facilitated innovation platforms, bringing together all value chain players to discuss challenges and ways of collectively handling value chain challenges to have a win-win situation for all players. Farmers, government partners from Ministry of Lands Agriculture and Rural Resettlement, representatives from the rural district councils, private sector partners participating in value chains participated in the formation of innovation platforms. The platform gave the chain actors the opportunity to discuss constraints affecting the value chains and how the constraints are going to be addressed. A lot needs to be done to ensure that that the chain sectors keep on interacting for the sustainability of the value chains.

Value chains, institutional arrangements, resilience and sustainability

The value chain approach strives to build resilient livelihoods by 'crowding-in' credible stakeholders/institutions to improve the functioning of market systems for the benefit of the poor (Heierli, 2013; Albu & Schneider, 2008). Kaplinsky (2004), defined a value chain as the organisational arrangements linking and coordinating actors working at different levels along the chain. The actors within a value chain are governed by rules and regulations (MercyCorps, 2008).

For Haggblade et al. (2012), Kirsten et al. (2009), laws, rules, regulations, international trade agreements and social norms and customs all contribute to the institutional environment. The development and functionality of value chain is influenced by the strength of these formal and informal rules or norms, and the way these rules are enforced in a value chain (Tschumi & Hagan, 2009). The vale chain approach emphasises how critical institutions are in creating conducive market environment, in which the Government is usually the key player in the setting and the enforcement of rules. The private sector is increasing becoming more important and effective in this role, especially in well-developed market systems or value chains (Ferrand et al., 2004). .

As Kirsten et al. (2009) aver, most agricultural developmental policies have succeed in Asia but failed in Africa hence the need to analyse institutions for sustainable agricultural development. Stakeholders such as the Government and the NGOs need to play a catalytic role to enable improvements in performance of value chains. The script by Ferrand et al., (2004) articulates the roles of institutions as facilitators of coordinated exchange of resources where buyers, sellers, consumers and other value chain players to effectively perform market functions, instead of playing an interventionist role themselves (Albu & Schneider, 2008; Tschumi & Hagan, 2009; Mutambara *et al.*, 2015).

In Zimbabwe, the Zimbabwe Resilience Building Fund (ZRBF) supported ECRAS project signed MOUs with private partners like Metbank, National Organic Produce (NOP), CBZ Bank, Klein Karoo Seed Marketing (K2) and Sidella to enhance the effectiveness of their participation in different value chains and to broker long term relationships with rural communities. For K2, the government's agricultural extension arm, Agritex was actively involved as seed multiplication is regulated and guided by government. The Ministry of Agriculture was also involved in the engagement of these private sector actors as a way of reinforcing their facilitatory role in value chains and building their capacity to continue engaging the critical value chain players beyond the ECRAS project transact in a reliable and sustainable way.

Sustainability of value chain is entwined with scaling-up and capacity to transform, therefore, the need to productively engage all critical actors is very critical (Tschumi & Hagan, 2009). This will ensure that even small or short term rural development projects have a scope to leverage the resources, actions and expertise of the private sector to bring about systemic and extensive impact (Tschumi & Hagan, 2009). The ECRAS project established a working whose main role was to pool together all the expertise at district level from different ministries and government departments (Vet, LPD, Agritex, NGOs and private sector players) to assist farmers in different ways in different value chains. Ultimately, this will increase the chances of rural projects to build resilience.

Institutional arrangements include contract arrangements, property rights as well as mechanisms of ensuring that the contracts are well enforced. No value chain can operate sustainably where the institutional environment is weak. An example of how the weak institutional environment has contributed to lack of sustainability of agricultural value chains is on Zimbabwe's cotton sector from 2004-2015. During this period, there was a proliferation of many cotton companies in the sector but governance of the value chain was weak. Lack of strict contract enforcement mechanisms resulted in serious forms of institutional failures such as side marketing, high agricultural loan default rates, rent seeking and opportunistic behaviour. This resulted in lack of sustainability in the once vibrant cotton sector.

Properly coordinated institutional arrangements result in win-win situations for all the value chain actors as these promote the development of profitable opportunities for investment. Availability of these incentives are a panacea for sustainable value chains necessary for resilience building.

Merging theory with practice: The market for poor approach (M4P) to resilience building

According to Mutambara *et al.* (2015), the M4P is an approach that can be used by developmental agencies to focus on fundamental constraints that inhibit sustainable development of market systems for the poor in different contexts. The approach emphasises on the participation of the private sector to reinforce the strengths of market systems Tshumi & Hagan, (2009) quoted in Mutambara *et al.*, (2015). (Mutambara *et al.*, 2015) posited that there is a lot to be done to understand smallholder farmers as potential markets for different value chains. In view of this it was recommended that there was need to invest into the M4P multi-disciplinary research to identify the bottlenecks to effective performance of markets for the communal farmers in Zimbabwe. Understanding these bottlenecks would be crucial in coming up with appropriate approaches to resilience building.

Under the ECRAS project implemented in Zimbabwe's Chiredzi and Mwenezi districts of Masvingo Province, a value chain assessment was done to identify gaps in the existing chicken, goats and cattle value chains. Evidence suggested that the farmers were failing to consistently supply the market and as a result, the rural farmers were not taken seriously by the output market (supermarkets and whole salers). The project engaged National Organic Produce and Met Bank to contract farmers in the commercial production of the indigineouls chickens. 48 000 birds were eventually produced and sold to the contract. The move was both historic and empowering for the rural communities coming from the magic of combining strength and weakiness of different actors in a value chain.

In the beef value chain, Montana Carswell Meats (MC) contracted farmers 143 farmers to participate in pen fattening under its Feeder Finance Scheme. Farmers were encouraged to group themselves and aggregate a minimum of 10cattle per group. The farmers were provided with stockfeed and vaccines which were deducted when the farmers delivered their cattle for slaughter. During the 2017 marketing season, 143 farmers participated in the pilot project and realised over $400000 within 4 month. For the goat value chains, the ECRAS project injected some improved goat breeds and promoted investment in goat breeding to ensure that the supply side of the value chain is improved before engaging the insatiable output market. The M4P requires that development practitioner understand what affects farmers'effective participation in value chain and find ways of addressing such barriers. The ECRAS project's success in these value chains is credited on the in-depth understanding of value chain bottlenecks and deliberate attempt to address the barriers in a more sustainable way. Fig 1 below shows the value chain actors participating at various stages of the beef value chain in Zimbabwe's Mwenezi District.

Figure 1: Participation of value chain actors a bridge to resilience building: Veterinary staff inducting cattle in Mwenezi (Golden Feedlot) (Top Left), Mwenezi Feeder Finance Farmers recording weights for their cattle at MC Abattoir, Masvingo (Top Right), MC staff slaughtering

cattle supplied under Feeder Finance Scheme (Bottom left and right). The farmers realised attractive remuneration from cattle sold under the MC Meats supported Feeder Finance Scheme.

The Value chain selection procedures and implementation framework

As Webber & Labaste (2010) note, selection of priority value chains for sustainable resilience is a process involving consultation of value chain stakeholders. As alluded to earlier, the value chain stakeholders comprise of the members of the community, input suppliers, producers, processors and consumers. Service providers such as transporters and financiers have critical roles in sustainable resilience building initiatives. Government stakeholders play vital roles in value chain governance. When using the value chain approach in resilience building, it is crucial to come up with priority sectors for the value chain interventions. The initial consultation process is meant to come up with the initial lists for screening. Lists can be obtained through consultations with keys stakeholders, previous assessments and choosing value chains that could have been identified as national priorities. To refine to list of potential value chains, markets analyses should be conducted and this can involve use of quantitative tools.

The selection of suitable value chains starts with identifying suitable chains that serve the needs of the targeted groups. For sustainability, it is advisable to start with existing value chains. Basic value chain assessment should be done to gather facts around what has been working and what has not. Women and the youths are usually the targeted groups who are mostly excluded from most opportunities that improve livelihoods. Sustainable value chains should empower and unlock opportunities for the marginalized communities including women and the youth and improve their participation in production and other activities of the value chain. The identification of the suitable chains should involve all stakeholders participating in the value chain. The stakeholders include the consumers, processors, farmers, buyers, inputs suppliers, government stakeholders and other chain supporters.

The original list of possible chains should be narrowed down to a few based on agreed selection criteria such as suitability to local geography, commercial viability. A SWOT analysis should also be carried on the value chain players in order to identify their strengths and weaknesses as well as opportunities and strengths within the value chain. This will assist in identifying areas where efforts should be channelled to smoothen the operations of the value chain. Examples can be drawn from the by Enhancing Community Resilience And Sustainability (ECRAS) project (implemented in Chiredzi and Mwenezi Districts in Zimbabwe) funded by the Zimbabwe Resilience Building Fund (ZRBF)- a multi-donor fund aimed at building the resilience of rural communities. It was revealed that there was mistrust between farmers and the private companies. Farmers in these areas accused the private companies of extractive behaviour whilst the private players had a perception that the farmers are not trustworthy. The ECRAS project focused on carrying out productive engagements between the farmers and the private sector players in order to build trust within the value chain. Building on the existing value chains before introducing new ones enables lessons to be learnt from the status quo. The lessons learnt from previous experiences can be useful in making corrective measures in new resilience building interventions.

Basing on the authors' experience with the ZRBF supported ECRAS project, the Value Chain Selection and Implementation Framework illustrates the several steps to be followed when selecting and implementing pro-poor value chains. The pro-poor value chains are meant to improve resilience of disadvantaged communities. The activities involved are as illustrated in Fig 2 below.

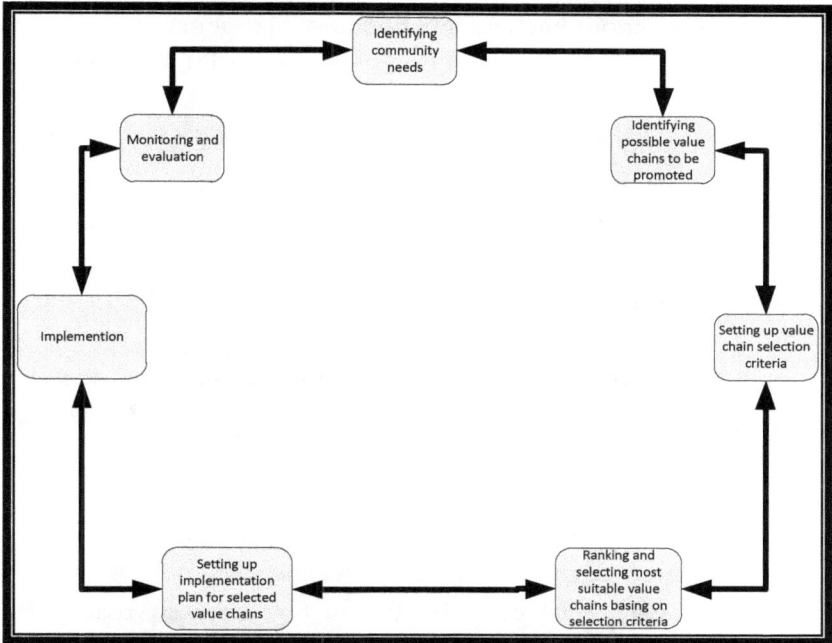

Figure 1 Value chain selection and implementation framework. Source: Authors (2017).

Step 1: Identifying community needs

Involves understanding the objectives of the targeted community. The objectives may vary from need to increase income levels, food security, improved livelihoods, and poverty eradication.

Step 2: Identifying possible value chains

Prepare a list of possible value chains that can be promoted in pursuit of addressing the above objectives. The list may include the crop and livestock value chains that are suitable for the particular area. Communities should be engaged to participate in identification of the value chains that they feel can make them move out of poverty.

Step 3: Setting up value chain selection criteria

This involve coming up with the value chain selection criteria basing on the following variables;

- suitability to local geographical environment

- conditions such as, soil conditions, topography, and climatic factors such as temperature, humidity, and rainfall pattern for the area.
- Unmet market demand
- Potential to improve household incomes
- Commercial viability of the value chain basing on the economics of production. For communities to sustainability participate in the value chain, the returns should be profitable in order to be attractive.
- Potential for participation by the marginalized members of the communities. These include women, youths, aged, disabled and the poor.
- Gender equality.
- Sustainable natural resource management.
- Ability to promote resilient livelihoods
- Existence of critical infrastructure such as roads, storage facilities,
- The potential for scaling up the operations.
- Ability of the prospective farmers to meet quality expectations.
- Period on return on investment
- Initial capital required by the farmer
- Current farmer knowledge
- Staff experience

Step 4: Ranking and selection of most suitable chains.

After setting up the value chain selection criteria, the value chains are ranked according to the agreed selection criteria. This will be followed by scoring the value chains in order to identify the most suitable options. The value chain that best suit the selection criteria will be implemented.

Step 5: Implementation

The implementation stage involves the practical application of the value chain concepts agreed upon by the stakeholders during the selection process. All stakeholders along the chain are supposed to be driven by the desire to create value. For sustainability, all stakeholders within the chain should derive benefits from the collaboration by all actors along the chain.

Step 6: Monitoring and Evaluation

Monitoring and evaluation is crucial in determining whether the project is achieving the desired results. It is meant to advice the stakeholders on whether the value chain activities under implementation are pointing towards the success of the project or not. This will assist in coming up with viable decisions.

Recommendations

While the value chain approach has been found to be useful in promoting communities to be improve their absorptive and transformative capacities, the concept does not operate in isolation. Value chain approach on its own may not be the panacea to development of resilient communities. The approach needs to be complimented with other institutional reforms such as improvements in institutional environment and stakeholder involvement at each and every stage of the value chain. Institutional environment refers to rules and regulations governing the value chains. The flow of information along the value chain should be smooth in order to reduce forms of institutional failure such as rent seeking, free-riding and opportunistic behaviour. The triangulation of the above strategies will ensure the development of sustainable resilient communities.

Basing on practical experience from the ECRAS Project, the value chains were identified through stakeholder engagements. The communities were engaged through the Community Adaptation Action Planning (CAAP). The CAAP approach was adopted following its successes in Ghana and Niger. The approach proved to be key for building motivation and capacity for action among communities, while also strengthening community participation and influence in local government decision-making (Daze *et al.*, n.d.). The approach was adopted following its successes experienced in Ghana and Niger. From the CAAP workshops conducted in the communal wards of Chiredzi and Mwenezi, the rural communities identified beef, sorghum, millet, and indigenous chickens as the main value chains that sustaining their livelihoods. The same results on the critical value chains from the CAAP were also similar to the findings from the key informant interviews conducted during the context analysis carried by ECRAS project. The project also carried value chain analyses research which identified lack of trust between value chain actors, lack of reliable markets, poor pricing policies among the major constraints limiting the smooth performance of value chains. It is therefore recommended that all the value chain actors and supporters be engaged at all the stages of planning and implementation in order to enhance community resilience and sustainability.

Conclusion

The value chain approach's magic in resilience building lies in its efforts to crowd-in credible actors for the smooth functioning of value chain. It underscores the importance of an enabling environment in which the Government play a critical role in the creation of laws, policies and their enforcement and that ownership of value chain interventions be in the hands of stakeholders with the wherewithal to continue performing the functions beyond the life of the intervention/project. The approach strives to build long term trade relationships premised on trust among the value chain actors.

The major success factors from the ECRAS project were, ensuring that all the value chain interventions are preceded by a value chain assessment to identify barriers/bottlenecks for farmers' active participation. Riding on existing value chain and value chain actors addressing the identified gaps, deliberate effort to ensure that the farmers derive some material value in their participation in the value chain, in a more sustainable way. It was also realised that quick win can be registered where private sector value chain players can be engaged to contract rural farmers, supplying the critical input and recouping the cost after sale of products.

Innovation platforms need to be facilitated in order for the value chain stakeholders to collectively identify bottlenecks hindering smooth performance of value chains. Such platforms enable all actors to contribute in identifying solutions to their problems. Building confidence and trust is enhanced and this will go away in ensuring sustainability of value chains and resilience building.

List of Abbreviations and Acronyms

AGRITEX	Agricultural Technical and Extension Services
CAAP	Community Adaptation Action Planning
ECRAS	Enhancing Community Resilience and Sustainability
FAO	Food and Agricultural Organization of the United Nations
GOZ	Government of Zimbabwe
USAID	United States Agency for International Development
WFP	World Food Program
ZimVAC	Zimbabwe Vulnerability Assessment Committee
ZRBF	Zimbabwe Resilience Building Fund

References

Albu, M., & Schneider, H. (2008) *Making Markets Work for the Poor. Comparing M4P and SLA frameworks. Complementarities, divergencies and synegies,* Bern: The Springfield Centre-Fauno Consortium.

Baker, D. (2006) *Agriculture Value Chains: Overview of Concepts and Value Chain Approach,* Bangkok: FAO.

Boudi, M., Laoubi, K., & Chehat, F. (2016) A Value Chain Analysis for Sustainable Development of Olive Oil Agro-Industry: The case of Algeria, *Journal for Agriculture and Environment for International Development,* 267-292.

Brown, D., & Kilig, J. (1996) The Concept of Resilience. Theoretical Lessons For Community Research. *Health and Canadian Society, Vol 4 No 1,* 29-52.

Canzanelli, G. (2001) *Overview and Learned Lessons on Local Economic Development,* Human Development and Decent Work. International Labour Organisation.

Daze, A., Percy, F., & Ward, N. (n.d.) *Adaptation Planning with Communities,* CARE International.

FAO. (2016) *South Sudan Resilience Strategy (2016-2018).* The Food and Agricultural Organisation.

Ferrand, D., Gibson, A., & Scott, H. (2004) *Making Markets Work for the Poor: An Objective and an Approach for Governments and Development Agencies,* Woodmead: Con mark.

GIZ. (2013) *Value Chains Development by the Private Sector In Africa: Lessons learnt and guidance notes,* GIZ.

GOZ. (2016) *Zimbabwe Vulnerability Assessment Committee,* Harare: Government of Zimbabwe.

Haggblade, S., Theriault, Staatz, J., Dembele, N., & Boubacar, D. (2012) *A Conceptual Framework fo Promoting Inclusive Value Chains: Improving the Inclusiveness of Agricultural Value Chains In West Africa.* Prepared for the International Fund for Agricultural Deveeloopment, Michigan State University, Department of Food and Resource Economics.

Heierli, U. (2013) *Market Approaches that work for development: How the private sector can contribute to poverty reduction,* Berne: Swiss Agency for Development and Cooperation.

Homann-Kee Tui, S., Adekunle, A., Lundy, M., Turker, J., Birachi, E., Schut, M., Mundy, P. (2013) *Innovation Platforms Practice Brief 1,* Addis Ababa: CGIAR.

Joshi, S. R., Rasul, G., & Shrestha, A. J. (2016) *Pro-poor and Climate Reslient Value Chain Development, Operational Guidelines for the Hindu Kush Himalayas.* International Centre for International Mountain Development, Kithmandu.

Kaplinsky, R. (2004) *Competitions Policy and the Global Coffee and Cocoa Value Chains.* Paper Prepared for United Nations Conference for Trade Development, Centre for Research and Innovation Management, University of Sussex, Brighton.

Kaplinsky, R., & Morris, M. (2001) *A handbook for value chain research.* Institute of Development Studies. University of Sussex.

Kirsten, J. F., Doward, A., Poulton, C., & Vink, N. (2009) *Institutional Economics: Perspectives on African Agricultural Development,* Washington DC: International Food Policy Research Institute.

MercyCorps. (2008) *What are markets and why should we pay attention to them?* Retrieved March 02, 2018, from www.mercycorps.org/files/file1203640666pdf.

Millet, D. (1999) *Disasters by Design. A reassessment of Natural Hazards in the United States.* Washingto DC: Joseph Henry Press.

Mitchell, J., Keane, J., & Cooles, J. (2009) *Trading up. How a Value Chain Approach Can Benefit the Rural Poor,* COPLA Global. Westminster: Overseas Development Institute.

Mutambara, S., Darkoh, M., & Atlhopheng, J. (2015) Making Markets Work for the Poor (M4P) Approach and Smallholder Irrigation Farming, *Department of Environmental Science: University of Botswana, Volume 4*(1), 1-9.

Pali, P., & Swaan, K. (2013) *Guidelines for Innovation Platforms: Facilitation, Monitoring and Evaluation.* ILRI Manual 8, CGIAR, Addis Ababa.

Paton, D., & Johnson, D. (2001) Disasters and Communities. Vulnerability, Resilience and Preparedness, *Disaster Prevention and Management, 10(4),* 270-277.

Reddy, A. A. (2013) *Training Manual on Value Chain Analysis of Dryland Agricultural Commodities,* ICRISAT, Andhra Pradesh.

Saarelainen, E., & Sievers, R. (2011) *The role of cooperatives and business associations in value chain development.* Value Chain Development Briefing Paper 2 November 2011, International Labour Organisation.

Stoin, D., Donovan, J., Fisk, J., & Muldoon, M. F. (2012) *Value Chain Development for Rural Poverty Reduction: A Reality Check and Warning,* Enterprise Development and Microfinance Vol 23 No 1, Practical Action Publishing.

Tollens, E. (2006) *Market Information Systems In Sub Saharan Africa. Challenges and Opportunities,* Paper Prepared for Presentation at the International Assocoation for Agricultural Econometrics Conference, Gold Cost.

Tschumi, P., & Hagan, H. (2009) *A Synthesis of the Making Markets Work for the Poor (M4P) Approach,* UK Department for

International Development (DFID) and the Swiss Agency For International Development and Cooperation (SDC).

Tshumi, P., & Hagan, H. (2009) *A synthesis of the Making Markets Work for the Poor (M4P) Approach.* Retrieved March 03, 2018, from UK Department for International Development (DFID) and the Swiss Agency for Development and Cooperation (SDC): https://www.eda.admin.ch/.../172765-unesynthesedemarche_EN.pdf.

USAID. (2008). *Value Chain and the Cluster Approach. Transforming Relationships to Increase Competitiveness and Focus on End Markets.* Micro Report #148, United States Agency for International Development.

Webber, M. C., & Labaste, P. (2010) *Building Competiveness in Africa's Agriculture. A guide to value chain concepts and applications,* World Bank.

WFP. (2016). *El-Nino 2015-16 Preparedness and Response Situation Report No 2,* Situation Report 28 January 2016, World Food Programme.

Woodhill, J. (2012) *Multi-Stakeholder Collaboration and Scaling of Inclusive Agri-Food Markets.* Centre for Development Innovation, University of Wageningen.

Chapter 5

Land Redistribution, Justice and Development in Africa: A Religious Survey of Successes and Failures of the Land Redistribution in Zimbabwe, 1985-2017

Tobias Marevesa & Prosper Hellen Tlou

Introduction

The question of land has been a controversial issue in Zimbabwe as elsewhere around the world for the past decades. At independence in 1980, Zimbabwe inherited polarised pattern of land distribution, with the minority of the settler's large-scale commercial farmers owning the prime and fertile land whilst the majority of Zimbabweans were squashed in infertile land and in areas where there were low rainfall patterns. This was against the African traditional religious and cultural belief systems of equitable distribution of the land against its own people favouring (*vauyi*) foreigners. According to Mbiti (1967) religion is pervasive, every person is religious. If this assertion is to go by, then a person is born in a particular culture and indigenous religion becomes innate. Religious and cultural perspective on land in Zimbabwe has a thin line that divides them. The chapter treats religion and cultural perspectives as one thing with regards to Land Reform Program. The idea that the indigenous farmers were forced to leave their cultural heritage by British settlers to infertile land resulted in the marginalisation of indigenous people in communal areas. In this regard, there is clear evidence of injustice in land redistribution in Zimbabwe because chiefs were not considered in the process as they are the custodian of the land This land imbalance between settlers and indigenous farmers led to the war of liberation to regain Zimbabweans' religious and cultural heritage.

The land issue has been perceived differently by different people. On one hand, some people regarded the land redistribution as a political gimmick where other political parties such as ZANU (PF) and MDC formations wanted to gain political mileage. On the other hand, some critics viewed the land redistribution as something that was long overdue because that was the major factor that led to the liberation struggle in Zimbabwe. This chapter focuses on land redistribution, justice and development from a religious and cultural perspective in Zimbabwe. We advance the argument that although the land redistribution process in Zimbabwe had its own shortfalls, it generally brought a lot of positive development in the country where many indigenous Zimbabweans have become successful commercial farmers. In pursuing this argument, we also explore the legality and justice system that surrounded the land redistribution in Zimbabwe, paying special attention to how it was perceived from the perspective of African religious and cultural heritage in Zimbabwe. The roles of the traditional leadership (such as herdsmen and chiefs), the traditional view of the land and that concept of the Mother Earth can contribute to land redistribution, development and justice in Zimbabwe. The legality of the land redistribution are explored from a religio-cultural point of view by looking at the multiple land ownership where some people are having more than one farm. This resulted in some people failing to own even a single farm. The chapter concludes that even though land redistribution process brought in some positive development to the indigenous people of Zimbabwe, there was a lot of injustice in as far as many traditional leaders were treated in the resettlement and land redistribution process, resulting in minimal land development. In addition, it did not auger well with human rights as the rule of law and rights of commercial European farmers were disregarded and grossly violated.

African traditional religious and cultural views on land

From a religious and cultural perspective, some beliefs and practices of the Shona and Venda shows their friendly approach to nature. According to Chiwara, Shoko and Chitando (2013); Taringa (2006), this friendly aspect is seen in the Shona attitudes to nature with regards to land, animals, plant life and water bodies. The environment is safeguarded by cultural traits or sacred taboos that control wayward behaviour and wanton destruction of nature. Taringa (2006: 12) however, posits that, "...the ecological attitude of traditional African religion is based more on fear or respect of ancestral spirits than on respect for nature itself". Taringa's view is significant in this study because the redistribution of land was done probably without the blessing of the ancestral spirits hence production from the land could be reduced. From the traditional religious and cultural perspective, there are mechanisms which are put in place in order to protect the land and to safeguard endangered species from extinction such as Rhinos and Tigers. These religious and cultural attitudes could have been used to address the pressing issues of land redistribution, justice and development. Sibanda (2017) raised a pertinent issue with regards to the land; he called the land 'Mother Earth'. Land in the indigenous religion is referred to as Mother Earth, where there is life, minerals, water, food from the fields among others. The Mother Earth concept is symbolic of the love of the mother to her children that she treats all her children equally.

Another important element to be looked at is the role of chiefs in society from a religious and cultural point of view, in relation to the issue of land in Zimbabwe. In the Shona and Venda religion and customs, the chief is an embodiment of tradition and culture (Chiwara, Shoko and Chitando, 2013: 41). He is the leader of all the people in his community and is the custodian of the land where people get life. According to Nkomo (1998: 14), chiefs are a combination of executive, ritual and judicial power and always enjoy the support of his subordinates and the people under his jurisdiction. The role of the chiefs therefore would be to stabilize societies for development. The major role of chiefs is to resolve conflicts and disputes through his traditional court *(dare)*. Chiwara, Shoko and Chitando (2013: 42) note that the chief is the last court of appeal for the village headmen refer cases to him which are difficult for them to settle. As the chief presides over his traditional court he is helped by his advisors *(machinda)* who advises the chief and make it a point that there is peace, harmony and unity within his kingdom. Bourdillon (1976) argues that the chief's court deals with a variety of cases which includes, divorce, quarrels, compensation, breaking taboos, theft of cattle among others. The chief is both a "religious and political ruler" (Bourdillon, 1976: 137). Among other roles of the chief is to mediate between his subjects and the spirit guardians in his area of jurisdiction (Shoko, 2007: 10). Related to the view of Shoko, the chief has the role of spearheading and overseeing the organisation of rituals such as *mukwerere* (rain making ceremony) to make sure that there is enough rain and fertility on the land. Given the importance of the traditional leaders to indigenous societies, the organisers of land redistribution could have utilised the involvement of traditional leadership in land redistribution, justice and development. What usually happens is that, chiefs are only used by some politicians to make sure that they remain in power.

Cultural values

Zimbabwe is full of good cultural values which could have been instrumental in Land Reform Programme. According to Chiwara, Shoko and Chitando (2013), the Shona cultural values are rich in good values which include ethics and morals through the concept of *Hunhu* that shows good behaviour and peaceful co-existence. This concept believes in working together rather than individual activities. Another pertinent issue in *Hunhu* is identity in relation to human rights. According to Chidester (1992: 82), "a human being is a human because of other human beings". In African cultural point of view, personhood is articulated in the course of giving through ancestral rituals, kingship, and inclusive acts of hospitality (Chidester, 1992: 82). The Shona concept which says, *munhu navanhu* (a person is a person through other persons), is vital in this study in that land was supposed to have been redistributed equally because every person is important. The Shona word *unhu* (personhood) is etymologically derived from *vanhu* (people) who determines what is to be *munhu* (a person) (Chiwara, Shoko and Chitando, 2013: 43). Based on this, a person has the right to life, security, and freedom in relation to a person's communal set of social and political ethics, all enshrined by belonging to the community of the living and the living dead. It is possible to construct an African understanding of land redistribution, justice and development in Zimbabwe given the richness of Zimbabwe's culture.

Land Redistribution in Zimbabwe

At independence in 1980, land acquisition and redistribution was the government's major aim in order to address the problem of poverty, household food security, social security, and empowering people economically. The land resettlement programme was in two phases, with the first one stretching from 1981 to 1987 (Chung, 2007; Moyo; 2000). About 2 million hectares were acquired by the government on the "willing seller-willing buyer" system which was funded by the British government during Margret Thatcher's tenure Chung, 2007. This was done according to the Lancaster House agreement of 1979, which the British Government was supposed to fund the redistribution of the land in Zimbabwe (Sachikonye, 2006; Chung, 2007 Chitsike, 2003. During the first phase of land redistribution, the process was well organized and the intended beneficiaries benefited and these were the poor peasant farmers, the landless who were displaced during the war of liberation, war veterans and the commercial farm workers. The first phase of the land redistribution was organised because the organisers identified land first to resettle the peasant farmers. The allocation of land was orderly and infrastructural development was subsequently done by the government. In 1980, there were a targeted number of households to be resettled as 18,000 on 1.5 million hectares in a period of five years (Chitsike, 2003; Juana, 2006). The number of resettled families was revised to 162,000 in 1982 on 8.3 million hectares of land because of financial constraints (World Bank, 1991). According to Juana (2006) and Chitsike (2003), there were a number of amendments of both the National Constitution and Land Acquisition Act, one of them being the new Land Policy of 1990 which further reduced the hectarage to 8.3 million hectares, but no changes to the targeted population. The policy highlighted that the hectarage was to be reduced because of shortage of funding. In the context of religious and cultural perspective, the way land was redistributed was not according to the dictates of traditional African beliefs and practices. The chiefs who are the custodian of the land were not involved in the redistribution.

Traditionally, chiefs were appointed and anointed by the ancestral spirits (Sibanda, 2017), so if chiefs were not involved in the redistribution of the land, then the ancestral spirits might be angry resulting in perennial droughts as Zimbabwe is experiencing. Even if many people were resettled by the Government as in Figure 1, traditionally, without the blessings of the chiefs it becomes futile. The new National Policy which was gazetted in 1990 also enunciated the Government's strategic aims for the sizes of various land tenure regimes. This can be summarised in Figure 1 below.

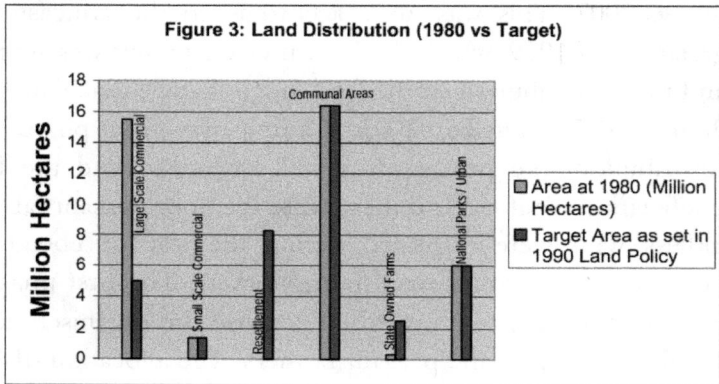

Figure 3: Land Distribution (1980 vs Target)

Figure 2 below shows the hectarage of land owned by various groupings just before Zimbabwe got independence and by the end of 1990s. This diagram shows that 3.6 million hectares of land that was acquired by the Government primarily from large scale commercial farmers to resettle the landless.

Table 1: Land distribution at and after independence

Land category	1980 (million ha)	1997 (million ha)	Increase/decrease in Land (million ha)	Percentage Change (%)
Communal areas	16.4	16.4	0.0	0
Resettlement areas	0.0	3.6	3.6	--
Smallholder areas	1.0	1.1	0.1	--
Large scale commercial area	14.8	11.3	-3.5	(23.68)
State farms	0.3	0.1	-0.2	(66.7)
National parks, wild life and urban settlements	6.0	6.0	0.0	0
Total	38.5	38.5	0.0	0

Source: CSO (1998); Rugube and Chambati (2001).

At the beginning of the land redistribution programme, the government adopted four models (A, B, C, and D) which were used to resettle landless families. These models were defined as below:

A) The model involves families being allocated residential stands in rural areas of about five hectares of land each for farming and for grazing (Juana, 2006; Chitsike, 2003). In the model, there were access roads that linked villages with the service centres where civil servants such as agricultural extension officers, healthy personnel and educational practitioners were based. This was the major model that was used in the Land Reform Programme in Zimbabwe.

B) This model was not extensively used in the land reform. It requires the creation of cooperatives to utilise the farms which were bought by the government from large scale commercial farmers. Cooperatives could be formed to do projects such as irrigation.

C) The model involves a "commercial estate or a processing facility and settler out growers" (Juana, 2006: 297). This model was introduced in order that those who benefited were re-settled near the estate where they provide labour for the estate and where they also get services from the estate. However, this model was not mainly used during the land reform in Zimbabwe.

D) This scheme was mainly done in the Southern parts of Zimbabwe in the low rainfall areas of regions IV and V. These areas were mainly used for commercial ranches for the development of livestock. According to Chitsike (2003: 5), this model was later rebranded and renamed the 'Three Tier Scheme'.

Models A and D were mostly used in the land reform programme, while models B and C were not intensively used. By the end of 1996, about 71,000 families were re-settled on 3.6 million hectares of land out of the targeted 162.000 on 8.3 million hectares in 1990 GoZ, 1999; CSO 1998. To date, the area of small-scale farms rose from 1 million in 1980 to about 1.1 million in 1997, while the hectarage of large scale commercial farms declined from 14.8 million hectares in 1980 to 11.3 million hectares in 1997 (GoZ, 1999; CSO, 1998; Chitsike, 2003). In the context of religion and culture in Zimbabwe, talking of models of land redistribution is unheard of, in fact, on all the models given above there is not even one which talks about a traditional approach to the redistribution of land.

After the 1987 land redistribution, the British government had a new leadership after the fall of Margaret Thatcher. Her successors Tony Blair and George Bush stopped funding land resettlement in Zimbabwe and they gave an excuse that there was corruption and patronage in the land redistribution programme. In reaction to Tony Blair's government, the government of Zimbabwe enacted a Constitutional reform which gave the government a mandate to repossess land for redistribution from white farmers to poor peasants (Gono, 2008). The British also retaliated by funding local people, media, civic societies and political parties to dislodge the ZANU PF regime. According to Kanyenze (2004), when financial support was not forthcoming to finance land redistribution this resulted in *jambanja* or fast-track programme in February 2000. It can be pointed out that there was a deep-rooted conflict between Zimbabwe and United Kingdom. The conflict led to Zimbabwe being sanctioned by Britain and her allies accused of not observing the rule of law when repossessing the land. The *jambanja* or fast-track resettlement programme was also named the Third Chimurenga. It was an episode where people were fighting for their religious and cultural heritage.

Fast-Track Land Reform Programme

The Fast Track Land Reform Programme is also known as Third Chimurenga or *Jambanja*. According to Sibanda (2017: 190), *jambanja* is a stage which refers to the period when there were haphazard and unpredictable incidents of land seizure from the commercial farmers during the Third Chimurenga, or *hondo yeminda* (war for the land) as it was also known. Raftopoulos (2009) notes that aggrieved by the defeat, ZANU-PF, in alliance with war veterans and land –hungry peasants, embarked on a violent process of land occupations that later became known as Fast Track Land Reform Programme (FTLRP). The major aim of the Fast-Track Land Reform Programme was to identify about 2 million hectares of land for redistribution to the poor peasant farmers who were squashed in rural areas. These peasant farmers were in dare need of land for their economic and agricultural development. There was also need for careful planning for basic infrastructural development for the resettlement area to be inhabitable. These include such amenities as boreholes, dip tanks, roads, and schools, among others. Furthermore, on all the farms which were to be acquired, there were other things which needed planning such as the demarcation of farms plots and villages where people would be settled. This could not be done overnight, but needed more time and dedication. According to Sibanda (2017), the Third Chimurenga commenced in February 2000 when a communal initiative of the people under the leadership of Chief Zenda of Svosve in Mashonaland East Province demonstrated against the government forcing it to embark on a revolutionary land redistribution programme that resulted in the Land Reform Programme. It should be noted that during the colonial era, chiefs were salaried. These were chiefs who were appointed and paid by the colonial rulers and these ended up supporting the colonial government. There were those chiefs who could not accept being paid or being put on the payroll because they thought they were being sell-outs; their chieftainship was taken away from them as punishment of not supporting them. According to Sibanda (2017), after independence, there were also those chiefs who were appointed by the government depending on how they supported the ruling ZANU PF party for instance, Chief Charumbira of Masvingo district. This could have been the same situation with Chief Svosve who led a revolutionary demonstration against the government in order to force to redistribute its religious and cultural heritage. The question which one may ask is that, was chief Svosve appointed by the government or was appointed by the ancestral spirits? Whatever the case could be, it is important to note that the chiefs were involved in the Land Reform Programme especially in the Third Chimurenga.

The move to acquire land from the Large Scale Commercial Farming emanated from the study carried out by the World Bank in the 1990s (Moyo, 2007). The research by the World Bank revealed that only 30% of the LSCF was used (Juana 2006). The 30% of LSCF could also be used to resettle small-scale farmers. The Zimbabwe Agricultural Policy Framework (thereafter ZAPF) 1995-1998 had targeted 5 million hectares for LSCF for resettlement. This move was supported by the 1998 Donor Conference on the Land Reform Programme. Each settler was to be allocated land that ranges from 5 to 50 hectares for crop based farming (Juana 2006).

There were two models which were formulated under the Fast Track Programme which are models A2 and A1. These models were meant to give indigenous access to land to participate in commercial farming. The scheme under the Agricultural Land Settlement Act (Chapter 20: 01) existed in four ways namely; Peri-urban, Small Scale, Medium Scale, and Large Scale Commercial Farm Settlement. The table below shows the amount of land that has been given to settled farmers from 2000 – 2002.

According to Hill (2003), in the late 1997, the government announced that 1 471 white farms were earmarked for compulsory acquisition. Some British settler farmers were not going to be compensated. This nationalization programme affected the country negatively because the country depended most on agriculture for its economic development. This resulted in shortages of maize, the staple diet, especially in drought years for example 1992. Former President Mugabe did not change his stance on compulsory acquisition of land; instead, he accused settler farmers of having the best or the prime land of the country which was stolen by their ancestors. It can be argued that, settler farmers had the monopoly of the large tracks of fertile land, while the majority of the indigenous peasant farmers were squashed in poor and infertile land. A critical analysis of this argument is that, first; the British government did not honour the Lancaster House agreement of 1979 to fund the land redistribution programme. Second, there was land imbalance between the white and black farmers. This imbalance was against the traditional African religion and cultural beliefs and practices of the Mother Earth concept which symbolises the land as a mother of a family. As a mother the land should be shared equally among its children. There was need to balance the resource that the country had. Therefore, the Zimbabwe government cannot be entirely blamed for the land redistribution because it was long overdue. However, the problem could be how it was carried out. It is important to note that land acquisition contributed immensely to conflict among political parties in Zimbabwe.

Justice in Land Reform Programme

Many Zimbabweans participated in the liberation struggle with the mission of reclaiming their religious and cultural heritage, thus the land from the colonial rulers. A number of people skipped the country's borders to countries like Mozambique, Zambia, Tanzania among others to fight for the injustice which was perpetrated by the British settlers in areas such as unjust distribution of land and racial segregation at work places. The liberation struggle was inspired and led by the ancestral spirits who were angry by the unjust distribution of the land by the colonial settlers. Soon after Zimbabwe attained its independence in 1980, legislations and policies which guided the Government on how the land was going to be distributed and used by settlers were formulated. According to Chitsike (2003), the first legislation was passed by Parliament in 1985 as a new Land Acquisition Act which allowed the Government the right to acquire some of the large scale commercial farms for resettling the landless. In 1990, Parliament passed the Constitution Amendment Act, which limited the degree of protection afforded by the Constitution against the acquisition of land for resettlement. In 1992, a new Land Acquisition Act was passed which guided the Government to manage the acquisition of land and how to redistribute land to the needy. Some of the legislations and policies which were enacted by the government of Zimbabwe to guide them to redistribute the land to the landless were noble, but it appears that the role of chiefs was not considered.

It is noted that during the first ten years of independence, nothing much was done with regard to land distribution since most of the Large Scale Commercial Farms remained in the hands of the former colonialists. This was influenced by the Constitution of Zimbabwe which obliged the government to acquire the land on the willing seller-willing buyer basis. A decade after independence, 75 000 families received 11% of the total farmland of Zimbabwe, but this land reform was hindered in two ways (Chitsike, 2003). First, the Lancaster House peace agreement said that farms could only be transferred from white to black farmers on a willing-seller, willing-buyer basis (Chung, 2007). The land offered to the government at an affordable price was primarily infertile land with less successful farmers. The willing seller-willing buyer policy had a loophole in the sense that chances of getting a farmer who disposes his/her farm of benefit to him or her were very slim given that whites came to Africa to exploit resources. On the other hand, chances of getting a potential buyer were also very slim since it could be afforded by the elite. Thus the policy was unjust for it discriminated the majority. In addition, history shows that initially the whites had acquired the land for free then how could they dispose with a charge. Cecil Rhodes in the 1890's recognised that agriculture was a potential business enterprise and gave large tracts of land to his fellow British settlers as gratuity of the victorious soldiers of World War II. Rhodes, therefore, evicted the indigenous farmers who were occupying the fertile land and replaced them with the British settlers (Manyengwa *et al*, 2014). To clear land for the new white farmers in just one decade (1945-1955) more than 100 000 African families were often moved forcibly, into communal areas and inhospitable and tsetse fly ridden unassigned areas (Palmer, 1997). In addition, people could not take their cattle to their newly resettled areas. Their houses in which they were living were also burnt, and they lost all their investments that they had made on their farms (Manyengwa *et al*, 2014: 19). The practice that was being done by the British settlers was against the motherhood of the land, that it belongs to everyone and no one should be landless. The land as a mother is not selective to its own children, that is, the indigenous Zimbabweans, but the local farmers were put into land which was infertile hence unjust and unfair. This suggests that land was supposed to be redistributed fairly. This was a clear indication of the gross violation of human rights by the minority white settlers. The question that this chapter needs to address now is: how just was it done? From a religious and cultural perspective, there was injustice because there were settlers who removed the indigenous farmers from their cultural heritage to places which were infertile. The roles of the chiefs of allocating land to their subordinates were overlooked. In addition, in African traditional religion people are identified by places of their origin, so to remove those from their places of origin may detach them from their identity.

In this scenario, as a way of trying to get answers many issues arise such as: (i) when the British settlers first took the land from the indigenous there were no notifications to that effect. (ii) There was no compensation done for their property, yet at Lancaster the European farmers demanded compensation from the Zimbabwean government. When the reverse of reclaiming land from the colonialists, was done in independent Zimbabwe by the ZANU PF Government it was viewed by critics as a political gimmick to win the hearts of the electorate. The Fast Track Land Reform Programme was more political than serving the interest of the people. It is interesting to note that the government amended the constitution in 2000 and 2001 to give them (Government) more power to acquire more land. Chitsike (2003) argues that orderly and planned land reform has been sacrificed on the altar of political expediency. Though land redistribution was meant to serve the community it led to even deeper suffering for community members while war veterans and politically linked individuals and their relatives enriched themselves.

The chapter admits that the Fast-Track Land Reform Programme was a noble cause because the indigenous people were reclaiming their religious and cultural heritage. The 2013 Constitution is silent on how the land redistribution should be done. The new constitution is also silent on the role of chiefs in land allocation because they (chiefs) are the custodians of the land. The Constitution may also guarantee rights to communities and access to justice in situations where their rights have been violated. Nyakudya (2013) posits that the MDC successfully campaigned against a new government- initiated constitution which would have allowed the government to seize farms owned by white farmers without compensation, and transfer them to local farmers in Zimbabwe. However, this did not stop the government or rather the ruling party to fulfil its aim of acquiring land. Sanctions are mechanisms which are employed by countries and international organizations to persuade a particular government or group of governments to change their policy by restricting trade, investment or other commercial activities (Gono, 2008: 91). In the case of Zimbabwe, sanctions were widened to include other elements such as diplomatic isolation, culture, and sport. Gono (2008: 91) claims that the sanctions which were imposed on Zimbabwe were illegal because they were not sanctioned by the UN Security Council, but by Britain and her allies, while Mashakada (2016: 2), an MP for MDC-T, alleges that these sanctions could be referred to as "restrictive measures." This means that the sanctions were targeted to specific individuals and companies perceived to have been supporting perpetrators of gross violation of human rights. Sanctions that have been imposed on Zimbabwe are generally perceived as a means to isolate Zimbabwe on the International map. Nyakudya (2013) highlights that the sanctions are perceived as punitive measures in retaliation for ZANU-PFs anti – imperialist policies and its radical assertion of Zimbabwean sovereignty. Given this, it is very clear that the colonial rule never had Africans at heart, but their land, thus for them to preach the gospel of anti-human violation is not justifiable for they do not practice it themselves (Nyakudya, 2013). While Britain, the United States and their allies castigated the ZANU-PF government for its authoritarian governance, human rights abuses and disregard for the rule of law, and went on to impose a raft of sanctions against it, most African leaders such as the former president of South Africa Thabo Mbeki and Edgar Lungu of Zambia stood by their counterpart, whom they adjudged to be fighting an anti-imperialist war against the West.

Land Development

There is a significant development in the Land Reform Programme in terms of the hectarage that has been targeted to resettle families. The landless, war veterans, farm workers and other people who needed land had been re-settled and their lives have improved. The traditional African religious and cultural beliefs and practices agree in principal that there is a marked development in terms of land reform programme in Zimbabwe. The chiefs are central figures of development because they control the economic system by redistributing land equally to indigenous farmers. When we talk of land redistribution, the implication is that, land will be productive if it is utilized well. Chiefs are responsible for the fertility of the land by leading in the rain making ceremonies (mukwerere).

According to Sibanda (2017); Taringa (2006), chiefs are custodians of the land which gives plant life, animals, minerals, water bodies and other things. When indigenous farmers now own land, it follows that they can now exploit minerals such as gold, copper, tin, diamond, platinum, among others which indigenous miners were given by their ancestors. When agriculture and mining are well exploited in Zimbabwe there could be meaningful development because the two (agriculture and mining) contribute significantly to the economy of the country.

After independence, in the modern setup, Chiefs are supporting the Land Reform Programme in that they are part and parcel of the land committees at all levels from district up to national level. The fact that there are involved in these land committees follows that there are part of developmental agenda. Chiefs are also involved in developmental issue such as the Communal Areas Management Programme for Indigenous Resource (CAMPFIRE) programme. It is a programme which is involved in the preservation of wildlife. According to Sibanda (2017), the programme benefits and develops the local community. Local people benefit from this programme in that it provides employment. When animals in the programme are sold, the money will be ploughed back in the community by providing infrastructural development such building of schools, clinics, bridges and other projects that are needed in that particular community. It can be argued that the land reform programme in Zimbabwe brought meaningful development to the local people as well as to the nation. According to Juana (2006: 294-295), the major aims of the Land Reform Programme were as follows:

i)   Alleviating population pressure in the communal areas;

ii) Extending and improving the base of productive agriculture in the peasant farming sector;

iii) Improving the standard of living of the largest and poorest sector of the population;

iv) Improving the problems of and rehabilitating those adversely affected by the war;

v)   Providing for the landless and the destitute;

vi) Bringing into full production the under-utilised land; and

vii) Expanding and improving the infrastructure and services that were needed to promote the well-being of people and economic production (Chitsike, 2003: 3; Lebert, 2003: 4).

To achieve these aims and objectives, different policies and legislation were put in place by the government in order to acquire and redistribute land taken from Large Scale Commercial Farms without compensation. However, after the redistribution of land, macroeconomic markers reveal that the gross domestic product has decreased by 6% in 2000 and 8% in 2001and was going to be worse by subsequent years (ECA, 2002). The decline in gross domestic product shows that there is no meaningful development brought by land reform programme. In sectors such as agriculture, mining, and manufacturing, there was a marked decrease in output by 2001, resulting in the closure of companies and many people losing their jobs. According to ACA (2002), about 25,000 people lost their jobs in the manufacturing sector only by the first three months of 2001. Therefore, the land reform did not bring the desired results because its viability is questionable. It appears the Land reform has brought relief from those who could only farm at a low scale, but at commercial level, there was a drastic decline in production. Since Zimbabwe is an agro economic country, if the agricultural sector is not performing well it follows that the whole economy is affected. It can be observed that the drastic decline in production was probably exacerbated by those who were greedy who ended up having multiple farms resulting in insignificant farming. Tracks and tracks of land were lying ideal without being productive. In addition, the people who were allocated farms had no interest and expertise in farming thereby leading to low production to the gross domestic product. The issue of those who had a number of farms did not bring development in the Land Reform Programme. Related to the Mother Earth, there is a concept which was brought by the Zimbabwean nationalists such as Ndabaningi Sithole, Joshua Nkomo, Robert Mugabe among others which is 'son of the soil'. This concept is seen even today, when national heroes are being buried, they usually write (*famba zvakanaka mwana wevhu*) 'go well son of the soil'. This implies the motherhood of the land with regards to land fertility and its productivity in terms of development. As has alluded above, the Mother Earth concept shows fairness in treating its people equally, but the idea of multiple farms shows an element of greedy which is not characteristic of the beliefs and practices of traditional African religion and culture. Therefore, it resulted in negative development in as far as land reform programme is concerned.

Another problem that could have resulted in the decline in gross domestic product could be that newly re-settled farmers had no capital and farming implements to utilise in their farms. They could not acquire loans from banks because the majority had no collateral assets which the banks wanted before they disburse loans. The white farmers had advantages because they qualified to be given some loans. Robilliard *et al* (2002) and Deininger *et al* (2002) carried out researches on the cost-benefit study on the impact of the land reform programme in Zimbabwe independent of each other. They both discovered that the land reform programme in Zimbabwe yielded positive results on the incomes and living standard of the targeted people. An analysis of Robilliard *et al* (2002) and Deininger *et al* (2002) reveal that their research only investigated micro-level benefits and costs without considering an economy-wide coverage. For instance, they could have also investigated the impact of land redistribution on non-agricultural sectors such as the performance of the manufacturing sector. They could have carried out their research focusing on the contribution of the land reform to the gross domestic product of the country. Another research was carried by Bautista and Thomas (2000) when they made a computable general equilibrium analysis of trade and agricultural policy in Zimbabwe. Their findings suggest that land reform policies cannot at the same time endorse overall income growth and equity. According to Juana (2006), the method which was used by Bautista and Thomas (2000) may not yield good results because its complex and it requires experts to interpret the data. Therefore, their findings and conclusions might be misleading. It can be observed that the two researches that were carried out produced positive results that there is development that was brought by the land reform.

Juana (2006) proposed to use a social accounting matrix multiplier method which investigates the impact of land redistribution on output growth, household income generation and gross value added. The study investigated the welfare and equity issues which were possibly be addressed by the Land Reform Programme, particularly in accordance with the rural folks (farmers). Juana's (2006) study utilised the 1991 social accounting matrix for Zimbabwe, which was aided by the 1998 household survey, information was supplied by the Central Statistics Office in Zimbabwe. Juana's (2006: 296) conclusion was that, had it been that the Land Reform Programme was carefully planned and cautiously implemented, it could have increased output and gross value added "and redistributes income from large-scale owner households to small-holder house-holds, hence could be generally beneficial for the economy of Zimbabwe". However, traditional leaders would not like the view of Juana because they were not part of first phase of the Land Reform Programme and to them it was not well planned. This result of Juana (2006) shows a positive development brought by land reform programme in Zimbabwe. However, the study also reveals that there was need to take measures to sufficiently compensate large-scale land owners, whose land was acquired and had been given to smallholders. It can be argued that the large-scale land owners cannot be compensated for the land because historically they did not buy it, but they were just allocated. In other countries like Britain, a foreigner is not allowed to buy an inch of a piece of land. If this is true, why then should foreigners be allowed to own our African religious heritage in Zimbabwe? Probably they could have been compensated for the structures which they developed and their assets not the heritage of Zimbabwe- the land.

Conclusion

This chapter concludes that the Zimbabwean government cannot entirely be blamed for the land redistribution programme, because it was long overdue. There are those critics who have vehemently argued that the land redistribution programme was a gross violation of human rights and that there was no rule of law in Zimbabwe. It can be argued that there was no equitable distribution of the land in Zimbabwe; hence there was need for readdressing the land question by redistributing the land to the needy. However, the problem lay in how it was carried out where it was used as a political tool to win the hearts of the electorate in the 2000 elections in Zimbabwe. The chiefs were side-lined when they had a big role to play in the distribution of land since it was their religious and cultural heritage. There is much debate on the question of the legality of the land redistribution especially on the fast track programme. The traditional leadership did not perceive the Land Reform Programme in a legal way. For them, they viewed it as a chance to reclaim the lost ancestral lands, graves, mountains and sacred places as well as reclaiming boundaries which had been greatly changed by the British settlers. There was minimum development in as far as the contribution of agriculture to the economy of the country, but there was a marked development in the number of hectarage and families who were resettled by Land Reform Programme. One would say that, far from being over, the land issue in Zimbabwe remains a contentious challenge. It can therefore be recommended that there is need to balance the resources that the country is having by equally distributing the land to the needy.

References

Bautista, R. M., and Thomas, M. (2000) *Trade and Agricultural policy reforms in Zimbabwe: A CGE analysis.* Paper presented in 3rd Annual Conference on Global Economic Analysis, June 2000. Available at http://www.monas.edu.au/policy/cof/71Thomas.pdf.

Bourdillon, M. F. (1976) *The Shona People: Ethnography of the Contemporary Shona with Special Reference to their Religion.* Gweru: Mambo Press.

Chidester, D. (1992) *Religions of South Africa*, London: Routledge

Chitsike, F. (2003) A Critical Analysis of the Land Reform Programme in Zimbabwe. *2nd FIG Regional Conference, Marrakech, Morocco.* Available at
http://www.fig.net/pub/morocco/proceedings/TS4-4-chitsike.pdf.

Chiwara, A. Shoko, T. and Chitando, E. (2013) African Traditional Religion and the Church: Catalysts for National Healing in Zimbabwe in the Context of the Global Political Agreement, in *Southern Peace Review Journal*, Vol. 2. No. 1, 35-55. (Special issue with OSSREA Zimbabwe Chapter).

Chung, F. (2007) *Re-living the Second Chimurenga: Memories from the Liberation Struggle in Zimbabwe.* Harare, Weaver.

CSO, (1998) *Statistical Yearbook* 1997, Harare, Zimbabwe.

Deininger, K., Hoogeven, H., and Kinsey, B., (2002) *Benefits and costs of land reform in Zimbabwe with implications for Southern Africa.* Paper presented at the CSAE, Oxford, UK. Available at http://www.csae.ox.ac.uk/conferences/2002-UPaGiSSA/papers/Hoogeveencsae2002.pdf.

Economic Commission for Africa (ECA), (2002) Zimbabwe- A crumbling economy. In *Economic Report on Africa 2002:* Tracking performance and progress, pp 109-135.

Gono, G. (2008) *Zimbabwe's Casino Economy: Extraordinary Measures for Extraordinary Challenges,* Harare, ZPH Publishers.

GoZ, (1999) *National Land Policy Framework paper.* Discussion Paper supported by Food and Agricultural Organisation.

Juana, J. S. (2006) A quantitative analysis of Zimbabwe's land reform policy: An application of Zimbabwe SAM multipliers, in *Agrekon*, Vol 45, No 3, pages 294-318.

Kanyeze, G. (2004) "The Zimbabwe Economy 1980-2003: a ZCTU Perspective" in D Harold –Barry, Zimbabwe: *The Past and the Future,* Harare, Weaver Press.

Lebert, T. (2003) *An Introduction to land and agrarian reform in Zimbabwe.* National Land Committee, Johannesburg, South Africa. Available at http://www.cerai,es/fmra/archivo/lebert.pdf.

Mbiti, J. S. (1969) *African Religions and Philosophy,* New York: Doubleday.

Moyo, A. (1987) Religion and politics in Zimbabwe. In: Peterson, K. H., Religion, Development and African Identity. Uppsala: Nordiska Afrikainsstitutet

Nkomo, J. (1998) Compiling Specialised Dictionaries in African Languages: Isichazamazwi SezoMculo as a special Reference. In: Chiwome, E. M. and Gambahaya, Z. (eds.) *Culture and*

Development: Perspectives from the South. Harare: Mond Books Publishers.

Nyakudya, M. (2013) 'Sanctioning the Government of National Unity: a review of Zimbabwe's relations with the West in the framework of the GPA', In: Raftopoulos, B. (ed.), *The Hard Road to Reform: The Politics of Zimbabwe's Global Political Agreement.* Harare: Weaver Press

Raftopoulos, B. (2009) The crisis in Zimbabwe, 1998-2008. In B Raftopoulos and AS Mlambo (eds), *Becoming Zimbabwe: A History from the Pre-Colonial Period to 2008.* Harare: Weaver Press.

Robilliard, A., Sukume, C., Yanoma, Y., and Lofgren, H. (2001) *Land reform in Zimbabwe: Farm-level effects and cost-benefit analysis.* International Food Policy Research Institute, TMD Discussion Paper No 84. Available at http://www.ifpri.org/divs/tmd/dp/papers/tmdp84. pdf.

Rugube, L., and Chambati, W. (2002) *Land redistribution in Zimbabwe: Five census surveys of farmland transactions, 1996-2000.* Broadening Access and Strengthening Input Market Systems, University of Wisconsin-Madison, USA. Available at http://www.ies.wisc.edu/Itc/live/bassaf0107a.pdf.

Sachikonye, L. (2011) *When a state turns on its Citizens: Institutionalized Violence and Political Culture.* Auckland Park: Jacana Media.

Shoko, T. (2007) *Karanga indigenous Religion in Zimbabwe: Health and Well-Being.* Aldershot: Ashgate Publishers.

Sibanda, F. (2017) "Rastafari perspectives on Land use and management in postcolonial" M. Christian Green, Rosalind Hackett, Len Hansen, and Francois Venter (eds.) *Religious Pluralism, Heritage and Social Development,* Stellenbosch: SUN MeDIA.

Taringa, N. (2006). How Environmental is African Traditional Religion? In: Exchange 35 (2): 15-25.

World Bank, (1991). *Zimbabwe Agricultural Sector Memorandum,* Vol 2: Main Report. World Bank, Washington DC, USA.

Chapter 6

(In-)securities and Ethical Dilemmas of the Field: Reflections on Insecurities and Ethical Dilemmas encountered by Male Researchers in a South African Place

Andile Mayekiso & Munyaradzi Mawere

Introduction

This chapter is a critical reflection on the ethical dilemmas generally encountered during fieldwork, and in particular during fieldwork carried out by one of the authors in Cape Town, South Africa. We also reflect on experiences involving men studying women participants. The latter is very complex especially when one has to visit women in their houses with their male partners absent. Conversations with women covered a whole range of issues, ranging from their sex life, labour, birth, boyfriends, witchcraft, HIV, rituals, and many more topics.

This chapter examines the security issues and ethical dilemmas encountered generally encountered by male researchers as they gather data for their researches from female participants in the field of sexuality, sensitive health matters such as experiences of giving birth and struggles of living with HIV in highly stigmatised communities.

Data for the Cape Town cases was conducted by the first author as part of his research for PhD studies at the University of Cape Town, South Africa during the period between 2008 and 2013.

Background and 'getting involved with women participants'

Getting to know participants has never been an easy task. One can never be sure how strangers will react towards you for the first time. The temptation to know more about someone is always there, but one needs to build trust and confidence first. This means that the more serious questions about people's past, present and even future always wait researchers as they negotiate their space and voice in the field. The suspicions and questions become even more rigorous when the researcher is male seeking to gather data from female interlocutors or vice-versa. Such was the situation encountered by one of the authors of this paper as he sought to harvest data on fatherhood in one of South Africa's low density suburbs of Cape Town City known as Gugulethu.

As the first author recounts:

> *Men in Gugulethu were initially suspicious of me. They thought I might be a police spy or a social worker of some kind. Some wanted to join the Infants Study only if they would be paid. Strangely, a few wanted to join if there would be a camera or a video tape so that they could appear on television. It soon became clear that one of the biggest challenges for young and resourceless researchers is the tendency of big companies, particularly those conducting quantitative research, to pay participants. People in Gugulethu specifically are used to short-term projects including participating in advertisements that pay them in return. This makes it difficult for projects like ours to get informants where the aim is to visit people in their homes frequently over a long period of time.*

This was the first dilemma the first author heretofore referred to as the researcher encountered in the field. The biggest question was how to manoeuvre such circumstances in a manner that would allow the researcher to harvest data without any compromise.

As the researcher progressed with his research, it became apparent that as the participants noted the "resourcelessness" of the researcher, all participants who participated in the projects willingly gave their consent, mostly verbally. They did not opt to commit themselves in writing as they normally do with big companies which normally conduct quantitative researches in the area. In fact, it soon became clear that many participants were hesitant to sign on a piece of paper as this felt like a contract to them and some were reluctant to sign despite being interested in the project.

The researcher took his time to explain the aims of the study to all the participants and told them that the material was for the purposes of attaining a PhD degree. He explained the objectives in their home language. It was stated clearly in the consent form (which the participants did not sign in any case) that participants have a right to withdraw from the study any time and they would remain anonymous if they so wish. Research ethics committees at the University of Cape Town approved the Infants Study design as per requirements of the National Institute of Health in United States of America. The second aspect of this project which focused primarily on fathers and children was approved by the ethics committee of the Department of Social Anthropology at the University of Cape Town (UCT), as mandated by the Faculty of Humanities Ethics Committee.

When the researcher joined the Infants Study in 2008, it was decided that a "white" female with two "black" African women should conduct interviews and home visits with female participants. The understanding was that female participants might feel more comfortable to speak to other women than speaking to a male interviewer. The researcher was to focus on men and other community members. But it soon became clear that female participants were getting concerned about a young female researcher frequenting their homes. They demanded that she stop visiting them because their neighbours started asking questions about this "social worker" who frequent them at home. This was a time HIV stigma was still rife in black communities of South Africa. We proposed the idea of a black man taking over those interviews with a female assistant always present. It was clear that the concerned female participants became more comfortable with this arrangement and this is how the researcher started working with them.

The researcher and his participants spoke about everything including details on giving birth, HIV, sex matters, feeding babies and many others. It was clear that women were enjoying these conversations and mostly because they could express themselves in their own language with the researcher as compared to when they had to talk through a translator before. However, this new arrangement – in which the researcher took over from the white female interviewer – soon raised eyebrows from the neighbours. Though female participants were quite happy to talk to the researcher, some of their lovers started asking questions about the nature of the conversations. At the centre of these conversations was how participants were dealing with HIV in their relationships where their partners were not aware of the pandemic.

Ethical quandaries and 'failed fatherhood'

This project has been an interesting but challenging exploration, to say the least, having to observe different forms of fathering practices or lack therefore by my participants. The two incidents shared in this piece had ethical implications for the research but also these stories show the insecurities and vulnerabilities that befall children when their fathers fail to perform fathering duties and responsibilities as prescribed by society. In both cases, fathers lived in the same household with their sons and therefore the possibility of them not knowing what was happening to the child was irrelevant. We offer narratives which show considerable complexity in household decision-making in a context in which the State is ill-equipped to address children's well-being and welfare. We have selected these cases because they provide us with an opportunity to better understand how fathering is practiced in the "new" model of nuclear family that seems to be emerging in Gugulethu. In Gugulethu, there seem to be a deliberate intension by residents to exclude relatives and other clan members. You hardly find three or even two generations living in the same household. The general living arrangement is for parents to live with their own biological children. Obviously the apartheid government planned for this as a way of destabilising black families by breaking those strong family ties. This was done by spreading people all over the Cape in what is now known as townships. A range of apartheid laws limited African people's access to urban lives in South Africa. Acts pertaining to Separate Development designated specified areas of the country as ethnic reserves. The Coloured Labour Preference Area, enacted in what was then the Cape Province, restricted African people's access to work in the Province. Influx control laws were cruelly enacted. Africans could only reside in urban areas if they held 'Section 10 rights'.[1] The effect

---

[1] The Bantu Urban Areas Act of 1964, for example, stipulated that African women had to receive permission to join their husbands in the city. This meant, if

was to separate labouring men from their wives and children, many of whom remained in the Bantustans, particularly the so-called 'independent' homelands of Transkei and Ciskei (designated as homelands for the AmaXhosa). A rich literature, of which Reynolds' work is an important component, explores the effects of these laws on the constitution of Black family life during apartheid. We are very critical of this model because we believe that black children benefited immensely from the way of life that valued and incorporated other kin members such as *omalume* (uncles), *otatomncinci* (child's father's younger brothers), and *otatomkhulu* (grandparents) in their everyday socialisation. We explicate the cases in some details here below:

Case One: Njabu's story

On 21 Feb 2012, when the researcher arrived for a routine visit to Sizwe, his girlfriend Minazana, mother of Njabu, worriedly told him that Njabu had been arrested at Spar in Gugulethu *Eyethu* Shopping Mall at around 14: 00. Njabu, at the time 2 years 11 months old, had accompanied Beauty, Sizwe's elder sister, who planned to steal from the shop. Intercepted by security guards, she ran away leaving Njabu behind. Beauty went home and told Minazana and Sizwe what had happened to Njabu. Neither Minazana nor Sizwe knew that Njabu had gone with Beauty to the Mall and both parents are on drugs (tik, dagga, mandrax, and alcohol). After Beauty told them, she went to her own bungalow (shack) where her boyfriend was waiting. They continued to drink cheap wine and beer there. Minazana took a taxi to Spar to see if she could come back with Njabu but the security guards and the manager were demanding R370, which is double the value of the milk stolen for his release. Failure to pay this money before 19: 00 meant Njabu would be taken to the police station where the police would see what to do with him. She did not have this money, so she came back home and told Beauty. Beauty told Minazana that she does not have such an amount they demanded at Spar. They only had to wait for her government

---

a 'section 10 woman' married a 'Homeland man', the apartheid state forced her to leave the city and join her husband in 'his homeland' (Bahre, 2002: 303).

grant[2]. Minazana told Beauty to borrow the money so that she can get Njabu back because he did not do any shoplifting at Spar. Beauty refused to borrow money. Sizwe was also at home, but he never went to Spar at any stage of his son's arrest. When the researcher asked him, what action had he taken to get his son back he said, *"I didn't take my son to the Mall. The person who took him there will bring him back."* It seems fair to view his response as irresponsible. But having worked with him for so long this did not surprise the researcher. In their encounters, the researcher was able to see that he feels proud being called a father, but he found the duties associated with this title quite challenging mostly.

It is important also to alert the reader to the fact that long before Njabu was born, there was a social worker visiting Njabu's grandmother, Mams, weekly to monitor her recovery progress after she had stroke on her right arm. Then without notice, the woman just stopped visiting Mams. Her sudden disappearance had devastating effects on Mams and other family members who relied on her to provide professional help to a stroke victim. Often when the researcher asked Mams how she felt about not having a social worker any more, she suggested that maybe she is the one to blame for not making speedy progress. *"Hey Andile, maybe she left me because she felt I was not getting better quickly but now I don't know. We had nice sessions, nice conversations which made me forget about the situation of this house. She even invited me to start going back to church and I was looking forward to that because I love church",* she remarked one day. Here, the failure in continuity of care of a state institution is internalised as personal responsibility and self-blame. In addition to the social worker, the police made numerous visits to the family arresting Sizwe at least three times during the researcher's fieldwork (Sizwe had been to prison 8 times in his life by the end of the researcher's fieldwork) for selling drugs, particularly dagga and tik. The police also frequented the house because of Beauty's troubles with the law. Beauty had been arrested for more than nine times at home and in shopping malls mostly for shoplifting. Generally, the family had a history of trouble

---

[2] Beauty is HIV-positive with her boyfriend, Lion, and are both receiving government grant for their status.

with the law due to drug dealing. Mams also made her living by selling drugs.

Mams' response to the researcher raises an important issue for us to consider before inviting external structures such as social workers into our participants' families and that is to consider the after effects of such interventions when we are long gone as field researchers (see also Cluver *et al*, 2014). If we facilitate children being taken away from their families, we also need to ensure that there are well functioning structures to assist them to cope better when they return from an institution to a dysfunctional home.

Njabu's incident raised a great deal of ethical quandary for the researcher. The researcher decided not to report this incident to the police or social workers[3]; instead he had a meeting with both Njabu's parents and his grandmother to warn them that if anything happens again he will report it and the child might be taken away from them. The researcher's decision to exclude authorities was informed by his knowledge that State structures have already failed this family despite being aware of the problems in the household. The researcher's decision therefore not to report this incident to the government organs was partly informed by these incompetences on the part of the government. It was also informed by the cultural model of responsible masculine identities the researcher had grown up with in his birth-village in the Eastern Cape, as is discussed below. But also, the researcher was concerned about the impact such a decision might have had on his [future] relationship with the family and the community, which he believed could jeopardise his fieldwork. Mfecane (2014: 1) warns us that "if friendships in the field need to be carefully managed, this itself is a two-way process, and our research subjects are just as much the authors of these relationships as we researchers are." The South African Children's Act requires professionals (police, social workers and psychologists) working with children who witness abuse to report it to the relevant authorities. It does not take a stance on researchers, although other legislation requires adults to report violence and neglect. The researcher's legal obligations were thus unclear. However, state failure in previous

---

[3] Minazana was relieved that no police were involved because her first daughter is with social workers in Khayelitsha after she left her alone

occasions did not give the researcher confidence in addressing Njabu's situation through these organs.

On the researcher's arrival at around 17: 00, Sizwe had gone to buy cigarette from the Somalian shop nearby. He was high on tik and dagga as always. He was so relaxed as if nothing had happened to his son. Considering his response when the researcher asked him what action had he taken to bring his son back, it became clear to the researcher that as an African man who understand traditional models of responsibility for children he had to step up and play the role he should have played had he gone beyond blaming his sister and considered the effects on the child. In his chapter on domestication, agency and subjectivity in the village of Bamenda in Cameroon, Nyamnjoh (2002: 113), raises an important feature of African culture which is relevant for this discussion as it contextualises the manner the researcher reacted to the situation he encountered during fieldwork. In his chapter: *A child is one person's only in the womb,* Nyamnjoh remarks that in its most common usage, this widely held [African] view about children reinforces the idea of the individual as a child of the community, as someone allowed to pursue the fulfilment of his/her needs, but not greed. "You belong to your mother exclusively only when still in the womb. Once delivered, you are expected to be of service to the wider community" (2002: 115), and that community becomes responsible for you. Because Sizwe failed in his responsibilities, the researcher felt that it was automatically expected of him to take responsibility for Sizwe's son because a child belongs to everyone or the entire community. *AmaXhosa* also have a similar idiom which goes: *umntana wam ngowakho, owakho ngowam* (my child is your child, [and] your child is mine). These traditional models of responsibility for children dictate that any man, regardless of paternity, must step in when a child's life in one's community is in danger. It was this kind of upbringing, teachings and communal expectation that led the researcher to play the fatherhood role after realising that Sizwe had completely ignored his responsibilities as a father. The researcher intervened and negotiated with the security guards and management at the shop, who eventually agreed to give Njabu over without any monetary exchange.

The researcher was very much aware of the belief that in order to remain impartial observers, it is advisable to continue with the research process and not intervene, and then after the fieldwork has finished go back to address issues or even alert authorities. As noble as this sound, the reality was that it might be too late to change the situation and in this case the trauma the child had endured being taken to the police custody or social workers had long term effects. For the rest of his life, the child will grow up with those images of incarceration. In other words, we would have left the frog in boiling water far too long for it to even attempt to crawl afterwards. The researcher did not pay for the child's release but the manager at Spar trusted him. She took his car's registration number and cell phone number as well as national identity card number. She did not trust the mother of the child even though the child was excited to see his mother again. The mother's dishevelled appearance had a lot of influence on the manager's lack of trust.

In a case in which state resources are unreliable, the researcher believed he had made the correct decision. This does not mean that the researcher is at ease with the child's situation. The failure to take action can have long-term emotional regrets for the researcher him/herself. A case in point is that of Sindiso Weeks, who decided not to report abuse of young women by South African soldiers policing the border, whose conduct was "partly enabled by local complicities with the soldiers' willingness to turn a blind eye to illegal border crossings by local people and their families on the other side of the border. That the soldiers were conspicuously well-armed and corrupt made the challenges of exposing their behaviour that much more complex for Weeks" (Ross & Posel, 2014: 11). Years after her fieldwork, Weeks regretted the fact that she did not report these incidents to the Public Protector. Yet, the researcher stood as a guarantor of the child's well-being in a context where family and state both failed. When crises occur, Nyamnjoh (2002: 115) suggests that in line with [African] traditional models of responsibility for children "you are not expected to decline rendering service to this or that person because they are not family." African traditional models demand that a man should avail himself in the best possible manner for the safety of children. In fact, it is not only men who are expected to fulfil this function, but any elderly person in the community including women because children belong to the community and not a particular family in the strict sense of the model. Even though the research ended in 2013, the researcher continued to monitor Njabu's situation mostly telephonically with family members.

Case Two: Sihle's story

Sihle, 11 years old in 2012, had been living with HIV since birth. His mother, a young woman from Port Elizabeth (PE), died four years previously in 2009 from an AIDS-related illness. Sihle's maternal family from Port Elizabeth in the Eastern Cape Province has never been involved in his life and he has never been to PE. Since his mother's death he has lived with his paternal family under the care of his father's mother, Nomonde. Sihle's father, Siyabulela (aged 34 at the time the researcher began research), refused to take his son to the clinic. This was despite the child having been very ill in the preceding few months. Siyabulela had an outburst one day towards his mother because she kept asking him to take his son to the clinic. He told Nomonde that he did not want *lenkwenkwe - 'this boy'* in the first place to come and live with them but Nomonde had taken him in after the child's mother died. He told Nomonde it was her responsibility to care for his health as she had taken him in without discussion. Siyabulela resigned from his job as a cleaner in December 2012. He had a history of drugs and alcohol abuse, and of violence including against his mother, Nomonde (then aged 67).

Despite his sickness, Nomonde and Siyabulela's sister, Zoleka (then 32 years old), refused to start giving him antiretrovirals (ARVs). His CD 4 count cell had dropped from 587 to 145 by end of March 2013 and doctors told the family to give him treatment right away. Zoleka, who was also HIV-positive, insisted that Sihle's CD 4 count would improve; he must just kept eating garlic, raw liver and other immune boosters as was controversially proposed by the late Manto Tshabalala-Msimang, the former health minister in President Thabo Mbeki's government.[4] Zoleka, together with her mother, feared that

---

[4] The former President came under a lot of criticisms for questioning the link between HIV and Aids. Often misunderstood, activists and other sections of the media blame him for the lives the country lost during his tenure as president.

once Sihle started taking ARVs he would have to take them for the rest of his life.

Unlike in Njabu's case, in Sihle's situation the researcher did not intervene or make an attempt to persuade the family to give him his medication. The researcher's decision, though complicated to make at the time, was informed by the presence of a medical doctor who has a legal right, even an obligation, to take the family to task for refusing to give the child a lifesaving treatment, or to force administration himself. Because the doctor knew about the family's decision to wait a bit longer and their attempts to get him recover by giving immune boosters such as garlic, it gave the researcher an opportunity to observe the effectiveness of the health system in this context.

Insecurities, complexities and relational complications: Returning to Anthropology 'at home'

Both stories shared above take us even closer to the realities of young children in the South African society, and in particular Gugulethu community. In effect, Njabu and Sihle have present fathers who are emotionally and responsibly absent.

In response to the situations described in the two cases above, the researchers decided that the researcher should continue visiting these two families even though his fieldwork was long completed. This shows empathy and compassion for fellow human beings as dictated by the African philosophy of Ubuntu which generally underlines the need for interdependence, sharing and co-existence among members of the community as is captured in the African dictum "I am because we are. We are therefore I am" (Mbiti 1969: 28). It also demonstrates some of the responsibilities of being an anthropologist 'at home', where the researcher has the obligation to satisfy certain requirements as is dictated by culture. The cases and responses to them demonstrate the complexities of research relations and raise questions about the duration of ethnographic research and the responsibilities it entails.

The advantage for the researcher to do this research 'at home', as it were, is that he was able to bridge the gap that is so complex and often undervalued of the interplay between entering and exiting the field in this situation. Had the researcher been working away far from his community, he would not have been able to follow what happened to Sihle after the end of his fieldwork. Both cases presented above raise mind boggling questions: "How (as researchers) do leave the field site? How do you (as a researcher) walk away and never go back? Is that ethically correct?" In short, situations as those herein presented raise ethically complicated questions about the beginning and ending of the research itself; about the beginning and ending of the interventions that the researcher may be obliged to take during (or after) fieldwork; about the beginning and ending of one's sense of humane connection (such as a social worker who just vanished) in the context where the State's interventions have completely failed to provide support and continuity to families in need.

Muzvidziwa (2004: 306-7) is very critical of researchers who do fieldwork away from home and who might lack commitment, and who can leave at any time. He quotes an example of Rabinow who studied locals in Morocco, who conceded that "I had a strong sense of being American. I knew it was time to leave." For Muzvidziwa (2004: 307), this kind of attitude is a sign of "…arrogance and lack of empathy not characteristic of non-citizen anthropologists; this could be regarded as a kind of deceitful behaviour. Such an attitude shows that to a great extent non-citizen anthropologists rarely fully assimilate into the communities they study." Our actions today in the communities we study will determine the future of other researchers who might be interested to investigate other social aspects in the same communities. Besides, what we do today has a direct impact on the growth of our discipline either positively or otherwise. This case raises serious questions: "How do we leave the field but remain connected to it? How could we walk away and never go back to the communities that build our professional profiles? Is it ethically correct to just walk away? We are not talking about driving pass the community and claim to still be in touch with them when you cannot even keep their mobile numbers on your phone.

The mutual benefit of ethnographic research lies in the fact that it enables the establishment of close relationships/friendships. Yet, the end of the fieldwork often symbolises the termination of contact between friends, researcher and participant(s). Of course, there is no written code that we should even keep their contact numbers and conversations on social media. We argue here that by ending our contact, we are actually showing that we do not care about their feelings. Emile Boonzaier and colleagues (2005) report on how participants expressed gratitude on the fact that he kept contact and visited them, taking his family and giving them an opportunity to also learn about his own personal life. The researcher also had the same experience in Gugulethu with family members asking about his wife and daughter showing real interest in the researcher and his life. Despite the fact that the researcher's fieldwork officially terminated in March 2013, he remains in contact with the participants through phone calls, text messaging (smsz), sometimes visits and unplanned encounters where they just meet.

This fieldwork has also had an effect at a personal level in that when the researcher's wife first accompanied him to some of the families, she could not hold her tears on returning home after seeing how people could survive in such poverty. As an educator, she is not used to see the kinds of background the children they teach come from. This research has been an eye opener for her as well. She is the one sometimes who reminds that we should go and see how our friends are doing. It is those small things that people sometimes appreciate more. Such interest shows that we are not just interested in our participants as research subjects, but as friends and fellow human beings. In this sense, the researcher have tried to give life to an ethic of *ubuntu* in the research process (see notes to the Principles of Conduct, Anthropology Southern Africa 2005).

Conclusion

The stories captured in this chapter, as others of the same nature, raise critical questions for morality, culture and society in general. Once confronted by the situations captured in the stories, you begin to think seriously about what we mean exactly when we talk about responsible fathering or parenting in general? We believe that the structure the studied households are taking greatly disadvantage children because other kin male members are excluded from the affairs of the family unit to a point where married women assume male functions, even leading family rituals. There is no division of labour as the one expected in a traditional [African] set-up. This is because in many contexts of South Africa (as is the case of Gugulethu), we now hardly talk of stable families where traditional [African] roles are still distinct and explicit. The family unit – which in itself is the smallest unit of society – was long destroyed by the apartheid regime which disrespected and disregarded African norms and values including African models of parenting. It is therefore important to note that family formations in Gugulethu are a structural consequence, a direct legacy of the apartheid system that radically destabilised black families. Like Mfecane (2014), our experience in the field particularly in an African place taught us that to manage friendships one must be willing to sacrifice, for instance, by taking people to the clinics, taking children to events where they might not have been able to go or by generally showing love to children and all other members in the community.

References

Bahre, E. (2002) Witchcraft and the exchange of sex, blood, and money among Africans in Cape Town, South Africa. *Journal of Religion in Africa*, 32(3).

Becker, H.; Boonzaier, E.; & Owen, J. (2005) From expose to care: preliminary thoughts about shifting the ethical concerns of South African social anthropology. Anthropology Southern Africa. *Vol. 28,* (2&4), Pp. 123-132.

Cluver *et al*, L. (2014) *The cost of action: large-scale, longitudinal quantitative research with AIDS affected children in South Africa.* In Posel, D. & Ross, F. 2014. Ethical quandaries in social research. Human Sciences Research Council Press. Cape Town.

Mbiti, J. (1969) *African philosophy and Religions*, Macmillan: London.

Mfecane, S. (2014) *Friends in the field.* In Posel, D. & Ross, F. 2014. Ethical quandaries in social research. Human Sciences Research Council Press. Cape Town.

Muzvidziwa, V. N. (2004) Reflections on ethical issues: a study of how urban women dealt with impoverishment. *Nordic Journal of African Studies.* 13(3), Pp. 302-318.

Nyamnjoh, F. B. (2002) A child is one person's only in the womb: domestication, agency and subjectivity in the Cameroonian Grassfields. In Werbner, R. Postcolonial Subjectivities in Africa. New York: USA.

Weeks, S. M. (2014) 'Insider, outsider: marriage proposals, advocacy and other ethical quandaries in law and society research', In Posel, D. & Ross, F. (2014) *Ethical quandaries in social research,* Human Sciences Research Council Press: Cape Town.

Chapter 7

Chaos and (In)security in the Nether: Repressive Media Policies in Zimbabwe in the Age of Political Paranoia

Last Alfandika

Introduction

This chapter critically reviews the media policy and regulation trajectory since the inception of print and broadcasting media in Rhodesia (colonial Zimbabwe). The contextual background in the chapter overviews the historical emergence and development of the issues which characterise the media sphere in the post-colonial Zimbabwe. This chapter is set to articulate the build up towards the government of Zimbabwe's perceived insecurities which prompted the promulgation of media and security laws such as the Broadcasting Service Act (BSA) (2000), Access to Information and Privacy Protection Act (AIPPA) (2002), Public Order and Security Act (POSA) (2002) and Interception of Communications Act (ICA) (2007), among other media debilitating policies.

Further, the chapter interrogates the inconsistencies and ambivalent nature of media policies which do not only characterise colonial Zimbabwe but also the first and second decades of Zimbabwe independence. It is, however, not within the purview of the present chapter to give a detailed historiography of the events that characterised media policy from Rhodesia to Zimbabwe. However, the chapter pays attention to the basic frameworks of the process of media policy development in this era in order to locate the historicity of the current contestations in Zimbabwe's media policy and regulations regime.

From Rhodesia to Zimbabwe: the political economy of the Media

To understand the debate surrounding media policy and regulation in Zimbabwe, it is important to dissect and plunge into the past and brings forward issues that invoked government's ire and insecurity suspicion which later informed the media policy framework at the beginning of the twenty-first century. The history of Zimbabwe is akin to the history of many African countries which had been subjected to colonialism by Western powers in the 19th Century. Throughout colonialism, the media industry was "aligned with the ideology and interests of the white ruling elite in Rhodesia" (Mukasa 2003; 172). More often than not, media would promote European cultural standards and denigrate Africans and their culture. This media politicisation intensified during Ian Smith's Unilateral Declaration of Independence (UDI) from Britain in 1965 which coincided with the heightened liberation struggle waged by the indigenous Zimbabweans. The Rhodesian Front regime manipulated the media to strengthen its rule in Rhodesia. In fact, to strengthen their colonial position, the government embarked on a propaganda warpath and the media became the centre of reliance. The information department of the regime introduced press censorship by moving government press officers into the Rhodesian Herald and Bulawayo Chronicle offices (Msindo 2009). African newspapers which dare cross the line were banned from operation in the then Rhodesia. In an effort to manipulate the masses, the Rhodesian government took over Rhodesian broadcasting in 1965 (Windrich 1980). The government would arrest and expel any journalist who threatened to expose the State or have alternative opinion contrary to the State ideology.

At independence in 1980, the new government in its effort to reconfigure the media into a public media found itself facing glaring contradictions emanating from the need to be a democratic nation guided by democratic principles and an authoritarian impetus informed by the soviet communist background (Ronning and Kupe 2000). Thus, the government's setting up of the Zimbabwe Mass Media Trust (ZMMT) a public trust that was to buy out the controlling share of the Rhodesia Printing and Publishing Company from the Argus group of South Africa in

In January 1981 was an articulation of the government's commitment towards democratic media policy in Zimbabwe (Mazango 2005). However, this arrangement did not work out well as the project was hijacked by the ruling party, ZANU PF, and became its tool for advancing its political power (Nyahunzvi 1987). In light of these contradictions and circumstances, media policy confusion was to follow in the 1990s with the adoption of the Western liberal economic policies. However, this era saw some opening up of the print media and an attempt to open the airwaves through the introduction of a TV station. Towards the end of the second decade after independence, the government encountered a host of challenges pursued by opposition political parties such as MDC and civil society backed by the former European settlers. In response to this political paranoia and insecurity the Zimbabwean government panicked and promulgated some repressive media and security legislation such as BSA, AIPPA and POSA. These repressive media policies became a centre of contestations in the current obtaining media environment in Zimbabwe.

The Press

The history of the press from Rhodesia to Zimbabwe is analysed alongside racial divide, the "white" minority who happens to be the elites and the "black" majority who represent the subjects. Zimbabwe was under colonial administration of the British South Africa Company (BSAC) which subjected the indigenous people to colonial bondage from 1891 to 1980. On 27 June 1891, the *Mashonaland and Zambesian Times* were published albeit in a hand-written form. These were to be replaced by, *The Rhodesia Herald* on October 20, 1892 as the country's major daily newspapers. The paper was later renamed *The Herald*, and survives up to this day but controlled by the government owned Zimpapers group. Initially, the publication was owned by a South African company, the Argus Company. On October 12, 1894, it opened another publication, the *Bulawayo Chronicle* in Bulawayo, Zimbabwe's second largest city. These two publications were for the white elites hence, they supported the British South Africa Company in its quest to continue ruling Rhodesia and later on supported subsequent ruling elites up to the current ZANU PF government. Mukasa (2003: 172) captures this development aptly:

> During the colonial era two types of press institutions emerged. Newspapers such as the Rhodesia Herald and the Bulawayo-based Chronicle, their sister weeklies the Sunday Mail and the Sunday News, as well as the Financial Gazette, were clearly aligned with the ideology and interests of the white ruling elite in Rhodesia. The journalistic ethos of the times was to promote European cultural standards while denigrating African culture and political agitation as the nemesis of western civilization and Christianity. Stories about Africans were largely, if not exclusively, negative and demeaning.

The structure of the media in the colonial era was made in such a way that it will advance the will of the elite class. It would be used as a tool of controlling the black people minority and influence their opinion. The indigenous Africans were to be forced to accept their position as second class citizens in the hierarchy of beings.

African newspapers in Rhodesia are traceable to the second decade of the 20th century. Most of these publications were based on missionaries' religious teachings and the promotion of literacy and culture (Dombo, 2014). The 'news' published by these newspapers were predominantly Christian religion and moral education (ibid). The Dutch Reformed Church produced the bi-monthly newsletter called *Munyai Washe* which was followed by the 1918's American Methodist Church publication, *Umbowo Hwe Ukristo*. These publications were to extend the evangelical work and publicise the good works of the church. At this time, the idea to provide newspapers for Africans was muted. In 1926, the Dutch Reformed Church published a semi-secular press called the *Rhodesia Native Quarterly*, then the *Mashonaland Quarterly* and later the *Rhodesia Quarterly*. Quoting Diana Jeater, Dombo (2014) explains that the main purpose of the publications was to help missionaries move towards a standardisation of the indigenous language. The publication was later taken over by the BSAC administration to disseminate "government news or policy, Legislation affecting natives, native agriculture, native education, the Native Affairs Department and its work, native medical needs" (Dombo 2014; 128).

The demise of the *Rhodesia Native Quarterly* marked the beginning of the *Native Mirror (Chiringiriro)* in Shona in 1931, or *Isibuko* in Ndebele. It was printed and distributed by the Rhodesian Printing and Publishing Company at the *Chronicle* offices in Bulawayo. The paper was printed in *Karanga, Zezuru* and *Ndebele,* as well as in English. The main focus of the paper was disseminating important government notices and reports in the vernacular languages. In the developmental stage of the press, the conflation of the State and the church to influence behaviour of the Africans was glaring. Based on such observations, one can conclude that from its inception the media was never meant to be democratic. Instead, it was established to advance elite agenda. It was used as an instrument of hegemonic power either to "legitimise" Christian domination or colonial political domination.

The launch of the *African Daily News* in 1956 marked a fierce ideological competition in Rhodesia mainly because of its objective reporting and a hard hitting stance on the colonial administration in Rhodesia. Although the press was white-managed, it was black-edited making it a counter hegemonic tool fighting for oppositional power in Rhodesia (Dombo 2014). In the process, it created a bifurcated narrative in Rhodesia as it advanced the plight of the subjected majority as opposed to the ruling elites. The establishment of the African oriented press advanced disgruntlement of the black majority to racial injustices and exploitation perpetrated by their white minority counterpart. At this moment, the emergence of an alternative voice at a time when Rhodesia was at war created insecurities and paranoia within the government.

To search for public consent and approval, the Rhodesian government embarked on a propaganda assault. In addition, it engaged its legislative machinery to churn out several security laws which impinge on media democracy. Law and Oder Maintenance Act (LOMA) of 1965 became the major security law to ruthlessly attack media democracy by prohibiting turning on a radio in a public place 'in case it picks up broadcasting which may be unfavourable to the State' (Moyo 2008: 15). Anyone found guilty of this offence could be jailed for up to two years (Zaffiro, 1984). In addition to the already suffering media democracy, Rhodesia introduced the Emergency Powers Act (1964). Under this Act, the State could hunt down the media which dare not toe the line and those who had divergent views to the State.

Under these laws, the *African Daily News* was banned by the Rhodesian Front government in 1964. Besides, this law empowered the State to create laws they deemed necessary on emergency basis, that is, without going through parliamentary formalities. Orders like the Emergency Powers (Censorship of Publications) Order of 1965 were enabled by these circumstances. Under this Act, publications were censored. As a result, many publications by indigenous Africans who were suspected of supporting the revolution by Africans were banned. For instance, Solomon Mutsvairo's first novel, *Feso* (1956) was banned by Rhodesian censors. In 1970, the Official Secrets Act was passed to empower the Rhodesian regime to further entrench information suppression on its policies and combat activism by Black Nationalist's social movements (Ndlela, 2003). It prohibited access to information by legalising refusal to disclose for any purpose, information prejudicial to the safety and interests of the State. Media was now at the service of the State.

Although other publications such as the *Moto, Parade, Umbowo*, among others, came in to criticise the Rhodesian government, they were closely monitored by a battery of security laws that had been created to guard against exposition of the ills of the State especially after the UDI by Ian Smith's government. These laws were also created to guard the dignity attached to the person of the president and to create an aura around a governing class so as to be untouchable by the exposing media.

Change without change? The end of an error and the beginning of another

The 1980 Independence from Rhodesia to Zimbabwe marked the end of a colonial administration that was highly debilitating to the development of media democracy and other forms of freedom. Naturally, one would have expected the beginning of a democratisation process from the ebbs of colonial regime to the much anticipated democratic freedom across the social, political and economic divide. However, to a greater extent, the media policy of the new Zimbabwe was laced with contradictions which were deep rooted in the colonial epoch when the press and broadcasting media served the interests of the government (Ronning and Kupe, 2000).

In a move which brought temporary hope and trust in the dispensation of 1980, the new government set up a "new" structure in 1981. The Zimbabwe Mass Media Trust (ZMMT) was set out as an articulation of a media policy in the new era of governance (Ronning and Kupe, 2000). In line with this media policy idea, the government did not want to be seen perpetuating a system they had been fighting against in Rhodesia. They had to disbar or morphs the configuration of the two daily newspapers in the country, The *Rhodesian Herald in Salisbury* and The *Bulawayo Chronicle* in Bulawayo, which were owned by the South African Argus Company (Ronning and Kupe, 2000).

Sadly, today, the mainstream media in Zimbabwe is tailored to serve the interests of the ruling class elites. Since independence, the Zimpapers press enjoys a monopoly of the press in Zimbabwe through its national dailies, national weeklies and regional weeklies publications. The national dailies are *The Herald* and *The Chronicle*, while the national weeklies include the *Sunday Mail*, and the *Sunday News*. Regional weeklies publications include *Manica Post for Mutare, H-Metro* for Harare, *B-Metro* for Bulawayo, *Kwayedza* for Shona speakers and *Umthunywa* for those who speak Ndebele in Matebeleland. From its inception, publications from this stable would promote the cause of the elite, especially the ruling class and at independence in 1980; the new government adopted this trend too.

On the other hand, alternative private press was promoting other voices since 1990s. This opening up of the media had come as part of the wider global liberalisation policy advanced by Western countries. Some newspapers such as; the *Independent*, the *standard*, and *Newsday* endeavour to provide alternative voice to the public in Zimbabwe. In addition, the *Financial Gazette* recently acquired by the

Associate Newspapers of Zimbabwe (ANZ), and the *Daily news* also form part of the private media in Zimbabwe. Besides these national publications, there is the Community Newspaper Group (CNG) owned and controlled by the government. These are community based newspapers. They are usually found in provincial capitals of Zimbabwe. These are *Masvingo Star* for Masvingo province, *Ilanga* for Matebeland North, the *Telegraph* for Mashonaland West, *Chaminuka* for Mashonaland East, *Nehanda* guardian for Mashonaland Central, *The Times* for Midlands province, *Pungwe* for Manicaland, and *Indosakusa* for Matebeland North.

There are also several regional private presses such as *Masvingo Mirror* and *TellZim* newspapers, among other private regional papers, which advance alternative voice in the media as a way of articulating media democracy in Zimbabwe. It is important to note that AIPPA caused closure to several publications and media establishments in Zimbabwe. The first causality of AIPPA was the *Daily news* which was closed after it failed to comply with the new registration requirements among other highly critical publications (Dombo 2014).

The broadcasting media

The history of broadcasting in Zimbabwe dates back to 1932 (Moyo 2004). Both the colonial and government in Zimbabwe have always been using broadcasting as a tool for political control and ideological manipulation of the masses all in the name of 'national interest' rather than 'public interest' (Kupe 2005, Moyo, D 2004). By 1932, broadcasting opened stations in Salisbury (now Harare) and Bulawayo (Miller 2007). Later in the years, other stations were built in the old Post Office building on Manica Road in Salisbury, but "from 1933 when radio broadcasting was first introduced in the country to the early sixties, the then Southern Rhodesia broadcasting relied on broadcasting from outside the country" (Mabika 2014; 2391). When the Federation was dissolved at the end of 1963, Southern Rhodesia became a separate country, and the Rhodesia Broadcasting Corporation (RBC) was formed. In 1968, the RBC expanded its services further with a number of local community stations such as Radio Jacaranda in Salisbury, Radio Matopos in Bulawayo and Radio Manica in Umtali. In 1975, the first FM stations opened in the Salisbury and Bulawayo areas and the network was gradually expanded to 22 stations covering the whole country (Miller, 2007). This expansion would improve the reach and access to information by the public although most of the information was of a hegemonic nature.

African radio broadcasting in Rhodesia served the purpose of disseminating government policies to the natives. Based on the fact that most of the natives could neither read nor write, the only means of communicating to them was through radio broadcasting using their own [mother] language (Moyo D, 2000). Broadcasting media was used as a tool to control the hearts and minds of the indigenous people described as too dangerous to be left idle as they can be easily manipulated by the communist ideologies (Masuku 2011). Having realised this, the Rhodesian government banned foreign communication as a measure to intensify its control of Rhodesian Broadcasting Corporation (RBC). The Ministry of Information embarked on propaganda assault through productions which paint a bad image of the speculated independent Africa to the Western countries. In fact, they wanted to portray an image which seems to suggest that Africans were happy and safe in the hands of the colonial regime.

Shortly after independence in 1980, the radio services were reorganised ostensibly to align them with the new dispensation in the new Zimbabwe. RBC was changed to Zimbabwe Broadcasting Corporation (ZBC). Today, the ZBC operates four radio channels namely, Sport FM, Radio Zimbabwe, Power FM and National FM. Sport FM broadcast for 24 hours a day in English, thus covering a broad spectrum of listeners. Its programmes include news and information, a variety of music, light entertainment, sport, comedy, quizzes and drama.

Radio Zimbabwe broadcasts for 24 hours a day, in Shona, Ndebele and other local languages. The station serves the majority of the rural and urban population that is largely indigenous Africans. Two thirds of the music played on Radio Zimbabwe is produced locally. The station's programme line-up includes discussions, features and drama on social, cultural, sporting and economic issues.

Power FM is a 24-hour commercial and music station aimed at the youths. It provides fast-paced music, entertainment, information and education. The majority of its listeners are young people who are highly receptive. The station broadcasts in English from Harare, the capital city of Harare. Its programmes include youth discussions, current affairs, commercially sponsored programmes and live phone in programmes.

National FM is an educational channel, which broadcasts for 24 hours a day in *Shona, Ndebele*, English and the minority languages of *Nambya, Chewa, Tonga, Venda, Kalanga and Shangani*. The audience demographics depend on the nature of the educational programmes being broadcast at the time. The station works closely with the Ministry of Education's Audio Visual Services, as well as other relevant government ministries and non-governmental organisations.

The 1990s saw the beginning of changes in broadcasting which have been known as "liberalisation of airways' in Africa (Article 19 2003). The liberalisation of airwaves demands for democratic reforms such as transforming state broadcasters into public service broadcasters that should enjoy editorial and programming independence as well as the licensing of private broadcasters as alternatives and competitors to the public broadcasters (*ibid*). In Zimbabwe, broadcasting remained a closed area with a single case trial which did not materialise when the government partnered a private player to start Joy Tv in the mid-1990s. The democratisation process of the 1990s was mainly a result of wider political changes taking place at the international level where Western liberal democracy was gaining ground ahead of the collapsing socialist and communist ideologies. The talk of deregulation, commercialisation and privatisation of broadcasting media during this time did not make an impact in the face of broadcasting services in Zimbabwe. Thus, demands for media democratic reforms such as transformation of State broadcasters into public service broadcasters and licensing of private broadcasters fell on a deaf ear in Zimbabwe, although to a lesser extent there was an attempt.

At the same time, an attempt to bring in some other players in the media industry other than ZTV was made. In this regard, to liberalise the airwaves the government engaged a British consultant, Peter Ibbotson to research and recommend on the issues of commercialising ZBC (Moyo 2004). The Ibbotson Report indicates that the then Minister of Information, Posts and Telecommunications, Joyce Mujuru wished to liberalise the market by ending ZBC monopoly of broadcasting and opening up the airwaves for other commercial companies. Although the Ibbottson Report had recommended total privatisation of TV2 and Radio 4, the government instead "leased TV2 to three private broadcasters namely, LDM, Munhmutapa African Broadcasting Corporation (MABC), and Joy TV (a.k.a. Flame Lily Broadcasting)" (Moyo 2004; 20). In addition, the other broadcasters did not have full control of the new station to enable them to be freely alternative voices in the true sense of the word as they were managed through government's involvement as a shareholder. Moreover, the coverage of TV2 was limited to only a 70km radius of the capital Harare and besides, the three broadcasters mostly carried entertainment (ibid). This only confirms the government's scepticism towards media liberalisation, freedom of expression, and access to information.

Currently, there are six national radio channels. ZBC owns four radio channels while the other two are owned by private players. ZBC operate *Radio Zimbabwe, Power FM, Sport FM* and *National FM.* Zimpapers operate *StarFM* while AB Communications operate *ZiFM.* In addition to these channels, other regional commercial licences have been issued to private players like, *FayaFM* owned by AB Communications in Gweru, *HevoiFM* owned by AB Communications in Masvingo, *YaFM* owned by Ray of Hope in Zvishavane, *BreezeFM* owned by Fairtalk in Victoria Fall, *SkymetroFM* owned by Fairtalk in Bulawayo, *KE100.4* owned by Kingstone and operate in Harare, *Nyaminyami FM* in Kariba owned by Kingstones again. These stations are more than just added commercial broadcasters. They compete with State-owned ZBC and *StarFM* and *ZiFM* which offer nationwide coverage. While *StarFM* and *Diamond FM* are owned, funded and controlled by *Zimpapers, Star FM* remains a national broadcasting station and Diamond operates in Manicaland region. *ZiFM* is owned by AB Communications which belong to the ruling ZANU PF legislator, Supa Mandiwanzira who is currently the Minister of Information and Communication Technology (ICT) and former deputy Minister of Information and Publicity (BAZ) falls under this ministry. In addition, Kingstones which operates two licences is a government owned company which sales and distributes stationery while Ray of Hope is owned by Munyaradzi Hwengwere who is a former government employee in the ministry of information and a Chief Executive Officer at ZBC. It is clear that there is a conflation of interest here as the government seems to licence their own proxies. Nevertheless, George Charamba, the permanent secretary in the Ministry of information defends such licencing structure:

> ...the British media power has never been democratic, it has been woven around media moguls or magnets such that you see that the notion of democracy does not come into play, so yes, and argument will be used to say the State is licencing its own. That is very consistent, we do so yes, they are ways just to show you that we are in the terrain of power not of democracy so I will make sure that by the end of digitalisation, ZBC has six channels to control and I will use the argument that it is a public media. We are imposing on it certain social burdens so it must have more channels. Then the other six there is a dog fight, which is not so general, these are people who are in print who are coming to electronic because they want to create an integrated media service (*Interview with George Charamba in Harare on the 13 of July 2017*).

Admittedly, the State uses the media as a tool for ideological manipulation. It has never envisaged the media in the terrain of democracy but in the terrain of power. This position indicates a tough task ahead of the media democracy lobby groups whose hope is to win the hearts and minds of the policy makers so as to reform media laws.

Chaos in the nether: the development of media policy in Zimbabwe

The period around 1990s saw new forces in international governance affecting national politics and the way the media sphere was configured and operates in Zimbabwe. In this new development often called the 3ʳᵈ wave of democratisation in Africa, neo liberalism was spreading much across the African continent in the work of adjustment policies that were being implemented during the same time. Among the countries that hid the call for economic adjustment programmes are Zimbabwe, Zambia and Malawi. Countries up north of the Zambezi had gone through processes of implementing the policy adjustments from the Washington consensus institutions like the International Monetary Fund (IMF) and the World Bank (WB). Naturally, the process of liberalising and deregulating the economies and different sectors means shrinking the role of the State in the economy and the media in this instance. In essence, neo-liberalism entails pushing government out of media spaces so that private players can come in and operate with very little government interference in terms of both financing and control.

Towards the year 2000, new media entities like newspapers, magazines, and other publications critical of the government's policies began to emerge. For instance, the Parade under the editorship of Andrew Moise began to hard hit the State exposing the government's ill dealings. With regards to this development, Moise explained that they were writing public interest stories which concern the national interest. Among the stories were concern about the Economic Structural Adjustment Programmes (ESAP), the colonially adopted education system, and the land question. These controversial issues were being aired out when not any other newspaper was doing so. At that time, it (Parade) had become popular and controversial that Nathan *Shamuyarira*[5] was writing letters to the publisher threatening the publication to change its

---

[5] Nathan Shamuyarira (29 September 1928 – 4 June 2014) was a Zimbabwean nationalist. He later served as the Information Minister of Zimbabwe and as the Information Secretary of ZANU PF.

149

editorial policy as averred by Andrew Moise, a former editor of the Parade:

> …saying you must do something about your Magazine because it is causing trouble. The government noticed that we were questioning their policies and *Gukurahundi*, turning people out on the street, revealing mass graves and the brutality of the elections. We would expose the lack of development in Bulawayo and centralised developments in Harare. The threats on our lives also increased, too many disappeared and some were found hanged mostly soldiers who were trying to expose ivory smuggling. Eventually, I was fired by the editor due to a directive from Nathan *Shamuyarira* and the ZANU PF government. I was given eight hours to leave the office. (*Interview with Andrew Moise on the 13th of July 2018, Harare*).

The minister's intervention in to the editorial policy of a publication indicates that the government had plunged into a state of paranoia hence such panic reactions. The act of writing threatening letters to the editor testifies how deeply troubled the government was due to press reports which were highly investigative revealing some corrupt activities by senior officials of the state.

On the side of the public media, the government had a firm editorial grip and the Ministry of Information continued to exert tremendous influence over Zimpapers publications. So pronounced was the State control of public journalism that some government officials complained that the media had lost all semblance of credibility (Chuma 2008). As a result of this monopoly, ZANU PF government receded into a comfort zone till such a time when the economy began to show some signs of exhaustion affecting the socio-economic life of the general population. In addition, the formation of MDC in 1999 and the defeat of the government in the 2000 Constitution referendum together with the birth of the *Daily News* was enough to send some chilling messages down the State's spine.

Earlier on, in the middle of the 1990s, equally hard hitting magazines like the *Horizon* had set up the tone after it was established by the editor fired from the Parade, Mr Moise. He set up the publication with the help of Judy Todd and some journalists who had worked with him at the Parade such as *Jacob Mutambara, Tendai Madima* and later, *Ray Choto*. [6] Although, the publication operated on a shoe string budget, struggling in terms of financial resources, it managed to keep the government on its toes by exposing corruption and other unscrupulous government dealings. In trying to frustrate the publication, the government opened a barrage of tricks to unseat the publication. Among their arsenal was to initiate several lawsuits for the stories published. For instance in November 1998, "Horizon" won an appeal case at the Supreme Court to reverse a Z$40 000 (US$1 100) defamation judgment. The defamation case against the magazine was brought by former army commander Solomon Mujuru. This further support the claim that law suits was used to muzzle the media or deter journalism from playing a watchdog role. Andrew Moise explained in an interview:

It was mainly government or government associated people or military like General Solomon Mujuru[7] and he was awarded damages but we appealed and the whole thing was thrown out and he was ordered to pay the costs of the suit. When we got the High Court Sherriff to collect what we were awarded from Solomon Mujuru, he pulled a gun and 'said get off my property or I will kill you' and that was the end of our cost...This was just one of the cases but it was most serious and the Supreme Court was interfering with the citizens right to freedom of expression (*Interview with Andrew Moise in Harare on 13th of July 2017*).

The State occasionally applied legal attacks on the private press. In 1992, two *Financial Gazette* journalists were summoned before a parliamentary committee investigating a financial scandal involving a private company after publishing leaked information. The committee used its legal powers to compel the paper's editor to reveal his source

---

[6] Judith Todd is the daughter of Garfield Todd (1908–2002), Rhodesian Prime Minister 1953-58, and a political activist in Zimbabwe. She was a manager at the Zimbabwe Trust when the Horizon Magazine was set up.

[7] Solomon Mujuru (born 5 May 1945 – 15 August 2011), also known by his nom-de-guerre, Rex Nhongo, was a Zimbabwean army general and politician.

or face jail. Two years later, two journalists from the *Daily Gazette* were detained and questioned under the Official Secrets Act for a story on tax evasion by ZANU PF-owned companies. In 1995, *Financial Gazette* publisher, editor and his deputy, were charged and convicted of criminal defamation and fined for a story about the alleged secret wedding of President Mugabe and his secretary, Ms *Grace Marufu*. However, incidents of arrests, detentions or legal action against journalists by State officials during the second decade after independence, compare favourably with the post-2000 era incidences.

The period stretching from 1989 to 2000 experienced an expansion of the press buoyed to a large extent by the liberal approach to the economy adopted by the government (Chuma 2008). This period saw a number of black privately owned publications developing. Elias Rusike teamed up with his business associates to buy Modus publishers, publishers of the *Financial Gazette* in 1989. In 1992, they launched the *Daily Gazette*, the first daily publication to challenge Zimpapers. Furthermore, they launched the *Sunday Gazette* (1993). Similarly, other private press such as the *Sunday Times* (1991) were registered. Trevor Ncube, Clive Murphy and Clive Wilson launched the *Independent* in 1996 and were later to add the *Standard* in 1997. These publications adopted a critical approach in their coverage of the government and ZANU PF issues (Chuma, 2008).

Although, some of the laws that are affecting the operations of media democratically in Zimbabwe have been in place prior to the formation of the main opposition [political] party in Zimbabwe, MDC in 1999, the intensification and selective application of those laws after the emergence of the MDC is of great concern today. There is no doubt about that but the aura that characterizes political space in Zimbabwe and the media regulation between 1980 and 1999 resulted in the establishment of the papers like the *Daily News* which became the biggest outlet of alternative voice. In the years 2000-2003 before it was shut down, the *Daily News* became the sole channel for opposition and civil society for critical mind about the state of Zimbabwe and that is why it was shut down. It allowed critical views to trickle into the public space thereby giving mileage to oppositional politics. It allowed for engagement on matters that were hitherto taboo in the State controlled media. In a way, this is why government is unwilling to let go of their stranglehold of the media because they know the impact of the media in terms of shaping public opinion, setting the agenda, mobilizing and energizing citizens, building citizen agents for citizens to demand and act on matters they feel have impact on their lives.

Liberalisation of the media had its own effects to the ruling class. The ruling elites became a subject of discussion in the hard hitting liberal media. Naturally, this created the need to dignify the person and office of the president. Thus, the creation of an honourable aura around a governing class to shroud power with some kind of mystery and induce fear and respect among subjects. To achieve this, laws that sought to create a larger than life identity in a ZANU PF leadership were created emphasising on clauses like 'bringing the office of the president in disrepute' would myth make the character of the President and will be portrayed as a larger than life character. This and other batteries of laws created for the same purpose would build some kind of assurance against the possibility of the media picking on that myth. What is debilitating in this issue is that a portion media democracy is taken away leaving media vulnerable to the laws and self-censorship.

Another argument in the same scenario indicates that, laws that govern the media in Zimbabwe prior to 2000 were usually class oriented laws. For instance, libel and defamation reflect some greater extent of class orientation; they deal with class preoccupation and class sensitivity, hence they are for the protection and security guaranteeing of the powerful class. The underlying reality is that the powerful classes are usually notorious in their pursuit of profit and would not want the world to know about it so they protect their hypocritical reputation by creating laws around libel and defamation to shoo off the media because it has the potential to undermine their reputations. On the contrary, a villager or a peasant has no reputation beyond that of attending to the earth, breaking the clod, making earth give some kind of well-withal for his poor family, he is not concerned about reputation because he has none. To protect this reputation, the elite class who is also the ruling class then abridge the freedom of the media.

Yet another way of looking at it is that, as Zimbabwean government became paranoid of the power of the liberal media, it began begging for the re-integration of the polarised society. Increasingly, the government began to make serious movements in order to win the minds and hearts of the people who had been polarised by liberalisation policies in the economy and the media. To do this they sought to touch on two vital issues in the history of Zimbabwe. The compensation of the liberation war heroes (War veterans) and the land question which land happened to be in the few hands of the whites. These movements created a sense of anxiety in the white community. To a certain point, the white farmers' community began to wonder whether the ZANU PF government could still be trusted with power. In the end, they concluded that the ZANU PF government could not be trusted to mind the status quo.

In fact, the white farmers' community in Zimbabwe's calculations were that, Lancaster House Agreement had within it builds in slow down mechanisms which were meant to empty, from the heart of the politician, the argument to change society in favour of the black majority. Instead, it would delay the process in such a way that several years later down the line there would emerge black elite whose interest become almost synonymous with interest the white settler. In which case, instead of having a conflict, there would have a sense of partnership thereby creating a comprador class. This model has worked well in South Africa and other parts of the world where independence had been given on a silver platter. In such scenarios, the emergence of black elites did not seek to transform society but rather joined the white elites in dominating the rest of the society.

The urgent need within the ZANU PF government to relook into the agenda of nationalism which was built around the land question marked a significant shift in the power relations in Zimbabwe. It changed the political economy of Zimbabwe in a way that created a variegation of classes. The black elites emerged replacing the white commercial farmers and became a class in itself. It became a class with self-conscious that would seek to defend its own interest and then landed peasantry with small holder pieces of land but still conscious enough that it had gained from the process of elites a set of finite assert on the base of which it could change its own circumstances. In these circumstances, there materialized in Zimbabwe, a true peasant class with land and which is ready to defend that land. In addition, there is also a middle class which is African and whose claim to class is ownership of a piece of land again, there are ready to defend it. In the same circumstances, there is the dearth of a class that was almost coincident with race by way of the ex-white commercial farmers. That's creating a new milieu in Zimbabwe as part of reclaiming the legacy under attack by the western oriented liberalisation polices of 1990s.

However, an interesting dimension is that, as the destruction of the settler class was taking place in Zimbabwe, some developments began to take shape where the white farmers in a counter attack did not only invest in MDC, but also invest in the Daily News and the broadcasting media through Capitol radio. This prompted the ZANU PF government to wonder, why does an ex-colonial class suddenly discover the need to redirect capital in a high risk area like the media with modest retains and where stability is not assured. Based on the knowledge that media is a crucial tool in the acquisition of power and its retention, and or the settlement of the political question. The State discerns the need to understand the motive taken by the ex-settler class in these new developments. As if to confirm the power of the media and its role in political manipulation, there appeared some former ZBC employees, led by Georgina Goodwill. The government strongly believed that this cabal was invited by the then Chief Justice, Anthony Ray Gubby.[8] The ZANU PF government still accept as true that the then Chief justice Gubby was working in cahoots with the white commercial farmers whose land has been dispossessed by the government as elaborated by Mr George Charamba in an interview:

> Chief Justice Gubby does two heinous crimes, contrary to the rules, he accosts the white farmers to come before his court with the land case, and promising that if that were to be brought before his

---

[8] Anthony Ray Gubbay (April 26, 1932) is the former Chief Justice of the Supreme Court of Zimbabwe. He served in the position from 1990 to 2001, when he was forced to take early retirement and replaced by Godfrey Chidyausiku.

bench, he would rule in favour of the farmers who happen to be white, the second aspect, he broadens the vista of that whole argument and he also, begins to as it were to encourage judgements which State monopoly in the media culminating in constitutional case called State versus Capitol radio…and the State lost… (*Interview with George Charamba, in Harare on the 13th of July 2017*).

This scenario created a legal vacuum in the administration of broadcasting services in Zimbabwe. The fact that there was now a judgement which confirmed that State of emptiness made it possible that whoever had ambitions of establishing themselves in the broadcasting media would do so lawfully. In the same spirit, armed with this judgement, Georgina Goodwill puts up her antenna on Monomotapa Hotel and began broadcasting. The State was caught napping; it did not have the technology to determine where the signal was coming from. Indeed, it was ill equipped in terms of both the law machinery and the technology to deal with this kind of broadcasting piracy. Politically, the State had not evolved an argument to defend State monopoly of the ZBC and overnight, it was caught flatfooted. To make matters worse, there was no ministry of information, but a department of information and publicity under the president's office. Now that the government found itself squarely facing an adverse judgement to remove any inhibitions or establishment in the industry or broadcasting so that anyone could declare themselves broadcasters, except they were going to so on the strength of a finite resource which is a national property called the frequency.

This is similar to what preceded the FCC in America. Americans had discovered that Frequencies were not freely available in a given polity, they could not be created, and they could only be misused or destroyed or used more efficiently. Based on the fact that it was a finite resource, they then naturally decided to create an urgency that would regulate access to it. Since frequency is a common property, whoever has access to it should be able to utilise it to the natural good, which may mean in class terms, "to the good of the dominant class". Following this unveiling, the American created FCC to regulate what they fear was going to be chaos in the nether. The FCC role was to after a process option the right of access to frequency to the broadcasters. That's, how the first generation of radio broadcasters in America came to be and this experience, informed the world that broadcasting must be regulated, yet in Zimbabwe, there was no law to that effect and Zimbabwe was on a fix.

Now in this case an adverse judgement had been handed down against the State. As non-believers in the democratic administration of justice, the State labelled the Supreme Court an adverse bench presided over by (Gubby) whom it believes sympathises with the ex-colonial class of white people in Zimbabwe. To make matters even worse, there was no technological knowledge to establish who was doing what in the broadcasting industry. More so, the State had no established authority that could handle the licencing process because there was no law to it. There was need for a statutory board but for it to be put in place, it was supposed to be backed by a statutory creature such as a law that underpins it. So as the monopoly of the State broadcasting was being challenged by the white interests, the State was found flatfooted and could not defend itself.

As for Capitol Radio, the State having realised the existing legal vacuum within the national media policy framework and the effects of such a broadcasting policy gap, panicked and sought all means possible to stop any broadcasting not sanctioned by the State in case they broadcast anything detrimental to its comfort. In addition, the State invoked presidential powers (temporary measures), mainly because if it was to wait, it would take time. This was possible given that the MDC was in parliament, and would surely oppose the bill. To expedite the law making process, the State picked up a law making instrument that would allow it to have a law overnight. There was a provision in the Zimbabwean Constitution which allows the president to make law on an interim basis, and specifically a period of six months. Thus, Presidential powers were invoked and regulations put in place creating provisions for licencing processes. The regulations made it criminal to smuggle transmission equipment into the country. Ultimately, the State closed down Capitol Radio and forfeited the equipment allegedly smuggled into the country. Because the regulations had a short life span of six months only, the State embarked on a process of crafting a new law to plug this gap.

Admittedly, the first draft of BSA was cobbled within a week and was mainly made up of plagiarised pieces of legislations from the Australia, South Africa, Ireland and Canada broadcasting legislations. No wonder why Charamba (2017) had this to say:

> If plagiarism is a crime, we were guilty of it. We went to the law of Australians, South Africans which was a derivative of the Australian law and to the Irish and the Canadians and out of their pieces of legislation we then hybridised our Broadcasting Service Act (*Interview with George Charamba in Harare on the 13th of July 2017*).

A simple comparison of these laws reflects a cunning similarity with the media laws of the nations cited above. Such action was taken for the two basic reasons which are expedience and time. The State had to quickly put together some legal framework because things in the broadcasting sector were happening ahead of legal reality. The expedience side was that Zimbabwe was beginning to pick a quarrel with the Western world over the land issue hence, looking for a law from the Soviet Communist States such as North Korea and China would create an easy way to challenge the Western countries. The plan was then to put in place a law that protects the national interest but which is built from the Western doyens of media democracy. For instance, Australia has always been a self-conscious society. Similarly, Canada lives in the shadow of the United States of America (USA) so it would not want to be overrun by Americans, and equally Australians do not want to be overrun by the Americans. It was then important to put up a nationalist legislation made up of pieces shopped from these four countries. In the process, it was essential that the State was conscious of accommodating its nationalist sentiments by making it difficult for the Western world to come back and attack it because the inspiration of the law making process had been the West.

As the government work on the broadcasting media policy vacuum, it also saw the need to consolidate the legal framework for the print imperative. In line with that, Access to Information and Privacy Protection Act (AIPPA) was mooted. AIPPA was structured in such a way that three quotas of the law concentrate on providing access to information, another section deals with the issues of registration and regulation of conduct of the journalist and publishers. However, the whole body of law of "access" seemed to be ignored by the media interest lobby groups creating, an acrimonious debate based on issues of registration, professional givens of practitioners and conduct of publishers.

It is important to note that all media laws passed in Zimbabwe prior to 2000 sought to regulate the media negatively because they all seek to prohibit certain media behaviour at the expense of administering it. In actual fact, every security law that felt affected or disturbed by the behaviour of the media would take away media freedom by inserting a clause that prohibit the media from upsetting the State by reporting it negatively. For instance, under LOMA, the Police would look at ways in which the media would inconvenience them when they want to enforce the Law and Order instrument. LOMA would then be used in such a way that it would show off the media at that critical time when the Police are enforcing Law and Order. As Charamba tells us:

> This is the situation we had in the country in the pre-2000 era. There was no composite law which deals with the media as an estate. Essentially what really prompted law making in 2000 and beyond was a bid on our part to then create one stop legal shop for the media industry (*Interview with George Charamba, in Harare on the 13th of July 2017*).

Due to this incapacitating aspect of media policy in Zimbabwe, an idea was mooted to put up laws which administer the operation of the media in Zimbabwe and regulate it in such a way that the media itself will have the opportunity to seek redress on issues that affect it such as failure to access 'public interest' information from the public bodies. Thus, the structure of AIPPA concentrate on access, and a small section of it concentrate on registration and conduct of the journalist and publishers. Ostensibly, the aspects of access as captured in AIPPA are supposed to guarantee democratisation of communication. Thus, democratisation of communication can only be guaranteed if people who hold information in the 'public interest' are compelled to release it in a way that empowers the citizens. This is where the issue of access becomes pregnant. In other words, the capacity of the citizen to compel a powerful person or board to release information that is needed by the public to fulfil their functions as useful conscious citizen demonstrate some level of communication democracy.

Regardless of the situation elaborated above, the motive prompting the State to put up media laws around this period could be aligned to ZANU PF government's panicked over the fall of other authoritative regimes which had accepted western liberal policies. For instance, shocking news from Zambia were that Kaunda Kenneth had been voted out, in Malawi, Kamuzu Banda had been replaced by his rival opposition party and in Zaire, Mobutu Sese Seko had been tipped off. These were enough signs to warn the ZANU PF government of their very soon fate if they had to continue with the liberal policies. It is prudent to note that MDC was rising and rising fast and in 2000 as it had influenced the masses to vote against the constitution on a referendum.

Other government's panic points includes, losing a court case in the State Vs Capitol Radio, lost in the referendum of 2000 as mentioned above, the rising of strikes, and riots led by a labour body once loyal to the State, the Zimbabwe Congress of Trade Union (ZCTU), as a result of soaring unemployment level, rising inflation and debilitating poverty. Quoting Bond and Manyanya, Chuma (2008) noted that 1997 recorded around 55 national labour actions, rising from the usual 15 per year which had characterised the last 10 years. . Among the issues leading to strikes was action against awarding the Zimbabwe National Liberation War Veterans Association (ZNLWVA) additional gratuities of Z$50,000 (equivalent to US$4000) which was a lot of money by Zimbabwean standards in 1998. In addition, early 1998 was characterised by nationwide food riots, Mass protests against the rise of food and other commodities (ibid).

Furthermore, the formation of the MDC and the financial support it got from the white community, increased anti-government sentiments from the alternative press like the Daily News. In another development of similar nature, the country witnessed challenges mounted by Econet wireless challenging the State's domination in the telecommunications industry. Econet won the case and was awarded a telecommunication licence effectively ending the State monopoly in this industry. The liberalisation dispensation buoyed the sprouting of private business entities right across the various sectors of economy including the media. The government became intensely interested in how it would control the media narrative. It therefore crafted pieces of legislations such as BSA, AIPPA, and POSA. These policies would aid the State and its agencies to control the activities of the media and the civil society. These media policies pushed in the post 2000 era were an immediate reaction by the authorities to avoid a seemingly certain regime change in Zimbabwe.

The government's State of paranoia at this point exudes the extent to which it understands the power of the media as a tool of media control. It backs the notion that media are critical fortunes of political actors without then power and politics will not nigh. Furthermore, there are some signs to justify that the processes that gave birth to a new opposition political party seem to be the same process that gave birth to the powerful privately owned media like the Daily News which was increasingly beginning to challenge the dominant imperative goings in the country. Thus, the reaction of the State was to reinstate the provision of a monologue in terms of interpretation of the status quo of the situation obtained in the country. To the State, it was important for the nation to embrace a univocal narration or interpretation of the political situation in the country. Through the media policies of 2000, the State sought to restore credibility of the Zimpapers publications and the ZBC as the only credible voices out there with no competing or contesting articulation.

To some extent, these policies achieved their objectives by closing down upcoming broadcasting such as the haunted Capitol Radio in Harare in 2000 and seizure of their equipment. We all witnessed the closure of the Daily News which had frustrated the State and in particular, the ruling party, ZANU PF's ambition to muzzle all alternative private media in the country. The State to a greater extent, re-established the State media status as the only sole provider of news.

The Zimbabwean Media regulation Framework

Regardless of the chaos which created the political obsession and insecurity within the ruling ZANU PF government and the creation of media laws, a mega first score was the creation of the 2013 Zimbabwe Constitution which recognise as official the sixteen languages spoken in Zimbabwe, freedom of expression and freedom of the media as well as access to information. This has become the supreme law to govern the media in Zimbabwe regardless of some contestations inherent. In addition to the constitution of 2013, there are two media laws acting as the principle laws in the Zimbabwean media governance. AIPPA in all its repressive form became a comprehensive law to administer the operations of the media in Zimbabwe. The BSA, on the other hand became handy in administering the operations of the broadcasting media in Zimbabwe.

However, there are other several security laws that impinge media freedom in Zimbabwe with some dating back as far as the colonial period. Due to these laws and regulations, the Zimbabwe media sphere has been described by Freedom House (FH), Media Institute of Southern Africa (MISA), Media Monitors (MM), Zimbabwe Association of Community Radios (ZACRAS), Zimbabwe Editors Forum (ZINEF), Zimbabwe Union of Journalists (ZUJ), among several media lobby groups as "not free". Among these security laws are the Criminal Law (Codification and Reform) Act (CODE), Interception of Communication Act (ICA), Official Secrecy Act (OSA) and Public Order and Security Act (POSA). In terms of Freedom of the Media ratings, Zimbabwe is rated 'partly free' in *Freedom in the World 2016*, Not Free in *Freedom of the Press 2015* and Partly Free in *Freedom on the Net 2015* (Freedom house, 2016). This means that there is inconsistence of media democracy in Zimbabwe. To further compound the situation in Zimbabwe, the abduction of Itai Dzamara[9], a journalist and a critic of the ZANU PF government in 2015 indicates the extent of media repression in Zimbabwe. For instance, AIPPA is supposed to make public information available to

---

[9] Itai Dzamara is a Zimbabwean journalist and political activist. He was abducted on 9 March 2015 in Harare's Glenview suburb.

both members of the public and the press. More so, it should ensure the protection of the citizen's rights to privacy (Chuma 2008).

Nevertheless, the private media and media lobby groups describe it as the best statutory creature on how not to access information in Zimbabwe. AIPPA provides that the print media is regulated by Zimbabwe Media Commission (ZMC) which is also created through a process that excludes the parent Ministry, the process that the president only enjoys the prerogative to either accept recommendations or reject them. Worse still, ZMC is manned by Commissioners as a constitutional body. It exists in Zimbabwe's Constitution as it [ZMC] is created by standing rules and orders committee (SROC) which is a committee of parliament. Thus, ultimately the process around the creation of ZMC is outside the executive. They are actually located within the legislature but for the purpose of bringing that into being they then have to send their recommendations to the executive. Also, because ZMC is a constitutional body, it falls under the Minister of Justice meaning that the Ministry of Information has nothing to do with ZMC except as a client. ZMC is required to account at the close of every financial year to parliament by way of originating a report which is tabled at the parliament.

Seemingly, in the broadcasting industry, BSA was established to deregulate the broadcasting media. However, contrary to the reasons of establishment, the Act makes it very difficult for private players to enter into the broadcasting industry except where there are strong links with the individuals in the ruling part, ZANU PF as what is happening in the current licencing dispensation where all licences have been given to ruling part proxies like Honourable Minister Supa Mandiwanzira and his AB communications as well as Zimpapers radios. This licencing regime creates plurality without diversity in the Zimbabwean broadcasting industry. The State appointed BAZ to run the regulatory portfolio under this Act. BAZ is a creature of statute. It is not a constitutional board like ZMC, although it subordinates itself unnecessarily to ZMC which is a higher board. The law that brings BAZ about is the BSA and is specific in terms of how the board is structured. In addition, the law provides for a balance of interests in the board by mixing up different interests which has something to do with broadcasting in Zimbabwe. For instance, chiefs are included as custodians of culture, women as the majority grouping in the society, while lawyers and accountants are meant to uphold probity, and broadcasters for their technical background as it is a highly technical field. As a result of the need for this comprehensive composition, the Minister of information and publicity has some saying in terms of making recommendations to the president but he does so within strictures provided at law.

In addition to media laws, another security law which was a direct replacement of LOMA came into being. POSA, which was passed in 2002, had strong implications on the media democracy in Zimbabwe. Besides being hard on the security sector (section 15) of POSA outlaws the publication of "false Statements prejudicial to the State". In the context of a paranoid State, a mild criticism can easily pass for a prejudicial Statement, resulting in criminal persecution and prosecution for the individuals or organisations concerned (Chuma 2008). A combination of BSA, AIPPA and POSA became the new media policy in Zimbabwe in the new millennium. This period was a classical return to the UDI Rhodesia (ibid).

Interestingly, the Zimbabwean Constitution amendment number 20 of 2013 provides on section (61) the right of establishment. In circumstances where there is need to prohibit broadcasters from establishing business on regulation basis, the State has no power to impose such prohibition except through a process of licencing. Thus, the licencing process is the only basis for denying one to broadcast in Zimbabwe. To assess the issuance of broadcasting licences, there is a "Public hearing" feature incorporated. To a certain extent, it is a way of genuflecting to the notion that frequencies are a common national property and the people (*demos*) must have a say in the licensing process, hence anyone who should eventually be licensed must be subjected to public scrutiny through public hearing.

Promoting the above argument, licensing may also be denied due to unavailability of frequencies. There are two distinctive services according to the International Telecommunication Union (ITU) namely, the primary service and the secondary service. In Zimbabwe, the primary service is that service which a society regards as critical to its survival. For example, when disaster strikes the society has to rely on primary service as well as any significant announcement. Secondary service is that service which is required in excess of that which is required for survival. In Zimbabwe, frequencies dedicated to primary services are protected at all costs because they deal with the survivability of a people in a polity and country. To protect such frequencies, the State ensures that there are no other services around primary service which can encroach to the point of interfering with the cleanliness of the signal so as to enhance wider coverage across the country. By the same logic, primary frequencies themselves can never interfere with secondary signals. Thus, here, primary services are given a privileged position in the structure of societal communication strategy.

Besides, planning frequency distribution services have been taken seriously by the State. Firstly, national coverage should entail coverage of the national territory by primary services. A whole set of radio stations which are meant to cover the whole territory of Zimbabwe have been created. There are four ZBC channels namely, 1 Starfm, (Zimpapers) and 1 Zifm (AB Communications) which covers the whole Zimbabwe and these channels are not allowed to be interfered with. In the event of a disaster or war, the government should be able to rely on these stations to disseminate information around the country.

The second level of planning is based on demographic survey. Areas of high concentration and human settlement must be served well at the primary level and having satisfied that, at any other level. The third level has to do with cultural distinctiveness. Cultural or linguistic distinctiveness is provided for in the Zimbabwean Constitution which makes provisions for 16 national languages. Those national languages must find expression within the airwaves, so the service plan must include every speech community in radio waves accessibility. This supports the notion of access to information as provided for in the Constitution amendment number 20 of 2013.

Another level of planning is uniqueness in terms of geographical and economic placement. For instance areas like *Gokwe* and *Malipati* were historically ignored because of their unique topographical, cultural and economic setup and they are distinguished language communities. The same applies to the eastern highlands and in places like *Bikita*, where the topography is very challenging as some locations are always in the signal shadow. Thus the topographic factor must always be taken into consideration. For example, in *Chimanimani*, there is a transmitter at *Gwindingwi*, a stone's throw away from *Biriviri* which is in the valley. To enhance service here, another sub transmitter has been erected in the valley. This means that more resources are being used over a very small area. Unlike in *Tsholotsho* or *Lupane* where the signal can go as far as *Binga* because of the nature of the land which is flat and there are no physical barriers.

While some areas in the rural parts of Zimbabwe are in media signal shadow, all urban conurbations are readily covered. The radio frequency plan ensures firstly that all national services in urban areas are given frequencies. However, the metro stations which were supposed to operate within a 40km radius around their towns of establishment need additional area of operation as they have a potential to reach as far as 60 km away. This was elaborated by Kindness Paradza, a member of the Parliamentary portfolio committee on Media in Zimbabwe, thus:

> …we only have commercial radios and mainstream radios and right now there is a problem with commercial radio stations. They were given a perimeter of 40km radius to broadcast and right now they are saying it is not enough because we are not getting enough business. Most of them are running on big loss right now because the radius they are operating on is not enough, they need to be extended, but we are saying, before the perimeters are extended satisfy that market first… (*Interview with Kindness Paradza, on the 10th of July 2017, in Harare*).

These sentiments were echoed by George Charamba who affirms that when they made a follow up to see how the newly radio stations were doing technologically and commercially, they discovered that transmitters were reaching over 60 km, yet these radio stations had been limited to 40 km radius only. Indeed, it would not make technological and commercial sense to confine station within a short range where there is few advertising business. This calls for a revision in terms of increasing the allocated radio station sphere of influence.

Conclusion

This chapter dissected and examined the historicity and political economy of the media from Rhodesia to Zimbabwe in a bid to create a background which builds an understanding of the [media] insecurity issues currently bedevilling media in Zimbabwe. The chapter has also interrogated the policies and regulations governing both the print and broadcasting media. At the pick of the discussion in this chapter was the revelation of chaos and media crisis that rocked the nation in the second decade of independence where the State suffered an ambivalence of accepting Westernised liberal democracy while its heart remained with the authoritarian communist ideology. It is during this period that the here described paranoia and insecurities discovered the need to come up with new media laws such as AIPPA and BSA and POSA. What emerges from this analysis is that from Rhodesia to Zimbabwe, the media industry has never been free, safe and democratic. It has been woven around the church, media moguls, elites and the State such that the notion of democracy could not come into play. This has been consistence throughout the ages up to the current epoch. It is also important to take into cognisance of our historical encounters to predict the future trajectories as history has significant influence on how the future is shaped.

References

Chuma, W. (2004) "Liberating or Limiting the Public Sphere? Media Policy and the Zimbabwe Transition, 1980 – 2004" in *Zimbabwe: Injustice and Political Reconciliation*, B. Raftopoulos and T. Savage (eds), Cape Town: Institute for Justice and Reconciliation.

Chuma, W. (2007) *Mediating the transition: The press, State and capital in a changing Zimbabwe, 1980- 2004*. Ph.D. Thesis. University of the Witwatersrand.

Chuma, W. (2010) Reforming the media in Zimbabwe: critical reflections in Chuma, W. and Moyo, D. (eds.), (2010), *Media policy in a changing Southern Africa, critical reflections on media reforms in the global age*, Pretoria, Unisa Press.

Chuma, W. (2013) The State of Journalism ethics in Zimbabwe; A Report for the Voluntary Media Council of Zimbabwe. Harare.

Chuma, W. and Moyo, D. (eds.), (2010) *Media policy in a changing Southern Africa, critical reflections on media reforms in the global age*, Pretoria, Unisa Press.

Chuma, W. (2011) *The press and power in a changing Zimbabwe.* Saarbrucken, Germany: Lambert Academic Publishing.

Compagnon, D. (2011) *A predictable tragedy: Robert Mugabe and the collapse of Zimbabwe.* Philadelphia: University of Pennsylvania.

Frederikse, J. (1982) *None but ourselves, masses vs media in the making of Zimbabwe*, Harare, Oral Tradition Association of Zimbabwe

Freedman, D. and Jonathan, O. (2015) Media reform: an overview, Fordham University Press.

Kupe, T. (2004) 'An Agenda for Researching African Media and Communication Contexts', *Ecquid Novi: African Journalism Studies* 25: 353-356.

Mano, W. (2005) *Press freedom, professionalism and proprietorship: behind the Zimbabwe media divide, Westminster papers in communication and culture*, Special Issue, November 2005: 56-70, University of Westminster, London.

Mosco, V. (1996) *The political economy of communication: Rethinking and renewal.* Thousand Oaks: Sage.

Moyo, D. (2010a) Reincarnating clandestine radio in post-independent Zimbabwe. *Radio Journal: International Studies in Broadcast and Audio Media.* 8(1) Moyo, D. and Chuma, W. (2010) Media policy in Changing southern Africa: A critical reflection on media reforms in the global age, Eds. Pretoria: UNISA Press.

Moyo, L. (2010b) The dearth of public debate. Policy, polarities and positional reporting in Zimbabwe's news media. In *Media Policy in a changing Southern Africa. Critical reflections on media reforms in the global age.*

Msindo. I (2009) 'Winning Hearts and Minds': Crisis and Propaganda in Colonial Zimbabwe, 1962–1970, Journal of Southern African Studies, 35: 3.

Ndlela, N. (2003) *Critical analysis of the media law in Zimbabwe.* Harare: Konrad Adenauer Foundation.

Ronning, O. and Kupe, T. (2000) The dual legacy of democracy and authoritarianism: The media and the State in Zimbabwe in Curran, J. and Park, M. (eds), (2000) *De-westernizing media studies*, London, Rutledge.

Ruhanya, P. (2015) Alternative media and African democracy: The Daily News and opposition politics in Zimbabwe, 1997-2010, Westminster University.

Saunders, R. (1991) *Information in the interregnum: The press, State and civil Society in struggles for hegemony in Zimbabwe* (unpublished PhD thesis).

Saunders, R. (1999) Dancing *out of Tune: A history of the media in Zimbabwe*, Harare, Edwina Spicer Production.

Saunders, R. (2000) *Zimbabwe's growth towards democracy 1980-2000*, Harare, Edwina Spicer Production.

Chapter 8

Cyber Communications, Social Media and National Security: Reflections on the Laws Governing Social Media and Online Communications in Zimbabwe

Golden Maunganidze

Introduction

National security is a concern of any national government. For this reason, national governments always invest immensely in security and as one of its top priorities to preserve sovereignty and freedoms of its people. Nevertheless, in the name of safeguarding sovereignty some governments end up enacting a raft of repressive laws that only seek to protect the interests of the elite while restricting journalistic enterprise, safety and professionalism. Zimbabwe is one such country, which in the name of safeguarding national security, has ended up putting in place some repressive media laws.

In light of the above, this chapter examines the laws that govern the operations of social media and cyber communications in Zimbabwe. The chapter takes a deep analysis of both the laws that are already in force as well as proposed laws that are likely going to be part of Zimbabwe's legislations. Although there may be no law which does not have its positive side, it seems some of the laws passed by governments in Africa are crafted to quash some descending voices that criticise sitting governments. It is from this realisation that in Zimbabwe, since the year 2000, the civic society in Zimbabwe especially organisations such as Media Institute of Southern Africa (MISA- Zimbabwe), Voluntary Media Council of Zimbabwe (VMCZ) and Zimbabwe Union of Journalists (ZUJ) have been on record accusing the Zimbabwean government for passing draconian media laws that restrict the free flow of information. It seems, the government became afraid of its shadows and managed to come up with laws such as Access to Information and Protection of Privacy Act (AIPPA), Interception of Communications Act (ICA),

Censorship and Entertainment Controls Act (CECA), and Criminal Law Codification Reform Act, among others. Presently, the government of Zimbabwe is in the process of proposing a new law aimed at regulating cyber and online communications in Zimbabwe, the computers and cyber security bill. According to Media Institute of Southern Africa (MISA Zimbabwe) reports, hundreds of journalists in Zimbabwe have been arrested and charged under these laws – a move that was widely viewed as intimidating strategy by the government which did not want the press to unearth certain under-dealings by the government of the day. Despite the fact that Zimbabwe managed to come up with a model constitution in 2013, it is regrettable that five years down the line, most of the media laws in the country are not yet in harmony with the dictates of the new constitution as the government remains reluctant to repeal the media laws in the country. Instead, the government is in a bid to come up with yet another law that govern the operations of social media and cyber communications. The former President of Zimbabwe, Robert Mugabe's government introduced a whole Ministry of Cyber Security, Threat Detection and Mitigation to deal with cyber communications issues. According to the Permanent Secretary in the Ministry of Media and Broadcasting Services, George Charamba, the ministry was meant to detect threats posed to the government due to abuse of social media (The Herald, 11 October 2017). There was an outcry from the media and civic society organisations over the introduction of this controversial ministry. The *Daily News* Newspaper carried a story titled" "Government presses panic button" on the 26th of September 2017. According to the story, the then minister of Home Affairs Ignatius Chombo had issued a statement warning journalists and social media users against posting articles about the economic crisis haunting Zimbabwe at the time. This was seen as a direct attack to press freedom and freedom of expression in the country. Civic Society Organisations (CSOs) condemned the minister for such a move. However, that did not stop the government from harassing perceived enemies using online media platforms to churn out "unpalatable" content to the international community. This was a clear indication of a government in a panic mode.

However, even in the so-called "new dispensation", when the new government took over in November 2017 and the President insisting that he was going to come up with a leaner government, he surprisingly re-introduced the cyber security element under the Ministry of Information Communication Technology and Cyber Security. To the generality of Zimbabweans, the new government seem to share the same fears with the former administration, hence the maintenance of same laws and government ministries. There is even a high possibility that the government likely going to be elected in 2018 may maintain the same laws much to the discontentment of the general public. This could be true if we go by Mukasa's (2003) observation that the Zanu PF led government maintained the laws that were inherited from their colonial masters. Mukasa further argue convincingly that although the constitution gives guarantee for freedom of expression and assembly, some laws are still viewed as stumbling blocks for the total enjoyment of the human rights. The irony with the most 'unpopular' law - AIPPA spells the word bad in Shona language. This chapter exposes the implications of both the existing and the proposed legislations to both the people as well as the government of Zimbabwe.

The dynamism of social media and the internet

The coming of internet has provided people with a unique platform where they can easily access instant information concerning things or events taking place throughout the whole world (Dauze, 2007). Through social media platforms such as Facebook, Twitter, WhatsApp and YouTube, among others, users can share information faster than before. This development, however, has sent shockwaves to many governments prompting them to come up with legislations that directly deal with the new developments. Social media platforms have become alternative public spheres which have successfully promoted candid debates regarding topical issues of the day. As Martin (2012) notes, unlike on the traditional media where the governments can use propaganda, the internet has proven to be completely different with users being able to promote their own agenda to counter government hegemony. Different individuals with

173

different personalities and various literacy levels that patronise online platforms have given headaches to ruling governments due to the content they circulate on social media platforms that may not cast the government and ruling Zanu PF party in positive light. It is for this reason that scholars such as Griffin (2000) has noted that the coming in of new technologies has disrupted communication patterns among media users. Griffin does not agree with Laswell's (1948) linear communication model that says communication is one directional from the sender to the user. According to Laswell, all media messages have a direct impact on the users, and the receivers are gullible and defenceless individuals. Upon bombarded by powerful media messages, the content consumers have predictable reaction. Lasswell's model was developed to study the media propaganda of countries and businesses at that time. Only rich people and the ruling class used to have the power to control communication mediums such as newspapers, televisions and radios which they used to disseminate preferred information. The information disseminated by the mass media during that time was targeted at creating a 'preferred culture' among the audience. The introduction of new media technologies such as the smart phones, which enable the users to freely access and distribute information via internet within the shortest possible time, has changed communication dynamics in different parts of the world. Due to technological advancement, the people have moved a step up in creating social media networks which they can now use as alternative sources of news.

In Zimbabwe, the internet has been unprecedentedly a platform for all as witnessed by the mushrooming of alternative news dissemination platforms (Chiyadzwa and Maunganidze, 2014). Most people now rely on mobile news for updates and also for updating colleagues and friends on events taking place in various parts of the country. Similarly, there are various social media platforms where citizens especially the youths use to vent out their beliefs, ideas, concerns and sometimes feelings. Faced with pressure from non-formal journalists, one of Zimbabwe's major newspaper company, Alpha Media Holdings (AMH) which runs *NewsDay*, *The Standard* and *The Zimbabwe Independent* newspapers is now incorporating citizen journalists in their daily operations (Chiyadzwa and Maunganidze,

2014). In this regard, one can note that the coming of social media has revolutionised communication processes in Zimbabwe as things have completely changed in as far as who can (and cannot) influence public opinion. Martin (1988) pointed out that we are living in the Information Society where the people's lives depend more on the availability of information rather than anything else. This justifies the ever-increasing demand for new channels of communication as well as social media platforms that try to outdo each other in creating user friendly services that allow for a two-way communication between the user and the consumer. The ever-rising need for gadgets such as smart phones and technologically enabling tools by both the youths and Zimbabweans in general is a clear testimony that the internet has become very critical in the everyday lives of the citizens. This resonates with Denhere and Mudhovozi's (2011) observation that young Zimbabweans especially university students are now depending on internet for almost every aspect of their lives.

According to the Internet World Statistics (2017), the Zimbabwean national internet penetration rate over the population lies at 41.1%, as data becomes more affordable, with millions getting access to cheaper data capable handsets. The internet growth from year 2000 up to 2017 is 13,343.9% which is a huge growth in Zimbabwe with social network being a major mover as mobile network operators drive cheaper social media data bundles. Zimbabwe has a 16.337,760 million population with 6,721,947 internet users as at 31 March 2017, a huge increase from 50 000 users in the year 2000 (see www.internetworldstats.com). The increase in usage of internet on mobile devices has helped the users to deposit more data on the internet and subsequently social media platforms thereby benefiting consumers of the content. The content generated on social media platforms do not necessarily conform or tally with what those who hold political power would want to see published, hence the interest by sitting governments to craft laws that gag communication processes. Dearing (1996) notes that the media have power to set the agenda for the public. This function has, on one hand, helped the media to be a very important tool in the hands of the government. The social media on the other hand try to set its own agenda, hence the dispute between the government social media users. The provision of posting and receiving 'undiluted' content has seen users flocking to social media platforms for information. In the process, governments have tried to retain control of the information disseminated through these channels by coming up with laws that govern social media platforms. Zimbabwe is not an exception since it had already started the process of coming up with Cybercrimes and Cyber Security Bill meant to heavily deal with those perceived to be 'abusing' the social media networks. Apart from the proposed new laws governing social media, the majority of people who use internet in Zimbabwe have accused the government of cyber bullying, spying or victimise the users because of various reasons, chief among them being governments' insecurity. A number of social media users have been arrested in Zimbabwe and in some serious situations, users would be charged with trying to overthrow the government using online media platforms. Martha O'Donovan, a young American lady in Zimbabwe is the latest victim of laws controlling social media usage in Zimbabwe after being arrested in 2017 over a twitter post which criticised former President Mugabe's wife and her son Russell for buying luxury cars while Zimbabweans were suffering (see https://twitter.com/zimmediareview/status/926440423538733056 ?lang=en).Subversion charges were preferred against her as if to imply that mere posting of one's opinion on twitter was worse than committing murder. Although she had been since freed, O'Donovan remains one of the people who suffered the government's insecurity as ordinary people ended up getting arrested for trying to express themselves online.

There are a number of reported cases concerning Zimbabweans who have been either arrested or harassed by state security agents because of their online activities for example in a 17 year old boy from the town of Chiredzi was found guilty of criminal insult by magistrate Tinashe Ndokera in 2012 after he posted a picture of a woman on his Facebook page and put a caption in Shona language 'these are Chiredzi's prostitutes' (see http://abcnews.go.com, 20 February 2012). The court ordered that the boy be caned twice. Apart from one Chiredzi boy (see http://abcnews.go.com), whose name was protected by the courts because he was still a minor, there are other several cases that saw some prominent politicians like Job Sikhala – a popular member of the opposition Movement for Democratic Change (MDC) was convicted on several occasions after he posted some "unpalatable" messages on Facebook. Another person who was arrested over content posted on Facebook is Vikas Mavhudzi who posted on the then Prime Minister, Morgan Tsvangirai's Facebook page on 2011 alerting him about what was happening in North Africa referring to the Arab Spring. Mavhudzi was arrested for trying to incite violence in the country. He was however, later acquitted of all the charges preferred against him.

The use of social media in Zimbabwe

Social media is any website that allows for social interaction which includes social networking sites such as Facebook, MySpace and Twitter (O'Keeffe et al., 2011). The use of social media has been rapidly rising in Zimbabwe since the turn of the new millennium with Facebook taking a significant lead on the number of subscribers. Arpan, Kumar & Rekha (2016) argue that between 2005 and 2013, the use of social networking sites among the youth increased from 9% to 90%. Thus, social media has become part of daily life for an increasing number of young people in many countries across the world and Zimbabwe is not an exception. Research by Drago (2015) revealed that 73 percent of Elon University students spent most of their time on social media networks. The study demonstrated that social media has indeed become part of the young people's lives. The way of living has completely changed with the youth taking advantage of these "new" platforms to even do things which they were previously not able to do for example video calling, WhatsApp chats, sharing of pictures and videos, among other things. This development, however, seem to have pushed governments to be afraid of the potential of social media thereby coming up with draconian laws that govern how social media could be used.

Social media have become a substitute for face-to-face communication for youth (Erwin et al., 2014). Where the youths used to interact physically, today, social media platforms have seen them coming up with a virtual community which allow them to interact freely even if they are not at one place. This may result in a situation where the young people may actively participate in things like political debates without necessarily attending a rally. In closed political environment such as Zimbabwe, during former President Mugabe's rule (1980 -2017), it was dangerous to be actively involved in opposition politics. There were several reports of torture and harassment where Mugabe's critics were severely punished for opposing the [former] President or the government. Activists like the missing Itai Dzamara who disappeared on 9 March 2015 at the age of 35 after staging a Mugabe Must Fall Campaign dubbed "Occupy Africa Unity Square" continued to remind the young people about the dangers of going in the streets to challenge the then ruling government. However, with the increasing number of young people using social media, a lot of social movements are fast gaining popularity in Zimbabwe.

Many social movements largely by the activists in the country have cashed in on the popularity of social media platforms to spread their ideologies to millions of anonymous online subscribers. These social media movements have harnessed the new opportunity for mobilisation of the masses offered by social media (Lopes 2014). In Zimbabwe, the rise of social media activism reached the climax on 6 August 2016 when an outspoken cleric Pastor, Evan Mawarire of His Generation Church managed to literary shut down the country following his successful #*ThisFlag* campaign. In his campaign, Mawarire urged both civil servants and those who work for the corporate world to stay away from work in order to let the government realise how the economic situation had deteriorated in the country. Interestingly, Zimbabweans did not go to work on the day leading to Mawarire's arrest for trying to overthrow a legitimate government – a charge he has since been acquitted of (see https://www.newsday.co.zw/2017/11/breaking-thisflag-pastor-evan-mawarire-acquitted/). With social media, consumption has gone from individual activity to one in which consumers have an opportunity to interact with others (Villi, 2015). By so doing, sharing content becomes central in social media as it involves social exchange on one hand and distribution and dissemination on the other hand (Wittel, 2011). Social media platforms in Zimbabwe have become "alternative channels of communication" that have opened new windows for the people to air their views as well as amplifying their voices so that they can be heard by solution holders. The picture collage below show popular social media user Pastor Evan Mawarire in handcuffs, just the same way any dangerous criminal could be handled by the police while the other picture illustrates how social media users abroad expressed themselves through online platforms.

File Pic 1. Pastor Evan Mawarire in handcuffs after being arrested for leading social media campaign dubbed #ThisFlag. Source: Google

File Pic 2. Shows people in the United Kingdom who reacted angrily to Pastor Mawarire's arrest and their subsequent demand for his immediate release.

Source: Google.

Many Zimbabweans who previously feared to openly express their views on issues to do with politics have found a new window which allows them to be actively involved in issues that used to be viewed as extremely dangerous. Those who do not want to go out of their homes and join others in the streets, can thus be able to follow the events live as they unfold in the streets. Besides, they can also spread the images and videos of what would be happening even if they are not physically at the scene. The new wave of protests is bringing to focus the role of social media, particularly Facebook, as the main force behind the recent popular movements (Lim, 2012).

In Zimbabwe, social media has played a critical role in public opinion formation movements such as *#Tajamuka* in 2016 and *#ThisFlag* in 2016. Through social media posts, Mawarire managed to convince his social media friends and followers to carry their flags as a way of reclaiming the pride of being a Zimbabwean which had been eroded by the Mugabe administration. Similarly, social media played a critical role in fast-tracking the free flow of information during the "Operation Restore Legacy" orchestrated by the Zimbabwe National Army in November 2017 as the military pushed for the former President Mugabe's ouster. Images and short video clips of demonstrations taking place in Harare were awash on social media in the country helping people outside the capital city to flow proceedings live as they were unfolding in Harare. At the end of the day, newspapers were left behind as social media took over in giving live coverage of daily events in the country. This was also the same case when the former Prime Minister and Movement for Democratic Change (MDC-T) leader, Morgan Tsvangirai died. Social media were the first to make the announcement. It took one of the MDC-T vice presidents, Elias Mudzuri to announce the death of his former boss on Twitter for the whole nation to know what had happened.

During Tsvangirai's funeral, Zimbabwe Broadcasting Corporation (ZBC) did not give priority to events that were unfolding especially the huge crowd which turned up at party headquarters (Harvest House) and Freedom Square to mourn Tsvangirai. The public broadcaster focused on the speeches made by President Emmerson Mnangagwa. However, it was social media which continued to give Zimbabweans an alternative voice on how events were unfolding at the opposition leader's funeral.

Although social media is a relatively young phenomenon in Zimbabwe, works on social media and collective action has been around as early as the 1960s, providing scholars with important information in order to understand the impact of social media as a tool of public opinion formation (Leenders and Heydemann 2012). While most of these studies have focused on specific case studies, particularly in the Middle East and North Africa following the Arab Spring, to demonstrate how social media shaped the public opinion and helped promote social movements, none has shown how the young Zimbabweans consume and distribute social media content particularly from Facebook and Twitter. And yet the government has shown keen interest in introducing laws that deal with social media users in Zimbabwe.

Laws governing social media in Zimbabwe: Some critical reflections

As has been noted in the preceding discussion, there are a number of legislations that have been put in place by the Zimbabwean government to govern social media operations in the country. In the preceding sections, I critically reflect on these laws.

Cyber Security Bill

The introduction of Cyber Security Bill by the Zimbabwean government in 2017 and the subsequent introduction of the ministry to closely monitor cyber operations in October 2017 was not seen in positive light by members of the public who feared that the law may be used to harass innocent individuals. Even if the government tried hard to justify the coming in of the controversial bill soon to be turned into law, civic society organisations and human rights lobby groups in the country expressed their worry as they view the move as oppressive, barbaric, and archaic
(see, http://zimbabwe.misa.org/2018/02/23/omnibus-cyber-bill-muddies-fundamental-rights/). During his presentation on the bill's weaknesses to Masvingo journalists on 26 August 2017, Media

Institute of Southern Africa (MISA-Zimbabwe) Director, Tabani Moyo noted that:

> The bill gives the police unnecessary power to extract electronic evidence from ordinary citizens' electronic devices such as cell phones, computers and other digital gadgets. Electronic evidence is a whole discipline out there which needs experts to manage. Why am I saying so is, because most of our Zimbabwe Republic Police (ZRP) stations still use type writers... how then are we going to assist a police force which is operating on type writers to manage electronic evidence so that it is not tempered with when it is submitted in courts? Electronic evidence, when you find it online has a way it should be stored with so that it remains in its original form. Once you temper with it, it means it is no longer useful (Moyo presentation 2017 at Charles Austin Theatre).

The other issue on this bill is what is referred to as illegal remaining. According to the bill, this occurs when electronic devices such as mobile phones and laptops remember recent online activities. According to this bill, it is a criminal offence for someone to take advantage of their gadgets' capability to remember things like passwords and ends up using Wi-Fi and hotspots before being given a new password to access internet. However, the argument by civic society in Zimbabwe is that, the fact that electronic gadgets manage to remember previous online activities should actually be seen as an advantage to society since technology is moving very fast.

The other aspect of the bill which has been widely condemned is the clause which seeks to make it a criminal offence for someone who refuses to help law enforcement agents with hacking in to someone's email. This clause connotes that the police have a right to summon anyone they suspect to be a technical genius to assists then in carrying out their investigations through helping with hacking the suspect's accounts. Refusing to corporate with the police is regarded as a crime. Hence, in one way or the other, every citizen shall become a police officer as granted by this bill, yet it is always unfair for anyone be forced to do police work if they do not want. In fact, the police should be equipped to do its business without necessarily forcing civilians they just meet along the road doing their business and punish them for refusing to comply. According to TechZim report of 5 September 2017, the Information and Communications Technology (ICT) minister, Supa Mandiwanzira, indicated that the proposed bill would be fast-tracked to become a law. The coming in of new government in Zimbabwe in November 2017 did not change any matters with regards to the introduction of the new law specifically targeting social media users.

Interception of Communications Act (ICA)

This law gives the government of Zimbabwe power to intercept private or personal communications such as telephone conversations, electronic mails (email), short message services (sms), video calls as well as printed communications that include letters and memorandums. According to the Act, the person who is being intercepted may not be aware of the whole process. The communications are just intercepted and the government uses the findings without alerting the people involved. Since the law enforcement agents have the privilege to intercept unsuspecting citizens, the general public therefore live in unnecessary suspicion and fear as they may be spied on unknowingly. For the reason, among others, the public can view the law as a weapon being used by the government to violate their privacy through accessing information that may have not implications to state security. The law also criminalises non-compliance or lack of cooperation by the service provider. In other words, service providers are compelled to show highest degree of compliance when the government shows interest in extracting a thread of communication from ordinary citizens. Although the Zimbabwe Internet Service Providers Association (ZISPA) raised serious concerns over the law, the government has not managed to disband unwanted sections in this legislation. The number of communications that have been intercepted by the government to date cannot be ascertained since it is widely believed that these processes are sometimes operated clandestinely by state security agents such as the much dreaded Central Intelligence Organisation (CIO). According to MISA-Zimbabwe Internet Governance Manual (2015), the law discourages interpersonal communication among the general citizens who may end up practising self-censorship. This violates the people's right to communicate freely in a democratic society.

Censorship and Entertainment Controls Act (CECA)

This piece of legislation prohibits the importation of physical undesirable material from beyond borders. Mostly, the prohibited material that is deemed pornographic in nature is not acceptable in the country through this legislation. However, artists and the generality of the citizens have complained that this law prohibits the enjoyment of fundamental human rights especially when they want to show their artistic expression, cultural expression and academic freedoms as enshrined in the constitution of the country. The Act also allows for the appointment of the Censorship board whose mandate is to screen material that is supposed to be consumed by the public. However, the board has been accused for being biased and failing to be objective thereby violating human rights in the process.

Criminal Law Codification Reform Act (CODE)

This law has been used several times by the government of Zimbabwe to arrest and prosecute individuals who would have expressed opinions, sentiments or posted materials on internet platforms such as Facebook. Many Zimbabweans have fallen victim of this law and they have been arrested. An American citizen Matha O'Donovan was arrested in 2017 after a tweeting information which was widely viewed as criminal. Subversion charges were preferred against her. However, she was later acquitted. Former *Sunday Mail* editor Edmund Kudzayi was arrested in 2014 (https://www.newsday.co.zw/2014/06/sunday-mail-editor-arrested-suspected-links-baba-jukwa/) after the government suspected that he was the one who leaked government secrets on Facebook under the pseudo name Baba Jukwa. The government went to the extent of sending a police officer identified as Assistant Commissioner Crispen Makedenge to Google head office in America to seek information which would help the government to track the 'notorious' Facebook character Baba Jukwa. However, Google refused top corporate resulting in Makedenge coming back clueless.

This however, shows us that the government can do whatever it takes to arrest perceived online state enemies. In the end, this discourages social media users to exercise their freedoms online thereby ending up practising self-censorship.

Access Information and Protection Privacy Act (AIPPA)

This is one of the most criticised media laws in Zimbabwe. When the law was introduced in Parliament in 2002, the late national hero and former Zanu PF secretary for legal affairs in politburo, Edison Zvobgo criticised AIPPA saying in its original form, the law was the most calculated and determined assault on our liberties guaranteed by the Constitution, in the 20 years that he served as Cabinet minister (see http://www.thezimbabwean.co/2013/09/moyos-nine-lives/). According to the law, all journalists in the country are compelled to register with the Zimbabwe Media Commission (ZMC). However, with the coming of citizen journalism, it becomes difficult for any person who runs micro-blogging sites to be accredited with ZMC. In another way, citizen journalists who can help in the promotion of access to information may fail to have access to critical information due to lack of accreditation cards.

Some recommendations

I have argued in this chapter that most of the laws being used to govern cyber communications in Zimbabwe are out-dated as they are not in harmony with the country's 2013 Constitution. As underlined in this chapter, there is need for the government to urgently repeal most of the laws that are being used today so that they are in harmony with the supreme law of the land. According to section 61 and 62 of the current Zimbabwean Constitution, the people have the right to freedom of expression and of the media as well as the right to access it. In light of the constitutional provisions, it is imperative for the government to quickly align the media laws to be in harmony with the laws of the land.

Besides, the government must also make sure that existing laws in the country are in accordance with the regional laws and international human rights laws. Zimbabwe is a signatory to several regional and international human rights conventions such as the African (Banjul) Charter on Human and People Right (1981) and The Universal Declaration of Human Rights (1948) and it is against this background that the government must honour its commitment to respect human rights.

Just like the traditional media, social media play a critical role in promoting free flow of information as well as ideas. In this regard, the government must make sure that the policies and laws crafted at any given time should not hinder free flow of information. The people in Zimbabwe are now relying more on the information they get from social media in order to get timely news updates of events taking place throughout the country so that they would be able to make informed decisions. Social media in Zimbabwe is playing a critical role as an alternative to the newspapers and radios already licenced by the government. However, media laws must not be used to regulate social media operations.

Conclusion

This chapter has argued that social media and online communications in Zimbabwe have helped in facilitating and strengthening democracy, lobbying for policy changes as well as raising important issues of and about governance. However, the government crafted 'draconian' laws to govern social media and cyber communications which ended up doing more harm than good. Although it is very important to come up with some regulatory frameworks, it is indeed sad that the laws that are being used in Zimbabwe hinder free flow of information on online platforms and social media in general. This is viewed as the government's desperate bid to stop citizens from playing a watchdog role – the duty which was previously reserved for the traditional media alone. The ever-increasing number of people using social media and online platforms in Zimbabwe is a cause for concern – a development that has seen the government finding itself in a panic mode. With fresh memories of the Arab Spring which saw the long-time Presidents in Libya and Tunisia being removed from power using the "force" of social media, the Zimbabwean government is on high alert as they even propose new laws such as the Computers and Cyber Security and Crimes Bill all meant to minimise social media activities.

References

Allern, S. (2002) 'Journalistic and commercial news values: News organizations as patrons of an institution and market actors', *Nordicom Review*, 23 (1-2): 137-152.

Denhere C and Mudhovozi P. (2011) *Gender and Differantian in Internet Usage: A case study of Great Zimbabwe University Students, Zimbabwe International Journal of Open and Distance Learning*, Volume 1 and 2.

Chiyadzwa, F. and Maunganidze, G. (2014) *Reflections on the implications of the empowered citizens at Alpha Media Holdings (AMH)*, IOSR Journal of Humanities and Social Sciences (IOSR-JHSS) Vol 19, Issue 3, Ver 11 (Mar 2014), PP 113-119 e-ISSN: 2279-0837, p-ISSN: 2279-0845.

Chuma, W. (2013) *The State of Media Ethics in Zimbabwe*, VMCZ, Harare: Zimbabwe.

Dauze, M. (2007) *Preparing for an Age of Participatory News, In Journalism Practice*, Vol. 1, No 3, 2007.

Feltoe G. (1993) *A Guide to Press law in Zimbabwe*. Harare, Legal Resources Foundations.

Gans, H. J. (1980) Deciding What's News: A Study of CBS Evening News, NBC Nightly News, Newsweek and Time. New York: Vintage Books, Random House.

McQuail, D. (2010) *McQuail's Mass Communication Theory*. SAGE. United Kingdom.

Martin, W. (1988) *The information society—idea or entity?*, Aslib Proceedings, Vol. 40 Issue: 11/12, pp.303-309, https://doi.org/10.1108/eb051115.

McLuhan, M. (1967) *The Medium is the Massage: An Inventory of Effects*. Penguin Press. London.

Messner, M. and Distow, M. (2008) *The source cycle: how traditional media and weblogs use each other as sources*, Journalism Studies 447 -63.

Mukasa, D. (2003) *Press and Politics in Zimbabwe*, African Studies Quarterly. Volume 7, issues 2-3.

O'Neill, D. (2012) No Cause for Celebration: Celebrity News Values in the UK Quality Press, *Journalism Education* 1 (2): 26–44.

Pfukwa, C. (2001) *Multimedia Communication*, Zimbabwe Open University (ZOU), Harare, Zimbabwe.

Tapscott, D. (1998) *Growing Up Digital: The Rise of the Net Generation*, McGraw Hill. New York.

The Access to Information and Protection of Privacy ACT No 5/2002 Harare, Government Printers.

Schultz, I. (2007) 'The journalistic gut feeling: Journalistic doxa, news habitus and orthodox news values', *Journalism Practice* 1 (2): 190-207.

Zimbabwe National Statistics Agency (ZIMSTAT) (2015) *Multiple Indicator Cluster Survey 2014*, Final Report, Harare, Zimbabwe.

Websites

http://abcnews.go.com

https://twitter.com/zimmediareview/status/926440423538733056 ?lang=en

https://www.dailynews.co.zw/articles/2017/09/26/mugabe-s-govt-presses-panic-button

https://www.herald.co.zw/govt-explains-cyber-security-ministry-role/

www.internetworldstats.com

https://www.newsday.co.zw/2014/06/sunday-mail-editor-arrested-suspected-links-baba-jukwa

https://www.newsday.co.zw/2017/11/breaking-thisflag-pastor-evan-mawarire-acquitted/

http://www.thezimbabwean.co/2013/09/moyos-nine-lives

http://zimbabwe.misa.org/2018/02/23/omnibus-cyber-bill-muddies-fundamental-rights/

Chapter 9

Fish Farming and Aquaculture in Zimbabwe: Revisiting Zimbabwe's Aquaculture development Enigma through the Lenses of Regulatory Framework

Henry Chiwaura & Munyaradzi Mawere

Introduction

Aquaculture is a fast growing industry in the world. It has become an increasingly lucrative industry with the potential to resuscitate economies of many countries. However, both the harvesting of fish and the practice of aquaculture in general have cosmic and legal implications that should be handled with care. This means that the expanding industry globally and nationally calls for adequate legal and policy frameworks, especially in African countries such as Zimbabwe where there is both an environmental and legal luxity to deal with the fish industry.

The increase in population provides aquaculture with the potential to close the protein gap particularly in rural areas of the country where an estimated 70% of the population resides (Machena and Moehl, 2000). Production from aquaculture has overtaken harvesting of fish from natural sources globally and Africa has witnessed a 10% growth in the industry (Herald, 2017). The development of aquaculture industry in Zimbabwe is made possible by the fact that the country has abundant water bodies in the form of dams and lakes, suitable climatic conditions and available organic materials used to rear the fish. Zimbabwe also boost of 60% of dammed water in the Sothern African Development Community (SADC) (Ibid). The country can exploit natural water bodies and artificially constructed water bodies. The initial formal aquaculture training programme in Zimbabwe was introduced in 1987 with the establishment of aquaculture training centre at Magamba Training Centre by the Ministry of State (Political Affairs). The training was introduced with the assistance of United Nations Development Programme (UNDP). This was as a result of the realisation that in order to have a sectoral development there is need for skilled manpower. The course has been running ever since its introduction and various non-governmental organisations (NGOs) have assisted predominately rural communities with the provision of resources in aquaculture.

We note that in as much as aquaculture was introduced in 1987 in Zimbabwe, it remains relatively new to most rural farmers. This is aggravated by the fact that while Zimbabwe has a promising small-scale commercial fish industry, the country is still in the process of developing a well-grounded regulatory framework for the referred industry. In fact, despite its great potential in feeding and sustainable development, aquaculture is given less attention by the government of Zimbabwe. Yet, the much needed regulatory framework is a complex one that involves international, regional and national legal and policy instruments which further complicates aquaculture operations. In Zimbabwe, this realisation has prompted fish farmers to establish The Zimbabwe Fish Producers Association (ZFPA) in March 2016 to promote and develop aquaculture as a fully-fledged and vibrant part of the livestock industry.

This chapter is a critical appraisal of Zimbabwe's regulatory framework for aquaculture. It explores and underlines legislative and policy issues that must be addressed in Zimbabwe in order to have an effective legal and policy frameworks of aquaculture in the country in a manner that promote nuanced understanding of environmentalities and ontologies, especially of relationships, social interconnectedness and interdependence between social 'actors' in the cosmos.

Fish Framing in Zimbabwe

Zimbabwe is a landlocked country with international borders with Botswana, Mozambique, and South Africa. The country is endowed with natural rivers that have been dammed to assist with water and agriculture provisions. The concept of fish farming was first introduced in Zimbabwe in early 1950s but has never fully developed up until 1987 when aquaculture was formally introduced at Magamba Training Centre by the Ministry of State (Political Affairs) with the assistance of the United Nations Development Programme (Dadzie, 1992).

Since the 1950s, the Eastern Highlands of the country have experienced commercial trout farming and stocking of farm dams, which increased with the formal introduction of aquaculture. The government assisted the farmers by introducing research at Henderson Research Station. The size of fish farms is relevantly small in Zimbabwe and most farmers use farm house manure as fish feed with others using commercial fish feed. The National Parks has been pivotal in providing fingerlings mainly to trout farmers. Major fish industries in Zimbabwe are bream, trout, kapenta, and tilapia fishing companies. 70% of farmers are producing tilapia at a small scale but with an increasing number of Oreochromis niloticus (Nile tilapia). In Zimbabwe, the latter is a non-indigenous species which needs permit to import. Catfish and carp are also farmed, though to a lesser extent. A fish evaluation programme by Swedish International Development Agency (SIDA) in southern Africa found out that aquaculture is yet to play an important role in the development of rural farmers (Gopper and Miller, 1989/2). Zimbabwe has got both small scale fisheries (SSF) and commercial ones. SSF, according Food and Agriculture Organisation (FAO: nd) of the United Nations are "artisanal, characterised by low technology, low capital and fishing practices that are undertaken by individual households and not companies. They tend to be firmly rooted in local communities, traditions and values". Zimbabwe and Zambia share Lake Kariba, an artificially created lake that supports the largest tilapia fish farming in Africa. However, a research carried out by FAO has shown that, fish farming is on the decline in Lake Kariba since the 1990s due to droughts, hydropower generation and uncoordinated management regimes from the countries that share the lake (see Ndlovu, *et al.* 2017). The government of Zimbabwe has come up with a plan to allow community participation in the exploitation of fish resources in Lake Kariba by developing a combination of Lakeshore Master Plan and fishery co-management programmes which were developed in the 1990s (ibid). These programmes are in line with the Communal

Area Management Programme for Indigenous Resources (CAMPFIRE) that share wildlife resources between the government through the Department of Parks and Wildlife and communities. Ndlovu *et al* (Ibid) note that this policy instrument is not working as expected. For them, there is lack of coordination in both plan formulation and implementation. This in itself calls for a coordinated policy framework from the central government as the situation in Kariba is a mirror image of what is prevailing in the rest of the country where SSF and commercial interest converge.

The recent opening of Tokwe – Mukosi Dam in Masvingo Province, the largest inland dam in Zimbabwe, puts the country on a good trajectory for aquaculture and in particular fish production and development in southern Africa. Tokwe-Mukosi was constructed to assist agriculture in Zimbabwe through irrigation and of late focus is now on aquaculture and fish farming to compliment irrigation (Mukwashi, 2017). Zimbabwe has the largest tilapia or rather vertically integrated tilapia farm in sub-Saharan Africa that is the Lake Harvest Aquaculture Fish farm (LHA) in Lake Kariba. LHA produced roughly 20 000 tons per annum in 2015 and sells 37% of this to domestic market, 50% to southern African market and 13% to the European market (ADBPSO, 2011). Besides Kariba and the recently constructed Tokwe-Mukosi, Zimbabwe has a number of artificial dams that can be utilised by communities and commercial sectors to develop aquaculture and fish industry.

The potential of aquaculture in the southern Africa region and Zimbabwe in particular is however betrayed by both regional policy framework and national legal and institutional instruments as is discussed in the ensuing sections.

Policy Framework for Sustainable Aquaculture Development in SADC region

Southern African Development Cooperation (SADC) was established in 1980 by member states in southern Africa comprising of nine member countries that are Angola, Botswana, Lesotho, Malawi, Mozambique, Swaziland, Tanzania, Zambia and Zimbabwe. Democratic Republic of Congo is the latest member. The main aim for establishing this regional block was to promote economic, regional independence and self-reliance using resources found within the member states. The community uses a decentralised system where members are responsible for various sectors. Malawi's Principal Secretary of the Ministry of Forestry and Natural Resources was named as the sectorial coordinator for forestry, fisheries and wildlife (Gopper and Miller, 1989/2). However, as noted by Gopper and Miller (1989), SADC does not represent a homogenous region in terms of aquaculture and fish farming. As the duo argue, there are countries with no fish tradition and others with very low consumption trends in the region such as Swaziland and Lesotho and those with marine fisheries that are mainly exploited by foreigners such as Angola and Mozambique and those that depend on fish for protein supply such as Malawi and Zambia. Thus, depending largely on need, Zambia and Malawi have the most developed aquaculture and fish industries in the region.

Having realised the disparities in aquaculture and fish industries in the region, SADC has come up with strategies to improve the industry in the region. SADC recognises the importance of aquaculture and fisheries in people's economic and social wellbeing in the region. In order to support national initiatives taken and international conventions for the sustainable use and protection of the living aquatic resources and aquatic environment of the region, SADC Member States signed the Protocol on Fisheries on 14 August 2001. As is captured in Article 4 of this Protocol:

...In the case of shared resources, State Parties shall cooperate with one another to ensure that the objective of this Protocol is achieved. State Parties shall endeavour to ensure the participation of all stakeholders in the promotion of the objective of this Protocol. State Parties shall take appropriate measures to regulate the use of living aquatic resources and protect the resources against over-exploitation, whilst creating an enabling environment and building capacity for the sustainable utilisation of the resources.

Further, Article 6 of the Protocol notes:

State Parties shall endeavour to establish common positions and undertake coordinated and complementary actions with regard to:

a). international fora conventions and agreements relevant to this Protocol,

b). international bodies relevant to this Protocol.

As can be seen, the protocol emphasises Member States' responsibility in managing shared resources. Since Zimbabwe is a signatory to this protocol, it has to harmonise its domestic legislation with regard to fisheries and management of resources shared by other countries in order to safeguard the environment as well as the fishing communities. The SADC Common Agenda is stipulated in Article 5 of the Protocol and is implemented through the Revised Regional Indicative Strategic Development Plan (RISDP) (2005-2020) as well as in the SADC Industrialisation Strategy to 2063.

It is worth noting that in 1995, the Southern African Community countries adopted a Code of Conduct for Responsible Fisheries (CCRF), which originated from Food and Agriculture Organisation international code for responsible fishery. The main aim of the code of conduct is to encourage countries and those who work in fisheries to preserve and carefully manage fisheries and their habitats. On this note, national governments are responsible for the careful and effective implementation of the code. The code also put the responsibility to develop and implement aquaculture and fisheries policies within the respective governments' jurisdictions. In 2004, SADC Member States agreed to implement short, medium and long-term plans to support food security by providing resources to small scale farmer's agriculture. The agreement was signed in Tanzania and became known as Dar es Salaam Declaration. The declaration recognised reasons for food insecurity within the SADC region as being a result of inappropriate national agriculture and food policies. It acknowledges that farmers in the region have inadequate access to inputs and markets. As such, SADC committed itself in the short-term from 2004-2006 to increase aquaculture and marine farming, and to improve fish stock management and fish product quality through pre- and post-harvest handling, processing and storage, in accordance with SADC protocol on fisheries (SADC Arusha Declaration, 2004). The medium and long-term (2004-2010) plans for SADC underline the need to promote conservation, management and sustainable utilisation of plants and animals, including fisheries, forestry and wildlife.

Other policy framework for sustainable aquaculture development in the SADC region include but not limited to the following: ACP Strategic Plan of Action for Fisheries and Aquaculture, 2012-2016 (and its Implementing Roadmap to 2020), the 2004 Regional Agricultural Policy (RAP, the 2014 Policy Framework & Reform Strategy for Fisheries and Aquaculture in Africa (PFRS), the 2015-2030 Agenda for Sustainable Development, the 2016 SADC Regional Aquaculture Strategy & Action Plan, and the SADC Regional Aquatic Animal Health. The vision for SADC is to have a common shared future and a region that has people with improved standard of life, social justice, economic wellbeing and security. Zimbabwe being a member of SADC and a signatory to the aforementioned protocols can use the same experience to come up with a National Aquaculture Policy that can harmonise its plural legal system on aquaculture and fish farming.

Legal and institutional arrangements in Zimbabwe

In Zimbabwe, as with many other countries in the region, there are a number of legal and institutional arrangements that affect aquaculture in one way or another. These are:

Ministry of Agriculture, Mechanisation, and Irrigation
The Ministry of Agriculture, Mechanisation and Irrigation has been involved in the support services for fish farming in Zimbabwe through its fish farming unit at Henderson Research Station. Fish farming services have also been provided by the same Ministry through its extension services provided by AGRITEX and the Veterinary services. The Minister of Agriculture, Mechanisation and Irrigation Developments in Zimbabwe made some regulations in terms of section 50 of the Agricultural Marketing Authority Act (Chapter 18: 24) cited as Agriculture Marketing Authority (Command

195

Agriculture Scheme for Domestic Crop, Livestock, Fisheries and Fisheries Production Regulations) of 2017. This initiative is meant to ensure that support services to fish farming in Zimbabwe is timely and sustainably provided.

Zimbabwe Fish Producers Association

People interested in fish farming production established a Zimbabwe Fish Producers Association (ZFPA) in March 2016. The association was established to promote and develop aquaculture as a fully sustainable livestock industry (Chronicle, 2 June 2017). It is important to note that the ZFPA's establishment came on the back of a fish building capacity project by the government of Zimbabwe funded by EU-Smart-Fish programme. ZFPA is made up of small and commercial fish farmers. The Ministry of Agriculture, Mechanisation and Irrigation Development is working with an EU-Smart-Fish funded project to develop the countries' aquaculture potential. Zimbabwe was called upon to emulate other African countries that have invested in aquaculture development with stimulus policies and programmes that promote strong and sustainable industries. Such countries as Ghana, Namibia, Kenya, Uganda and South Africa have vibrant aquaculture industry simply because they provide enabling environments that sustain the industry (AcquaFeed.com Staff, 04/12/2016). ZFPA as a stakeholder in aquaculture industry contributed to the draft policy by drawing up a position paper on fish farming to ensure that fish farming is well represented in the National Fish Policy and be in a position to actively contribute to food security and national economic development.

Parks and Wildlife Act Chapter 20: 14 (1975)

The Zimbabwe Parks and Wildlife Management Authority (ZPWMA) is a government parastatal established to protect and manage national parks, botanical reserves and gardens, sanctuaries, safaris and recreational areas. The agency's main objective is that of conserving the biodiversity found in these areas. According to the Parks and Wildlife Act Chapter 20: 14, hunting and collection of animals and plants in the aforementioned areas is restricted by the agency. One of the functions of ZPWMA as outlined in the Act, Part 11, section 4 (1) b (iii) is the conservation and utilisation of the fish resource of Zimbabwe. Part XIV of the Act deals specifically with fish conservation. Under section 83 (1) of this part of the Act, the Ministry is entitled to declare any person to be appropriate authority for fishing water. As captured in section 84 of the Act, the Ministry can also declare in the interest of fish conservation any water in Zimbabwe to be controlled fishing waters. The Act defines 'controlled fishing waters' as waters which have been declared in terms of section 84 to be controlled fishing waters. Section 85 (1) stipulates that, subject to section eighty-six, no person shall fish in any waters other than those specified in a notice made in terms of sub-section (2), except in terms of a permit issued in terms of section 86 by the appropriate authority for the waters. Section 86 thus is about permission to fish, while section 87 prohibits use of explosives in fishing. On the other hand, section 89 deals with protection of fish and aquatic life and section 90 (1) regulates control of business of catching and selling fish where no person is allowed to carry on the business of catching fish in any waters and selling such fish except in terms of a permit issued in terms of section 94 of the Act. ZPWA, for instance, regulates "41 camps and villages along the lake shore, of which six are fishing camps and 35 are fishing villages" (Ndlovu, *et al.* 2017). The camps are registered under the Ministry of Small and Medium Enterprises (SMEs) and Cooperative Development. More so, "the fishing villages or camps are in communal areas and are regulated by the Rural District Councils (RDCs) through block permits that are received from ZPWMA as part of the co-management requirements" (Ibid: 3). The statutory instrument 362 of 1990 does not permit farming and rearing of livestock within the camps and communal areas. ZWPA regulates fishing by SSF in most wildlife safari areas and National Parks.

Water Act Chapter 20.24 (1998)

The major legislative framework for water use, management and conservation in Zimbabwe is the Water Act Chapter 20: 24 of 1998. The Act recognises different uses of water, one of which is fish farming. The act also prohibits privatisation of water which gives rights of use to communal farmers. Previously before amendment to the Act, commercial farmers had exclusive rights to water use in the country. Section 6 of the Water Act has provisions for ensuring that all citizens have access to water for primary use and to meet the needs of aquatic and associated ecosystems, particularly when there are competing demands. Local Authorities that include rural and urban district councils as well as municipalities all have a stake in water management within their areas of jurisdiction. Each rural district has a unit of the District Development Fund (DDF), which oversees the construction of small to medium-sized dams (Latham, 2002). The ideal situation is that local authorities should act in conjunction with Zimbabwe National Water Authority (ZINWA) and the responsible ministry in order to ensure that their capacity to provide water in their areas of jurisdiction is promoted and enhanced. ZINWA now has the exclusive obligation of water resources management countrywide – a position that has affected local authorities to discharge water duties. Therefore, most local authorities lack capacity to develop water resources, and this has in turn affected ZINWA's operations in terms of water provision (Chibememe, *et al.* 2014). Public participation in water management is limited by the Water (Catchment Councils) Regulations of 2000, which was established under the Water Act in Zimbabwe. ZINWA has catchment councils that operate under it that have administrative and institutional authority over matters such as planning and water distribution, district development planning and implementation, and the installation of and maintenance of boreholes in rural areas (Maro and Thame 2002). The Water (Catchment Councils) Regulations 2000, clarifies the functions of Catchment Councils in Section 11(1) to include: preparation and updating outline plans for river systems; deciding and enforcing water allocations and reallocation; determining applications for the use of water and imposing necessary conditions; monitoring activities of sub-catchment councils; and maintaining all registers of permits issued for access by members of the public. Under section 12(1), Catchment Councils have the power or mandate to grant or refuse applications for a provisional permit or temporary permit for use of water; carry out inspections; revise or cancel permits; grant permits for construction of water storage works; and ensure compliance with the Water Act.

Furthermore, the Catchment councils function as stated in the same section: regulating and supervising the activities of permit holders in the use of water; monitoring water flow and use in line with allocations made under the permit; ensuring that water meters are functional and in good order; promoting catchment protection; and assisting in collection of data and planning. There are seven catchment areas in Zimbabwe managed by catchments council which are Gwayi, Manyame, Mazoe, Runde, Umzingwane, Sanyati and Save Catchments. The Regulations identify stakeholder groups such as Rural District Councils, communal farmers, resettlement farmers, and small-scale commercial farmers as being eligible for election to the sub-catchment council. The provision offers an opportunity for participation of communal farmers as members of sub-catchment councils. So far, many communities have benefited from aquatic resources that come from the rivers that form the seven catchment areas (Chibememe, *et al.* 2014).

Proposed National Fish Policy

Governance principles have always been applied in various sectors of any jurisdiction. Since aquaculture is relatively new, there is need to apply pragmatic concepts and principles to the sector so that it becomes a lucrative and sustainable industry. Lack of properly coordinated systems will always result in environmental damage, outbreak of preventable diseases, and low buy in by local communities (Hishamunda and Ridler, 2014). Also, without effective policies in place there will be probably misallocation of resources, environmental degradation and low growth rate for the aquaculture industry. In order to unlock aquaculture potential in Zimbabwe, the country has to come up with a policy framework guiding and regulating the industry.

Zimbabwe recognises aquaculture as a form of livestock production with potential to contribute significantly to sustainable livelihoods, food security, and economic development, through value addition and export of processed fish product, but no aquaculture policy has so far been put in place. The European Union is currently funding a government process to craft a National Aquaculture Policy on Zimbabwe. The Ministry of Environment, Water and Climate is leading the consultative process and has tasked ZEPA to come up with a position paper with regards to fish farming in the proposed policy framework. The drafting of the National Aquaculture Policy seeks to rationalise the fishing industry and any other related to it. High on the policy agenda is to determine whether fish farming and fisheries should operate as separate entities or under a single legislative framework. A conducive policy framework is reached at by reviewing the existing institutional and legislative frameworks. This is a long process that should involve participation of relevant government institutions, public sector, individuals and the civil organisations. Machena and Moehl (2000) advocate that the proposed policies should incorporate appropriate aspects of Code of Conduct for Responsible Fisheries (CCRF). Fish consumption is relatively decreasing in relation to an increase in population. Zimbabwe has underutilised water resource, favourable climate, high fish demand and inexpensive labour attributes that are not being utilised by the aquaculture and fish industry. Use of these resources has been hampered by lack of infrastructure and inputs. According to Machena and Moehl (2000: 340-1), "the potential for expansion is nevertheless considerable, but requires several enabling factors that include: a positive perception of aquaculture, sound policies at the national level, strong public institutions, availability of nutrient inputs, conducive investment policies to attract increased private-sector participation, and access to credit for commercial-scale enterprises". The drafting of a National Fish Policy should be aimed at rationalising legislation and other strategic issues relating to fish and optimise production. As such, the process of drafting a National Fish Policy will ultimately determine whether fish farming and fisheries should operate as single entities under separate policy frameworks, or under a single mandate (Herald, 2 June 2017). It is envisaged that for aquaculture development to take place, the proposed National Fish Policy should come up with different Boards for each fishery management area that will be responsible for the respective fishery catchment area as is the case in Zambia (Mudenda, 2009).

Conclusion

The Zimbabwe Aquaculture and Fish industry has a regulatory maze that need to be harmonised. As discussed in this chapter, the maze need to be harmonised by having a policy framework coordinating the different regulations regarding the industry in question. We have argued that the government should aim to promote community participation in the legal and policy reform process so that access to information is enhanced. We further noted that although civil society organisations are assisting in the crafting of the national policy, they must improve their advocacy with regards to issues that affect SSF on legal and community rights when dealing with aquaculture. An informed community will be able to ask for its rights thereby forcing authorities to provide them. Thus, we conclude by calling for the closure of the gap between SSF and commercial entities in aquaculture and fish industries in Zimbabwe if at all goals set by United Nations and SADC are to be achieved and sustainable aquaculture and robust fish industry attained.

References

African Development Bank Private Sector Operations. (2011) The Lake Harvest Aquaculture, *Project Brief*, Zimbabwe.

Chibememe, G., Dhliwayo, M., Gandiwa, E., Mtisis, S., Muboko, N and Mupika, O. L. (2014) *Review of national laws & policies that support or undermine indigenous peoples and local communities, Zimbabwe.* Ford Foundation.

Dadzie, S. (1992) 'An overview of aquaculture in eastern Africa', *Hydrobiologia*, 232(1): 99–110.

Dar-es-salaam Declaration on Agriculture and Food Security in the SADC Region, (2004) Dar-es-salaam, Tanzania.

Food and Agriculture Organisation (FAO). (2015) Voluntary Guidelines for Securing Sustainable Small-Scale Fisheries in the

Context of Food Security and Poverty Eradication; FAO: Rome, Italy.

Goppers, K and Miller, J. (1989/2) SIDA evaluation report rural development, southern Africa. Fish Farming for rural development, SIDA

Government of the Republic of Zimbabwe. (1975) Parks and Wildlife Act Chapter 20: 14, Harare, Zimbabwe.

Government of the Republic of Zimbabwe. (2001) Parks and Wildlife Amendment Act No 19.

Herald. (2 June 2017) Fish farming, comprehensive aquaculture policy in Zimbabwe, Harare, Zimbabwe.

Hishamunda, N. and Ridler, N. (2014) Policy and governance in aquaculture: lessons learned and way forward. FAO Fisheries and Aquaculture Technical Paper 577, Food and Agriculture Organisation of the united nations, Rome, Italy.

Latham, C. J. K. (2002) Manyame Catchment Council: a review of the reform of the water sector in Zimbabwe. *Physics and Chemistry of the Earth.* 27(11-22): 907-917.

Machena, C. and Moehl, J. (2000) 'African Aquaculture: A Regional Summary with Emphasis on Sub-Saharan Africa', In: R. P. Subasinghe.; P. Bueno; M. J. Phillips; C. Hough.; S. E. McGladdery & J. R. Arthur, Eds. *Aquaculture in the Third Millennium. Technical Proceedings of the Conference on Aquaculture in the Third Millennium*, Bangkok, Thailand, 20-25 February 2000. pp. 341-355. NACA, Bangkok and FAO, Rome.

Maro, P. & Thame, L. (2002) Policy, Legislative and Institutional Framework. In Hirji et al. (eds.) *Defining and Mainstreaming Environmental Sustainability in Water Resources Management in Southern Africa.* SADC, UICN, SARDC, World Bank: Maseru, Harare, Washington DC.

Mudenda, H. G. (2009) Assessment of national aquaculture policies and programmes in Zambia. Sustainable Aquaculture research in sub-Saharan Africa, EC FP7 Project. Project Number 213143. Lusaka, Zambia, SARNISSA.

Mukwashi, T. (2017) 'The Victimhood of Communities Induced by Infrastructure Projects in Zimbabwe: Case of Tokwe-Mukosi', *The International Journal of Humanities & Social Studies*, 5 (7): 50-60.

Ndlovu, N.; Saito, O.; Djalante, R.; and Yagi, N. (2017) 'Assessing the Sensitivity of Small-Scale Fishery Groups to Climate Change in Lake Kariba, Zimbabwe', *Sustainability, 9, 2209*: 1-18.

Water (Catchment Councils) Regulations (Statutory Instrument 33 of 2000).

Water (Permits) Regulations, 2001 (Statutory Instrument 206 of 2001).

Water (Subcatchment Councils) Regulation (Statutory Instrument 47 of 2000).

Water Act (Chapter 20: 24).

Chapter 10

Extractive Engagement of Key Value Chain Actors: The Major Barrier to Resilient Livelihoods and Economic Growth for Rural Farmers in Zimbabwe?

Solomon Mutambara

Introduction

Rural farmers have always been part of market systems as consumers, producers or buyers. These markets, for the farmers have been instrumental in reducing poverty and sustaining agricultural production in other countries outside Africa (DFID, 2012). Therefore, there is a growing interest amongst development agencies to identify and address the barriers that currently prevent markets from effectively working for the poor farmers in Africa to sustain agricultural interventions (Ferrand *et al.*, 2004; DFID, 2012). Considering that the possible solutions for development challenges clearly depend on what is chiefly causing it (Garrette & Karnani, 2009; Magombeyi *et al.*, 2012), this study adopted a multidimensional and multidisciplinary approach to explore the role of contextual (individual and structural) factors affecting farmers' access to the output market which ultimately affect the resilience of smallholder farming systems in Zimbabwe. The study is guided by the Market for the Poor Approach (M4P).

M4P conceptualises market systems as consisting of core markets, supporting functions, and the formal and informal rules that affect how it works (Martin *et al.*, 2011; Dunn, 2013; Mutambara *et al.*, 2015). The core function of the market system provides a platform for the exchange of goods or services guided by formal and informal rules and a set of supporting functions. Figure 1 shows the M4P multi-function and multiple-player arrangement structure of a market system.

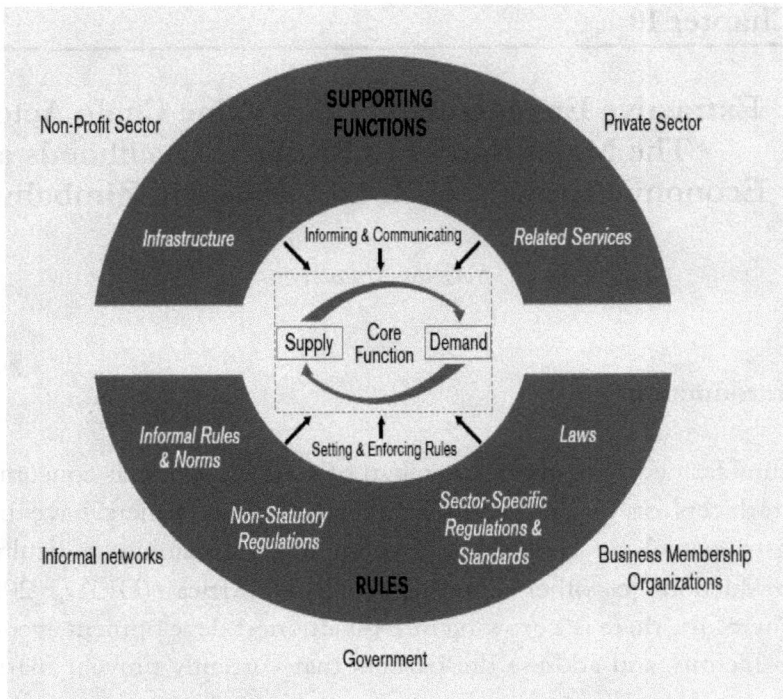

Figure 1. The structure of the M4P approach
Source: Mercy Corps (2008: 2)

The M4P approach facilitates the identification of external influences in developmental programmes and shows where the poor are placed within a market system (Dunn, 2013). The functionality of markets is influenced by the strength of formal and informal rules or norms, and the way these rules are enforced (Tschumi & Hagan, 2009). The M4P approach shows how critical institutions are in creating conducive market environment and how different factors can conspire to marginalize the poor (Ferrand *et al.*, 2004; Mutambara *et al.*, 2015).

M4P requires that development agencies such as the Government and the NGOs play a catalytic role to enable genuine market players to effectively perform market functions instead of performing market roles themselves (Albu & Schneider, 2008; Tschumi & Hagan, 2009; Mutambara *et al.*, 2015). The argument being that NGOs, and governments at times, have no legitimate long-term roles within a market (Ferrand *et al*, 2004) and efforts should be made to 'crowd-in' other credible stakeholders to improve the functioning of market systems for the benefit of the poor (Heierli, 2013; Albu & Schneider, 2008). In keeping with the M4P's strategic commitment to crowding-in, Tschumi & Hagan (2009) proposed three guiding principles to be considered as multiple stakeholders are roped-in. The principles are; that market interventions be strategically resourced to avoid displacement of market mechanism, that transactional relationships be premised on trade exchanges and that ownership of interventions lies in the stakeholders with the wherewithal to continue performing the functions beyond the life of the intervention (Tschumi & Hagan, 2009; Mutambara *et al.*, 2015). The approach is more system-centric, and recognises that the poor people's participation in the market as welfare-recipients provides a poor basis for lasting or sustainable development (Ferrand *et al.*, 2004).

The Asian countries such as China that have been more successful in reducing poverty tend to have done better at getting poor people into markets effectively (Perry, 1997; World Bank, 2008). It has been proved that markets were more successful in influencing sustainable rural development programmes in Asia than in Africa (Perry, 1997; World Bank, 2008). Jenkins & Ishikawa (2009), drawing examples from Bangladesh, demonstrated that enabling the poor people to buy, by accessing markets creatively and designing affordable products for the poor, breaks the long-held assumption that 'Bottom of the Pyramid' markets are not viable. Markets were also at the heart of successful economic activities in Asian irrigation schemes, providing the structure and processes to determine what is produced and consumed (Ferrand *et al.*, 2004).

That said, this chapter exposes the way rural farmers are trapped in the vulnerability quagmire by different value chain players, including the government (through policies and practices), wholesalers, retailers, formal traders, and other private sector. The chapter further examines the rural farmers' own attitude towards livelihood strategies that can potentially put them in the resilience pathway.

Research methodology

Smallholder rural agriculture involves multiple stakeholders from multiple sectors and disciplines, whose 'multiple viewpoints, perspectives, positions, and standpoints" need to be considered (Johnson *et al.*, 2007). A commitment to inter-disciplinarity is often seen as a necessary precondition for successful resilience research, connecting people's time use patterns with their spatial and material footprints (Fahy & Rau, 2013). Therefore, considering the multivalent character of smallholder farming operations, an interdisciplinary approach or more specifically the mixed method design, drawing on various methods to generate qualitative (textual) and quantitative (numeric) data, was used for this study (Carter & Beaulieu, 1992).

The mixed method research design took the form of a Convergent Parallel Design whereby the researcher collected quantitative and qualitative data and analysed the two data sets separately and then mixed the two databases by merging the results during interpretation or during data analysis.

The study targeted irrigation schemes as they are the only rural farming entities with a commercial focus, where a link between farmers and buyers could be easily traceable. Eight community small-scale irrigation schemes in the south-eastern Lowveld and the Midlands Province of Zimbabwe were purposively selected for this study. The Southeastern Lowveld area lies within the agro-ecological region V which receives very little rainfall (less than 400mm per year) and very high atmospheric temperatures making cropping under rain-fed not only risky but usually impossible(Mutambara *et al.*, 2015). The Midlands Province, especially the targeted Gweru Rural District is within agro- ecological region III which receives an average rainfall of about 650mm per annum. The selection of irrigation schemes from different agro-ecological regions and locations broadened the scope of the inquiry and reduced area specific biases. This improved the generalisability of the findings on the sustainability challenges of smallholder irrigation schemes as the research was based in 3 provinces and 3 districts.

The multiple stakeholders involved in different value chains of smallholder irrigation schemes were also selected for interviewing for this study to assess how their levels of engagement were impacting on the sustainability of the schemes. These stakeholders included Irrigation Management Committees (IMC), traditional leadership, relevant Government departments such as Agritex, Department of Irrigation, NGOs, relevant private companies (Cairns Zimbabwe, Farm and City, agro dealers, TM, OK and banks such as the Commercial Bank of Zimbabwe, Steward bank, Agribank and BANC ABC).

From the identified schemes, a simple random sampling method was used to select participating farmers through a self-weighting system or proportional representation. A total of 316 farmers (205 females and 111 males) were interviewed from the 8 irrigation schemes, Tsvovani (48), Dendere (32) and Rupangwana (32) in Chiredzi District, Zuvarabuda (33) and Vimbanayi (60) in Chipinge District, Insukamini (42), Mutorahuku (34) and Mambanjeni (35) in Gweru District. Purposive sampling was used to determine the FGD participants. The discussions targeted male and female farmers from the eight targeted irrigation schemes to understand farmers' attitudes, feelings, experiences, perceptions and reactions to smallholder irrigation schemes' challenges. The researcher selected those whom he felt, could provide the needed information and selected those who were in the irrigation scheme, 10 years preceding the day of the FGDs. Therefore, a cumulative total of 81 (43 females and 38 males) farmers from the 8 irrigation schemes were interviewed through FGDs.

Judgmental sampling (also known as purposive sampling) was used to select key informants for interviewing in the study. The researcher chose the sample based on who was judged appropriate for the study focusing on the role of the stakeholder and the position of the person within a particular organisation or institution. The key informant interviews allowed the researcher to obtain information from knowledgeable people with a wealth of experience in dealing with irrigation farmers in the different subsystems of the scheme, tapping from their expertise and unique viewpoints. A total of 37 key informant interviews were conducted with government departments, opinion leaders and other stakeholders who were deemed relevant and had different interests in smallholder irrigation schemes. The following is the list of key informants who were interviewed for the study: 8 Irrigation Management Committees (IMCs), 8 Agritex officials, 8 Department of Irrigation officials, 6 informal agricultural produce buyers (*makoronyera*), 2 agro processors (Cairns Zimbabwe and Chegutu Canners (Pvt) Ltd) and 5 supermarkets officials.

Data from the questionnaire survey was processed in SPSS and was subjected to both descriptive and advanced statistical analysis. Qualitative data from FGDs and key informant interviews were analysed using the thematic framework analysis approach.

Research findings

Age and Gender of the farmers
A total of 316 farmers (205 males and 111 females) from 8 irrigation schemes were interviewed. The average age of the farmers in the schemes was 51 years while the modal age was 58 years. The irrigation schemes had a sizeable number of elderly people as 12% of the respondents were over 70 years of age. Twenty nine percent of the farmers in the 8 irrigation schemes had not attained any level of education, 34% had attained primary level education, 11% ended in form 2, 22% had attained ordinary level of education while 1% and 3% had attained Advanced level and tertiary education respectively.

Irrigation schemes are mainly for crop production but surprisingly, crop and vegetable production were not the major livelihoods for over 40% of the irrigation famers. According to the FGDs conducted in the 8 schemes, the irrigation schemes could not satisfy the food requirement for some plot holders let alone their monetary requirements. One FGD participant said;

> *Our irrigation plots are too small to allow us to produce enough food for our families, we have to supplement with rainfed fields and other activities.*

Ikerd (1997) argued that if an agricultural project cannot enable the people working on it to meet basic needs and foster a good quality of life, it would be difficult to sustain. The range of livelihood activities farmers were engaged in mirrored Hassan, Qureshi and Heydari's (2007) findings in Iran where some of the irrigation farmers remained subsistence and were engaged in off-farm income generating activities, such as carpet weaving and other crafts to achieve modest living in many rural areas. Sacks (2014) confirmed that a typical situation surrounding irrigation schemes in Southern Africa is the simultaneous engagement of farmers in both rain-fed agriculture (outside the irrigation scheme) and irrigated agriculture.

The livelihood activities farmers engaged in, were not earning them much – USD71 from crop production, US$60 for vegetable production and US$67 from livestock production per month. This confirms that the interviewed households were poor. Considering that the average household size was 6, each person was living on USD0.39 per day, for the households solely depending on crop production. This finding confirms the FAO (2010) findings that 50 % of Africa's population lives on less than US $1 per day which implies a general inability by the people to effectively express demand for food from market sources. The income level of the respondents therefore suggests that large segments of populations were not only unable to meet their food needs from market sources but were also not able to provide a viable market for agricultural inputs (FAO, 2010).

Assets ownership level

The plot holders in the 8 irrigation schemes generally owned very small plots. Vimbanayi, Mutorahuku and Zuvarabuda each farmer owned 0.1 hectare plots while Mambajeni, Rupangwana and Insukamini farmers owned 0.2ha plots each. Each farmer in Dendere owned 0.4 hectares although they were only able to utilise 0.1ha at a time due to water shortage. Tsvovani farmers owned 3 hectare plots. Thirty-four percent of the households did not own cattle and those who had cattle owned an average of two beasts each. Forty-five and 90 % percent did not own any goat and sheep respectively and those who owned goats had an average of 3 goats each. The majority of the sampled households owned chickens (86%) with an average ownership of 7 birds each.

In Zimbabwe, the minimum survival threshold for a household of 6 members is at least 3 beasts for cattle and 5 beasts for goats (Chawatama, 2008). Thus 64 % and 70 % of the interviewed households were below the cattle and goat survival thresholds, respectively. The livestock and physical asset ownership level showed that the farmers in the smallholder irrigation schemes were under-resourced as their livestock ownership levels were below the survival threshold and the majority did not have basic agricultural implements for communal agriculture.

Barriers to farmers' effective participation in the output market

Informal output marketing arrangement

With the smallholder irrigation schemes, the marketing arrangements were highly informal. Farmers grew a range of crops like cabbage, rape, tomatoes, maize and wheat. These crops had no recognisable marketing board or consistent institutional buyers with which arrangements could be made for stop order payments. Without stop orders and formal buyers, the banks and private sector buyers were not happy to invest in the smallholder farming. The risk of non-payment was very high as the culture of non-payment had allegedly gripped farmers and has been reinforced for decades in Zimbabwe.

Subsistence mind-set of the farmers

Eighty-five percent of the farmers indicated that their production in the scheme was for both household consumption and for sale. Fifteen percent reported that their production was solely for sale with Dendere having the greatest proportion of farmers (88%) who were producing solely for sale. Three percent of the farmers felt their irrigation plots were too small for serious commercial engagements. The pattern suggests that the irrigation farmers were into subsistence farming, defined as "a system of farming intended to provide a self-sufficient lifestyle for the farmer and family where crops and livestock are maintained to support family need with little or no excess produced for marketing" (Business Dictionary, 2014: 1).

The difference in the production objectives of the farmers across the 8 schemes was shown to be statistically significant using Chi-square tests while the differences amongst the farmers by gender and marital status were proved to be insignificant. For farmers of different educational background, the goal of their production in the scheme was found to be statistically significant ($\chi^2=2.069$, df=14, p=0.000), with those who had not attained any level of education and those who attained primary level of education having the greatest proportion of farmers reporting that their production was aimed at satisfying their household food needs.

FGDs confirmed that even those who were growing tomatoes and other leafy vegetables (high value crops) were doing so to satisfy their household grain requirements by barter trading the vegetables with grain. Most farmers were growing a variety of crops on their 0.1 hectare to avert the possible negative effects of market glut resulting from specialising in one crop and to enhance their household food security. Figure 2 below shows how a variety of crops were grown at the same time in different schemes.

Figure 2: A variety of crops grown (a little of everything) at Zuvarabuda and Rupangwana irrigation schemes.

Source: *Author's own shots*

Farmers' crop choices/ preferences

Farmers had different reasons for growing different crop types in their respective schemes. Twenty five percent selected crops that had the potential to give them cash, whilst 34% selected crops that were easy to sell, while some crops were selected for being easy to grow (7%), compatible with small hectarage (5%) and gave high return per unit area (3%) as shown in Figure.

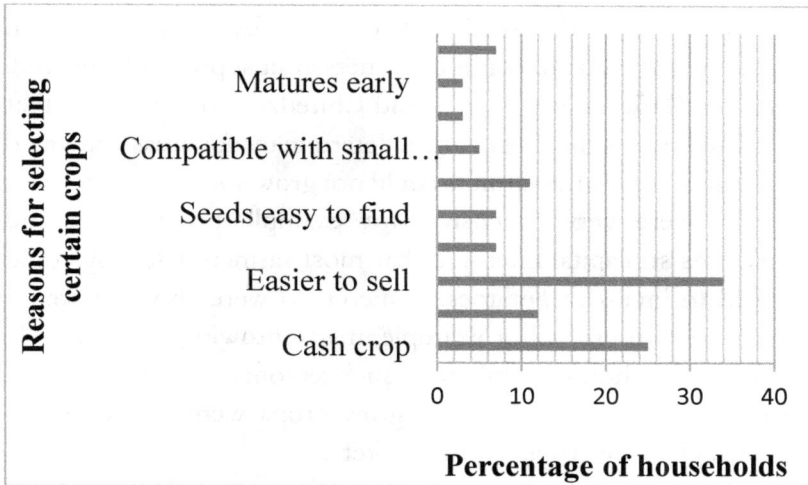

Figure 3. Reason for crop preferences

Source: *Author*

Preference for high-value crops

Only three percent of the farmers said their choice of crops was restricted to high value crops where the return per hectare was high. This largely informed those who were following the market-driven cropping calendar as they strived to grow crops when demand was high even if at times it entailed growing crops off-season when the costs of production would be very high. Farmers in Rupangwana and Vimbanayi regarded tomatoes as the favourite crop for their scheme as they could yield better than any other crop and if well timed (if not grown where there is a market glut). Farmers in Zuvarabuda, Vimbanayi and Rupangwana preferred tomatoes, especially the tomatoes star varieties (Starke Ayres, 2014), because they were able to produce more even after cultivating very small hectarages.

Preference for easy or cheap-to-grow crops

Three percent of the farmers selected early maturity varieties so that they could quickly harvest and sell and plant the next crop while the other 3% grew the crops because the seed was donated and was available at no cost. This was the case with the sugar bean crop that was grown in Zuvarabuda as a donation from Parsel and Zim-AIED. The purchase price for sugar beans ($30 per 5kg) was very high unlike maize (US$11 per 5kg) and reportedly, over 50% were not growing sugar beans unless the seed was donated by someone or an arrangement was made to contract farmers after supply of bean seed. The Agritex Officers in Chipinge and Chiredzi also confirmed that seed availability was the most critical determinant for areas cultivated under sugar beans. Some farmers could not grow some crops because the inputs were very expensive, for example potato seed and fertilizer, was so capital-intensive that most farmers felt they could not afford to invest in potatoes. Some crops were chosen because they were easy to grow. For example, maize growing was relatively easier than other horticultural crops such as tomatoes and potatoes. Unfortunately, easy and cheap to grow crops were not as highly paying as high value crops on the market.

Preference for non-perishable crops

If the product was perishable, the farmers indicated that they would be placed at a very weak bargaining position as the produce could rot in their hands. This would eventually force them to accept any price the market offered. For Mutorahuku, the use of public transport restricted the quantities of produce they could send to the market at a time. One farmer said:

> *We usually watch our tomatoes rotting because of lack of transport. The only bus that service us can only carry 60kg per farmer to the urban market and at the peak of tomatoes harvesting, many crates of tomatoes will rot by the roadside.*

This partly explains why maize and sugar beans were very popular crops in the 8 irrigation schemes. Both have a long shelf-life which will allow the farmer to look for a better market for their produce

Preference for easy-to-sell crops

Thirty-five percent of the irrigation farmers selected crops for production that were considered easy to sell. This shows that output marketing was a critical variable in the selection of crops to produce. The researcher's experience in the irrigation schemes revealed that although many horticultural crops, namely, cabbage, tomatoes and onions, attracted high prices on the market in times of product scarcity, it was difficult for most farmers to sell because of their high perishability and poor road networks linking the schemes to the markets. Perishable vegetable required efficient transport system to allow them to reach the market before the produce was spoiled as the largest consumer market was found in urban centres. Farmers across the 8 schemes reported that transportation of the produce to the market increased the costs, which made it difficult for farmers to recoup as their produce competed with those of other farmers operating closer to towns. Some farmers had had to time their cropping cycle to ensure that they harvested only when the crops were scarce in the market. One farmer in Rupangwana said:

> *I grow my tomatoes during the summer when there is no one with the produce around and in the country. I don't get any headache in selling the harvest because even the middlemen (makoronyera) will humble themselves before me as the only supplier around. I determine the price or at least have a strong bargaining power as the crop will be very scarce.*

In the targeted irrigation schemes in Chiredzi and Chipinge there is a high potential for better harvest for butternuts during the winter but farmers usually opted for sugar beans. Their argument being that, if they failed to secure the market for butternuts at the point of harvesting, they would have limited options but to either dispose the produce at very low prices or feed them to cattle. The worst case scenario was for the farmer watching his produce rot in storage. Farmers needed market assurance to produce such crops as butternuts. But the problem with the available buyers was that they were not interested in written guarantees or contracts, but only verbal ones. Farmers interpreted such practices as unprofessional and

217

unscrupulous behaviour bent to short-change them should buyers find cheap produce elsewhere.

The major problem affecting the smallholder irrigation farmers was the high volatility and unreliability of market prices that defied any form of planning on the part of the farmers. A crate of tomatoes which was selling at $15 in June 2014 was selling at $7 during the first week of August 2014. In July 2013, the same crate was selling at $24. The farmers that had grown tomatoes in 2014 had used their previous years' experience to determine the planting time and harvesting so as to make the peak selling time coincide with the previous years' peak selling month. Their demand forecasting and planning gave negative outcome as the 2013 peak selling time coincided with a serious glut in the market during the same mouth in 2014.

Preference for staple crops

Twelve percent preferred crops that satisfied their household food needs. That explained why 66% grew maize in their scheme while 24% were not growing maize. The difference amongst the 8 schemes on the number of farmers growing maize was proved to be significant by the Pearson's Chi square test at $P=0.05$ ($\chi^2=1.061$, $df=7$, $p=0.000$). Zuvarabuda and Vimbanayi had 39% and 41% respectively, of their farmers growing maize while 100% were growing maize in Mambanjeni, Dendere and Tsvovani.

Discussions with farmers confirmed that their dryland plots were not producing much of the needed maize because of the extreme arid conditions of the areas in the regions 5 and 3 in which the targeted irrigations schemes were situated and farmers would make sure they include maize in their annual irrigation cropping cycles. One farmer from Dendere had this to say:

> *Kuno kunopisa, saka chibage unotochiwana muirrigation, saka ndinototi ndirime chibanje chesadza muno (this a dry area and maize only does well under irrigation condition, so will make sure I have grown maize in the irrigation scheme).*

In the event that farm gate buyers fail to purchase staple crops, farmers would not seek alternative marketing mechanisms for example, conducting roadside sales or approaching private company buyers because the objective of producing staple crops was two-pronged: to preserve the greater part for household consumption and the rest for sale. They would preserve some for household consumption. Unfortunately, these staple crops were usually not as highly paying as was needed to offset high production costs in the irrigation scheme. Also the fact that farmers would devote the whole cropping cycle for household consumption suggests that their motives were subsistence and would not leverage farmers to acquire high yield enhancing technologies such as yielding crop varieties and fertilizers in the subsequent cropping cycles. Some farmers in Dendere , Tsvovani and Rupangwana, reported that for the purposes their food security, they would usually deviate from the normal cropping calendar in their scheme and grow tomatoes from September onwards to barter for maize from the adjacent Chipinge district across the Save river. Therefore, even those who were growing commercial high value crops were doing the same to enable them to access grain for household consumption.

Unreliable buyers for agricultural produce

Sixty-three percent were selling their produce to the middlemen at the farm gate, 25% were selling to the local people, and 9% were selling to wholesalers while 2% were selling to supermarkets. One percent was not selling to anyone. The difference in the types of the buyers who were buying from the 8 irrigation schemes was statistically significant at P=0.05 (χ^2= 1.203, df= 28, p=0.000), with proportionally more farmers in Chiredzi and Chipinge reporting selling to informal middlemen than those from Gweru district. This was possibly because most of the schemes were located over 60 kilometres away from urban centres where most buyers were found. The farmers had special reasons for selling to these buyers and were encountering different challenges from dealing with each of them. These challenges are discussed in the subsequent sections.

The middlemen (Makoronyera)

Sixty three percent of the farmers were selling their agricultural produce to the middlemen. The middlemen or the *makoronyera* were individuals who were buying from the farmer for purposes of reselling. In Zimbabwe, formal trading channels had become limited as there was a high rate of company closer thereby increasing competition in the existing markets that were struggling to keep afloat. Many companies including supermarkets and other formal companies were closing down and the informal middlemen, operating from the growth points, town or cities' green market moved in to cover the gap. Most of the *makoronyera* were highly unscrupulous with some swindling farmers in different ways. Farmers from the 8 schemes reported that the common ways the *makoronyera* short-changed farmers was through misrepresentation of facts around the consumer price of agricultural products to farmer, directly stealing from the farmers, use of misleading scales, using unclear quality grading of products to force prices down and bullying tactics. According to the farmers that participated in FGDs across the 8 schemes, the fact that the *Makoronyera* were popular buyers did not necessarily mean that they were the ideal buyer but was attesting to the lack of viable alternative buyers in the market. For example, a bucket of tomatoes bought at $3 in Rupangwana in August 2014, was sold at around $13 to vendors in Masvingo by the *makoronyera*. Therefore, the *makoronyera* were getting super profits while farmers could hardly breakeven.

The wholesalers

Twenty percent of the farmers were selling their produce to the wholesalers. The wholesalers that were buying from the farmers included Jasbro, Manica Produce and Marigold located in Bulawayo, Mutare and Harare, respectively. The challenge that farmers encountered from wholesalers was that they were not supporting the production process, (that is provision of inputs on credit, guaranteeing a market after production, offering contracts), but would hunt for the product once farmers had harvested. One famer in Dendere said:

> *All the available wholesale buyers are not helping us with an input support; they all become fly-by- night buyers.*

They were also offering low prices which would only be adjusted upwards after farmers' resistance and were using unfair grading system when buying from the farmers. This conduct by wholesalers made them as informal and unscrupulous as the *makoronyera*. The wholesalers reported that the smallholder irrigation farmers lacked consistency in their production level which made it difficult for them to depend on them. One wholesaler official said:

> *We need farmer who can reliably supply us throughout the year and the majority of our smallholders farmers have no capacity.*

The supermarkets

As was the case with the wholesalers, the supermarkets were not engaging in contact farming arrangements with the irrigation farmers to support the production of high value crops they wanted. The problem farmers had with supermarkets was that they were buying few quantities at any given time which would require staggered cropping to ensure smooth supply over time. One farmer from Mutorahuku irrigation scheme reported:

> *These supermarkets are not reliable buyers, they only take a small fraction of my harvest in small quantities and if you consider the transport costs involved, you can see that the business is not viable at all.*

Dealing with supermarkets also required efficient transport system to ensure that daily deliveries were made before shops opens at 8am. It was clear from these requirements that the farmers from Zuvarabuda, Rupangwana and Vimbanayi who were over 70km away from these supermarkets, besides facing challenges in matching the quality needed, would find it difficult to meet the logistical requirements to sell to supermarkets.

Supermarkets blamed the farmers for lacking consistence and commercial scale needed for continuous supply to supermarkets. One official from TM supermarket reported:

> *We need 200 bundles of rape every day and the local farmers can't supply us enough consistently. Farmers were also blamed for lacking market information which*

prevented them from following market driven cropping calendar and responding to the different tastes of the urban consumers. As a result, they were more comfortable in dealing with wholesalers like Wholesale fruiters and FAVCO who could supply a variety of vegetable as at and when needed. It was also revealed that farmers were more comfortable with cash transactions. Cash on delivery payment arrangements were not always possible for organisations like supermarkets as they had a chain of approvals needed before the money could be released. Some supermarket such as TM and Bon Marche were only paying through the bank and this excluded the majority of the farmers as most of them had no bank accounts.

The local community buyers

Twenty-five percent of the farmers were selling to local buyers. The local people were the most reliable buyers for the farmers. Unfortunately, most of the local farmers lacked money, especially following the introduction of multiple currencies in 2009 and the economic melt-down affecting Zimbabwe. They, as a result, would buy in very small quantities. Farmers also expressed the challenge of saving money that came in USD 0.50 or USD 1.00 trickles, which usually resulted in them not being able to plan for the next cropping cycle. One farmer from Rupangwana said *"...kunongouya vemakapu, apo nepapo. Zvino mari yacho ingaungana here?"* (Only local buyers come to buy in as small quantities as 250ml cups after some time, which challenge us on the saving of the proceeds as the money comes in trickles). More so, the local buyers would usually buy in kind or barter trade with grain or small livestock like chicken and goats depending on the volumes involved. The farmer would then sell the barter traded items to get money. In Insukamini, the farmers were getting fewer local buyers as the scheme was facing competition from other new farmers who were beneficiaries of the Government's fast tract land reform program who were growing the same crop the farmers in the scheme were growing.

Information asymmetries

Sixty percent of the farmers did not have contact details for reliable buyers by the time of the survey and the differences in the 8 schemes on the number of farmers with contact details for good buyers was found to be significant using Pearson's Chi-square test

(χ^2= 1.938, df= 14, p=0.000). All the farmers in Dendere and Mambanjeni had no contact details for the buyers while 76% of the farmer in Zuvarabuda and 58% of the farmers in Vimbanayi had contact details for the buyers they thought were good. Unfortunately they had contact details from the *Makoronyera* who usually misrepresented market information to manipulate the farmers. This suggests that farmers needed an independent source of market information.

Competition from South African producers

The Zimbabwean smallholder farmers were also facing competition from South African producers. A range of agricultural products from South Africa were flooding most of the urban markets in Zimbabwe, from onions, tomatoes, potatoes, eggs, to apples and oranges, and were delivered in 30 ton trucks. This was happening although the Zimbabwean Government had imposed a ban on the importation of agricultural products into the country. Farmers that participated in the FGDs argued that the smuggling of agricultural products into Zimbabwe shows that the borders were highly porous, possibly due to corruption. Thirty ton haulage trucks were used to smuggle these products showing that the corruption was institutionalised. All this was happening to the detriment of the smallholder farmers who could not match the quality and price of South African products. The South African products were selling fast and had remained preferable to consumers because they were very cheap. One 15kg pocket of dried onion from Zimbabwe cost $10 in April 2014 yet the South African onions were costing US$4 or US$5. This huge price difference ensured that the local onions would only sell after the South African got finished or the local producer would be forced to reduce the price to match the South African price which at times would mean selling at a loss. The cost of production was cheaper in South Africa (where a bag of Urea cost USD 10 against US$ 35 in Zimbabwe) than Zimbabwe and therefore, the smallholder farmers could not compete with South African farmers (Government of Zimbabwe, 2013). The smallholder farmers needed protection from outside competition.

Pot consumption substituting industrial consumption

All the farmers in the 8 schemes complained that the economic meltdown of the Zimbabwean economy manifesting itself in the folding up of industries and high levels of unemployment was marking agricultural markets poorer than was the case 10 years before the survey (Chitiyo & Kibble, 2014). The major reason being that, agro based industries like Cairn, that used to be responsible for processing agricultural produce like tomatoes into tomato sauce and jam had closed most of their processing centres in Zimbabwe. Therefore, all the horticultural farmers were just producing for household consumption or what farmers in Rupangwana called "pot consumption". That partly explains why the market for horticultural products was now easy to flood than 10 years ago as industrial consumption of the produce had long ceased and was replaced by the pot consumption. One Agritex Officer in Mutare and officials from Cairns Zimbabwe charged that if Cairns (Pvt) Ltd Company was still functional, one would have discovered that there was going to be a critical shortage of tomatoes in the market. Therefore, the market was poor because of economic hardships affecting the country and the industry, compromising the industrial consumption of agricultural products.

Interviews with Cairns officials confirmed that they used to help in absorbing the tomatoes produced by farmers to manage the glut. One of the officials said:

> *When we were still processing tomatoes, you could hardly see any glut in the market, but now tomatoes are flooded throughout the year as there is no longer any industrial demand for the product.*

They had long stopped the processing of tomatoes due to viability challenges as the company was under judiciary management by the time of the survey leaving Chegutu Canners (Pvt) Ltd as the only processor of tomatoes in the country. Interviews with officials from Chegutu Canners confirmed that the company was operating at 40% production capacity due to challenges with old machines and lack of capital to revamp the agro- processing plant. This showed that its tomato processing capacity was constrained.

Compromised purchasing power

Thirty percent of the respondents said that the market had become poorer because there were now fewer buyers in the market and 18% of the respondents said money had become scarce. FGDs with farmers and interviews with buyers revealed that the high level of unemployment had, to some extent, reduced the purchasing power of the customers. Vegetable vendors in Chiredzi, Gweru and Checheche Growth Point in Chipinge District unanimously emphasised that they were no longer selling as higher volumes as they used to do in the five years preceding the survey. Many of them said *"vanhu havasisina mari"* (People no longer have money).

Weak contract farming arrangements amongst irrigation farmers

Fifty-two percent of the farmers in all the 8 schemes were never involved in contract farming and 48% had some form of contract farming in their history of farming (Figure 6.9). The differences of farmers' involvement in contract farming amongst the different schemes was found to be statistically significant (χ^2=92.36, df=7, p=0.000) as 100% of the farmers in Dendere and 97% of the farmers in Mambanjeni had never been involved in contract farming. Seventy-four percent of the farmers in Insukamini and 75% of the farmers in Tsvovani were involved in contract farming. Differences amongst farmers of different sex, educational background and marital status on their involvement in contract farming were found to be statistically insignificant by chi-square test. This suggests that the personal characteristic of a farmer was not very important in determining one's being contracted into contract farming. Usually, the contractors targeted schemes, the overall potential of the farmers and the sizes of the plots in the schemes. For instance, although the performance of Tsvovani farmers was not very good, private companies were attracted to the scheme by the size of plot each farmer commanded (3ha), which, *ceteris paribus*, could produce higher volumes of produce than Dendere and Vimbanayi where each farmer commanded 0.4ha and 0.1ha respectively. That possibly explains why farmers in Dendere had not engaged in contract farming. Water availability was another critical variable that influenced a scheme's involvement in contract farming. The schemes that faced perennial water challenges had a low chance of being selected for contract farming. It was only if a private company got into a scheme that considerations about personal characteristics of the farmer like the production history and credit worthiness of the farmer were made.

Cottco (Pvt Ltd), Chishawasha (Pvt Ltd), Masuku (individual) and Better Farming Company were the institutions that have been involved in some contract farming with the farmers. With Better agriculture contracting farmers in Tsvovani in the growing of African bird eyes chilies while Chishawasha contracted farmers in Insukamini farmers the assistance of Zim-EID. By the time of the survey, only 11% were engaged in contract farming mainly from Tsvovani for the production of chillies with Better Farming Company.

The major problem faced by 10% of the farmers in contract farming was the failure by the contracting companies to supply enough inputs to leverage best yields on the contracted crops. Specifically, companies were failing to supply adequate fertilizers. Farmers from Insukamini Irrigation scheme, who were contracted to grow sugar bean by Chishawasha Company, complained that the company did not give them sufficient basal and top dressing fertilizer. The company failed to live to its promises after harvesting. They took all the horticultural products the farmers had produced to Harare and came back with literally nothing. One farmer gave the company 200 dozens of carrots packets; she was given US$5 by Chishawasha instead of at least US$100. The explanation given by Chishawasha was that the market was flooded, yet when they started the contract farming arrangement, they had promised to pay a fixed price for their produce. The company failed to buy a single cabbage from the farmers. According to the farmers, the justification given by the contractor for failing to buy was that cabbages were flooded in the market and the price for cabbages had become too low for any meaningful trading transaction. One farmer from Insukamini said;

Akauya pano akati kabheji razara mumarket uye mitengo yacho yadhakwa saka handikwanisi kuatenga kutindizoatengesa. Asika, dei kusiri kuti market inonetsa zvimwe tingadai takanyorerana pasi. (He came here and said that there is a glut for cabbages in the market and I can't buy them and resell at that price. But were it not for the tricky market for agricultural crops, maybe we could have entered into any contractual agreement over the matter).

In in the next season, Chishawasha Company failed to buy the sugar beans at the contracted price and farmers subsequently dumped the company.

The other contractor was Masuku, who was backed by Care international and Zim-AEID (NGOs) in the production of sugar beans in Insukamini. Like Chishawasha, Masuku failed to supply enough fertilizers for the contracted crop and farmers felt the company was buying the sugar beans at lower than the market price. As a result its relationship with farmers could not last for 2 seasons. It was well understood by the farmers, that the quintessence of contract farmers was to guarantee a market for the produced harvest and the failure by the contracting company to buy the produce defeated the purpose of contract farming. What could be deduced from the behaviour of these contactors was that they were not prepared to shoulder any risk of market failure but wanted the farmer to bear all the risks. Farmers explained this as part of the unscrupulous and extractive behaviour of the private companies and as consistent with the capital thinking of the private companies bent on maximising profits. If the prices on the market for the product were below the contracted price, the company would adjust the price downwards, but if the market price was higher, the contractor would never increase the buying price. The contracting companies always made sure the farmer was the bearer of all risks.

Better Farming, which was contracting Tsvovani farmers in the production of the African's bird eye chilly, also had the problem of not supplying enough seedlings to the farmers. Fewer farmers were contracted and the hectarage commanded was very low (25ha shared among 60 farmers). The seedlings were prepared in Harare and transported to the scheme. Controlled hectarage was done to ensure that the crop management standards could be adopted successfully by the farmers since the crop was labour intensive.

None of the companies, besides Better Farming Company, had written contracts with the farmers. The contracts were purely verbal which allowed them to shift goal posts at the detriment of the farmers. *Better Farming Company was providing 80% of the input to the farmers and was expecting the farmers to contribute the other 20% (4 bags of compound C and 3 bags of AN fertilizer were given to a farmer for every 0.5 ha). Better Farming was offering some imbedded services in the form of extension advice to the farmers through their agronomist. The agronomist was also running a demonstration site where the farmers were learning by seeing how different activities were done. According to the agronomist, the demonstration site was a critical component of the extension support since some of the farmers were illiterate and were learning better through practical demonstrations. The Better Farming officials revealed that they once experienced a problem of side marketing by some farmers although the problem was not very prevalent. Anyone caught side marketing the chilli was removed from the contract farming arrangement. Interviews with Cairns Mutare officials also revealed that side marketing was one of the major problems the company faced when it was contracting farmers in the production of tomatoes in Manicaland.*

Discussion of findings

The major threat to the sustainability of the irrigation schemes was the output market that had grown highly informal and unfavourable to the irrigation farmers. The middlemen (makoronyera) dominated the output market and were swindling farmers to get super profits when farmers could hardly breakeven. This was making the farmer-to-middlemen relationship unsustainable as the farmers were usually not able to make use of their proceeds to finance the procurement of inputs (fertilizers and certified hybrid seeds) for the subsequent cropping cycles. This was in line with Mati's (2008) findings that in Kenya the middlemen were ripping off farmers by offering ridiculously low price even if consumer prices were favourable. Even the few wholesalers and super markets who were buying from the farmers had become as informal, and at times as unscrupulous, as the *makoronyera* as they had unfair grading system and were not supporting the production of agricultural products in any part of the value chain. Johnson (2005) discovered that in Vietnam, even the most proficient company could not continue to be effective if serious inefficiencies along the supply chain could not be conquered. This suggests that the supermarket, wholesaler and agro processors' failure to support the production process of farmers can also compromise the sustainability of their businesses.

The supermarket and wholesalers blamed the farmers for lacking consistency in their supply with indication that they were more comfortable in dealing with wholesalers like Wholesale fruiters and FAVCO and South African suppliers who could supply a variety of vegetable as at and when needed. Conversely, researches in Vietnam have indicated that numerous smallholder farmers groups regularly supply supermarkets with different agricultural products (Smith, 2005).

Although over 80% of the farmers had cell phones, farmers still had challenges in obtaining accurate information for the market possibly due to their reliance on *makoronyera* and lack of platform for exchanging market information. This suggests that farmers needed an independent and credible source of market information. In Rwanda, although agriculture was intensive, farmers' lack of access to information on best practices, quality seeds and other inputs kept their productivity level very low (Shah, & Keller, 2009; Tschumi & Hagan, 2009; Obidike, 2011). Conversely, a research by Jenkins & Ishikawa (2009) in Bangladesh reveals that poor smallholder farmers that lived in rural communities where there were mobile phone networks were enjoying improved access to relevant information such as market prices for inputs and outputs database for suppliers and buyers as well as market trends.

The output market for agricultural products was shown to be generally weak and this weak demand was attributed to the substitution of industrial consumption of agricultural products with "pot consumption' or household consumption following the closer of the agricultural processing industry in Zimbabwe. In 2013 the average capacity utilisation of Zimbabwe's manufacturing sector was estimated at 39.6% down from 44.9% in 2012 (Government of Zimbabwe, 2013). At least 4 500 companies had closed shop since 2011, sending more than 55 443 employees onto the streets and a 3,2 percent GDP growth predicted for 2015, suggested that the limping economy would be largely stagnant in 2015 (Chitiyo & Kibble, 2014). Many of the wholesalers indicated that they were finding it difficult to engage into contract farming as the economic conditions were unstable and unpredictable, security of investment was not guaranteed, agro processing industries were closing down and corruption in different value chains was getting institutionalized. The closer of companies gave rise to very high level of unemployment (which stood at 90% in 2008 and 70% in 2013) (Chitiyo & Kibble, 2014). This together with the liquidity challenge that dovetailed these economic challenges was compromising the customers' purchasing power resulting in further weakening of markets for agricultural products. The identification of such underlying causes of market failure is consistent with the M4P provision that interventions should be premised on a sound understanding of why market systems are not currently working for the poor, and a realistic vision of how they might work more effectively for the poor in the future (Albu & Schneider, 2008; Tschumi & Hagan, 2009). A supportive agro processing industry was needed to enhance sustainable production in the irrigation schemes.

Some of the schemes were located over 60 kilometres away from urban centres and the majority of them were linked to very bad dusty roads which increased transport cost and logistical challenges to markets. Researches in Africa have revealed similar challenges in different countries. In most East African countries, over 50% of the population lives over 5 hours away from a market centre (Omiti, Otieno, Nyanamba, Mccollough, 2009; UNDP, 2012). In Uganda, 30% of the communities had no access to 'all-weather' roads and two-thirds had no bus or taxi connections (Salami et al., 2010). In Kenya underdeveloped rural roads have reduced farmers' competitiveness leading to high transport costs for agricultural products to the market and farm inputs to the farmers (Salami et al., 2010). In Uganda coffee exports fell both in volume (8 per cent) and value (23 per cent or USD 10 million) in January 2009 (compared with January 2008), due to transport and storage problems (Salami et al., 2010). The M4P approach highlighted that for the markets to work for the poor, basic services and infrastructure need to be available (Tschumi & Hagan, 2009).

Contract farming arrangements were found to be the most ideal arrangement to enhance the sustainability of irrigation schemes as different markets (input, outputs, financial markets) were combined by the same players that had mutual interests in the profitable production in the irrigation schemes. The farmers' modest gains from contract farming in Tsvovani confirms that production incentives, in the form of a guaranteed market with less transaction costs for farmers was important for the sustainability of an irrigation scheme. Unfortunately, the majority of the private sector player that engaged farmers in contract farming could not own up some of the basic commitments such as supplying adequate inputs and offering extension support and ascertaining the market for the produce. What was common with most of the contractors was their extractive engagement with the farmers. Conversely, experiences in Asia revealed that smallholder irrigation schemes were well supported by private companies under active contract farming arrangements. India had a number of companies that realised additional business opportunities by organizing the value chain of different crops from smallholder farmers from end-to-end. For example, Jain Irrigation Systems was the world's largest manufacturer of irrigation systems and was also a leading processor of vegetables and fruits from smallholder irrigation farmers (Heierli, 2013).

Recommendations

Basing on data harvested during research, to ensure that the major barriers to resilient livelihoods and economic growth for rural farmers in Zimbabwe are addressed, I recommend the following:

- The government should provide functional legal framework for the operation of contract farming which ensure that both farmers and private companies are protected in the different value chains.
- All the farmers in irrigation schemes need to be trained in farming as a business and market linkage to inculcate a business mentality in the operations and production systems in the irrigation schemes.

- Policies with enforcement mechanisms should be put in place to ensure that aid in the form of outright hand-outs to farmers is discouraged to avoid debilitating dependency and to enhance farmers' level of ownership and responsibility in the irrigation schemes. Providing assistance through markets will also crowd-in private sector players which will ensure sustainable engagement as both parties will be having mutual benefits in their relationship.

- It is also recommended that all sectors in Zimbabwe, from politicians, the humanitarian, the business community, farmers' organisations and the farmers themselves need to be educated on the need to avoid extractive engagement when dealing with farmers. Farming in smallholder irrigation schemes has investment phases and different economic and natural shocks which require the patience and resilient thinking of all the stakeholders to sustain productivity and long-term linkages with farmers.

Conclusion

The farmers' low levels of production, the low usage of fertilizers and hybrid seed varieties, the preference for staple, easy to sell, easy to grow and non-perishable crops, and the lack of motivation to change ways of farming epitomises the subsistence nature of the farmers. Their subsistence mentality could not provide them with sufficient incentives to leverage commercial and sustainable production to consistently supply the output market. The most popular buyer for most of the irrigation schemes was the middlemen, *makoronyera*. The popularity of *makoronyera* was not because they were the ideal buyers, but was due to the lack of viable alternative buyers, as the Zimbabwean economy was ill-performing and ever-growing informal. Unfortunately, the formal players such as wholesalers and supermarkets were behaving more like the *makoronyera* in that they were not supporting the production process and using unfair grading and pricing systems. They were not interested in written contract which made their engagement with farmers as extractive and unscrupulous as that of the *makoronyera*. Some supermarkets preferred dealing with wholesale companies than individual farmers who lacked consistency in the supply of products. Some were buying from South Africa where quality of products was much better than the locally produced products. *The smallholder farmers were blamed for not being consistent, organised and not being very responsive to the market needs in their production cycles.* Local buyers (community members) were facing serious liquidity challenges that prevented them from engaging in cash transactions and trading in high volumes with the farmers. Contract farming was ideal for farmers in the irrigation schemes as it combined different markets (inputs, outputs and financial market) under one umbrella. Unfortunately most of the companies excluding Better Farming Company could not satisfy the basic objectives of contract farming namely, the provision of adequate inputs, offering extension support and ascertaining the market for the produce. What was pervasive with most of them was their extractive engagement with the farmers and their lack of commitment for long term relationship with the farmers.

The smallholder community irrigation farmers were facing competition from South African agricultural products. On the other hand, the demand for agricultural products was warping as industrial consumption for agricultural products was replaced by pot consumption. The general population also had its buying powers reduced due to economic hardships and high levels of unemployment following the closure of companies.

References

Albu, M., & Schneider, H. (2008) *Making Markets Work for Poor Comparing M4P and SLA frameworks: Complementarities, divergences and synergies.* Bern: The Springfield Centre-Fauno consortium.

Business dictionary. (2014) *Subsistence agriculture.* Retrieved from http://www.businessdictionary.com/definition/subsistence-agriculture.html.

Carter, K. A., & Beaulieu, L. J. (1992) *Conducting A Community Needs Assessment: Primary Data Collection Techniques.* Gainesville, FL: University of Florida—Institute of Food and Agricultural Sciences.

Chawatama, E. (2008) *The socio economic status of smallholder livestock production in Zimbabwe*, Harare: IDS.

Chitiyo, K., & Kibble, S. (2014) *Zimbabwe's International Re-engagement: The long haul to recovery*, London: Royal Institute of International Affairs.

DFID (Department of Foreign and International Development). (2005) *Making Market Systems Work Better for the Poor (M4P): An introduction to the concept, Discussion paper prepared for the ADB-DFID 'learning event*. Manila, ADB Headquarters.

Dunn, E. C. (2013). *Individual Advanced Research Opportunities (IARO) Program. Final Research Report: Making Markets (Not) Work for the Poor: Market Ideology and Development Assistance in the Republic of Georgia*, Washington DC, US Department of State's Title VIII Programme.

Fahy, F., & Rau, H. (2013) Researching complex sustainability issues: Reflections on current challenges and future developments', in F. Fahy and H. Rau (eds.) *Methods of Sustainability Research in the Social Sciences* (pp. 193-208), London: Sage.

FAO (Food and Agriculture Organization). (2010) *The State of Food Insecurity in the World: Addressing food insecurity in protracted crises*. Rome: FAO.

Ferrand, D. Gibson. A., & Scott, H. (2004) *Making Markets Work for the Poor: An Objective and an Approach for Governments and Development Agencies*. Woodmead: Con mark

Garrette, B., & Karnani, A. (2009) *Challenges in Marketing Socially Useful Goods to the Poor, Working Paper No. 1135*. London: Social Sciences Research Network.

Government of Zimbabwe. (2013) *The 2014 National Budget Statement*. Harare: Ministry of Finance and Economic Development.

Hassan, U. I. M., Qureshi, A. S., & Heydari, N. (2007) *A proposed framework for irrigation management transfer in Iran: Lessons from Asia and Iran*. Colombo, Sri Lanka: International Water Management Institute.

Heierli, U. (2013) *Market Approaches that work for development, how the private sector can contribute to poverty reduction*. Swiss Agency for Development and Cooperation: Berne.

Ikerd, J. (1997) *Toward an Economics of Sustainability*. Dept. of Agricultural Economics, University of Missouri. Retrieved from www.ssu.missouri.edu/faculty/JIkerd/papers/econ-sus.htm.

Jenkins, B., & Ishikawa, E. (2009) *Business Linkages: Enabling Access to Markets at the Base of the Pyramid, Report of a Roundtable Dialogue*. Jaipur: International Finance Corporation.

Johnson, A. (2005) M4P week 2005: Proceedings of a series of review and planning events held by Making Markets Work Better for the Poor (M4P) during the week 31 October to 4 November 2005, Asian Development Bank.

Magombeyi, M. S., Morardet, S., Taigbenu, A. E., & Cheron, C. (2012) Food insecurity of smallholder farming systems in B72A catchment in the Olifants River Basin, South Africa. *African Journal of Agricultural Research, 7*(2): 278-297. Retrieved from http://www.academicjournals.org/AJAR.

Martin. C., Tschumi, P., Rahm, A., & Sahlen, O. (2011) *M4P HUB Conference Proceedings, Developing Market Systems: Seizing the Opportunity for the Poor*. Brighton, UK: Institute of Development Studies.

Mati, B. M. (2008) Capacity development for smallholder irrigation in Kenya, irrigation and drainage. *Irrigation and drainage, 57*, 332–340.

Mercy Corps (2008) *What are markets and why should we pay attention to them?* Retrieved from www.mercycorps.org/files/file1203640666.pdf.

Mutambara, S., Darkoh, M.B.K., & Atlhopheng, J. R. (2015) Making Markets Work for the Poor (M4P) Approach and Smallholder Irrigation Farming. *Irrigation Drainage System Engineering, 4*(130), 1-9.

Obidike, N. A. (2011) Rural Farmers' Problems Accessing Agricultural Information: A Case Study of Nsukka Local Government Area of Enugu State- Nigeria. Library Philosophy and Practice (e-journal). Retrieved from http://digitalcommons.unl.edu/libphilprac/660

Omiti, J., Otieno, D., Nyanamba, T., & Mccollough, E. (2009) Factors influencing the intensity of market participation by smallholder farmers: A case study of rural and peri-urban area of Kenya. *Afjare 3(1), 45-59.*

Perry, E. (1997) *Low-cost irrigation technologies for food security in Sub-Saharan Africa FAO: Irrigation Technology Transfer in Support of Food Security.* Rome: FAO.

Sacks, J. D. (2014) *Culture, Cash or Calories: Interpreting Alaska Native Subsistence Rights. Retrieved from scholarship.law.duke.edu/cgi/viewcontent.cgi?article=1325&context.*

Shah, T., & Keller, J. (2009) *Micro-Irrigation and the Poor: A Marketing Challenge in Small-holder Irrigation Development.* Accra: Agric marketing.

Smith, D. (2005) *M4P: Cross-cutting Issues in Agricultural Value Chains, M4P week 2005.* Proceedings of a series of review and planning events held by Making Markets Work Better for the Poor (M4P) during the week 31 October to 4 November 2005, Asian Development Bank.

UNDP. (2012) *Africa Human Development Report: Towards a Food Secure Future.* New York: United Nations Development Programme Regional Bureau for Africa (RBA).

Salami, A., Kamara, A. B., & Brixiova, Z. (2010) Smallholder Agriculture in East Africa: Trends, Constraints and Opportunities. Avenue du Ghana: African Development bank group.

Starke Ayres (2014) *Star 900 Tomato.* Retrieved from www.starkeayres.co.za/com_product_docs/STAR-9008.pdf.

Tschumi, P., & Hagan, H. (2009) *A synthesis of the Making Markets Work for the Poor (M4P) Approach.* UK Department for International Development (DFID) and the Swiss Agency for Development and Cooperation (SDC). *https://www.eda.admin.ch/…/172765-unesynthesedemarche_EN.pdf.*

World Bank. (2008) *Mobilising public-private partnerships to finance infrastructure amid crisis.* Washington DC: World Bank.

Chapter 11

Herdsmen, Farmers and the National Security under Threat: Unveiling the Farmers and Fulani Herdsmen Violence and Conflicts in the Niger Delta Region of Nigeria

Odeigah, Theresa Nfam & Munyaradzi Mawere

Introduction

Cattle rearing and farming are both occupations that are common to the people of Nigeria. Though now practised at commercial level, the activities are still being practised at subsistent level. Nigeria and especially the Niger Delta Region is blessed with vast fertile land, vegetation, favourable climatic conditions and a large human population. The favourability of climatic conditions have, however, generated fertile grounds for violence and conflicts between farmers in the Niger Delta and the nomadic Fulani herdsmen. Conflicts between herdsmen and farmers have also become common in the Niger Delta Region of Nigeria because of the cattle open-grazing system. Because of the open-grazing system, the Fulani herdsmen's cattle often eat up most of the crops on the farms. The consequent violence between the farmers and the herdsmen has resulted in loss of lives, wanton destruction of crops, herds of cattle and other property. The herdsmen in the Niger Delta Region are mainly of Fulani ethnic group and this has brought ethnic and religious colouration to the conflicts and resulting violence (Nairaaproject.com, 2018).

The security challenge in the Delta Region is serious especially because some of the herdsmen are from the neighbouring countries such as Benin, Cameroon, Chad, Niger Republic and Equatorial Guinea as well as from amongst members of the Boko-Haram the Islamic fundamentalist sect that is opposed to Western education and that is trying to create an Islamic State in Nigeria. Herdsmen have been implicated in the assassination of prominent people in the Niger

Delta Region. They have also been implicated in armed robbery, cattle rustling and other forms of criminality rampant in the region. Open-grazing of cattle has been known to cause "road traffic accidents" involving road crashes that attract reprisals from the herdsmen. The elite and highly placed Nigerians are also reportedly said to own herds of the cattle being reared by the herdsmen. The new and dangerous security challenge in the Niger Delta Region, arising from conflicts between farmers and herdsmen, is that some of the herdsmen are now well armed with sophisticated weapons such as automatic rifles and pump action guns, knives, daggers, bows, arrows and dane guns. The farmers who are more in number, on the other hand, are usually poorly armed with only machetes and hoes as their farm implements (Nairaproject.com, 2018). This means that the farmers remain vulnerable to attacks by the herdsmen. More so, their farming activities are interrupted exposing themselves and the nation to food insecurity and related problems.

This chapter critically examines the conflicts, the resulting violence and criminality that have been associated with the relationship between herdsmen, farmers and the generality of the people of the Niger Delta Region. A historic-structural and multidisciplinary approaches are adopted in this study owing to the complexity and multifarious nature of the problem(s) under investigation. The study reveals that conflicts and violence between herdsmen and farmers of the Niger Delta are not new. They have a long history dating back to the colonial period – a period that first exposed the Niger Delta farmers to land and food insecurity. Concurring with Animasaun (2016), the chapter advances that the recurrent herdsmen and farmers conflicts and the resulting pockets of violence are a national security threat that should be nipped in the bud.

The Fulani Herdsmen of the Niger Delta Region

The Fulani herdsmen are referred to as a group of people in northern Nigeria, also known as nomadic or Fulani pastoralists. The Fulani (as they are also fondly known) are populated and spread all over Africa, but predominantly in West Africa. The main Fulani in

238

Nigeria are in Fulbe Sokoto, Fulbe Adamawa, Fulbe Mbororo and Fulbe Gombe, among other areas (Nairaproject.com, 2017). These people are engaged in random movement with their cattle, goats and sheep from one destination to another, and returning later after several months or years to their original camps. The Fulani herdsmen are mostly found in the Northern part of Nigeria and other parts of West Africa (facts.ng 20018). The bulk of the beef consumption in Nigeria is from the livestock supplied by the herdsmen. The cattle, however, are owned by very privileged Nigerians in politics or business. These cattle owners have powerful union known as the Miyetti Allah Cattle Breeders Association of Nigeria (MACBAN) which is said to be a very powerful group that has tremendous influence on the government of the day. Some people have alleged that this group is a very powerful and influential group and that this could be one of the reasons why herdsmen have not been arrested, tried in the court of law and convicted for criminal offences so far in Nigeria (Toromade, 2018).

Figure 1: The Fulani herder, grazing inside a farm
Source: Vanguardngr.com, 2018

The main occupation of the Fulani herdsmen is to manage the herds, by moving them around in search of grazing sites. In northern Nigeria, the business of rearing of cattle is dominated by the Fulani and they have migrated to other parts of the country. The Fulani herdsmen provide security around their settlements by making security tools like dane guns, knives, bows and arrows towards protecting themselves and their livestock.

Over the years, the movement of the Fulani herdsmen had been peaceful and not much of violence was recorded because of the general low population density especially along their grazing routes (Soriola, 2018). The fact however remains that, the Nigerian population, including that of the Fulani herdsmen, has over the years grown to about 180 million (Vanguardngr.com, 2018). This increase in population around the country has encouraged blockage of the grazing routes of the Fulani due to personal and official structures being built as well as increased population of the herds of cattle over the years. As a result of this obtaining reality and the increase in the rate of consumption of livestock meat in Nigeria, the Fulani herdsmen move with their cattle to places where water and grass are sufficient for their herds. As noted earlier, the herds are usually owned by individuals who are into business and trade. More so, the rearing of cattle is expected to boost agriculture from livestock farming and also to increase the agricultural yield of farmers and not to encourage violence and conflicts (Gambari, Agwai *et al*, 2018).

The random and planned trans-human movement of the Fulani herdsmen is primarily because of the grass and water that their cattle need in a seasonally changing environment. Because of the riverine terrain and the vegetation of the area in the Niger Delta, most Fulani herdsmen bring their cattle to the region in search of good pastures and water. The herdsmen, most of the time, would carefully study a particular area before embarking on any journey with their cattle. The availability of grass for their cattle is always the most important factor and prized priority considered by the herdsmen, and also to ensure reduction of excessive grazing in a particular spot. It is also pertinent to note that cattle's grazing in Nigeria is a private business and not a government venture. The political elites and rich people in Nigeria are the main group of people in cattle business in the country, using the Fulani herdsmen, whose main occupation is cattle. This also could explain the enormous influence that the herdsmen wield such as the privilege of carrying Ak-rifles as they move from one location to another (Abubakar, 2017).

Fulani herdsmen and farmers conflicts in the Niger Delta Region

Decades ago, the Niger Delta farmers and the Fulani herdsmen have somehow lived together in harmony. In the 1960s, the Federal Government of Nigeria made attempts to introduce legislation to guarantee major grazing routes for the nomadic cattle herdsmen to avoid destruction of farmlands. However, because cattle rearing are a private business, this move could not be achieved and the plan was eventually aborted. Part of the failure of the proposed legislation was that farmers and other citizens of Nigeria were not ready to cede any part of the land to the herdsmen. The Federal Government of Nigeria in the heat of the crisis mooted the idea of the establishment of cattle colonies for grazing (or grazing reserves), but this was vehemently opposed by some States like the southern Nigeria (Toromade, 2018).

But when exactly the Fulani herdsmen and farmers' conflict and violence started did, remains a mind boggling and critical question. The question is critical in that it lays bare the genesis of the conflicts and violence in the Niger Delta. In view of the question, we note that the Fulani herdsmen and farmer's conflicts and violence have always occurred in the past, but it was always limited in scope and to some areas. Only between 1996- 2006 about one hundred and twenty one people were killed by the herdsmen having conflicts with farmers (Ohuabunwa, 2018). The cattle herdsmen have also reportedly encountered several cattle rustlers and a lot of such complaints had gone to the government and the necessary authorities. Unfortunately, attempts to solve these problems have failed as the Fulani headsmen keep trespassing farmlands, destroying valuable crops. Farmers, most of the times, are overpowered because of the weapons and firepower of the Fulani herdsmen (Adetula, 2016). In 2016, over one million three hundred herds of cattle were said to have been rustled in Katsina State of Nigeria one of the thirty states in Nigeria which predominately a Fulani state (Vanguardngr.com). Several herdsmen also loss their lives in the attacks by the cattle rustlers and some people believe that the frequency of these attacks on herdsmen and their cattle informed the sophistication noticeable in the arm they now wield. It has also been alleged that at times, the cattle are poisoned by the farmers leading to the death of several herds of cattle, while at other times the cows are said to be shot dead by angry farmers (Effiong, 2018). Below is a picture showing a herder holding across a sophisticated weapon. Below is the picture showing the herdsmen holding weapons, this is one of the weapons used by herdsmen in attacking the farmers.

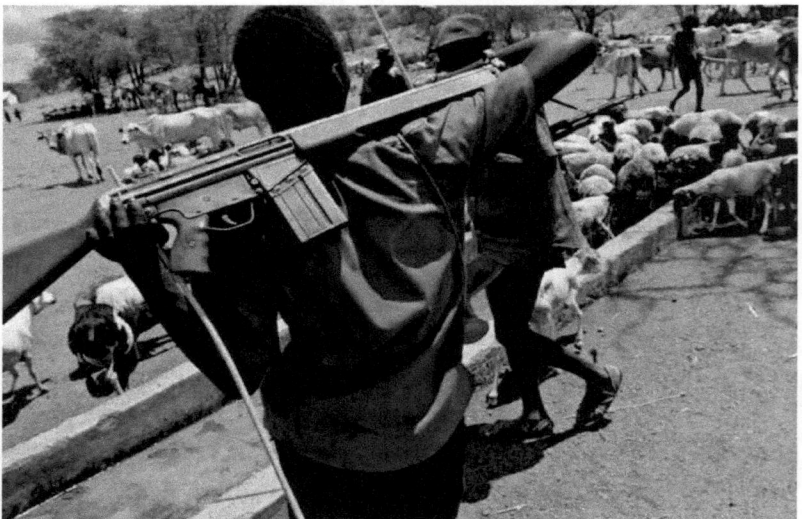

Fig 2: dailypost.ng. 2018, herders grazing their cattle.

Fundamentally, the Fulani herdsmen have been known to wreak havoc in many communities in the Niger Delta Region. About some decades ago, a cow was found dead in Ogoja Ndem in Cross River State and this issue became a major problem among the community and the Fulani herdsmen. The issue resulted to conflict and the herdsmen poisoning one of the streams in the community leading to the death of several community members who drank the water (Edoko, 2010). In recent times, the conflict between the farmers and Fulani herdsmen has become very frequent with massive loss of lives and property posing a threat to food and national security in the region and Nigeria in general. Since 2015, the violence has increased infrequency and scope because the cattle herdsmen now carry automatic weapons against the farmers who most of the times are unarmed, resulting in multiple clashes and fatal reprisal attacks (Odey 2017).

These attacks have also occurred in several other parts of Nigeria such as Benue, Nasarawa, Taraba, Ondo, Cross River, and Delta States, among others (Ohuabunwa, 2018). In the Niger Delta Region, these same attacks have occurred and maintained a regular crescendo engulfing farmlands and farmers. In the Niger Delta states and especially in Bayelsa State, people have been thrown into mourning following recurrent attacks by the Fulani herdsmen and this has led the people suffering unprecedented hardship and insecurities in the hands of the herdsmen. Perennial suffering and tears of sorrow following as incidents of killing, rape, robbery, destruction of farmlands have always been afflicted on the people. In a recent incident, the Fulani herdsmen attacked a 52 year old woman and her 18 year old daughter on the farm from Ofumwengbe village in Ovia South West Local Government area of Edo State using machetes on them (Osagie, 2018). Such attacks have become a major threat to farmers who are no more able to do their business because of the fear of being attacked by herdsmen (Nairaproject.com, 2018).

In their quest to find good grazing sites for their cattle, the Fulani herdsmen have also attacked the people of Okuku in Yala Local Government area of Cross River State living a lot of people dead and several others displaced (Calabarreporters.com, 2018). Some of the victims were students of the Cross River State University of Technology, Okuku campus. Consequently, most farmers in the Niger Delta Region have abandoned their farmlands because of fear of the Fulani herdsmen (Abdul Abdul-Rasheed, 2017). It has also been reported that the Fulani herdsmen in the process of grazing, raped a women and injured three other people in the Delta State in Aniocha North and Ughelli South areas of Delta State (Nseyen, 2018). The recurring attacks of Fulani herdsmen have become a problem to farmers, especially amongst Cross River State indigenes (Abdulsalam Abdullahi, 2018), who feel insecure and vulnerable not only to attacks by the Fulani herdsmen but also to famine and hunger. Attacks have become a routine in Cross River State; in the 7th of

December, 2017, the Fulani herdsmen attacked Mbiabong Ito community in Odukpani Local Government area following an invasion of the herdsmen living over 200 hundred families homeless (Ike, 2017). This community was also invaded by the herdsmen who took their cows into the farmlands of the people. During the conflict, it was discovered that the Fulani herdsmen had sophisticated weapons that were used against the farmers, which led the community fleeing from their farmlands and homes (Effiong, 2018).

On a separate incident, it was reported that the officials of the Nigerian National Petroleum Corporation were attacked by the suspected herdsmen at Tse Torkula, a border town between Nasarawa and Benue States, during their official duty on petroleum pipelines (Duru, 2018). Many of the workers were injured and taken to the hospital for treatment. Worse still, there have been regular incidents and attacks of this nature in the Niger Delta communities and Nigeria as a whole and this has caused a lot of hardship to farmers and the people (Ohuabunwa, 2018), in general who remain exposed to both land and food insecurity. As reverberates with Tope's (2018) report on the Urhobo people when he notes that the issue of Fulani herdsmen and farmers conflicts has become terrifying and caused communities like the Urhobo and other ethnic groups in the region to live in fear and unable to enjoy a good quality of life.

Factors prompting the Herdsmen and famers conflicts

There have been a lot of theories and concern over the identity of the people behind the attacks in the Niger Delta. There are three main schools of thought. The first one views the Niger Delta conflict and violence as a result of the Fulani herdsmen being manipulated by the *Boko- Haram*. The second school of thought views the violence and conflict as a result of the *Boko-Haram* members masquerading as Fulani herdsmen. More others are of the opinion that the herdsmen are from other West African countries that have illegally migrated into Nigeria. This could be as a result of poor management of the Nigerian borders. The Nigerian Immigrations Surveillance Office has not really lived up to expectation. Whatever the real force and people behind the violence and attacks could be, what remains clear is that the Fulani herdsmen clashes are driven by a combination of factors ranging from climate change, environmental factors, political factors and land scarcity (Adetula David, 2016).

Climate change, which is one of the critical factors affecting the cattle business, is one of the reasons prompting the Fulani herdsmen to move from one place to the other in search of grazing sites. The change in temperature has prompted the herdsmen to move to areas that have comparatively lower temperatures such as the Niger Delta Region where there is adequate rainfall almost all the year round. The environment in the northern part of Nigeria has contributed immensely to the conflicts in the Niger Delta because it gets very dry and at times with very little rain in the year causing the land to dry up and unable to sustain cattle grazing. This climatic challenge is a poses a big problem for herdsmen, who then embark on pastoral nomadic movements as they search for better pastures for their cattle.

More so, the focus on grazing has also shifted because the Fulani herdsmen have been involved in other forms of criminality such as armed robbery, kidnapping, assassination and rural banditry. All over the Niger Delta, the issue of the Fulani herdsmen eventually has the potential to limit agricultural production and the involvement of the people in arable farming, because the farmlands are no longer conducive and safe for farmers (Odey, 2017).

The Niger Delta Region is undergoing several security threats that have in turn impacted negatively on the people economically, politically, socially and religiously. Adding on to the conflicts that arise as a result of oil exploitation, the Niger Delta remains a shimmering pot with prickled holes. In fact, the frequent attacks on oil installations by the militant groups has been a source of concern to the people and therefore adding the problem of the Fulani herdsmen and farmers conflicts is a serious challenge to the region (Nimo, 2017).

Beyond the Fulani herdsmen and Farmers conflict

The Niger Delta Region, with its abundant natural and human resources, has become both a source of hope and despair to the people of Nigeria. Even though, the Niger Delta is known for the rich production of oil and gas and account for the bulk of Nigeria's foreign exchange earnings, agriculture remains one of the dominant occupations of the people. The Niger Delta happens to be rich in both oil and fertile soils suitable for agriculture. This exposes the region to people from almost all works of life, who are attracted either by the rich oil reserves or by the fertile tracts of land.

Taking it from a sociological perspective, where there are more people there is likely to be more conflicts as well. This is because conflicts are inevitable where numbers are high. This has been the case in the Niger Delta where the problem of the conflicts between the Fulani herdsmen and farmers is gradually affecting the farmers' agricultural output and exposing people to personal insecurity. As noted by the Global Terrorism Index (2015), the Fulani Militants are the fourth deadliest terrorist group in Nigeria as far back as 2014. It is for this obtaining reality that the herdsmen's activities and associated violence have resulted to fear, hunger and starvation in the land (Omawumi, 2018). The recent attacks by the Fulani herdsmen on Ossissa Community in Ndokwa East and Abraka Community in Ethiopia East Local Government areas of Delta State, for instance, has led to the killing of not fewer than sixty people (Osagie Otobor, 2018). The attack also resulted in the displacement of people and destruction of property worth several millions of naira. All these attacks have imposed danger and brewed insecurity to socio-economic activities of the people in the region (Animasaun, 2016).

Food security has become a problem in the Niger Delta Region where supply of food has become limited as a result of the Fulani herdsmen's conflicts with the farmers. The farmers now find it difficult to go to their farms for fear of being attacked by the Fulani herdsmen who can strike any time of the day. Consequently, the conflicts have resulted in an increase in the prices of basic food commodities thereby causing hardship for the ordinary people in the region (Adetula, 2016). A recent empirical research carried out by the Global Humanities Organisation with the British Department for International Development (BFID) between 2013 and 2016, has revealed that the negative effects of the conflicts between the herdsmen and farmers in Nigeria are a perennial one that has negatively affected the country's economic development (Global

Terrorism Index 2015). As the Global Terrorism Index further reveals, the States affected by the Fulani herdsmen and famers conflicts loss an average of 47 percent of their revenue from agricultural produce. This poses serious threats to the country's food security and Gross Domestic Product.

The Fulani herdsmen and farmers conflicts has also created unfavourable atmosphere for business. It has stirred and created unprecedented fear in the minds of [potential] foreign investors, with the result showing down on economic growth and national development.

The Way Forward

The solution to the Fulani herdsmen and farmers conflicts and violence are not easy to come up with, owing to the complexity of the problem itself. During the gathering of data for this research, it became apparent that the cattle are owned by individuals who are wealthy and highly placed in government and politics. More so, cattle's rearing in Nigeria is a private business and not a government venture. The major solution therefore is for the government to enact a legislation that outlaws the open grazing of cattle, but before that there should have been sensitisation of the herdsmen on this new approach. This approach is likely to be successful because cattle are healthier when they are ranched since they are not exposed to diseases and stress on open grazing.

More importantly, the herdsmen should be educated on this new approach and if possible given soft loans by the government, to facilitate a smooth transition from their current way of life. The soft loans may also help to lure the nomadic herdsmen, especially in the Benue State (of Nigeria) – the middle belt which is the food basket of the nation.

We further argue that the establishment of cattle colonies or national grazing reserves is likely to intensify conflicts. This is because the national grazing reserves would warrant government needing to acquire peoples' land or may result in government using land for a purpose that most Nigerians feel is a private business.

More so, we note that security agencies such as the Police and Immigration Service should mop-up the various arms and ammunition in the hands of the people who are not licenced. Those who are apprehended should be made to face the wrath of the law of the land. The security agencies especially the Immigration Service should control and monitor the country's porous borders to ensure that people from within and others from neighbouring countries are not involved in this criminality.

The inability of the Nigerian the national security agency to contain this mayhem for this long remains a challenge to the people and the national economy. In view of this problem, we urge that the government properly train and equip the Police, so that they can better handle conflicts and violence. Most importantly, the Federal Government should facilitate dialogue and education among the Fulani herdsmen and the farmers (Gambari, Agwai *et al*, 2018) to avoid unnecessary violence and conflicts.

Conclusion

Fundamentally and historically, the Fulani herdsmen have always grazed their cattle in the open along the roads and farmlands in almost all the parts of the Niger Delta Region. But recently there has been an upsurge in the herdsmen trespassing of farmlands and destruction of crops and other valuable products, exposing the people of the Niger Delta to both land and food insecurity. Besides, the menace has caused a lot of violence leaving a number of people dead and property worth millions of dollars destroyed. The herdsmen are involved in crime, and violence leading to unprecedented fear to till the land among the farmers eventually. This has negatively impacted on the land and food security in the Niger Delta. Although the government has proposed grazing reserves to address the conflict and violence problem between the Fulani herdsmen and farmers in the Niger Delta, we submit that this is not likely to work in Nigeria because cattle rearing is a private business. We note that the enactment of anti-open grazing bill has not produced the derived results and so there is need for proper sensitisation and involvement of the herdsmen at every stage of the bill.

References

Adetula, D. (2016) Understanding the Fulani Herdsmen Crisis in Nigeria: Here is everything you need to Know, venturesafrica.com.

Adetula, D. (2016) Understanding the Fulani Herdsmen Crisis in Nigeria: here is everything you need to know, https://ww.venturesafrica.com. Accessed 12th October, 2017.

Alabi, T. (2018) Herdsmen Attack NNPC official in Benue State, https://www.informationmng.com. Accessed 15th January, 2018.

https://www.calabarreporters.com, 2018.

Animasaun, D. (2016) https://www.vanguardngr.com. Accessed 10thMarch, 2017.

Duru, P. (2018) Herdsmen attack NNPC Officials Working on Pipe Line in Benue State, Accessed February, 2018, https://www.vanguardngr.com.

Effective of Fulani herdsmen and Farmers Crisis on Food Security in Abraka Delta State, Nigeria, https://nairaproject.com Accessed 12 January, 2018.

The Fulani Ethnic Group Nigeria, (2018) https://www.Fasts,ng. Accessed 3rd March, 2018.

Gambari Ibrahim, Agwai, M. L., Ibrahim J,. Jeja Attahiru,. Kwaja Chris, Balla Fatima,. Muhammed-Oyebode Aisha,. YA'u Y. Z. (2018) How To Resolve Herdsmen Crisis-Nigeria Working Group.www.premiumtimes.com. Accessed 5th February, 2018.

Global Terrorism Index (2015) Institute for Economics and Peace, Nigeria.

How to Resolve Herdsmen Crisis-Nigeria Working Group, (2018) www.premiumtimesng.com. Accessed 6th March, 2018.

Ike, U. (2017) Herdsmen Sack 200 Family in Cross River. www.vanguardngr.com, Accessed, 28 December 2017.

Mazi, S. O. (2018) Routing the Fulani Herdsmen Militants Calls for external Help, https://vanguardngr.com. Accessed 13th February, 2018.

Ohuabunwa, S. (2018) Routing the Fulani Herdsmen Militants call for External help). www.vanguardngr.com, Accesses 7th January, 2018.

Olu, O. (2018) Rampaging Fulani Herdsmen a Threat to Nigeria Unity, ttps://www.realnewsmagazine.net. Accessed 6th March, 2018.

Oral Interview with Abdul Abdul-Rasheed, 66+ years, status male, Occupation cattle rearing, place of interview Ogoja, Cross River State, 2017.

Oral Interview with Abdulsalam Abdullahi, 69+ years, status male, Occupation cattle rearing, place of interview Makudi, Benue State, 2018.

Oral Interview with Briggs Nimo, 78+ years, status male, Occupation business, place of interview Port- Harcourt, River State, 2018.

Oral Interview with Effiong Asuquo, 70+ years, status male, Occupation famer, place of interview Odukpani, Cross River State, 2018.

Oral Interview with Musa Abubakar, 72+ years, status male, Occupation cattle rearing, place of interview River State, 2017.

Oral Interview with Odey John , 71+ years, status male, Occupation cattle rearing, place of interview Ogoja, Cross River State, 2017.

Oral Interview with Nseyen Nsikak, 64+ years, status male, Occupation famer, place of interview Ughelli, Delta State, 2018.

Oral Interview with Edoko Paulina, 73+ years, status male, Occupation Civil Servant, place of interview Cross River State, 2011.

Oral Interview with Yahaya Zainab, 67+ years, status female, Occupation Cattle Owner, place of interview Oncha-Ugbo, Delta State, 2017.

Osagie, O. (2018) Herdsmen Attack Woman, daughter in Edo https://www. thenahiononline.ng.net.

Toromade, S. (2018) What You Need to Know about Fulani Herdsmen and Anti- opening Grazing Law, Miyetti Allah, hpps://www.pulse.ng.

Osagie, O. (2018) Herdsmen Attack Woman, daughter in Edo. Thenationonlineng.net. Accessed 11th September, 2017.

Soriola, E. (2018) History of Fulani Herdsmen in Nigeria and today's Crisis, www.naija.ng. Accessed 2nd February, 2018.

Wifa, B. A. (2018) Problems and Challenges Afflicting the Niger Delta Region, particularly the Core Niger Delta, www.focusnigeria.com.

Chapter 12

The Creation and Performance of Secure Agricultural Processes and Practices in Colonial Zimbabwe: Tackling Food and Land Tenure Insecurity through Learning Resource Conservation Lessons from the Bromley Farming District

Simeon Maravanyika

Introduction

This chapter examines the creation and performance of intensive conservation processes on settler farms in colonial Zimbabwe to demonstrate the extent to which the settler administration was willing to tackle insecurities in the 'white' agrarian sector. The chapter utilises a case study, the then Bromley farming district of Zimbabwe. The Bromley farming area is located in Mashonaland East Province along the Harare-Mutare Road (Salisbury and Umtali in the colonial period), about fifty kilometres from Harare and 30 kilometres from Marondera. As happened in all the other settler farming districts in the colony from the early 1940s onwards, an Intensive Conservation Area (ICA) was established in Bromley to superintend over the construction of conservation works to ensure the sustainability of the settler farming sector and to inculcate new farming knowledge, skills and business cultures.

Improvement of settler agriculture, it was envisaged, would once and for all put to rest the question of African competition, which for a long while posed a persistent headache to settler farmers and policy-makers. A number of extra-market forces were crafted to diminish African agriculture, with two pieces of legislation namely, the Land Apportionment Act (of 1930) and the Native Land Husbandry Act (of 1951), perhaps constituting the most severe blows to African agriculture. African agrarian success challenged, in the colonial psyche, the very foundations of European supremacy. Apart from insecurities created by stiff competition from African farmers, which impacted on African labour availability, agricultural marketing and pricing permutations also posed a challenge as the volume of African produce had the effect of pushing prices of commodities down. Improving sustainability of settler capitalist agriculture – both in terms of equipping it with modern farming technologies and methods and increasing not just yields but also the quality of crops – was projected to be the most effective way of shoring up the economic status of European farmers, and of the colony, to the level of a neo-Britain (Maravanyika, 2010). Without such success, the chances of economic prosperity for the colony would be severely curtailed as, apart from agriculture, mining was the only other viable pillar of the economy till the early 1940s when manufacturing emerged as an important third sector of the economy whose strength lay in its industrialisation and urbanisation thrust.

This chapter examines the establishment of an ambitious agricultural and resource conservation programme in the colony's settler farming districts, then termed the "Intensive Conservation Areas" (ICAs) Programme, from the early 1940s. The programme turned out to be a major driving force of the colonial agricultural sector, as evidenced by the fact that the majority of ICAs continued to function after Zimbabwe's attainment of independence, without much government support. The performance and legacy of these ICAs is an area that needs scholarly scrutiny as the story of colonial conservation on settler farms, often not given prominence by economic historians, partly explains the success of settler agriculture in the colony. It also explains why, on a comparative basis, Southern Rhodesia's farmers largely succeeded while their counterparts in colonial Zambia were only relatively successful and in colonial Malawi, apart the company-run tea estates in the highlands, they were an outright failure. The story of the ICAs also explains Zimbabwe's agricultural successes in the 1980s and early 1990s. A strong base had been created in the colonial period, on whose basis Zimbabwe earned the title of being the "food basket" of the region and the food security portfolio in the Southern Africa Development Community (SADC).

This chapter adds to the literature on the colonial settler agricultural sector, which is timely in an era where Zimbabwe's new post-Mugabe government has fingered the agricultural sector as a low-hanging fruit that can act as a springboard for catapulting the country out of its decades-long economic malaise. The Mnangagwa administration has promised to revisit the land reform programme with a view to correct the tripartite challenges of multiple farm ownership, low agricultural output and lack of title, which inhibits access to agricultural finance (Zimbabwe Situation, 1 February 2018, Daily News, 2 February 2018). It is also timely on another level; the status of agriculture in the southern African region has recently been further brought into the limelight by the South African government's declared intention to follow post-colonial Zimbabwe's path of land alienation from white landowners without compensation (IOL, 28 February 2018).

This chapter draws lessons from ICA operations in the settler farming district of Bromley in colonial Zimbabwe. The chapter investigates a programme pursued by the colonial administration to tackle insecurities in settler agriculture, a feat which registered - though at the expense of African agricultural productivity - remarkable successes for white farmers. There is no need for policy-makers in the Mnangagwa administration to re-invent the square-wheel when it moves to craft and implement its resource conservation and preservation policy in the agricultural sector. A lot of important lessons on tackling insecurities in agriculture can easily be drawn from the past and improved to address contemporary post fast-track land reform challenges.

Old wine in new wine skins? Agriculture and participatory resource governance approaches

Advocates of Community-Based Natural Resources Management (CBNRM) have, since the 1980s, come to regard it as one of the most effective natural resources management methods. This is so because Community Based Natural Resources Management emphasises inclusion and participation of local residents in areas where the target resources are located in planning, decision-making and management. This is meant to ensure that interventions and outcomes are people-centred, people-driven and sensitive to customs, beliefs, knowledge-systems, local micro-economic and bio-physical contexts and other peculiarities of target communities (Murphree 2002; Mawere 2015). This management approach is premised on the thinking that for sustainable conservation and development to take place, local communities should play a key role in the formulation and implementation of projects and, in the process, benefit in tangible ways from proceeds of such initiatives (Berkes, 2004).

CBNRM is a reaction to top-down exclusionary resource management policies historically pursued by governments in the management of natural resources, both in the colonial and post-colonial eras (Gibson, 1999). Colonial and even post-colonial correspondence by officials in government's agricultural, forestry, fisheries and wildlife departments, among other units, often blamed local communities for resource degradation, which, in the majority of cases, resulted in conservation interventions being planned and enforced centrally, from the top, without local input (Vallema and van de Breemer, 1999). This was in spite of the fact that African communities utilised local indigenous knowledge systems in their interface with natural resources, which worked in favour of resource preservation. Top-down resource management methods bred local resentment in many communities, as such methods were in the majority of cases premised on restricting access to such resources, and levying high penalties on community members caught utilising resources in their localities (Dzingirai, 2005; Mawere 2015).

African discontent against top-down resource management often manifested itself in increased poaching and illegal harvesting and utilisation of natural resources, as local resources were important sources of livelihoods. Top-down management disempowered local leadership structures from encouraging sustainable harvesting and use of resources, and from promoting compliance with indigenous knowledge and resource-use traditions. A good example of this is the case of the Mafungautsi Forest Reserve in Gokwe where local communities from villages such as Matashu, Maruta and Mafa have for long illegally harvested forest products such as broom and thatch-grass, firewood, fruits, herbal medicines, timber and small game because of high-handed policing mechanisms employed by the

Forestry Commission of Zimbabwe (Mutimukuru-Maravanyika, 2010; Maravanyika, 2012).

Top-down resource management promotes vandalism and wanton destruction, as important infrastructure such as boundary fences, water-harvesting infrastructure, electrical installations, to mention a few, erected for the purpose of resource conservation and preservation, got run-down, sabotaged or destroyed by communities living on the margins of protected areas as there was no perception of ownership of this infrastructure, and a lack of understanding of how these were meant to also benefit locals (Murombedzi, 1994).

This chapter argues that participatory resource management approaches, as elaborated above, are not a new intervention. They are 'old wine in new bottles' meant to undo vulnerabilities and insecurities of the locals. While the nomenclature and terminologies ascribed to co-management initiatives may be, and may, indeed, keep changing from time to time to suit changing contexts, when it comes to praxis, these approaches have been in circulation for much longer as the example of the Intensive Conservation Areas Programme demonstrates. Dzingirai and Breen (2005), among other applied social science and development practitioners, have argued that resource management programmes in Africa were, till the 1980s, always been top-down, exclusionary and characterized by heavy-handed policing by government departments. They further argue that it was only a combination of the fall of the Soviet Union, on one hand, and a rising tide of "people power", as more and more people pressed for democratic governance, on the other, that led to the adoption of participatory approaches to conservation, such as community-based natural resources management. These postulations, juxtaposed with the evidence on the ground, clearly lack accuracy.

Attempts to time-line and contextualise joint-management opens up two issues related to community-based conservation for discussion. The first is that the view that co-management is a phenomena of the late 1980s whose roots lie in the decay of the Soviet Union and the rising tide in favour of democracy is ahistorical. Although CBNRM might not have been known by that name before the 1980s, its implementation in colonial Zimbabwe dates back to the

1940s, as the case of the Intensive Conservation Areas Movement aptly demonstrates. Contrary to the argument that community conservation is a phenomenon of the 1980s, I argue, it began in the years immediately after the Great Depression. From the early 1940s, right up to the end of colonial rule, the minority government of colonial Zimbabwe set up intensive conservation systems on settler commercial farms. The Intensive Conservation Areas (ICAs) were indisputably an early form of community-based soil management which yielded positive results for the settler agrarian sector.

Secondly, the CBNRM approach did not gain as much traction as development practitioners allege. Co-management programmes have traditionally been initiated and pushed mainly by Non-Governmental Organisations (NGOs), and not governments. Though already popular among development practitioners in the NGO sector, by the time the Fast Track Land Reform Programme (FTLRP) was launched in the year 2000, joint resource management was completely ignored by the government of Zimbabwe. Non-Governmental Organisations in the resource management sector who tried to advocate for uptake of the framework by the Zimbabwe government were often cast as purveyors of neo-imperialist discord, whose agenda was to help the anti-land reform opposition to dethrone the then Mugabe government. The NGO sector was thus not viewed as a partner, but as a foe. This is quite paradoxical because, as this chapter reveals, the colonial government, led by Prime Minister Sir Godfrey Huggins, fully embraced community-based soil and water management, and utilised it as a tool to improve the fortunes of the settler agricultural sector.

Participatory resource management would have been very beneficial, I postulate, to the Zimbabwean agrarian sector if it had been considered in formulating and implementing the FTLRP and the post-2000 agrarian and conservation agenda. CBNRM would have been instrumental in tackling some of the challenges and insecurities that the land reform programme wrought, such as the massive degradation that is taking place on the country's tobacco lands (Zembe *et al*, 2014). In light of this observation, documentation of the colonial ICAs programme is critical as it adds to be body of knowledge, and to options, on how the Zimbabwe government, particularly after the general elections of mid-2018 and other administrations in the future, may implement their agrarian agenda to improve the agricultural sector drawing on experiences from the past. This, indeed, is the function of historical enquiry, for present generations not to repeat past mistakes, but to leverage on the past to improve the quality of life in the present and in the future.

Land reform and community-based participatory resource conservation

Zimbabwe's 'fast-track' land reform programme launched in the year 2000 after land-hungry villagers, led by veterans of the country's struggle for independence, has for the past eighteen years been a subject of controversy and debate among scholars. Two main schools of thought have characterised scholarship on the programme. One views it as President Mugabe's "land grab" – a disorderly process motivated by a combination of political considerations of the ruling Zimbabwe African National Union Patriotic Front (ZANU PF) in the wake of declining support and the birth of a vibrant opposition party (the Movement for Democratic Change (MDC) in September 1999), and a scheme meant to line the pockets of greedy, corrupt politicians. The second school of thought argues that the programme was an essential part of the *Chimurenga*, the struggle for decolonisation and self-determination, meant to redress colonially-induced land hunger among Africans (Mlambo, 2005).

Debates by the two schools of thought have mainly focused on three contested positions. The first school of thought focuses on what Neil Thomas and William Shaw have characterised as "ethical and moral" arguments for or against land reform (Thomas, 2003). The body of literature that takes this line of thought preoccupies itself with the ethics and morality of the programme; whether its central premise of seeking to address a colonial injustice still holds water, and whether there is any utility in addressing past injustices by resorting to revenge and retribution. Drawing inspiration from post-Apartheid South Africa's example, where the Mandela-led African National Congress government chose truth-telling and reconciliation over retribution and justice, this school of thought further questions the practicality and utility of the methodology used to redress the land question. The second body of literature examines the notion that the programme was "chaotic, violent and unplanned" (Chaumba *et al*, 2003).

On the basis of the argument that land reform was chaotic, scholarship in this school of thought has attempted to locate reasons why the government opted for 'chaos' and, in many instances, seems to conclude that considerations outside the land issue influenced the programme. Among such considerations are the emergence of a strong opposition, the Morgan Tsvangirai-led MDC in September 1999 and discontent among the war veterans who, under the leadership of the vibrant and charismatic Chenjerai Hunzvi, had managed to squeeze concessions from the regime such as heavy pay-outs and monthly pensions for their role in the liberation struggle. In addition to this, there was also the general loss of political support in urban areas due to the plunge of the economy, particularly after the twin miscalculations of unbudgeted payments to war veterans and the misadventure in the Democratic Republic of Congo, where the army's deployment in support of Laurent Kabila was a massive drain on the Zimbabwean national fiscus. The third body of literature enquires on whether the land reform programme has any direct causal relationship with low agricultural productivity on the farms, the decline of the national economy, the spike in political violence and polarisation, and American, European and Australian economic sanctions on Zimbabwe (Scoones *et al*, 2010).

While recent literature on the success of resettled farmers has created a lot of interest and refocused debate in current Zimbabwean agrarian discourses (Hanlon *et al*, 2013), there is also a vivacious body of literature that casts the land reform programme as having had a deleterious impact on the national economy. Examples of such literature include Maravanyika's work (2009) on the impact of agricultural activities of 'new farmers' on forest land in Mafungautsi State Forests and Mapedza (2003), and Mutimukuru-Maravanyika's (2010, 2011) ground-breaking research on sustainability in northwestern Zimbabwe. It is surprising, however, that there is not much scholarly research on the environmental impacts of the fast-track land reform programme on farmland in the Mafungautsi reserve. Meanwhile, research on state forests has shown that by 2006, the Mafungautsi State Forest had deteriorated rapidly especially in relation to soil erosion, water sources, small-game and indigenous trees, due to the recent farm invasions by, mostly, the local Shangwe people, who had earlier been evicted from the forest by the colonial regime and were now reclaiming their ancestral land (Mutimukuru 2004, Mapedza 2007, Mutimukuru-Maravanyika 2010, Maravanyika 2012, Maravanyika 2018).

Similarly, literature on the invasion of game parks and conservancies in general shows that the deterioration of natural resources in protected areas is taking place at an alarming rate (Ferreira 2004, Wolmer et al, 2004). Though no comprehensive study or survey has been carried out yet on resource conservation and preservation on former white farms where African farmers have been settled, there is significant suggestive evidence from press reports of the depletion of timber resources.

As the land reform was taking place, a number of community-based conservation projects were underway in the country. These projects focused on forestry and wildlife and not soil conservation and preservation. One such project was the Community Areas Management Programme for Indigenous Resources (CAMPFIRE), which James Murombedzi has characterized as perhaps one of Africa's most successful and progressive contemporary conservation and resource preservation initiatives (Murombedzi, 1999). The programme allowed African communities to participate in the management of wildlife in their localities, and to have a share in the benefits that accrued from it. The Adaptive Collaborative Management (ACM) programme in the forestry sector is yet another example (Mutimukuru-Maravanyika, 2010). ACM provided a framework for local communities residing on the margins of protected forests to co-manage the forests with the Forestry Commission, and to benefit from access to non-timber products such as broom and thatch grass, honey, mushrooms, access to the forest for grazing purposes and revenue from the sale of forest products.

The joint resource management programmes mentioned above demonstrate that community-based conservation can be a useful tool in ensuring the conservation and preservation of natural resources such as soils, water, trees and small game in the Zimbabwean countryside. They further reveal that co-management, when properly conceived and implemented can contribute to improved output, be it in agriculture, forestry, wildlife or soil management. The Bromley case study unravels how the colonial government set up a community-based conservation strategy to successfully deal with depressed agrarian conditions of the late 1920s and early 1930s.

Back to the past: the case for a colonial settler agrarian sector

The settler agricultural sector was, from the turn of the 20th century, viewed as an important basis upon which Southern Rhodesia could transform itself to prosperity. After the failure to achieve as much success as had been anticipated in the gold-mining sector, reality soon dawned on the British South Africa Company (BSAC) administration that there was no possibility of locating a "richer rand" than the one that had been discovered at Witwatersrand in South Africa in 1886 (Phimister, 1988). The BSAC turned to its other valuable asset, the land, and enunciated a White Agricultural Policy in 1908 (Machingaidze, 1980). Accompanying this move was the introduction of an array of measures to facilitate the growth of the white agricultural sector, among them the setting up of agricultural training institutions, demonstration farms, extension support as well as a coherent white settlement policy, a land bank to provide agricultural finance and promulgation of measures to suppress African agriculture and mobilise African labour for the sector, both from within and from without the colony's borders (Blank 2015; Palmer 1977; Kwashirai 2006).

Making the settler agricultural sector successful, having suffered a number of setbacks during the First World War of 1914 – 1918 related to lack of financing, marketing bottlenecks and an unstable world economy, rose on the colonial list of priorities after the end of First World War. The matter increased in importance from 1923 onwards, after the expiry of the British South Africa Company's Royal Charter. The expiry of the Charter precipitated a referendum, where the settler community in the colony was given the choice to either govern themselves under an arrangement that gave them a lot of autonomy from Britain, called the "Responsible Government" or to join the Union of South Africa as its fifth province (Mackenzi, 1978). The settlers chose self-rule. In other words, they elected to curve their own space under the sun where they would thrive on their own terms without suffocating superintendence from the colonial power, Britain. They found this to be a better option than to be swallowed and incorporated into a more established colony which carried a "bad class" of 'whites', as racially-chauvinistic Southern Rhodesian whites often viewed Afrikaners (Maravanyika, 2010).

The desire to establish a vibrant agricultural sector grew and reached proportions of a crusading zeal in the 1930s because of fatal blows inflicted by the Great Depression on the colony's economic sectors, which brought a lot of uncertainty in a young colony that had just passed its fortieth birthday (Report of the Committee of Enquiry into the Economic Position of the Agricultural Industry of Southern Rhodesia, 1934). A major highlight of this uncertainty was the migration of young white men who did not see much light ahead of the tunnel, and often did not share their parents' optimism about the future of the colony (Mlambo, 1998; Report of the Select Committee to Investigate the Problem of Unemployment in the Colony, 1932).

The unflinching desire to succeed stubbornly accelerated a little over a decade later as a new wave of white immigrants came to the colony after the Second World War, attracted by the tobacco boom (Maravanyika, 2014) and after the shock victory of the nationalistic Afrikaner political outfit, the National Party in the plebiscite of 1948, which wrung alarm bells in London and in her territorial possessions in southern Africa the region.

Putting the white capitalist agricultural sector on a sound footing was absolutely necessary considering the fact that upon colonisation of Southern Rhodesia, the majority of white people who ventured into settler farming were not of the right stamp in terms of their capital possession and farming skills. Rich, educated 'whites' seldom chose to be pioneers. They usually migrated to well-established colonies such as New Zealand, Australia and South Africa. This means that those the colony attracted were often poor fortune-seekers who anticipated opportunities for upward economic and social mobility mainly because of exaggerated news of riches comparable to the biblical King Solomon's mines in the new territory. In the case of Southern Rhodesia, such news was mainly propagated by commercial interests linked to the British South Africa Company (BSAC), a commercial entity which also doubled up as the government, to attract bigger numbers and, in the process, generate more money for the company and its shareholders. Significant white populations were viewed as the only basis upon which a sustainable colonial enterprise could be premised.

In the case of Southern Rhodesia, such exaggeration mainly had to do with the extent of mineral wealth lying in the colony's belly. This meant that the majority of those who ventured into farming needed a lot of support to transform them into successful farmers. It is in this context that the colonial government, led by Prime Minister Godfrey Huggins, prioritised uplifting the status of settler commercial agriculture from the late 1930s, a remarkable programme which wrought so much success that at the dawn of independence the sector had grown to leaps and bounds, to a point where it was capable of exporting huge volumes of cash crops and beef to Europe, and providing most of the region with grain, which earned it the moniker of "bread-basket of the region."

In the early 1940s Bromley, like the majority of farming districts in the former British colony, faced significant challenges related to soil erosion and rampant cutting down of trees. The massive cutting down of indigenous trees was the result of the tobacco boom that had commenced at the end of the Great Depression in the second half of the 1930s. Natural resource conservation was not a priority for the majority of settler farmers as they sought to make quick returns after a severe depression that had begun in the 1927/28 farming season and had left almost all farmers in debt and struggling to stay afloat. As this was happening, the colonial government of Godfrey Huggins was in the process of bringing all settler farming areas under a conservation framework.

Towards intensive conservation processes, 1934-44

The first half of the 1930s, when the world was battling with an unprecedented Depression, is a vantage point from which the agrarian crisis colonial Zimbabwe was facing prior to the launch of the ICAs movement in 1944 can be understood. A Committee appointed in 1932 to enquire into the problem of white unemployment in the colony found that it had reached alarming levels, especially among the white youths (Report of the Select Committee to Investigate the Problem of Unemployment in the Colony, 1932). White youths were leaving the farms for urban areas and, in some cases, leaving the country altogether in search of greener pastures abroad. In 1934, another Committee of Enquiry appointed to look into the state of the agricultural industry reported, "There can be no doubt that the farming community is facing a crisis... The issue that has to be faced is whether it is possible to build up a white colony on any basis other than a white agricultural population" (Report of the Committee of Enquiry into the Economic Position of the Agricultural Industry, 1934: 1).

Poor soil management was cited by the Committee as a major contributor to the poor state of affairs on the farms. The Committee recommended a number of measures to address the problem of soil erosion, which in its view was negatively affecting the agrarian sector. The Committee revealed the extent to which it believed that sound soil management amounted to a national priority by stating that; "…soil erosion [was] a national question and [was supposed to be] treated as such." The Committee (1934: 2). It further noted:

> What thirty years ago was good land and grew good crops… is now desert country, where white farmers can no longer make a living … the question of water conservation and the prevention of soil erosion should be in the forefront of the government's agricultural policy.

The effect of the agricultural crisis was felt in the political arena. Two premiers, Howard Moffat and George Mitchell, were voted out in 1933 by an overwhelmingly agrarian-based white electorate. Their fall was not entirely because of their failures though. They were unfortunate to preside over elections in an era where the Great Depression was biting so hard. As the economy screamed and livelihoods were shattered desperate voters, not considering the international nature of the economic slump, hoped that a change of guard at the top would automatically place the economy on the path to recover.

The election of October 1933 ushered Godfrey Huggins (later knighted Lord Malvern) and his Reform Party into office (Murray, 1970). Huggins, a surgeon and a farmer, rose to power mainly because of his two attributes. As a medical doctor he was renowned for his sterling work together with his colleagues in the medical fraternity in fighting the influenza epidemic after the First World War. As a farmer, his passion for agriculture was well-known (Gelfand, 1971). He never settled in town, but chose to permanently reside at his Craig Farm on the outskirts of the capital, Salisbury. Huggins' campaign was bolstered by his in-depth knowledge of the agricultural crisis and his eloquent articulation of a programme of action to rescue the sector and the economy at large, which excited a huge portion of the settler community and consequently delivered to him the premiership (Gelfand and Gann, 1964).

The Huggins administration embarked on a number of interventions to rescue the ailing agrarian sector. It introduced the Farmers Debt Adjustment programme in 1935 to advance loans to farmers who had saddled themselves with debts they were unable to settle (NAZ, S1215/1085/4, Farmers Debt Adjustment Act, 1935, Correspondence). A fund was established in 1938 to enable farmers to finance their operations on easy repayment terms (NAZ, S987/1, Oral Evidence to the Natural Resources Board Farming Enquiry). The government also negotiated the Tripartite Labour Agreement with Northern Rhodesia and Nyasaland in 1936 to ameliorate the colony's agrarian labour shortage (Mtisi, 1994). The government also enacted the Compulsory Labour Act in 1942 to provide for forcible recruitment of Africans to work on farms during the Second World War in response to a severe food deficit (Johnson, 1992). Lastly, the Huggins administration set up control boards in the 1930s and marketing boards in the 1940s to enhance the marketing of the colony's major agricultural products (Rukuni, 1993) and appointed the Natural Resources Commission in 1938 to enquire into the status of the colony's resources (Report of the Commission into the Preservation of Natural Resources of the Colony, April 1939), among other measures.

The Natural Resources Commission's report of 1939 further highlighted the parlous state of the agrarian sector. It revealed that the colony's prime agricultural land had been deeply impoverished by erosion of the soil, and some of it "ruined beyond repair" (NRC, 1939). The Commission recommended that the government enact the requisite legislation and establish a statutory board to superintend over natural resources in the colony. Following the Commission's report, the government promulgated the Natural Resources Act in August 1941 "to make provision for the conservation and improvement of the natural resources of the colony and other matters incidental thereto" (Statute Law of Southern Rhodesia, 1941. The Natural Resources Act, 1941, Proclamation Number 19 of 1941, p. 349). The Act provided for the formation of the Natural Resources Board whose mandate was:

> to exercise general supervision over natural resources, to stimulate by propaganda and such other means as it may deem expedient a public interest in the conservation and improvement of natural resources, to recommend to the Government the nature of legislation it deemed necessary for the proper conservation, use and improvement of natural resources.

Sections 27 to 33 of the Act provided for the formation of ICAs in all the colony's settler farming districts (Statute Law of Southern Rhodesia, 1941. The Natural Resources Act, 1941, Proclamation Number 19 of 1941, p. 350).

Bromley before the ICAs movement

By the 1940s, Bromley had established itself as a relatively prosperous district, thanks to a tobacco boom, first in the mid-1920s and then from the second half of the 1930s onwards. Though successful as a tobacco growing district, Bromley had not prospered at the same level as other white farming districts in the Marandellas region, such as Virginia and Wenimbe-Ruzawi (NAZ, F450/6, Bromley ICA, File 1). Bromley had both big and small farms.

The small farms were mainly a result of sub-divisions, as many farmers cut up and sold portions of their farms in order to remain afloat during the Depression. There were 33 sub-divisions south of the railway line, all of them not exceeding 500 acres in size (The Conservation Officer, R. K. Harvey's Report for 1946). Because of Bromley's proximity to Salisbury, the colony's capital, the majority of these small-holdings were held by people who were not involved in agriculture to any significant scale, but who desired to stay out of the city. Some of the buyers worked in Salisbury, while others held the properties as country homes where they could go to rest during vacations. As for the holdings where farming was being carried out this was on a small-scale because of the size of the farms. There were also big farms in Bromley. The majority of these were located north of the Salisbury-Umtali railway line, while the majority of subdivisions were in the south of the railway line. This zoning pattern, where small holdings were on the south of the line of rail, while big farms were on the northern side, was probably determined by the market, as the settler who bought the small sub-divisions preferred the southern side which gave them closer proximity to the main thoroughfare to Salisbury, as well as the railway siding. Farmers on the northern side ventured deeper into the interior, away from the Salisbury-Umtali road and therefore further away from Salisbury and Marandellas ((NAZ, F450/6, Bromley ICA, File 1, The Conservation Officer, R. K. Harvey's Reports).

Tobacco had become the prominent crop in Bromley in the second half of the 1930s. While some Bromley farmers may have attempted tobacco production in the 1920s, market conditions discouraged mass uptake, especially after the fall of the tobacco market in the 1927/28 cropping season. From that time, till the country began to recover from the Great Depression, tobacco farming nose-dived. This situation altered drastically in the second half of the 1930s. As the crop increased in popularity among farmers, more and more land was cleared and put under tobacco. Tobacco production increased, while maize production declined.

Increased production of tobacco was because the crop fetched higher prices in comparison with maize, whose price was controlled by the state from the early 1930s. With the genesis of maize control from 1931, there was general dissatisfaction among farmers with maize pricing policies (see NAZ, S881/181/3979, Report of the Commission of Enquiry into the Maize Industry of Southern Rhodesia, NAZ, S1180/2/51 [5], Maize Enquiry Committee Report, 1930, NAZ, S1180/1, Oral Evidence to The Maize Enquiry Committee and the Maize Control Amendment Act, Number 17, 1934). In 1931, Britain had left the gold standard, a move that resulted in the devaluation of the sterling in the second half of the 1930s (Eichengreen and P. Temin, 1988). The depreciation of the sterling fuelled Southern Rhodesia's tobacco boom. This was because British trade with the sterling areas increased as Britain traded more with her colonies in response to the dollar crunch.

Apart from the devaluation of the sterling, the Second World War brought with it a huge market for the colony's tobacco. Tobacco consumption naturally increased because men fighting for the Empire consumed more and more tobacco at the war front. Another dynamic was that the war prolonged the dollar crunch, which necessitated the Empire to be more inward looking in terms of its trade (Scott, 1952). It became a priority for Britain to confine the bulk of her trade within the Sterling area. This meant that the colony's tobacco had a ready market in Britain, regardless of its quality.

Tobacco farming in Bromley and other districts took place without much attention to conservation measures. Because of poor farming methods on tobacco lands, hundreds of tobacco farms in the late 1930s and early 1940s were infested by nematodes, while production was "gravely reduced" (Phimister, 1986). The farmers' attitude towards the soil was unhealthy as they "did not care what happens... as long as [they] can get as much wealth out of the land as quickly as possible" (Southern Rhodesia Legislative Assembly Debates, I June, 1938). Farmers' disregard for soil conservation on their tobacco lands generally resulted in a scenario where Mashonaland, of which Bromley was part, "contained thousands of acres of wreckage by the start of the 1940s" (Phimister, 1986). Tobacco cultivation demanded the application of soil conservation measures and the setting up of timber plantations on the farms to ensure a source of wood energy for flue-curing. In the absence of these measures, soil erosion and depletion and massive deforestation took place.

By the mid-1950s, all of the colony's farming districts had been covered by the programme. Though settler commercial farm lands cannot be regarded as common property resources as they were privately owned, the ICAs programme put in place a framework for collaboration, joint-monitoring and joint-management at a local level to ensure water and soil conservation. In his examination of the Virginia ICA in the 1990s, David Hughes argues that community-based intensive conservation practices helped farmers to create "mutuality with the land", which led to the evolution of what he calls an "environmentalist form of identity" (Hughes, 2006)

Colonial natural resources legislation and the introduction of ICAs

An ICA was a farming area, usually composed of around 100 settler farmers or farms. African farmers were excluded from the ICAs. The programme was tailor-made for the benefit of settler farmers (and later, though in a limited way, African purchase areas (Shutt, 2002). The ICAs were mandated by the Natural Resources Act of 1938 to:

> ...inaugurate and undertake the construction of works and other measures for soil and water conservation and improvement of soil and water supplies in [their area, generally to cooperate with and assist the [Natural Resources] Board in carrying out [the] objectives and purposes of [the] Act, construct and maintain such works as it may deem necessary for soil and water conservation and improvement and to superintend or perform, or enter into contracts for the superintendence or performance of all such acts, matters and things as are incidental to soil and water conservation, maintenance or improvement.

Once an ICA was created, the farmers elected a committee which led the district's conservation programme in collaboration with the conservation officer for the area. The Natural Resources Act spelt out the procedure for the demarcation of an ICA. It could only be declared in a particular farming district or area once at least two thirds of farmers in the proposed district had agreed in writing that their farms needed rehabilitation work (The Natural Resources Act, 1941). This was a very important aspect of the programme, as it was based on farmers agreeing to participate and not on force.

Belonging to the ICA movement was voluntary. This was because of a number of factors. The main one was that the Huggins Government, which to a large extent comprised of people with vested interests in agriculture, did not want to be on a collision course with the settler farming community, especially since farmers constituted an important political constituency in the colony. The Natural Resources Bill was presented to parliament at a time when the world had plunged into the Second World War. Southern Rhodesia joined the war on the side of the United Kingdom and the Allied powers. Among its other contributions - such as "(feeding) Italian prisoners of war" - colonial Zimbabwe was also assigned to provide food for the war effort (Phimister, 1986). Because the government was mobilising farmers to produce more food to meet increasing domestic demand (and for the war effort), officials did not want conflict with the farmers over the conservation programme.

An attractive sweetener was offered to farmers who elected to become part of the ICAs movement. They were eligible for state subsidies, loans, grants-in aid and other government support. It is because of the availability of such incentives for settler agriculture that JoAnn McGregor (2005) has observed that, "For settlers, conservation entailed financial and other incentives: for Africans, it entailed coercion and punitive restrictions on resource use. From 1948, when the Department of Conservation and Extension (CONEX) was created under the Directorship of Charles Murray, ICAs became an even more attractive proposition as they received preferential treatment from CONEX and its conservation officers (CONEX, 1949).

As already stated, had to voluntarily apply to be co-opted into the programme. The Act stated that:

271

If the owners of land in any area wish on their own initiative to undertake the construction of works and other measures for the conservation or improvement of natural resources in such area, they may petition the Minister in writing to declare such area to be an intensive conservation area. Such petition shall clearly describe the boundaries of the said area and shall contain such other particulars as may be prescribed by regulation (The Natural Resources Act, Proclamation Number 19 of 1941, p. 358-9).

Upon receipt of an application for the declaration of an ICA from a group of farmers, the Minister was required to publish that petition in the media for the public to examine it. This was done so that, in the event that the petition had been prepared and sent to the Ministry of Agriculture and Lands without adequate consultation in the concerned farming district, landowners whose farms were located in the area described in the application, but did not wish to be part of the proposed ICA could disagree in writing and give reasons for their not being satisfied with the petition for their inclusion in the programme. In the event that two thirds of landowners in the proposed ICA agreed with the proposition, the ICA was, by Notice in the Government Gazette, declared by the Minister of Agriculture and Lands (NAZ, S989, The Natural Resources Act, 1941: 7).

While the first ICA was declared at Inyazura (renamed Nyazura after independence) in 1944, it was not until the mid-1950s that all settler farming districts were covered by the ICAs programme. The delay was because in almost all farming districts there was resistance from some of the farmers. The major reason for resistance was that farmers were not satisfied that the programme would be carried out without, at some point, the state turning around to coerce them to use more and more of their own resources to finance conservation work (such as contour ridging, crop rotation, soil conservation, tree planting, the fencing off of grazing areas, and animal husbandry). This concern was understandable, considering that this programme was introduced in a context where, less than a decade from 1944, the majority of the farmers were bankrupt and saddled with debt.

Such a situation resulted in farmers fearing for a return to the crisis years where, in the absence of a government bail-out, a vast number of farmers were on the brink of either losing their farms to creditors or closing shop altogether on their own accord because of viability challenges. Apart from fearing that they would be forced to embark on a costly soil conservation programme, many farmers also questioned the ability and competence of conservation officers in the country. This was partly because the Department of Agriculture and Lands had for many years been understaffed, and this staff shortage impacted negatively on the provision of extension services (NAZ, S989, The Natural Resources Act, 1941, p. 7) Farmers were only acting true to their nature. As observed by D. Aylen, an agricultural official responsible for combating soil erosion, "the farmer is naturally a conservative person who, before he spends any money wishes to see with his own eyes that the proposed remedy is a certain cure and, therefore, worthwhile" (NAZ, A1510/32, D. Aylen, Erosion Policy, The Dangers of Soil Erosion and Methods of Prevention).

The birth of the Bromley ICA

By August 1941, when the Natural Resources Act was promulgated, soil erosion in the Bromley District was high (NAZ, F450/6, The Bromley ICA, File 1, The Conservation Officer, R. K. Harvey's Report for 1946). A few farmers had initiated soil conservation measures on their farms, but the percentage of land under the plough that had been protected was low. Urgent soil conservation measures were needed on the majority of farms in the area. The conservation officer's Report for 1946 reveals that almost all of the district's tobacco lands needed protection. The district also required better pasture management practices to be put in place and for paddocking to be undertaken. Tree planting was also necessary as by 1941 only four percent of the total area under cultivation was covered by trees. This situation was worsened by the fact that the area did not have any forest reserves. This means that there was need for afforestation work on the farms, better animal husbandry methods and, more importantly, soil conservation work.

In the early 1940s, a number of Bromley farmers, through the Bromley Farmers' Association showed interest in having their area declared an ICA. This was because they anticipated that their farms would benefit considerably from subsidized work done by government tractor and road construction units and also from government funding in the form of subsidies, grants-in-aid and loans. The farmers thought that their farms would also benefit from provision of equipment by the government for the improvement of their lands. Most of their information about the benefits of joining the ICAs programme came from agricultural officers who, in a bid to market the ICAs programme, utilised every opportunity when they came into contact with farmers to provide information about the programme. Apart from the publicity given to the ICAs in newspapers, particularly *The Rhodesia Herald*, rapport with farmers at individual and community levels - such as at Farmers' Association meetings - was an effective tool (NAZ F450/6, The Bromley ICA File 1. Unless otherwise stated, all following references are from this file).

Farmers in Bromley sent their petition to the Minister of Agriculture and Lands for their area to be declared an ICA in June 1946. Upon receipt of the petition, the Department of Agriculture and Lands published the petition in *The Rhodesia Herald* on 19 July 1946. A number of farmers responded to the petition. However, some objected to their area being declared an ICA. Four main reasons were given for this opposition by some farmers. Some farmers were unhappy with the fact that there was no adequate consultation prior to the submission of the petition. There were also doubts among farmers about whether the Ministry of Agriculture and Lands had the capacity to roll out a programme of the magnitude envisioned by the Natural Resources Act. Other farmers needed more time to familiarise with the Act and to understand what it implied for them while still others objected because of the exclusion of their farms from the map of the proposed ICA.

The impression that agricultural officials were not competent enough to carry out a soil conservation programme of the scale envisioned by the Natural Resources Act was a result of poor staffing in the Irrigation Department. In addition to past omissions, a government Tractor Unit deployed to the area to carry out soil protection work between May and September 1946 had carried out unsatisfactory work, adding to the notion that the Ministry of

Agriculture could not carry out the programme. The work done by the Tractor Unit was not up to standard, as the repair work that needed to be done was not done meticulously, with the effect that many farmers were left unhappy with both the unit and Harvey, the conservation officer assigned to the area to supervise the construction of soil protection works by government tractor units (Letter from the Secretary, Bromley Farmers' Association, to the Secretary, Department of Agriculture and Lands, dated 12 January 1947). This development reduced farmers' enthusiasm to joining the ICA programme as Harvey, the man who had made the recommendation to the Bromley Farmers Union that their district stood to immensely benefit from the ICAs programme, had proven his inability to supervise such work.

Because close to fifty farmers out of 106 landowners in Bromley objected to the ICA, declaration of the ICA was postponed. Because of this, the original notice published in the Government Gazette of the 24th of May 1946 had to be cancelled as developments on the ground had rendered it not actionable. A new notice was subsequently published on 5 July 1946, after the petition had been revised. After a massive blitz by the Department of Agriculture and Lands and Bromley farmers, who were in support of the ICA, to persuade the farmers to withdraw their objections, a number of farmers withdrew their letters of objection, leaving only 33 objectors. This, therefore, met the constitutional requirement that the ICA would be adopted once two thirds of landowners had agreed to the declaration of an ICA (Letter from the Director of Irrigation, to the Secretary, Department of Agriculture and Lands, dated 20 January 1947). The Bromley ICA was duly declared on the 11th of April 1947 and its first elected Committee inaugurated on 2 August, 1947. L. C. E. Collingwood was appointed the first secretary of the Bromley Soil Conservation Area Committee. On 2 August 1947 the Committee was given its first grant-in-aid to meet its initial expenses.

The Bromley ICA at work

The Bromley ICA was made up of 106 farmers. This was not the first time these farmers had been involved in an organisation focussed on the furtherance of their interests. They had been, since the end of the First World War, members of the Bromley Farmers' Association. The formation of the Bromley ICA added another dimension to their co-operation. Once two-thirds of farmers in a particular farming district consented to their area being declared an ICA and the ICA was gazetted, farmers became subject to the collective decisions made at ICA meetings. Members elected an ICA committee, which was responsible for the ICA's day-to-day operation. The Committee and the conservation officer for the area, made frequent inspections of farms under their jurisdiction and recommended the construction of conservation works where they were needed.

In the event that the farmer could not afford to pay for the projects, the Committee approved farmers' applications for government loans, subsidies and grants. The ICA committee could also construct conservation works for free for poor farmers, using resources from profits it would have made by leasing its equipment such as tractor units and dam-building equipment to neighbouring ICAs and schools such as Peterhouse and Diggleford, among others. There were, however, instances when the ICA committee had to contend with lack of cooperation from some farmers. From 1953 the Bromley ICA had a problem, for example, from J. Nel of Belmont farm, who refused to construct contour ridges on his farm. It was only after he was reported to the Natural Resources Board in 1954 that he began to cooperate, fearing prosecution by the Natural Resources Court.

The Bromley ICA was formed at a time when the colony was experiencing a huge food deficit and insecurity. The Bromley ICA Committee worked hard to encourage increased food production in the district. Increased urbanisation as a result of the growth in the colony's industries, particularly the manufacturing sector, and drought such as the devastating 1942 drought, the obligation to house and feed Italian prisoners of war and to feed Empire forces during the Second World War. With increased production of tobacco at the expense of maize in the 1940s (Report of the Secretary, Department of Agriculture and Lands, 31 December 1946: 13), the government sought to put in place measures that would encourage food production. One such measure was the requirement under the Land Settlement Scheme of 1944 to have ex-servicemen produce food on a certain percentage of their land (Phimister, 1986). With the formation of the ICAs, ICA Committees were also tasked, apart from the conservation drive, to push for more food production.

The Bromley ICA Committee encouraged every farmer in Bromley to produce adequate food to satisfy their requirements on their farms. Apart from spreading awareness to farmers that it was not in the best interest of the country to import food, the Committee also talked about the role of food production in the industrialisation of the colony (Bromley ICA and Food Advisory Committee, Newsletter Number 5, 26 April 1950). The food production gospel was an integral component of the conservation movement, as the ICAs worked to promote sound farming methods and to protect the soil from erosion. The ICAs encouraged increased production. The cost of food imported from dollar countries increased in 1949 after the sterling devaluation and, in response to this, the ICAs increased their calls for the production of more food. At the 1949 Annual Congress of the Rhodesia National Farmers' Union, farmers were encouraged to produce "more food, more food, and still more food." In Bromley there were notable increases in food production, with the result that in 1951, four years after the formation of the Bromley ICA, the district got the first prize at the Agricultural Show's Inter-District Exhibit Competition.

The district also did well in terms of pasture management. This was a result of its being close to the Grasslands Government Experimental Station in Marandellas. The district's pasture management efforts were aided by J. A. H Hughes, a farmer in the district who donated a portion of land at his Farm, Bain's Hope, to the ICA for the establishment of a grass nursery. The ICA Committee encouraged all farmers to utilise the piece of land to sharpen their knowledge, and to get seed for planting grass on their farms. The ICA Committee encouraged the farmers to, "plant grass to restore the soil and at the same time turn it into milk and beef!" (NAZ F450/6, NAZ F450/7, Bromley ICA Files 1 and 2). The ICA also employed African fire rangers to patrol the district and to give an account of how every fire started. The rangers, attested as Special African Constables in firefighting, were tasked to;

> ...warn the natives about veld fires, cultivation of stream banks, digging out holes in contours and other conservation matters. They [were] to report veld fires, and to give assistance in putting them out. They [were] to arrest any native found unlawfully setting fire to the veld... (NAZ F450).

The ICA Committee also encouraged the preservation of natural timber through disseminating propaganda in its monthly newsletters.

Farmers were encouraged to avoid indiscriminate cutting down of trees and to plant exotic trees such as gums for tobacco curing, as well as a transition from the use of wood by converting to use of coal in their furnaces (Bromley District Intensive Conservation Area and Food Advisory Committee Newsletter, November 1950). The ICA utilised grants-in-aid, loans and other government grants to purchase tractor units for the construction of conservation works on farms and dam-building. The ICA's first dam-building unit, established in February 1949, had by July 1949 built eight small dams, with a capacity of three million gallons of water (Bromley ICA and Food Advisory Committee Newsletter, 29 July 1949). In its September 1949 Newsletter, the Committee noted:

> The need for water conservation is becoming obvious. Small dams in vleis not only provide water for stock, but by raising the water table and holding back run off, immensely benefit the vleis and the water supplies of the country as a whole (Bromley ICA and Food Advisory Committee, Newsletter, 12 September 1949).

At the end of 1949 the Unit had built 13 inland dams. At the end of the Federation of Southern Rhodesia, Northern Rhodesia and Nyasaland in 1963, over 110 dams had been built in Bromley, with a combined carrying capacity of one and half billion litres of water (Bromley ICA Newsletters, 1948-62).

In addition to the dams, aerial surveys and farm plans were carried out on all farms in the district. Farm planning involved the compilation of data and drawing up of detailed maps of each farm. The first map showed the land use patterns at the farm, the second classified the type of land on the farm while the third showed "recommended modification to existing protection layouts and future layouts for virgin lands – also potential dam site..." (Minutes, Meeting of Bromley ICA Committee, 5 April 1956: 3)

Farm planning paved the way for the deployment of units to construct works such as contour ridges and storm drains, and, in collaboration with the Melfort Road Council, to construct farm roads. The ICA was successful in putting pressure on farmers who would not on their own have carried out conservation work on their farms. Government funding for some of these projects was a useful carrot to lure reluctant farmers into adopting conservation initiatives. The elected ICA committee also had the power to report farmers who failed to comply with the Natural Resources Board's instructions. The Board had a Natural Resources Court, with the same powers as the magistrate's court, to prosecute offenders.

Community-based conservation in agriculture: Some lessons for the Zimbabwean agrarian sector

Elinor Ostrom has argued that if local communities are given the opportunity to participate and play a leading role in resource management and development programmes in their localities, it becomes possible to overcome the "tragedy of the commons" (Hardin, 1968) where individual greed, selfishness and the profit motive impede collective management of common property resources (resources that belong to and are used in common at community level). A situation where the profit motive superseded the need for conservation on the farms existed before the launch of ICAs. Ian Phimister (1986: 265) has aptly captured this mindset at the beginning of the 1940s when he says:

> Many farms had an air of impermanence. When they changed hands, 'windows ... and everything that could possibly be turned up' were removed from them. Land was simply abandoned after two successive crops, stripped of tree cover and exposed to the elements

with the result that Mashonaland contained 'thousands of acres of wreckage...

The ICAs programme was mooted to address the high turnover and environmental degradation on the settler farms. The majority of farmers needed a change in the way things were being done in the colony. Farmers' Associations had, since the 1920s called for the state to take more action to ensure that there was sound soil management on the farms (The Rhodesia Herald, Friday February 19, 1924: 18).

For Ostrom (2000), certain "design principles" are an essential pre-requisite to successful implementation of community-based conservation projects. Table 1 below lists some of Ostrom's design principles:

Table 1: Elinor Ostrom's "design principles"

Design Principles
• Rules that clearly define who has rights to use a resource (clarity of rules)
• Congruence between the rules that assign benefits and costs
• Possibility/flexibility to modify rules
• Monitoring and conformance (a monitoring mechanism)
• Graduated sanctions for offenders
• Conflict resolution mechanisms using clearly defined rules
• Recognition of rules by external users
• Application of rules, both across and up and down hierarchical levels

ICAs fit into Ostrom's framework in a number of ways. The Natural Resources Act clearly defined how an ICA could be formed. Joining the programme was voluntary. Two-thirds of farmers in a particular farming district had to agree to have their area declared an ICA. Once declared, the procedure concerning the appointment of an ICA committee, its functions, the nature of assistance and loans it could get from the state was also clearly stated. The presence of conservation legislation meant that the process could be enforced utilising legal instruments. Rules were clear and enforceable, offenders could be referred to the NRB, which had a court with magisterial powers, and monitoring mechanisms were also present in the form of the elected ICA committee, conservation officers, the NRB and the Ministry of Agriculture and Lands. The ICAs fit into the description of "communities" as they were set up in existing farming districts, where a sense of community had been fostered by farmers long before the 1940s, for example through their Farmers' Associations (Letter from E. O. Martyn of Danga Lima Farm, Bromley, to the Secretary, the Department of Agriculture and Lands, Salisbury, dated 17 June, 1946).

The ICAs strengthened this sense of community as ICA meetings, field days, farming competitions, the sharing of ICA equipment, government loans, grants and grants-in-aid, among others which, all acted as valuable social capital that facilitated and fostered closer community relations. Though some farmers initially resisted being included in the programme, there is no evidence of any farmer who explicitly said that they did not want to construct conservation measures on their farms. The resistance was because of lack of clarity about what the Act stipulated, and what such stipulations implied to the farmers. Resistance was, as already mentioned, also out of fear that the programme could involve pumping out huge amounts of money from farmers' coffers. Farmers, having reeled on the edge of bankruptcy and indebtedness in the 1930s, did not countenance other financial uncertainties.

A number of important lessons can be drawn from the ICAs for the benefit of the Zimbabwean agrarian sector today. The first is the vitality of effective legal instruments for conservation work, as was the case with the Natural Resources Act of 1941. In post-colonial Zimbabwe, this exists as the Environmental Management Act Chapter 20: 27 of 2000 (The Environmental Management Act, Chapter 20: 27 as amended in June 2005). The deficiency of the Act is that Sections 133 and 134 allocate the responsibility for conservation in communal and resettlement areas to rural district councils, as does the Rural District Councils Act, Chapter 29: 13 of 2005. This presents a challenge in that most rural district councils do not have the capacity and competence to carry out such tasks. Another dimension to this is that from 2000 to 2013, some rural district councils are controlled by the opposition parties such as the

Movement for Democratic Change, whose land policy differs with that of the ruling ZANU-PF.

Other lessons that can be learnt from the experience of the ICAs are that conservation policies cannot be implemented on a one-size-fits-all basis. They must take into account the opinions, aspirations and circumstances of the local people. In the case of the ICAs, the programme ensured that the majority of landowners in any farming district gave their informed consent to the declaration of an ICA in their district. This was the case of Bromley. In addition to this, they participated in the election of their ICA committee, where people who were respected by their community, and who were known for excelling on their own farms, were elected to attend to the day-to-day operations of the programme. In this way, the ICA committee performed an adequate role as far as each farm and its conservation requirements were concerned.

Local people participate effectively when they have "ownership" of their projects, and when they stand to benefit in tangible or visible ways. In the case of Bromley, farmers soon came to realise that the benefits of the programme outweighed the costs incurred. Because the ICA got government loans to buy its own tractor units and dam construction equipment, it was able to construct mechanical works and dams at a cheaper cost in comparison to market prices. Conservation works and dams, apart from helping increase agricultural output, also made the farms beautiful, scenic "Edens" (Hughes, 2005). A tourist in then Rhodesia described the farms in 1969 in this way:

> To the traveller, Rhodesia's countryside is a panorama spangled with the flashing mirrors of a thousand lakes and dams. From the vast reaches of Lake Kariba to the humblest farm pond, every one of these is a legacy of the ingenuity and enterprise of generations of Rhodesians. Nature formed Rhodesia without lakes; each one of them has been built by the hand of man (Hughes 2005: 277).

The role of the state is also important in the implementation of conservation programmes.

The ICAs were well supported with access to loans for the purchase of equipment, grants-in-aid and subsidies. They also had the support of conservation officers. A major challenge faced in the new farming areas in Zimbabwe is the lack of security as the vast majority of farmers do not have title or leases. This creates uncertainty, which discourages people from making long-term investments in soil improvement. The state needs to address the issue of security of land tenure, and to support conservation programmes financially and epistemologically as well as from a manpower point of view by appointing more conservation officers.

Conclusion

The creation of ICAs on settler farms is a major benchmark in conservation in Zimbabwe's agrarian history. This chapter has shown that the ICAs in general and the Bromley ICA were among the first attempts at community-based soil and water management projects in the country, contrary to the view by many natural resources management scholars who have argued that community-based management (co-management or joint-management as it is sometimes called) is a phenomenon of the 1980s. The ICAs transformed the ailing settler agricultural sector to a success story. They helped conserve natural resources that were rapidly degrading in these areas. The fast-track land reform programme has brought a new reality to former commercial farms.

Many "new farmers", as they are called in Zimbabwe, have moved into former settler farms. A land audit is yet to be carried out to determine who exactly is settled on which piece of land and their type of land-use. To guarantee food security, it is necessary for conservation programmes to be introduced in these new resettlement areas to arrest land degradation before parts of the former commercial farming areas are transformed into wreckage by poor farming methods. In coming up with this, there is no need to reinvent the wheel. It is possible to learn invaluable lessons from what has been done with the ICAs in the past, and to improve on such initiatives to come up with appropriate interventions. The agrarian sector and post-independence Zimbabwe can be turned again to a net exporter of surplus food, as was the case in the 1980s.

References

AFFCOMNET, "Zimbabwe's Forests Go up in Smoke amid Energy Crisis", http://www.affcomnet.org/index.php?option=com_content&view=article&id=13: zimbabwes-forests-go-up-in-smoke-amid-energy-crisis&catid=9&Itemid=101.

Africa News, "Zimbabwe: Indigenous Tress under Siege from Farmers", http://www.africanews.com/site/Zimbabwe_Indigenous_trees_under_siege_from_farmers/list_messages/41584.

Berkes, F. (2004) "Rethinking Community-Based Conservation", *Conservation Biology*, 18 (3): 621-630.

Bromley ICA and Food Advisory Committee, Newsletters.

Campbell, L. M. and Vainio-Mattila, A. (2003) Participatory Development and Community-based Conservation: Opportunities Missed or Lessons Learned?, *Human Ecology*, 31 (3): 417-437.

Chaumba, J., Scoones, I. and Wolmer, W. (2003) From Jambanja to Planning: the Reassertion of Theocracy in Land Reform in South-Eastern Zimbabwe, *Journal of Modern African Studies*, 41 (2): 533-554.

Child, G. (1996) The Role of Community-based Wild Resource Management in Zimbabwe, *Bio-Diversity and Conservation*, 5 (3): 355-367.

Department of Conservation and Extension (CONEX), (1949) Annual Report for the Year, p. 1.

Dzingirai, V. and Breen, C. (Eds) (2005) Confronting the Crisis in Community Conservation: Case Studies from Southern Africa, Durban, University of KwaZulu-Natal.

Eichengreen, B. and Temin, P. (2000) The Gold Standard and the Great Depression, *Contemporary European History*, 9 (2): 183-207.

Ferreira, S. (2004) Problems Associated with Tourism Development in Southern Africa: The Case of Transfrontier Conservation Areas, *GeoJournal* (60): 301-310.

Gann, L. H. and Gelfand, M. (1964) Huggins of Rhodesia: The Man and His Country, London, George Allen and Unwin.

Gelfand, M., and Ritchken, J. (1973) Godfrey Martin Huggins, Viscount Malvern 1883 – 1971: His Life and Work, *Central African Journal of Medicine*, Salisbury.

Gibson, C. (1999) Politicians and Poachers: The Political Economy of Wildlife Policy in Africa, Cambridge University Press: Cambridge.

Hamilton, J. D. (1998) The Role of the International Gold Standard in Propagating the Great Depression, *Contemporary Economic Policy*, 6 (2): 67-89.

Hanlon, J., Manjengwa, J., and Smart, T. (2013) *Zimbabwe Takes Back its Land*, Kumarian Press: Virginia.

Hardin, G. (1972) The Tragedy of the Commons, *Science*, 162 (3859): 1243 – 1248.

Hughes, D. M. (2006) Hydrology of Hope: Farm Dams, Conservation and Whiteness in Zimbabwe, *American Ethnologist*, 33 (2): 269-287.

IOL, Can Learn from Zim's Flourishing Farms", http://www.iol.co.za/mercury/we-can-learn-from-zim-s-flourishing-farms-1.1508335#.UZoADKYaJMs;/ http://mg.co.za/article/2013-04-05-00-coming-back-from-the-brink-of-disaster.

Jackson, A. (2006) *The British Empire and the Second World War*, Hambledon Continuum: London.

Johnson, D. (1992) Settler Farmers and Coerced Labour in Southern Rhodesia, 1936-46, *Journal of African History*, 33 (1): 111-128.

Kwashirai, V. (2006) Dilemmas in Conservationism in Colonial Zimbabwe, 1890 – 1930, Conservation and Society, 4 (4): 541 – 561.

Mapedza, E. (2007) Forestry Policy in Colonial and Post-Colonial Zimbabwe: Continuity and Change, *Journal of Historical Geography*, 33 (4) 833-851.

Mapedza, E., Wright, J. and Fawcett, R. (2003) An Investigation of Land Cover Change in Mafungautsi Forest, Zimbabwe, using GIS and Participatory Mapping, *Applied Geography*, 23 (1): 1-21.

Maravanyika, S. and Mutimukuru-Maravanyika, T. (2009) Resource-based Conflict at a Local Level in a Changing National Environment: The Case of Zimbabwe's Mafungautsi State Forest, *African Economic History*, 37 (2009): 129-150.

Maravanyika, S. (2010) A Failed Neo-Britain: Demography and the Labour Question in Colonial Zimbabwe", *African Nebula*, 1 (1): 18 – 33.

Matose, F. and Maravanyika-Mutimukuru, T. (2009) Squatting as a Means of Establishing Authority over Forest Land in Zimbabwe: A Missing Dimension to Land Reform", http: //0-www.indiana.edu.innopac.up.ac.za/~wow4/papers/matose_wow4.pdf, 2009.

Mawere, M. (2015) *Humans, Other Beings and the Environment: Harurwa (Edible Stinkbugs) and Environmental Conservation in Southeastern Zimbabwe*, Cambridge Scholars Publishing: Cambridge.

McGregor, J. (2005) Conservation, Control and Ecological Change: The Politics and Ecology of Colonial Conservation in Shurugwi, Zimbabwe", *Environment and History*, 1 (2005): 257-279.

Mlambo, A. S. (2005) Land Grab' or 'Taking Back Stolen Land': The Fast-Track Land Reform Process in Zimbabwe in Historical Perspective", *History Compass*, 3 (1): 1-21.

Mlambo, A. S. (1998) Building a White Man's Country: Aspects of White Immigration into Rhodesia up to World War II, *Zambezia*, 25 (2): 123 – 146.

Mlambo, A. S. (1999) Some are more White than Others: Racial Chauvenism as a factor in Rhodesian Immigration Policy, 1890 - 1963", *Zambezia*, 27 (2): 139 – 160.

Mtisi, J. P. (1994) The Political Economy of Labour in Southern Africa, *Department of Economic History Seminar Series*, University of Zimbabwe.

Murombedzi, J. C. (1999) Development and Stewardship in Zimbabwe's CAMPFIRE Programme, *Journal of International Development*, 11 (2): 287-293.

Murombedzi, J. C. (1994) The Dynamics of Conflict in Environmental Management Policy in the Context of the Community Areas Management Programme for Indigenous Resources (CAMPFIRE), *PhD thesis*, University of Zimbabwe.

Murphree, M. W. (2002) Protected Areas and the Commons, *Common Property Resource Digest*, 60, (2002): 1-3.

Murray, D. J. (1970) *The Governmental System of Southern Rhodesia*, Clarendon Press: Oxford, pp. 50-54.

Mutimukuru-Maravanyika, T. and Almekinders, C. (2011) Learning from Learning: the Experiences with implementing Adaptive Collaborative Forest Management in Zimbabwe, In: van Paassen, A., (Ed), *Knowledge in Action*, Wageningen Academic Publishers: Wageningen.

Mutimukuru-Maravanyika, T. (2010) Can We Learn Our Way to Sustainable Management?: Adaptive Collaborative Management in Mafungautsi State Forest, Zimbabwe, *PhD Thesis*, Wageningen University, pp. 146-154.

National Archives of Zimbabwe (NAZ), F450/6, Bromley ICA File 1.

National Archives of Zimbabwe (NAZ), F450/7, The Bromley ICA File 2.

NAZ, A1510/32, D. Aylen, Erosion Policy, The Dangers of Soil Erosion and Methods of Prevention.

NAZ, F450/6, The Bromley ICA, File 1, The Conservation Officer, R. K. Harvey's Report for 1946.

NAZ, S1180/2/51 [5], Maize Enquiry Committee Report, 1930, NAZ, S118O/1, Oral Evidence to The Maize Enquiry Committee and the Maize Control Amendment Act, Number 17, 1934.

NAZ, S1215/1085/4, Farmers Debt Adjustment Act, 1935, Correspondence.

NAZ, S881/181/3979, Report of the Commission of Enquiry into the Maize Industry of Southern Rhodesia.

NAZ, S987/1, Oral Evidence to the Natural Resources Board Farming Enquiry.

Nehanda Radio, "Zimbabwe Takes Back its Land from Who?",

http://nehandaradio.com/2013/02/05/zimbabwe-takes-its-land-back-from-who/

Nemarundwe, N. and Kozanai, W., (2003) Institutional Arrangements for Water Resource Use: A Case Study from Southern Zimbabwe", *Journal of Southern African Studies*, 29 (1): 193-206.

New Rhodesia, 18 October, 1940.

Newton, C. C. S. (1984) The Sterling Crisis of 1947 and the British Response to the Marshal Plan, *The Economic History Review*, 37 (3): 397-408.

Ostrom, E. (2000) Collective Action and the Evolution of Social Norms, *Economic Perspectives*, 14 (2000): 137-158.

Ostrom, E. (1990) *Governing the Commons: The Evolution of Institutions for Collective Action*, Cambridge University Press: Cambridge.

Palmer, R. H. (1977) *Land and Racial Domination in Rhodesia*, Heinemann: London.

Phimister, I., "Discourse and the Discipline of Historical Context: Conservationism and Ideas about Development in Southern Rhodesia, 1930-1950", *Journal of Southern African Studies*, 12 (2): 1986.

Phimister, I. (1988) *An Economic and Social History of Zimbabwe 1890 – 1948, Capital Accumulation and Class Struggle*, Longman: London.

Report of the Commission into the Preservation of Natural Resources of the Colony, April 1939.

Report of the Committee of Enquiry into the Agricultural Position of Southern Rhodesia, 1934.

Report of the Committee of Enquiry into the Economic Position of the Agricultural Industry, 1934, p. 1.

Report of the Select Committee to Investigate the Problem of Unemployment in the Colony, 1932.

Rukuni, M., (1993) 'The Evolution of Agricultural Policy, 1890-1990', In: M. Rukuni and C. K. Eicher (Eds), *Zimbabwe's Agricultural Revolution*, University of Zimbabwe Publications: Harare.

Scoones, I., Marongwe, N., Mavedzenge, B., Murimbarimba, F., Mahenehene, J. and Sukume, C., (2010) *Zimbabwe's Land Reform: Myths and Realities*, Weaver Press: Harare.

Scott, P. (1952) The Tobacco Industry of Southern Rhodesia", *Economic Geography*, 28 (3): 189-206.

Shaw, W. H. (2003) They Stole Our Land': Debating the Expropriation of White Farms in Zimbabwe", *Journal of Modern African Studies*, 41 (1): 75-89.

Shutt, A. K. (2002) Squatters, Land Sales and Intensification in Marirangwe Purchase Area, Colonial Zimbabwe, 1931-65", *The Journal of African History*, 43 (3): 473-498.

Southern Rhodesia Legislative Assembly Debates, I June, 1938.

Statute Law of Southern Rhodesia, (1941) The Natural Resources Act, 1941, Proclamation Number 19 of 1941, p. 349.

The Guardian Newspaper, "Britain's Mugabe-phobia has Obscured the Good News from Zimbabwe", http://www.guardian.co.uk/commentisfree/2013/jan/23/britain-mugabe-phobia-zimbabwe.

The Herald, "Let Us Not Be Axe-happy", The Herald, http://www.herald.co.zw/index.php?option=com_content&view=article&id=53425: let-us-not-be-axe-happy&catid=42: features-news&Itemid=134#.UZyhavcaJMs.

The Mail and Guardian, "Coming Back from the Brink of Disaster", http: //mg.co.za/article/2013-04-05-00-coming-back-from-the-brink-of-disaster.

The Rhodesia Herald, Friday February 18, 1924, p. 18.

The Standard "Deforestation Still Rampant in Zimbabwe" http://www.thestandard.co.zw/2012/11/11/deforestation-still-rampant-in-zim/

The Sunday Mail, "Deforestation Rate Alarming", http://www.sundaymail.co.zw/index.php?option=com_content&view=article&id=34931: deforestation-rate-alarming&catid=46: crime.

Thomas, N. H. (2003) Land Reform in Zimbabwe", *Third World Quarterly*, 24 (4): 691-712.

Vallema, B. and van de Breemer, H., "Natural Resource Management in Africa: Approaches, Constraints and Opportunities", In: Vallema, B. and van de Breemer, H. (Eds) (1999) *Towards Negotiated Co-Management of Natural Resources in Africa*, Rutgers, Transaction Publishers.

VOA News, "Tobacco Farming Negatively Impacts Zimbabwe's Indigenous Trees",
http://www.voanews.com/content/zimbabwe-trees-sacrificed-to-tobacco-farming-135992498/149782.

Wolmer, W., Chaumba, J. and Scoones, I. (2004) Wildlife Management and Land Reform in South-eastern Zimbabwe: A Compatible Pairing or a Contradiction in Terms, *Geoforum*, 35 (1): 87-98.

Zembe, N., Mbokochena, E., Mudzengerere, F. H., and Chikwiri, E. (2004) An Assessment of the Impact of the Fast-Track Land Reform Programme on the Environment: The case of Eastdale Farm in Gutu District, Masvingo, *Journal of Geography and Regional Planning*, 7 (8): 160 – 175.

Chapter 13

Women, the Poor and Energy Developmentalists on the Margins: The Politicisation of Development by the Global Elites

Joseph Mupinga & Munyaradzi Mawere

Introduction

Increased poverty and food insecurity are persistent insecurities in Africa affecting mostly the sustainable development of African rural areas. Rural women remain the most affected group with insecurities of all sorts always creeping their lives and crying loudly after them. The women are always at the brinks of development as they constitute 70% of the bulk of producers in agriculture. However, majority of them are living in abject poverty, with food and energy insecurity soaring by day incapacitating them to engage in agricultural mechanisation.

Worse still, key factors to development such as availability of energy and especially energy infrastructure have been left out, without being given their deserved attention and priority. Most African countries have adopted agriculture-based economic growth strategy in their bid to achieve sustainable development. However, different results have been yielded chiefly because of the marginalisation of women in many development projects in one or all of the stages of development project such as project formulation, planning, implementation, monitoring, and evaluation. In many African countries, this has been aggravated by the exclusion of some key sectors of development such as energy.

Energy poverty continues holding back Africa's development, most especially African women development. It is either there is no enough energy to meet demand or the little there is, is dame expensive and largely unreliable. For example, there are frequent electricity outages which cause damages to electric gadgets, heavy losses to business people, and loss in national Gross Domestic

Product (GDP). This reality is true for almost all African countries. It is for the same reason that in some African countries like Nigeria, people, in a humorous tone to make sense of frequent outages, have turned the formerly National Electricity Power Authority (NEPA), the parastatal that ran the Nigerian grid to "Never Expect Power Always". When the company changed its name to Power Holding Company of Nigeria (PHCN), again, humour quickly adapted to "Please Hold Candle Nearby" (The World Post, 21 February 2017). As further revealed by the World Post, "globally, of an estimated 1, 3 billion people lacking access to electricity, 700 million of them are Africans. In sub-Saharan Africa (which includes Zimbabwe), more than two-thirds of the population doesn't have access to electricity" (Ibid). Such sky-high level of lack is in spite of the fact that Africa needs to create millions of new jobs every year, and this calls for rapid growth in labour-intensive sectors such as manufacturing, which in turn requires access to reliable and affordable energy services. Thus, there is no doubt that such high levels of lack [of energy] stunts socio-economic development, most especially for women who always directly face the burden to improve healthcare and education for themselves and their families.

As one tries to think through Africa's energy problems, mind boggling questions arise: Why Africa suffer acute energy poverty when it is endowed with enormous energy resources ranging from solar and wind to hydro-electric power to geothermal power? How can renewable energy programmes promote gender equality, poverty reduction, employment generation and development for rural women in Africa? What are the energy needs of the rural women in respective countries which should contribute towards sustainable development and poverty reduction? To what extent can renewable energies meet the growing energy demands of the rural women? These are questions this chapter grapple with.

In view of the aforementioned questions, this chapter demonstrates how the provision of energy services to rural population, and rural women in particular, is a prerequisite for sustained socio-economic growth and development intervention for women in the rural areas of Africa. In so doing, the chapter unveils development naivety and emergent insecurities in the context of energy poverty that women experience which deter them from rapid socio-economic development.

Energy poverty among women in rural Africa

While energy poverty is not exclusively a women's problem, in Africa, rural women are the most affected group. As Connelly (2000) observes, generally, "African countries are characterised with increasing poverty mostly in the rural areas with women being vulnerable victims" (p. 95). Increasing poverty, social injustice, social instability, ethnic conflicts, general political instability and uncertainty, and increased corruption are some of the key emerging issues and insecurity concerns that haunt many African countries as they worsen livelihoods and production capabilities of women in the rural areas. Hardt and Negri (2000) add that "other key emerging issues include increased human trafficking within countries, regions and the continent at large where young rural women become targeted victims" (p. 105). In the health sector, there are emerging serious health conditions and diseases affecting mostly vulnerable populations of women in rural Africa. Women are affected directly and indirectly as health care-givers for their children and husbands amid health disasters that continue taking toll in Africa. Such health disasters which are increasing their occurrence as a result of poverty and undesirable life styles include cervical and breast cancer conditions, sugar diabetes, HIV and AIDS, tuberculosis and cholera. According to the World Health Organisation and the United Nations AIDS Programme (Sefasi 2010), as of 2008, 34. 4 million people were living with HIV/AIDS and AIDS had resulted in more than 25 million deaths since the first clinical evidence was reported in 1981. Further, 79 % of older people provide daily care and financial support to HIV/AIDS patients or orphans in Africa have limited or no information about HIV/AIDS. Majority of these care-givers are women, which makes them [women] the greatest victims of AIDS (Chimwanza & Watkins 2004) and other contagious diseases. Efforts by [national] governments to empower women socially and economically in the rural areas are eroded by the above emerging issues and insecurities (Frank, 2017). Nevertheless, the fact that women poverty has to be done a big blow remains factual.

Mawere (2016; 2017) along with Frank (2017) stress that [Western] theories on the causes of poverty are the foundation upon which poverty reduction strategies in Africa have been based on. Unfortunately, most of these theories are inapplicable to contexts such as those of Africa where they are applied on the basis of one-size-fits-all philosophy thereby rendering them useless (Mawere, 2017). More so, they do not take into account the various dimensions and forms of poverty such as energy poverty, which is rampant in most of the African communities. Poverty always expresses lack of something fundamental. As such, energy poverty is lack of access to modern energy services. It refers to the situation of large numbers of people in developing countries and some people in developed countries whose well-being is negatively affected by very low access and consumption of energy, use of dirty or polluting fuels, and excessive time spent collecting fuel[wood] to meet basic needs (EIA, 2017). While energy poverty is inversely related to access to modern energy services, it is distinct from fuel poverty, which focuses solely on the issue of affordability.

According to Frank (2005), rural areas are predominant in developing countries, and they do not have modern energy infrastructure. They rely heavily on traditional biomass such as fuel wood, charcoal, crop residual, pellets and so on. Because of lack of modern energy infrastructure like power plants, transmission lines, and underground pipelines to deliver energy resources such as natural gas and petroleum that need high or cutting edge technologies and extremely high upfront costs, which are beyond their financial and technological capacity (De Beer & Swanepoel, 2000), rural areas of developing countries remain lagging behind socio-economically at least development-wise. Frank's assertion resonates with the Energy Poverty Action Initiative (2014: 15) of the World Economic Forum's observation that "access to energy is fundamental to improving quality of life and is a key imperative for economic development. In the developing world, energy poverty is still rife. Nearly 1.6 billion people still have no access to electricity". As a result of this obtaining situation, a new United Nations (UN) initiative has been launched to coincide with the designation of 2012 as the International Year for Sustainable Energy for All, which has a major focus on reducing energy poverty among the people of the world.

It should be reiterated that energy poverty though not only confined to rural communities of developing countries, it is largely a phenomenon common in these countries. Cliches (2005) observes that although some developing countries like BRICs have reached close to the energy-related technological level of developed countries and have financial power to provide energy to their citizens, still most developing countries are dominated by traditional biomass. According to the International Energy Agency (IEA) (2017), "the use of traditional biomass will decrease in many countries, but is likely to increase in South Asia and sub-Saharan Africa alongside population growth". We add that even in these developing countries, women are the most affected.

Research conducted by the UNDP (2000) has found out that poor women in rural Zimbabwe generally have a more difficulty time compared to men because of their social and cultural roles and responsibilities. The research concluded that women often spend long hours collecting fuelwood and carrying it back home over long distances. Connelly (2000) reverberates that the time and labour expended in this way exhaust the women and compromise their capabilities to engage in productive and income generative programmes and activities. The UNDP has further asserted that rural women's opportunities for education and income generation are limited by lack of modern energy services and as a result their families and communities remain trapped in deep layers of poverty (UNDP, 2001). In a different study, Morrison, Raju and Sinha (2007) observe that factors such as women's age, education, number of children, poor family income and wealth lead to gender poverty and inequality. In countries such as Zimbabwe, such scenarios have been worsened by energy poverty. In an attempt to move its people out of this poverty situation, the Government of Zimbabwe has come up with its economic blue print known as Zimbabwe Agenda for Sustainable Socio-Economic Transformation (ZIM-ASSET). According to the ZIM-ASSET (2013), government has adopted a vision to move people out of poverty towards an empowered society and a growing economy.

Further, the government of the Republic of Zimbabwe has adopted a mission to provide an enabling environment for sustainable economic empowerment and social transformation to the people of Zimbabwe. However, even though the government is so committed to this vision and mission, women in rural Zimbabwe continue experiencing serious energy poverty in spite of the fact that energy is key enabler to productivity and development. This is largely because the government of Zimbabwe has no tangible policy on renewable energies. In fact, what has to be underlined is that the government of the Republic of Zimbabwe has come up with the ZIM-ASSET but has no policy on renewable energies to enable development for the rural women. This is worrying in view of development and also the fact that the Constitution of the Republic of Zimbabwe Amendment (Number 20) 2013, Section 17 (i) provides that: "the State must promote full gender balance in Zimbabwean society and in particular (a) the State must promote the full participation of women in all spheres of Zimbabwean society on the basis of equity with men". In fact, the case of unsolved energy poverty which affects rural women shows that government still has a lot of interventions to make to move women out of poverty and achieve sustainable development through energy initiatives in rural Zimbabwe.

Even though it can be noted that the Zimbabwe Gender Policy (2013) supports the view that Zimbabwe should work towards gender equality between men and women in terms of resource ownership, resource control and access, the policy only focuses on women and development issues of women and energy issues are not given much attention especially on how they affect [rural] women. We therefore underscore that although a gamut of literature support empowerment of women, gender equality and women participation in socio-economic development and poverty reduction, the government of Zimbabwe is yet to come up with tangible and sustainable policies to implement its commitment to empower the whole society especially in terms of women and development with particular reference to women and energy. Women in rural areas remain highly marginalised as far as energy accessibility and availability is concerned, thereby creating high levels of energy poverty. It is partly out of this realisation that the present chapter has sought to interrogate energy poverty and the potentials of renewable energy in promoting sustainable development and poverty reduction among women in rural Zimbabwe.

Demography and methodological issues

To carry out this research, mixed methods were employed. Mixed methods research is a methodology for conducting research that involves collecting, analysing and integrating quantitative and qualitative research. Mixed methods have merit over quantitative and qualitative methods used separately because where the methods are deployed; they provide strengths that offset the weaknesses of both qualitative and quantitative research. This is so because, quantitative research used separately has the demerit that it bears the potential for biased interpretations made by the researcher besides that it tends to generalise findings to a large group. On the other hand, qualitative research has a bias towards open-ended information and fails to cater for close-ended information such as that which should measure attitudes, behaviours and performance instruments. This is to say that, mixed methods provide more complete and comprehensive understanding of the research problem than either qualitative or quantitative method alone.

In total, seventy interlocutors were researched with around the ten provinces of Zimbabwe. The demographic data of the interlocutors were as follow:

Interlocutors	Age	Number
Married women	20-60 years	30
Girls	13-19 years	20
Married men	23-60 years	10
Boys	13-22 years	10
Total		70

Energy poverty, women and development: the experiences of women in rural Zimbabwe

The question on why Zimbabwe suffer acute energy poverty when it is endowed with enormous energy resources ranging from solar and wind to hydroelectric power to geothermal power, remains perennial and indeed topical even today. From data gathered during interviews by one of the authors of this chapter, it was discovered that many people in the rural areas are quite aware of energy poverty that haunt them in their respective communities. In fact, 75% of the respondents were aware that Zimbabwe suffers tremendously from energy poverty due to lack of investment in both renewable and non-renewable energy in the countryside. As a result, these respondents admitted that they were living in acute energy poverty, despite their awareness of the fact that Zimbabwe is endowed with enormous energy resources such as solar, wind, hydro-electric power, and others.

More so, it was revealed during research that the majority of the respondents were aware of the abundance of untapped renewable energy sources like solar, hydro-electric power and geothermal power. For instance, 85% of the respondents indicated that they were aware of the availability of the renewable energy sources of solar and water, but lacked expertise, technology and capital to tape the resources. As such, it was observed during research that only a few households in the Zimbabwean rural communities use solar energy for lighting and cooking.

This was further aggravated by the fact that no programmes were running in the rural areas with the sole objective of promoting poverty reduction among rural women. While 75 % of the respondents acknowledged that renewable energies can relieve women from spending more hours collecting firewood and cooking and instead give them [women] time to do income generating projects like their male counter parts, it was noted that nothing is being done by both the government and the private sector to promote gender equality, poverty reduction and employment generation and development for rural women in Zimbabwe. Majority of the respondents (85 %) even noted that programmes such as those that promote gender equality and energy poverty reduction among rural women would help to arrest deforestation, improve health standards, and create employment among women.

Basing on their knowledge of possible benefits of renewable energy, many households (80 %) noted that renewable energies will certainly improve food production, food security, and nutrition in their communities. The same respondents added that with provision of renewable energy they would improve their living standards, life expectancy and economic growth, most especially through solar-powered agricultural projects and other income generating projects. This expectation was quite in tandem with our observations in the rural communities where we observed that generally, households with solar energies had improved living standards, improved literacy level and increased participation in development activities.

It was hoped by the majority of the respondents that availability of renewable resources in rural areas will improve their lifestyles and promote creativity and innovation among women and other rural dwellers. In fact, 90 % of the respondents indicated that communities can improve lifestyles and promote innovation if solar energy is availed by government for cooking, lighting, irrigation, poultry, information and communication technologies, radio, television and internet services. It was observed that rural communities prefer solar energies and few households have installed solar energy at their homes for lighting. To the same effect, some schools and clinics also preferred solar energy as evidenced by solar-power systems installed on most of the workers' houses and administrative buildings of such institutions.

Noticeably, prevalent in discussions with interlocutors during research was the topic of access to energy and its impact on women and girls. O'Dell (2005), Peters and Whartosn (2009) whose literature is in agreement with these findings have noted that all things being equal, rural areas with renewable energy are likely to be more developed than those without. Whartson (Ibid), for instance, postulates that, energy is a key enabler to productivity and socio-economic development in any given country, and without access to energy services rural women remain poor and marginalised such that they can hardly contribute to socio-economic development of the nation. This is worrying if we are to consider the Zimbabwean situation where women in the rural areas are seriously suffering from acute energy poverty which is lack of access to the very energy services that should improve their lives.

As O'Dell, Peters and Wharton (2009) observed, the well-being of large numbers of rural women in Zimbabwe is being negatively affected by very low level of access to energy resulting from unavailability of energy, excessive time spent collecting fuelwood to meet basic needs and use of dirty polluting and health hazardous fuels. The net effect of such a scenario is a plethora of problems such as economic, environmental, health (pollution), land degradation and deforestation (O'Dell, Peters & Wharton, Ibid).

In parallel issues to the research findings, reliable, affordable energy is increasingly recognised by the international development community as an enabler of economic growth. The United Nations launched its Sustainable Energy for All (SE4A) initiative and declared 2014–2024 the Sustainable Energy for All Decade. Likewise, in 2013, President Barack Obama launched Power Africa, an initiative that was targeted to double the number of people with access to power in sub-Saharan Africa, where two-thirds of the population then and even now are without access to power energy. Similarly, in Asia, the Asian Development Bank launched the Energy for All Partnership, which aims to provide access to safe, affordable modern energy for an additional 100 million people in the region by 2015.

In Zimbabwe, energy poverty is aggravated by gender inequality – an imbalance between people of different gender. Gender imbalance is highly prevalent in Zimbabwe because culturally and historically women are tasked with firewood collection and meal preparation, exposing them to effects of energy poverty more than their male counterparts. This situation has created gender imbalances between women and men in terms of sustainable development and poverty reduction as women are being locked in vicious circles of energy poverty. The problem has worsened in Zimbabwe since independence in 1980 because land is a finite resource with its finite products for energy, yet the Zimbabwean population has quadrupled since 1980 (Vurayai, 2011).

Although the Government of Zimbabwe has a vision to drive the nation, "towards an empowered society and a growing economy" (Wharton 2009) with a mission "to provide an enabling environment for sustainable economic empowerment and social transformation to the people of Zimbabwe, energy poverty is increasingly becoming a serious problem highly prevalent at a macro-level affecting women and development in rural areas of Zimbabwe". The well-being of large numbers of rural women in Zimbabwe is being negatively affected by very low availability of energy.

Deforestation activities in search of firewood are worsening the problem. The Government of Zimbabwe and Civil Society Organisations have not seriously considered renewable energies as an alternative solution which can be affordable, immediate, clean and safe. The problem of energy poverty is being accentuated by the fact that no significant study and documentation have been done so far with regard to the topic. It is in view of this observation that this study has focussed on the need to interrogate the potential of renewable energies in promoting sustainable development and poverty reduction among women in rural Zimbabwe.

Rural women and the potential for renewable energies: Lessons for Zimbabwe

The majority (80 %) of the respondents who were interviewed by one of the researchers and co-authors of this chapter were very knowledgeable of renewable energy issues especially solar energy despite general attitudes of the majority of the populace in Zimbabwe that rural women are illiterate and do not know much concerning energy. The respondents expressed awareness of energy poverty and their marginalisation although Zimbabwe is endowed with enormous energy resources. This can be a lesson for most Zimbabweans who look down upon women in rural areas to take cognisance of the fact that if given equal opportunity with availing renewable energy, these women can do just as much as those in urban areas. They can as well even do better than their male counterparts who are running income generating projects with the use of energy.

301

Again, if the interviews and observations made during research are anything to go by, the majority (75 %) of the respondents supported the above assertion by indicating that solar can be easily used for lighting but very expensive for heavy uses like heating, cooking, and irrigation purposes. Of the several renewable energies available in Zimbabwe, women noted that if government or the private sector is to intervene, solar can be easily accessed by every household in rural areas especially women. Unlike small hydro-powered generators, which could only be accessed by those near perennial running streams, solar in Zimbabwe is an annual supplier of power to rural women, a lesson that the government and private investors can take advantage of and invest in that area.

At a different level, it was noted that energy programmes can help promote gender equality, poverty reduction, employment generation and development for rural women in Zimbabwe if energy sources are fully utilised with a view to improve the standard of life of women to at least the position at par with their male counterparts. Where there are solar powered irrigation schemes, it has been observed that women are as hardworking and productive as their male counterparts. Through availed solar powered irrigation for horticulture projects in Masvingo Province run by both women and men, it has been proven that women can produce just like men without distinctive difference. This should be an impeccable lesson by most investors in both the public and private sector, including non-governmental organisations in Zimbabwe. They should understand that given the provision of energy, women are capable of producing and generating income as much as their male counterparts.

Further, it was noted that sustainable development and poverty reduction initiatives work in a hand and glove kind of relationship. Once sustainability is certain, poverty reduction is imminent and vice versa. This is true owing to the visible relationship noted during research between women and renewable energies for coking, heating, lighting, education and health facilities, information and communication technologies. To be more specific, women in rural areas have been observed to be spending much of their time collecting firewood for cooking and not on social and economic development projects and activities. The lessons learnt here were that lack of energy compromises social and economic development and that rural women need energy for income generating projects which has to occupy them most of the time.

Despite doubts and unfound negative perspectives on rural women as far as energy is concerned, it can be taken as a found lesson that renewable energies can meet the growing energy demands of the rural women specifically on production. Adequate and reliable energy is required on daily basis for improved livelihoods and for economic growth in rural areas. It has been observed that rural communities require energy on daily basis just as much as energy is required in urban areas for economic growth and improvement of livelihoods.

Basing on data harvested during our research, we noted that the idea that industrialisation is urban bound and male dominated is a patriarchal gender biased way of thinking. All households whether they are rural or urban need energy for lighting, heating, cooking, charging cell phones for communication, use of radio and television for information on development. These are just but basics of energy usage, a lesson most Zimbabweans need to learn. Therefore, provision of renewable energy is of no doubt an imminent issue despite gender polarisation in favour of males and urban dwellers as being more productive than females in rural areas. Zimbabwe needs to learn that women can produce as much as men once energy is availed, and this can be the genesis of poverty reduction.

Another lesson learnt for Zimbabwe is that women in rural areas are living uncomfortably and in misery, yet they often do not express their misery. As we observed, women in rural areas seem to be highly uncomfortable with the situation that they find themselves in and they are economically unproductive save for the fact that they play part in their nutrition and food security as subsistence farmers. Poverty is usually uncomfortable and indeed painful, but is worsened by lack not only of tangible assets but of resources such as renewable energy which should be a vehicle through which sustainable development can be achieved.

On another level, both NGOs and the responsible government sectors seem to be playing truant yet they are aware that women in the countryside are living in abject poverty. They are deliberately avoiding real interventions that propel development concentrating on food hampers, fertilizers, and food and nutrition issues, ignoring renewable energy issues yet, they are the most empowering interventions that can initiate and sustain actual and sustainable development.

Last but not least, there is no doubt that renewable energy has the potential to uplift the standards of living of the general population and in particular women in rural areas. This resonates with Hardt and Negri's (2000) observation that renewable energies initiatives have the potential of promoting sustainable development and reducing poverty among rural women in Africa. Such initiatives are important in a number of ways. Most countries in Africa have adopted and implemented initiatives on energy considering urban areas neglecting their rural areas where most of their rural women are living under subsistence farming because of energy poverty. We therefore argue that it is critical that African governments and Zimbabwean government in particular assess and address growing energy needs of rural women in order to promote sustainable development and reduce poverty in the rural areas. This is important because adoption of renewal energies and vigorous implementation of renewal energy initiatives can also help address issues of deforestation and climate change concerns. It is also for the same realisation that scholars like Clancy (2003) postulates that it is anticipated that renewable energy programmes can relieve rural women from the burden of fetching and using fuelwood and allow them to concentrate on development initiatives like their male counterparts. This will promote gender equality, poverty reduction, employment generation and most importantly sustainable development for the rural women, respective countries and Africa at large.

Conclusion

Drawing on data harvested during research which culminated into this chapter, we conclude that most of the women in rural Zimbabwe are aware of both renewable and non-renewable energies – both tapped and untapped ones. However, they are also aware of the reluctance of both the non-governmental and government sectors in investing in these energies, especially renewable energies like solar energy possibly due to limited availability of resources and also due to anticipated cost involved. Worse still, there is also a sense of naivety of the women in rural Zimbabwe as they are quite aware of the attitudes of both the private sector and the public sectors in their perpetual marginalisation of women as a weaker sex which cannot be involved in production at equal level with their male counterparts.

More so, most of the women in rural Zimbabwe are still engaged in long periods of time sourcing manual energies in form of cow dung or firewood. Because of the scarcity of trees which have been cut down due to increased populations, the distance to be travelled by women to fetch firewood has been unimaginatively increased. In some cases, forests have been totally removed and there is nowhere else to look for firewood since people have been densely settled in rural areas. Seeking for energy sources by women is taking too long to an extent that it has become an occupation taking all their time. The net effect of energy poverty in rural areas on rural women is nothing but a plethora of problems such as absolute poverty whereby women lack in economic production, environmental problems where wanton cutting down and burning of trees and shrubs become prevalent, land degradation, deforestation and health disasters which are resulting from air pollution.

We therefore conclude that women in rural areas need energy for cooking and lighting as basic purposes. However, some stressed that energy can be provided to facilitate operations of income generating projects especially for irrigation purposes, poultry production, and heating systems. As such, there is a huge demand for energy by women in rural areas for basic requirements like cooking and lighting, yet a huge demand is there on energy consumption for income generating projects. Women in rural Zimbabwe and Africa at large really need actual poverty reduction and sustainable development rather than empty promises and politicisation of social and economic development by the Global Elite.

References

Alcott, W. (2003) 'The underdevelopment of Africa by Europe,' *Africa, the arrival of Europeans and the trans-Atlantic slave*, Video available at:
revealinghistories.org.uk/credits.Html#WashingtonAlcott.

Bartle, P. (1967) *The dependency syndrome*, Community Empowerment Collective: USA.

Chambua, S. E. (1994) 'The development debates and crisis of development theories: The case of Tanzania with special emphasis on peasants, state and capital,' In: Himmelstrand, U. *et al.* Eds. *Introduction to African perspectives on development: Controversies, dilemmas and openings*, James Currey: London.

Clancy, J. (2003) *Household energy and gender: the global context.* www.sparknet.info.

Cliche, P. (2005) *A Reflection on the Concepts of "Poverty" and "Development,"* Canada: Canadian Catholic Organisation for Development and Peace.

Connelly, M. P. (2000) *Feminism and development: Theoretical perspectives*, Oxford University Press: Oxford.

De Beer, F. and Swanepoel, H. (Eds). (2000) *Introduction to development studies*, 2nd ed, Oxford University Press: Oxford.

Frank, A. G. (2017) *Capitalism and underdevelopment in Latin America: Historical studies of Chile and Brazil*, Monthly Review Press: New York.

Frank, A. G. (2005) "The Development of Underdevelopment," Development: Critical Concepts in the Social Sciences: Washington DC.

Government of Zimbabwe (2013) *Zimbabwe Agenda for Sustainable Socio-Economic Transformation (ZIM-ASSET)*, Government Printers: Harare.

Government of Zimbabwe. (2012) *First Annual Medium Term Plan: 2011-2015 Implementation Progress Report* Fidelity Printers and Refiners, Harare.

Government of Zimbabwe. (2013) *Constitution of the Republic of Zimbabwe Amendment (no.20)* Fidelity Printers and Refiners: Harare.

Hardt, M. & Negri, A. (2000) *Empire*, Harvard University Press: Cambridge, MA.

Harris, J. M. (2000) *Basic Principles of Sustainable Development.* Metford: Global Development and Environment Institute, Working Paper No. 00-04, Tufts University.
http://www.reegle.info/policy-and-regulatory-overviews/zw

Leedy, P.D/ (1980) *Practical Research: Planning and a Design.* MacMillan: New York.

Mawere, M. *(2017)* The Political Economy of Poverty, Vulnerability and Disaster Risk Management: Building Bridges of Resilience, Entrepreneurship and Development in Africa's 21st Century, *Langaa RPCIG: Bamenda.*

Marrisen, A.; Raju, D. and Sinha, N. (2007) Gender Equality, poverty and Economic Growth, *World Bank Policy Research Working Paper 4349.*

Moyo, S. *et-al* (2002) *Master of Educational Management (MED) Dissertation Guideline (Module DEA 570),* Zimbabwe Open University, Harare.

Silverman, D. (2006) *Interpreting qualitative data: Methods for analyzing talk, text and interaction.* Sage: New York.

Sefasi, A. P. (2010) Impact of HIV and AIDS on the elderly: A case study of Chidzulu District, Malawi, *Malawi Medical Journal* 22 (3): 101-103.

The World Post. (21/02/20117) "The energy poverty is holding Africa back and it's time to fix it", Washington DC, USA.

Todaro, M. P. (1992) *Economics for a Developing World.* Longman: London.

UNDP (2000) *How is gender related to sustainable energy related policies?" Karlsson, G. and Clancy, J. in Sustainable Energy Strategies: Materials for Decision Makers,*
www.undp.org/energy/publications/200/2000a.htm.

Wolcott, H. F. (2002) Writing up qualitative research ... better. *Qualitative health research. 12 (1) 91-1003.*

Zimbabwe Ministry of Finance and Economic Development (2016) *Zimbabwe Interim Poverty Reduction Strategy Paper (I-PRSP) 2016-2018,* Government Printers: Harare.

Zimbabwe Ministry of Women Affairs, *Gender and Community Development (2013) National Gender Policy*, Government Printers: Harare.

Chapter 14

The Bitter Harvest of Militant Agronomics in Mugabe's Zimbabwe, 2000-2017

Fidelis Peter Thomas Duri

Introduction

One forgettable legacy of Robert Mugabe's rule in Zimbabwe was the use of coercion by the state to enforce economic development policies on the ordinary people. In particular, this chapter examines the use of force by the Zimbabwean government in the implementation of agrarian policies as it sought to improve the food security situation, among other things, during the period 2000-2017. In an effort to demonstrate how the Zimbabwean government used "squeezing tactics" as an instrument of agrarian reform (Volin, 1951: 469), the chapter focuses on the Fast-Track Land Reform Programme, the so-called Third *Chimurenga* (2000-2005), Operation *Maguta/ Sisuthi* (2005-2006) and the Targeted Command Agriculture (2016-2017).

Furthermore, the government's use of militant terminology, such as *chimurenga* (war), 'operation' and 'command,' in naming these agrarian programmes is also quite illustrative of the combative and militarised manner in which they were implemented. As the Solidarity Peace Trust (April 2006: 13), a human rights non-governmental organisation based in South Africa, rightly noted:

> The Zimbabwe government has developed a liking for terming all its large-scale policies in a language more associated with the military. It is the military that undertakes 'operations,' not municipalities and farmers. However, this is no coincidence: the army, police and the Central Intelligence Organisation (CIO) have been intimately involved in all these 'operations.'

These sentiments were reiterated by Mabhena (2013: 58) who observed that in independent Zimbabwe, "it had become a norm in government circles to refer to any aggressive policy as an operation."

In addition, the manner in which the ruling Zimbabwe African National Union Patriotic Front (ZANU-PF) government sought to implement these agrarian policies also involved a lot of coercive political canvassing. Pius Ncube, a Zimbabwean Roman Catholic Bishop, cited by *The Truth Seeker* (18 January 2007: 1), explained the primacy of political dynamics in the implementation of many government policies in Zimbabwe during the 21st century:

> These operations remind the population who is the boss. They remind people that they are subjects, not citizens. They keep them off balance, terrified and compliant…Of course, the regime knows it is hated, that it would never survive a genuinely free election, so it practises continuous and overwhelming intimidation.

That said, this chapter argues that elitist mechanisms to spur economic development through a dissonant and contradictory combination of populism, centralisation/statism and coercion, often fail to achieve the desired results for reasons that seem very apparent. The use of force, for example, is not an effective instrument to motivate people to produce. In addition, the state's centralisation of production and marketing processes is a disastrous top-to-bottom approach that demotivates producers by killing off competitiveness. As examples from Zimbabwe during Robert Mugabe's rule, particularly from 2000, illustrate, statist machinations are often unsustainable and monocultural in nature because, in addition to stifling economic diversity, they underestimate the initiatives and competitiveness of various stakeholders in the production process.

Antecedents of militant agronomics in world history

The use of state force in the implementation of agrarian policies has taken place in many other parts of the world across historical times. It is cogent to note that most of these militant agrarian programmes did not yield the desired results. One common reason

310

for their failure was that disgruntled farmers resisted impositions from above. This section examines a few examples in order to historically contextualise the Zimbabwean experience.

Sparta, a city state in ancient Greece, which was at the peak of its power during the period 600-370BC, provides one of the earliest examples of a militarised agricultural economy driven by brutal force. Conquered people were forcibly turned into *helots*, serf-like labourers or unfree servants, who were literally slaves (Cartledge, 2002; Forrest, 1968). Among other things, they were forced to work in the fields after which they surrendered 50% of the harvest to their conquerors (Tran, 2016). As a result of this forced arrangement, *helots* were "notorious perennial rebels whose brutal suppression occupied much of Sparta's energy" (Hunt, 1997: 142).

In some parts of Africa, European colonial administrations sometimes subjected Africans to coercive agrarian programmes. A notorious example can be drawn from Portuguese colonial rule in Mozambique where the cultivation of export crops such as cotton and rice was imposed on Africans from the early 20th century. In 1926, for example, the Portuguese passed a decree that forced Africans in the northern Mozambican provinces to grow cotton while European companies were contracted to buy, process and market the produce (Isaacman and Isaacman, 1985). In 1938, the government set up the Cotton Marketing Board (CMB) to provide seeds and buy cotton from Africans, usually at very low prices (Roberts, 1986). In 1942, the compulsory cultivation of rice was introduced (Roberts, 1986). During forced crop cultivation, Africans were ordered to prepare the fields by hand, cultivate given pieces of land and sell a stipulated quota of the harvest to the government failure of which they were flogged or imprisoned (Munslow, 1983; Newitt, 1985). In addition, Isaacman and Isaacman (1985) report of ill Africans who were severely assaulted for failing to complete their work on time in the cotton fields of Cabo Delgado Province and central Mozambique.

On the whole, Portuguese command farming in Mozambique was both unproductive and unsustainable. Forced crop cultivation, particularly of cotton, resulted in chronic hunger among many Africans since they neither had the fertile land nor adequate time to cultivate their own food crops. By 1951, as Spence (1951: 54) noted, African food crops had "reached almost famine production figures" in northern Mozambique. Thus, the Portuguese were shooting themselves in the foot by incapacitating the very African labour force which they regarded as the flywheel of the colonial economy.

The Portuguese administrators of Mozambique also suffered many losses and often failed to meet production targets due to African resistance. Among others, in the fields, African labourers employed various forms of passive resistance such as feigning illness, roasting seeds before planting and consuming a large part of the yield (Isaacman and Isaacman, 1985; Newitt, 1981). Some Africans "voted with their feet" as thousands fled into neighbouring countries (Munslow, 1983: 40). At other times, African resistance was overt. In 1947, for example, some 7 000 women from the Buzi area in the Sofala Province went on strike and refused to accept cotton seed from the colonial administration (Munslow, 1983). As well, in 1955 and 1958, there were large-scale boycotts in the Gaza Province during which Africans refused to sell their cotton to the CMB (Munslow, 1983). Various forms of African resistance rendered forced crop cultivation economically unproductive and unsustainable. This largely forced the Portuguese to discontinue the practice in 1961 (Duffy, 1961; Munslow, 1983).

In the then Soviet Union during the period 1928-1933, Joseph Stalin, in his First Five Year Plan, imposed a state collectivised agricultural system to replace the predominantly individual farming enterprises. Peasants were forcibly drafted into cooperatives to work on *kolkhoz* (collective farms) and *sovkhoz* (state farms) in the countryside (*Global Security*, 5 June 2016; Wedlund, 2008). The collectivisation programme had disastrous consequences and the horrendous famine of 1932-1933 attests to this (Wedlund, 2008). Many rich peasants (*kulaks*) resisted collectivisation, scaled down production and withheld produce, among other strategies of defiance (*Global Security*, 5 June 2016). The withdrawal into subsistence farming by peasant farmers starved the urban areas of raw materials for industries and food for the urbanites (Wedlund, 2008). Consequently, state grain collections during the period 1928-1929 nosedived by more than 30% below the level of two years before

(Ibid). Many peasants also killed hundreds of thousands of their head of livestock, including horses, rather than surrender them as common property in the collective farms. This deprived the agricultural sector of the much-needed animal draught power before the widespread use of tractors (Volin, 1951).

From late 1928, Stalin, in retaliation, launched the *dekulakisation* campaign which entailed the "liquidation of the kulaks as a class" (*Global Security*, 5 June 2016: 1). An estimated one million kulak families (about five million people) were deported. Many remaining peasants were displaced from their private farms and forcibly resettled in state-controlled collective farms. Other measures instituted to force the peasants to produce included 'terror famine' during the period 1932-1933 in areas such as the Ukraine in which the state imposed high grain quotas, removed any other source of food and cut off any assistance from outside from reaching starving populations. As a result of these brutal measures, about 97% of Russian peasant households had been collectivised by 1940. Lamentably though, an estimated 14.5 million people, five million from Ukraine alone, lost their lives during the period 1930-1937 as a result of Stalinist terror against the peasants (Ibid). On the whole, forced collectivisation "brought the economy to the verge of a total collapse" forcing Stalin to abandon the programme in 1933 (Wedlund, 2008: 223).

Similarly, in North Vietnam in December 1953, the ruling Vietnamese Communist Party (VCP) passed the Land Law which called for the seizure of land from people classified as landlords and rich peasants and converted it into collective farms to be worked by the peasant majority under the supervision of brigades. During the ensuing land grabs, many landowners lost their property while others were arbitrarily killed. There was also an obligation for the new farmers to sell a quota of grain to the state at fixed prices in exchange for provisions such as fertilizer, gasoline and bricks (Raymond, 2008). The fact that the government charged high prices for goods manufactured and distributed by the state while buying agricultural produce from collective farms at miserably low prices failed to incentivise the new farmers. During the period 1978-1979, for example, the price of grain on the free market was eight times higher than that offered by the government (Long, 1988). In addition, as Raymond (2008: 44) established in the collective farms, "the attitudes of individuals undermined collective efforts." Food shortages became rampant and the country was plunged into an economic crisis which forced the government to abandon collectivised production in 1988 (Ibid). After collectivisation had been abandoned, agricultural production shot up. By 1991, for instance, individual small-scale farmers produced 97% of North Vietnam's agricultural output, accounting for an estimated 40% of the country's Gross Domestic Product (Vickerman, 1986). In 1992, Vietnam became the world's third largest exporter of rice (Ibid). The Vietnamese experience illustrates the disastrous effects of coercive state-driven agricultural programmes.

In China during the period 1957-1961, the ruling Chinese Communist Party under Mao Tse Tung also introduced a crash agricultural programme known as the 'Great Leap Forward' in which people were forced to cultivate in collective units called Communes (MacFarquhar, 1983; Yang, 1996). Landowners were stripped of their property and rural peasants were forced to produce crops such as grain and cotton to feed the local population, supply domestic industry with raw materials, as well as for export. People who opposed to the plans were executed. By 1958, for example, 550 000 people had been killed (Yang, 1996). In addition, many cities were evacuated as the government forcibly relocated urban dwellers to the rural areas to work in collective farms (*History Place*, 1999).

Collectivisation/communisation of agriculture did not yield the desired results in China partly because it "impaired peasant incentives...and inhibited productivity and growth" (Kueh, 2006: 701). To aggravate the situation, local leaders often exaggerated crop yields as they competed for favours from the central government resulting in presumed surplus grain being exported, a development that caused chronic food shortages across the country (Yang, 1996). By the spring of 1959, the grain reserves had become depleted and a chronic famine set in, forcing people to abandon their homes to scavenge for food (Ibid). As chaos unfolded, hungry militias became predatory as they roamed the countryside seizing grain, assaulting people and raping women (Ibid). In their pursuit of livelihoods, more than 30% of peasant farmers abandoned the communes and started working on their individual plots (Ibid). It is estimated between 16.5 million and 40 million people died during the period 1957-1961 as a result of starvation, making the Great Leap famine the largest in world history (Friedman, 1985; Yang, 1996).

In Cambodia, during the period 1975-1979, Saloth Sar, popularly known as Pol Pot (*History Place*, 1999), and his ruling Khmer Rouge party sought to forcibly nationalise and centralise the peasant farming community virtually overnight, in accordance with Maoist and Stalinist agricultural models (Alvarez, 2001; Mydans, 17 April 1998; PPUI, 1975). Pol Pot conducted a brutal campaign to create an "agrarian society and turn people into revolutionary worker-peasants" (Mydans, 17 April 1998: 1). This involved turning Cambodia "back to a primitive 'Year Zero,' wherein all citizens would participate in rural work projects, and any Western innovations would be removed" (Krkljes, March 2017: 2).

Urban dwellers were forcibly relocated to the rural areas where they were supposed to provide agricultural labour. On 17 April 1975, for example, "Khmer Rouge soldiers, young peasants from the provinces, mostly uneducated teenage boys who had never been in a city before, swept through town. They set to their job right away, evacuating Phnom Penh (the capital city) and forcing all of its residents to leave behind all their belongings and march towards the countryside" (Ibid, p.2). During the process, as Joel Brinkley (2011: 40) noted, "Hospital patients still in their white gowns stumbled along carrying their IV bottles. Screaming children ran in desperate search for their parents." In addition,

> ...the ill, disabled, old, and young who were incapable of making the journey to the collectivised farms and labour camps were killed on the spot. People who refused to leave were killed, along with any who appeared to be in opposition to the new regime. Residents of entire cities were forcibly evacuated to the countryside...Children and parents were separated and sent to different labour camps...Due to conditions of virtual slave labour, starvation, physical injury, and illness, many Cambodians became incapable of performing physical work and

were killed by the Khmer Rouge as expenses to the system (Krkljes, March 2017: 3).

Mydans (17 April 1998: 1) also provides a vivid account of the forced relocation process: "Everyone (the elderly, the blind, the sick, even infants) was ordered right away to return to the villages. Some 20 000 hospital patients were forced to move out, some on wheeled beds. Tens of thousands of people died of starvation and disease in the first weeks…Many others were killed outright…" An estimated two million inhabitants were evacuated from Phnom Penh on foot into the rural areas at gunpoint and approximately 20 000 lost their lives along the way (*History Place*, 1999).

In the labour camps, 10 to 15 families lived together under a chairman appointed by the government. All decisions on work to be done in the fields were made by armed supervisors (Ibid, 1999; Jackson, 1978). Every working day lasted 18 hours from 4am to 10pm with only two rest periods. Every tenth day was reserved for rest. There were also three rest days during the Khmer New Year Festival (*History Place*, 1999). All farm work was virtually done by hand, without machinery (Mydans, 17 April 1998). During working days, as *History Place* (1999: 1) noted:

> Millions of Cambodians, accustomed to city life, were now forced into slave labour in Pol Pot's 'killing fields' where they soon began dying from overwork, malnutrition and disease, on a diet of one tin of rice (180 grams) per person every two days…Khmer Rouge soldiers (were) eager to kill anyone for the slightest infraction. Starving people were forbidden to eat the fruits and rice they were harvesting. After the rice crop was harvested, Khmer Rouge trucks would arrive and confiscate the entire crop.

Consequently, in January 1979, the majority of Cambodians "had reached an advanced stage of starvation and exhaustion" (Gough, 1986: 15). In addition, the brutal means used to implement agrarian reforms resulted in the death of more than 25% of the country's population of about seven million within a period of three years from starvation, overwork and executions (*History Place*, 1999; Krkljes, March 2017; Mydans, 17 April 1998).

Pol Pot's agricultural policy was self-destructive (Mydans, 17 April 1998). There was no motivation for Cambodians to embark on productive agriculture because of state brutality and the fact that the government expropriated up to two-thirds of the communal crop production (Jackson, 1978). In addition, many farmers had problems of marketing whatever surplus produce they had because industrial growth in the urban areas from where a ready market could have been available among workers had been decimated by the forced relocation of people to the rural areas (Jackson, 1978). Furthermore, the Khmer Rouge waged a relentless campaign that demonised the urban workers and idealised the peasantry as the class from which the nation in general and the agricultural economy in particular prospered. Most former urban workers, together with many other Cambodians became unpaid agricultural labourers and the country was turned into extensive rice fields watered by irrigation canals. The Khmer Rouge slogan became: "With water we have rice, with rice we have everything" (Democratic Kampuchea, August 1977: 11).

While the futility of coercive state-driven agrarian programmes has been laid bare in this section, some critical insights on sustainable development can be drawn. It is quite apparent that people cannot be incentivised to produce through the use of force. In addition, the planning of development projects by governments and non-governmental organisations should be inclusive in approach by taking into account the needs and welfare of the ordinary people. As the next three sections demonstrate, the disastrous agrarian policies discussed above were repeated in Zimbabwe, particularly from the year 2000, as the ruling ZANU-PF party under the leadership of the then President Robert Mugabe sought to improve the food security situation as one of an array of desperate strategies to restore its waning political fortunes.

The Land Reform Programme and the Third *Chimurenga* (2000-2005)

In 2000, the ZANU-PF government launched a militant land acquisition and agrarian scheme, officially known as the Fast Track Land Reform Programme, that involved repossessing land occupied mostly by commercial white farmers and redistributing it to the majority indigenous Zimbabweans, supposedly to economically empower them (Mugabe, 2001). Border Gezi, the then Governor of Mashonaland Central Province, proclaimed the programme as 'The Third *Chimurenga*' ('The Third Liberation War') thereby positioning it within a series of violent struggles against colonial rule dating back to the early 1890s (Alexander, 2003). It was not surprising, therefore, that the process was dominated by invasions, land grabbing and widespread violence. Thus, the evictions of white commercial farmers were widely known by the Shona slang, *'jambanja,'* denoting the centrality of violence in the pogrom (Pilossof, 1 December 2010).

The political dynamics that prevailed in Zimbabwe at that time largely account for the violent and vindictive nature of the land reform exercise. The legitimacy of the ruling ZANU-PF Party was waning as a result of mounting socio-economic hardships countrywide and the rising popularity of the Movement for Democratic Change (MDC) Party which had been formed in September 1999 under the leadership of Morgan Tsvangirai, with considerable funding from white commercial farmers (Meredith, 2002). The Land Reform Programme was, therefore, a multi-pronged political populist strategy by ZANU-PF to regain support from land-starved indigenous Zimbabweans and thwart the advances of the MDC. It was also meant to immobilise and pauperise commercial white farmers in order to prevent them from becoming a viable financial support base of the opposition MDC (Alexander, 2003; Raftopoulos, 2003). These political dynamics largely explain the violent nature of the programme, otherwise if ZANU-PF genuinely wanted to address land inequalities, it could have exploited its parliamentary majority since independence in 1980 to push through constitutional amendments for a non-violent land reform exercise which had the potential to win many local and international sympathisers (Sithole, 10 February 2012).

The impetus for the countrywide land invasions was provided by the government's belligerent nationalist rhetoric of repossessing lands lost to the whites and "reverse the colonial legacy of racialised land economic inequalities" (Hammar and Raftopoulos, 2003: 11). As the 2000 presidential elections drew closer, the ruling party proclaimed: "ZANU-PF has decided that 20 years is long enough to be polite to white farmers and Britain, and has now started taking back your land" (*Zimbabwe Independent*, 9 January 2004: 1). Mugabe set the tone for a violent land repossession exercise when he instructed farm invaders to "strike fear in the heart of the white man, who is the real enemy" (Masunungure, 2004: 176). With the government's consent and support, veterans of the liberation war were "at the forefront of these land occupations" (Pilossof, 1 December 2010: 2). Most white-owned commercial farms around Harare, for example, were seized in military style by homeless civilians under the leadership of so-called Commanding Committees comprising war veterans and ZANU-PF loyalists (Chitekwe-Biti, 2009). Together with personnel from security sectors such as the Zimbabwe Republic Police (ZRP), Zimbabwe Defence Forces (ZDF) and the Central Intelligence Organisation (CIO), the war veterans' structures mobilised civilians, mostly rural peasants, to invade white commercial farms in various parts of the country (Alexander, 2003; Alexander and McGregor, 2001). Most of the food, vehicles and other forms of support for the land invaders were provided by the ZDF (Alexander, 2003). The government-sponsored seizures of white commercial farms commenced on 26 February 2000. By 8 March 2000, approximately 400 farms had been grabbed (Meredith, 2002). The number of farms confiscated skyrocketed to 1 500 by June 2000 (Alexander, 2003). At the end of June 2000, the Commercial Farmers Union reported that 1 525 farms had been seized (Pilossof, 1 December 2010).

In July 2000, the Zimbabwean government officially pronounced the Fast Track Resettlement Programme in order to speed up the land invasions, stating that more than 3 000 farms were urgently needed for redistribution (Human Rights Watch, 8 March 2002).

Consequently, the year 2000 alone witnessed the confiscation of more than 1 600 commercial farms, mostly white-owned (Moyo, September 2000). Between 2000 and 2001, an estimated 3 000 white farmers were evicted from their farms (Chibber, 26 July 2014). By the end of 2002, 11.5 million hectares of commercial farmland had been seized without compensation (Sachikonye, 2003).

As a result of the farm invasions, the number of white commercial farmers in the country fell from 4 500 to only 450 by February 2004 (Cross, 4 February 2004). By 2007, more than 4 000 farms had been confiscated (Duri, 2014; *Financial Gazette*, 26 July- 1 August 2007). Land invasions continued after the setting up of the Government of National Unity (GNU) in February 2009 soon after which the General Agriculture and Plantation Workers Union of Zimbabwe (GAPWUZ) estimated that around 225 farms were seized (Zimbabwe Human Rights NGO Forum, 2010). By 31 December 2009, far less than 300 white commercial farmers remained on their farms (*Voice of America*, 31 December 2009). The Internal Displacement Monitoring Centre approximated that more than 3 000 white commercial farmers were evicted during the period 2000-2010 (Zimbabwe Human Rights NGO Forum, 2010).

On the whole, the land occupations were "highly confrontational and violent" (Pilossof, 1 December 2010: 2). In April 2000, for example, two white farmers who resisted the invaders were shot dead by marauding war veterans (Chitiyo, 29 April 2007). From mid-February to June 2000, six white farmers were murdered (Mamdani, 2008). At the besieged commercial farms, many workers and their families were also caught up in the violence at the hands of war veterans, soldiers, intelligence officers and police details. In March 2003, for instance, some Zimbabwean soldiers killed one farm worker and whipped 80 others during the invasion of Ruwa Farm, about 10 kilometres south of Harare (Meldrum, 21 March 2003). At Charleswood Farm, in the Chimanimani District, belonging to Roy Bennett, a white MDC Member of Parliament, war veterans abducted three female farm workers and flogged them on 6 February 2004; a soldier reportedly fired at farm workers killing one of them on 8 February 2004; policemen broke into the house of a male farmworker and took turns to rape his wife on 26 March 2004; and 17 children of

320

farmworkers aged between eight and 17 years who were on their way home from a football match were assaulted by soldiers on 2 April 2004 (Amnesty International, 5 April 2004).

The so-called Fast Track Land Reform Programme was an economic disaster that derailed the development agenda by employing a militant, divisive and exhausted brand of racial nationalism when repossessing commercial farms (Bond and Manyanya, 2001). The programme laid the foundations of a severe and multi-layered socio-economic crisis that made Zimbabwe critically food-deficient, among other things. Agricultural production fell drastically because most of the beneficiaries of the land redistribution exercise, the so-called 'new farmers' in public discourse, either lacked the requisite skills, adequate capital and even the enthusiasm to engage in commercial farming (Richardson, 2005). The extent of commercial farmland under productive use therefore fell over the years from 200 000 hectares during the 1999-2000 season, 90 000 in 2000-2001 and 50 000 in 2001-2002 (Ibid). In 2005, over 50% of the seized farms were either unclaimed or neglected (Duri, 2014; Richardson, 2005). In addition, some of the outgoing white farmers either looted or damaged farming equipment and infrastructure thereby scuttling the prospects of economic recovery in the near future (Organisation for Economic Cooperation and Development, 2004). To aggravate the situation, many disinterested 'new farmers' and criminals looted property from unclaimed and underutilised farms. Some ZANU-PF supporters allegedly melted irrigation pipes and sold them as scrap metal or coffin handles (Godwin, August 2003).

The country became critically food-insecure as a result of these chaotic developments. The production of maize, groundnuts, cotton, wheat, soya beans, coffee and livestock sank drastically from 50% to 90% during the period 2000-2003 (Richardson, 2005). Communal maize production fell by 60%, from 1.091 million tons in the period 2000-2001 to 315 000 tons in 2003 (Ibid). As the production of basic food crops dwindled, the country began to depend on food imports from the year 2001 (*Reuters Alert*, 20 March 2007). In May 2003, the country had no official grain reserves and people in the rural and urban areas who had some disposable income formed long queues outside shops to purchase grain and maize meal at exorbitant prices (Church World Service, 24 July 2002).

Zimbabwe's foreign currency reserves increasingly became depleted as a result of the drastic fall in the production of export crops, investor flight, deindustrialisation and the country's isolation from the greater part of the international community (Raftopoulos, 2003; Richardson, 2005). As a result of foreign currency shortages, the government faced severe challenges when it came to the importation of food. In addition, revenue inflows (in the form of royalties and corporate tax) into government coffers dwindled considerably owing to investor flight and industrial closures. The government increasingly became bankrupt, and therefore incapacitated, to import basic commodities that were scarce thereby forcing the country to increasingly depend on donor agencies for food (United Nations, 11 September 2008).

Chronic hunger became part of life for many Zimbabweans. It should be noted, however, that the number of people on the verge of starvation tended to vary upwards or downwards over the years depending food supplies that were routinely availed by international donors and sometimes by the government. In May 2002, about 25% of Zimbabwe's 12 million people were starving (Flanagan, 26 May 2002). During the same month, food shortages reached critical levels in the Masvingo Province where more than two million people were urgently in need of food aid (Bara, 2 May 2002). By July 2002, an estimated 7.8 million people, including 5.4 million children, were faced with hunger (SMH, 12 July 2002). In September 2002, the United Nations reported that about six million Zimbabweans were in need of emergency food aid (Ruhanya, 9 September 2002). During the same month, child malnutrition resulting from severe food shortages was estimated at 8% countrywide (*Daily News*, 11 September 2002). By the close of 2003, approximately 6.7 million Zimbabweans were food insecure (Mushita and Mpande, 2003; Schrimpf and Feil, 2012). During the 2003-2004 season, five million Zimbabweans were critically food deficient (Amnesty International, October 2004; Solidarity Peace Trust, November 2004).

The limited quantities of food which the government managed to procure locally and abroad through the Grain Marketing Board

(GMB), a state-owned company with the sole monopoly to import and distribute grain supplies in the country, were often politicised as the ruling party privileged its supporters while famishing opposition sympathisers. While threatening opposition supporters in early 2002, Abednico Ncube, a ZANU-PF government minister, for example, said, "As long as you value the government of the day you will not starve...You cannot vote for the MDC and expect ZANU-PF to help you...You have to vote for ZANU-PF candidates...before the government starts thinking your entitlement to this food aid" (Meredith, 2002: 231). Also speaking in August 2002, at a time when an estimated 50% of Zimbabwe's population was in a state of starvation, Didymus Mutasa, a senior ZANU-PF politician, clearly articulated the government's position on the manner in which food aid was distributed: "We would be better off with only six million people, with our own people who support the liberation struggle. We don't want all these extra people" (Meredith, 2002: 231; Solidarity Peace Trust, November 2004: 2).

It was largely as a result of the government's ill-conceived Fast Track Land Reform Programme from the onset of the new millennium that Zimbabwe became critically food insecure as the staple maize and other basic commodities became scarce. Notwithstanding this, however, there is no doubt that droughts aggravated the food insecurity situation. The 2001-2002 drought, for example, was the worst to hit Zimbabwe in decades (*Reuters Alert*, 20 March 2007). It should be noted, however, that most of the evicted commercial farmers had the financial capacity to mitigate the disastrous effects of droughts though setting up irrigation schemes, among other initiatives. By the year 2000, Zimbabwe's commercial farmers had developed 80% of the continent's irrigation dams, with a total of 10 747 dams and reservoirs 3 910 square kilometres in extent (Freeth, 22 August 2016). These measures "enabled agriculture to become the most important economic sector, despite the country being prone to intermittent drought conditions" (Ibid, p.1). Despite the catastrophic effects of the so-called Fast Track Land Reform Programme, Mugabe's ZANU-PF government launched another disastrous agrarian scheme known as Operation *Maguta/ Sisuthi* in 2005 as it desperately sought to improve the food security situation as part of relentless efforts to restore its waning legitimacy and cling to power at any cost.

Operation *Maguta/Sisuthi* (2005-2006)

In November 2005, as the food crisis continued to worsen, the government launched a military-style agricultural programme known as Operation *Maguta* (in the Shona language) and Operation *Sisuthi* (in the Ndebele language), which literally means 'Eat Well' (Solidarity Peace Trust, April 2006). This agrarian initiative, which was to be funded by the government to the tune of Z$15 trillion (Solidarity Peace Trust, April 2006), projected to have 1 500 000 hectares of land under maize production during the 2005-2006 season and to produce 2 250 000 tonnes of maize (Mukaro, 28 January 2005; *Zimbabwe Independent*, 18-24 November 2005b). In addition, the programme aimed to produce 90 000 tonnes of tobacco, 49 500 tonnes of maize seed, 210 000 tonnes of cotton, 750 000 tonnes of horticultural crops and 8 250 tonnes of tea (Matonho, 24 November 2016; Mukaro, 28 January 2005; Solidarity Peace Trust, April 2006).

The scheme was primarily meant for rural small-scale farmers with the government supposed to loan each family household 300 kilogrammes of Compound D fertiliser, 200 kilogrammes of Ammonium Nitrate fertiliser and 25 kilogrammes of maize seed. The recipients were required to pay back after harvesting their crops at an interest rate of 50%, either in cash or in the form of produce through the GMB (Mudzonga and Chigwada, 2009).

Operation *Maguta* was jointly headed by the Ministers of Agriculture and Defence. The Agriculture and Rural Development Authority (ARDA), a government parastatal, the Agricultural Research and Extension Services (AREX), a department under the Ministry of Agriculture, together with personnel from the ZDF, the Zimbabwe Prison Services (ZPS), the ZRP and the CIO were directed to coordinate in improving the food security situation in the country. The government empowered these organs to identify land and farming equipment, supposedly underutilised, in various parts of the country and put them to productive use in order to boost agricultural output, particularly of the staple maize (Solidarity Peace

Trust, April 2006). Despite this arrangement, the army completely sidelined AREX and ARDA officials in the management of the scheme (Ibid). In February 2006, Gideon Gono, the then Reserve Bank Governor, actually eulogised the army for its involvement: "We applaud the Zimbabwe Defence Forces for taking up the challenge by strapping their guns on their backs and rolling up their sleeves to till the land under Operation *Maguta*" (*Chronicle*, 1 March 2006: 2). The involvement of the security sector in the programme signalled "the intensification of the militarisation of Zimbabwe, as the army now usurps control of food production" (Solidarity Peace Trust, April 2006: 15).

From November 2005, marauding soldiers, armed police details, ZPS officials and war veterans invaded commercial farms in various parts of the country such as Mwenezi and Chiredzi Districts and seized farming machinery, without compensation, supposedly on grounds that it was not being fully utilised (Phiri, 27 July 2006; *Zimbabwe Independent*, 13 January 2006). Some farms that had previously been grabbed from commercial white farmers and were not being fully utilised by the new farmers were also taken over by the army. Most of these farms were along the Harare-Mutare Highway and included Kondozi Farm, a property then famed for the production of flowers for the export market (Solidarity Peace Trust, April 2006).

In early 2006, in several parts of the country such as the rural irrigation plots in Matabeleland, soldiers forced small-scale farmers to sell all maize in excess of 100 kilograms, which they had harvested after using their own inputs prior to the launch of Operation *Sisuthi*, to the GMB, the state company with the sole monopoly to procure and distribute grain. The plight of the producers was exacerbated by the fact that the GMB bought the grain at below-market prices (Ibid). A fascinating irony that emerges from such moves lay in that, the government's miscalculated strategy to boost the country's food reserves in actual fact brought about a state of impoverishment, starvation and food insecurity among the majority of agricultural producers.

In August 2006, Didymus Mutasa, the then Minister of State Security, announced that resettled farmers were compelled to cultivate crops such as grain on their portions of land (Mabhena, 2013). In the communal areas of Matabeleland, for example, the army "commandeered irrigation schemes that were previously run by communities under the guidance of ARDA and AREX" (Ibid, p.10). In the Matabeleland South Province, for example, soldiers forced villagers in three irrigation schemes to produce maize and went on to destroy any other crops they were cultivating. In the Ngwizi Irrigation Scheme in the Plumtree District, "a well-established and flourishing paprika crop was ploughed under. Paprika is a lucrative export crop with a guaranteed market" (Ibid, p.17). In the Silalabuhwe Irrigation Scheme in the Insiza District, reported the Solidarity Peace Trust (April 2006: 17), "long established vegetable gardens … (were) totally destroyed. Tomatoes, spinach, sweet potatoes, groundnuts were forcibly ploughed under in December 2005, by the army. The army harvested anything salvageable from this action and ate it." On 14 December 2005, in the Makwe Irrigation Scheme in the Gwanda District, "men and women were forced to uproot banana trees and some fruit trees. There was a huge crop of vegetables, cabbages, carrots, spinach, sweet potatoes, pepper, paprika; all that was to be history in a few hours' time" (Mabhena, 2013: 60).

It is a fact that ZANU-PF's agrarian programmes had serious political considerations. It is not surprising that the ruling party's militant agrarian programmes were most brutally implemented in the Matabeleland provinces. "Since 2000," as Farai Shoko, a *Mail and Guardian journalist*, noted, "Matabeleland has been a stronghold for…Morgan Tsvangirai and his Movement for Democratic Change (MDC-T). In the 2008 parliamentary polls, Tsvangirai took Bulawayo and two-thirds of Matabeleland North and South."

The brutal and insensitive measures employed in the implementation of Operation *Maguta* severely ruined the market garden economies of many families in the rural areas countrywide. The destruction of the market gardening economy and the imposition of a monoculture in maize, for example, limited the survival options of many communities to the extent that some children in the Matabeleland provinces dropped out of school during early 2006 after their parents had failed to pay school fees (Solidarity

Peace Trust, April 2006). In April 2006, the Solidarity Peace Trust complained: "The destruction of productive market gardens can be viewed as part of the pattern of abuse of communities by government. The destruction of the economic base of these communities is either an act of unbelievable stupidity, or furtherance of a policy aimed at impoverishing rural communities as a means of controlling them" (Ibid, p.6). Furthermore, as the Solidarity Peace Trust also observed: "Plot holders now have to beg for the very maize they themselves have laboured to grow, and soldiers have the power to say yes or no" (Ibid, p. 6).

Soldiers allegedly brutalised villagers in various parts of the country after accusing them of being uncooperative. From December 2005 to March 2006, for example, there were nine recorded cases during which the army severely assaulted plot-holders in Matabeleland South Province (Solidarity Peace Trust, April 2006). One such case took place at Irrigation Scheme One and involved "an irrigation scheme committee member, who was summoned to a disciplinary meeting at the army camp and formally beaten; his crime - challenging at a public meeting the common sense in the army demanding that people work day and night to finish planting their fields" (Ibid, p.23). For speaking out against the army, the man "was forced to collect water for the soldiers, before being made to lie down and receiving five strokes with a stick. The beating was so severe that his leg remained numb three months later" (Ibid, p.24). A similar incident involved a woman in her fifties who was accused of "not…working hard enough" after which the soldiers flogged her in the face, "permanently damaging the metacarpal-phalangeal joint of the index finger of her hand when she tried to protect herself" (Ibid, p.24). At the Makwe Irrigation Scheme, "a lot of people who did not complete ploughing as per instruction were severely beaten, some had to be hospitalised" (Mabhena, 2013: 61). There is also abundant evidence that soldiers reportedly evicted some villagers from their homes while others were arbitrarily fined for not working enough to produce the targeted maize yield (Ibid).

Operation *Maguta* was indeed a form of "state-sanctioned slavery" (Phiri, 27 July 2006: 1). In January 2006, for example, military trucks drove into the Silalatshani Irrigation Scheme and a farm in

Insiza District that had been seized from a white farmer, and off-loaded farming equipment which included disc harrows and planters. The soldiers disembarked and went on to set up military bases in the area from where they forced local villagers to work on the irrigation scheme and the farm. Gift Phiri, a journalist of the *Zimbabwean* newspaper, described in vivid detail how the army coerced rural communities to cultivate the winter maize crop at the Silalatshani Irrigation Scheme in July 2006:

> It is the end of another long and hungry Friday. Insiza villager, Lydia Sibanda, was woken by a piercing siren just before dawn and force-marched by a team of soldiers to plough a winter maize field under sub-zero temperatures in an official programme termed Operation *Maguta*...She has no idea what price she will be paid for her efforts and the compulsory acquisition of the crop when it is ready for harvesting. In the late afternoon shed, conversations among the farm workers are punctuated by bitter complaints about the state-sanctioned slavery on Silalatshani Irrigation Scheme...Anger simmers but is kept in check by fear of roving soldiers supervising the impoverished farm workers. Some of her neighbours, wary of beatings and harassment by soldiers...send disapproving glances...Military men have set up camps...and are ordering them to grow mainly maize, the country's staple food. Teams of soldiers are forcing other farmers to plough up other crops such as onions, tomatoes and potatoes in other areas...Villagers at Silalatshani Irrigation Scheme in Insiza are being coerced by soldiers to weed a winter maize crop using very short hoes. Gun-toting soldiers would literally herd the farm workers, clad in tattered garb, with some of the armed forces poking fun at their subjects. The famished villagers, who are forced to start tilling the land at 6am, are denied water, and only get a break at 12pm for 'lunch,' which constitutes a plate of boiled vegetables and stale sadza. Reports that the soldiers were flogging 'defiant and lazy' farm workers using *sjamboks* could not be independently verified. But the forced labour gave a graphic illustration of the true horror of the army-led Operation *Maguta*, which is deliberately fostering a situation where notions of human decency are debased, and where this debasement is celebrated (Phiri, 27 July 2006: 1).

The Zimbabwean government failed to raise the Z$15 trillion needed to implement the ambitious programme (*Zimbabwe Independent*, 18-24 November 2005a). Consequently, soldiers often came with inputs such as seed and fertiliser late into the season. To make matters worse, the soldiers instructed villagers under the scheme not to plant crops before the government availed inputs (Solidarity Peace Trust, April 2006). Corruption was also rampant among state officials and in late November 2005, before the scheme had hardly taken off, 60% (Z$70.8 billion) of the Z$118 billion allocated by the government for agricultural inputs such as seed, fertiliser and diesel vanished before ever reaching the intended recipient farmers (Solidarity Peace Trust, April 2006; *Zimbabwe Independent*,18-24 November 2005b). The programme was also derailed by some farmers and senior state officials who abused the heavily subsidised agricultural inputs by selling them on the black market (Human Rights Watch, 2009; *Zimbabwe Standard*, 12 February 2006). A senior GMB official told the Human Rights Watch (2009: 16) that Operation *Maguta*, which was primarily meant for small-scale farmers, "had mainly benefited the ZANU-PF elite" and that "seed and stock were also used to buy off war veterans before the March 29, 2008 elections."

By January 2006, it had become apparent that Operation *Maguta* was a monumental failure. Masvingo Province, which was set to harvest 10 000 tonnes of maize, for example, only harvested 10 tonnes from the army-run Nuanetsi Ranch (Mukaro, 28 January 2006). In Manicaland Province, a mere 40 hectares out of a possible 224 hectares had been put under maize cultivation at Kondozi Estate after six senior government officials, including Didymus Mutasa, the then Minister of State Security, and Joseph Made, the then Minister of Agriculture, allegedly took away farming equipment from the estate (Ibid). In Mashonaland West Province, the prospects of a good harvest at Hunyani Farm waned owing to late planting (Ibid). Farmers' organisations predicted a countrywide maize harvest in the region of 600 000 to 800 000 tonnes, which translated to only 30% of the operation's target (Ibid). Predictably, 5.8 million rural Zimbabweans (Freeth, 22 August 2016), constituting approximately 52% of the population, were dependent on international donor agencies such as the World Food Programme (WFP), for maize in January 2006 (Solidarity Peace Trust, April 2006). Only 45 000 tonnes of tobacco, constituting around 50% of the projected yield, were delivered to the action floors (Mukaro, 28 January 2006).

Despite the implementation of Operation *Maguta/Sisuthi*, the 2006 maize harvest was 1.1 million tonnes against a human consumption demand of 1.4 million tonnes (Mudzonga and Chigwada, 2009). The critical shortage of basic commodities was compounded from June 2007 by a government directive which compelled manufacturers and retailers to slash the price of goods by 50%. This triggered serious nationwide shortages of staple foods and other basic commodities as the few remaining factories either scaled down or ceased production in defiance (*Zimbabwe Times*, 23 July 2008). In 2008, the country's maize yield was estimated at 575 metric tonnes, a 28% drop from the poor harvest of 2007 (Ibid; Human Rights Watch, 2009). Data released by the United Nations World Food Program (UNWFP) on Zimbabwe in October 2008 indicated that the proportion of people who had gone for a full day without eating anything had risen from 0% to 13%, while those who afforded only one meal a day shot up from 13% to 60% since 2007 (Dugger, 22 December 2008). During the same month, the UNWFP stated that more than two million people were desperately in need of food relief (*Zimbabwe Situation*, 16 October 2008). In January 2009, more than 75% of Zimbabweans were living in abject poverty (Nsingo, 20 January 2009). During the same month, approximately 30% of Zimbabwean children under the age of five years were undernourished (Human Rights Watch, 22 January 2009; Nsingo, 20 January 2009). Between January and March 2009, over 5.1 million people needed emergency food assistance (Tarisayi, 2009). For the greater part of the first decade of the new millennium, maize was unavailable in most shops and where it was available at the black market, it was charged against the United States dollar. In November 2008, for example, a 20-kilogramme bucket of maize-meal cost US$20 at a time when teachers were earning an average of US$4 per month (Human Rights Watch, 22 January 2009).

It was not surprising that in late September 2006, Joseph Made, the then Minister of Agriculture, admitted that Operation *Maguta* had flopped (*ZimOnline*, 2 October 2006). The government, however, officially abandoned the operation in May 2010 (Ndlovu, 30 May 2010). The reasons for the failure of Operation *Maguta/Sisuthi* are quite apparent as history has shown. As Mbago Sithole (10 February 2012: 1), a Zimbabwean economic analyst, aptly put it: "It does not matter how good a policy is. If the implementation model is wrong, the benefits may be very limited." The Institute of Public Affairs in Zimbabwe (30 March 2017: 1) reiterated: "Economic transformation cannot be achieved through sheer militarism and the Goliathan logic of force." It was a "tried and failed, Stalinist farming system" (Matonho, 24 November 2016: 1). Having been coerced, abused and brutalised, rural communities had no enthusiasm to produce surplus grain for the GMB. Thus, as Mabhena (2013: 56) observed, command agriculture is "one of those top-down rural development models that fail to recognise local knowledge in development planning."

Targeted Command Agriculture (2016-2017)

The Targeted Command Agriculture was an agricultural programme announced by the Zimbabwean government in August 2016 (*Pindula*, 2016). Its main purpose was to boost agricultural production, starting from the 2016-2017 season. The agrarian programme was necessitated by the alarming food insecurity situation which had deteriorated from an estimated 12% in 2011 to 42% in early 2016 (Matonho, 24 November 2016). This dispensation, which had its roots in the farm invasions from 2000, and the inability and incapacity of the government to adequately address the inexorable food crisis, was aggravated by persistent droughts. The drought that was experienced during the 2014-2015 season, for example, wiped out 50% of Zimbabwe's maize crop (*Thomson Reuters Foundation*, 18 January 2016). During the next season, an El Nino-induced drought ravaged the whole country, with the most hit areas being the historically drought-prone Regions 4 and 5 in the provinces of Masvingo, Matabeleland North and Matabeleland South. Even Regions 1, 2 and 3 in the provinces of Mashonaland that traditionally received considerable rains were adversely affected (Government of the Republic of Zimbabwe, 2016). By February 2016, the maize crops in many parts of the country had wilted with 75% having been written off in Masvingo Province and 65% in Matabeleland South Province (Ibid). The situation became so desperate that on 4 February 2016, President Mugabe declared a State of Drought Disaster (Ibid). As a result of the El Nino weather pattern, the number of rural families without adequate food in the most drought-hit areas shot up from 30% in June 2016 to 79% three months later in August (Nicholson, September 2016). By September during the same year, an estimated 4.5 million people were food insecure (Ibid).

During the initial phase of the Targeted Command Agriculture scheme, the government identified 2 000 farmers near water bodies who had the capacity to cultivate a minimum of 200 hectares of maize per individual. Each farmer was obliged to harvest at least 1 000 tonnes of maize of which five tonnes per hectare were to be surrendered to the government as part of repayment of loans that had been advanced to cover costs of irrigation equipment, seed, fertiliser, chemicals, mechanised equipment, electricity and water. The farmers were allowed to retain surplus maize in excess of the mandatory 1 000 tonnes (*Pindula*, 2016).

From the onset, the Institute of Public Affairs in Zimbabwe (30 March 2017: 1) expressed concern at the militarisation of the agricultural programme:

> Our concern is the implication of the logic of all things 'command.' Our argument is very simple: the rush into things all 'command' will trigger a descent into militarism and this poses grave consequences for our pernicious walk to a democratic polity. Command economy will place into the hands of the security network such enormous political and economic power through bureaucratic usurpation and the net effect is to render irrelevant if not totally displace the constitutional republic. A country in which the security establishment is the centrepiece of economic production is nothing short of a military dictatorship with a civilian face. The question is: to whom and how will the men and few women in uniform with artillery and grenades account to? ...This reveals the actual operation of how a command economy will be run.

Even though Command Agriculture was administered by the office of Vice-President Emmerson Mnangagwa, the military was actively involved in its implementation with Perence Shiri, the then Air Force Commander, as the head of the programme (Mhlanga, 14 August 2017). The scheme was, therefore, another "Stalinist project" (*Zimbabwe Standard*, 26 March 2017: 1). In June 2017, Constantino Chiwenga, the then ZDF Commander, castigated Professor Jonathan Moyo, the then Minister of Higher and Tertiary Education, for criticising the programme. Chiwenga justified his involvement in civilian issues arguing that food self-sufficiency is critical to national security (Kwaramba, 28 June 2017). In August 2017, Lieutenant-General Phillip Valerio Sibanda, the then Zimbabwe National Army (ZNA) Commander, confirmed that more than 1 000 soldiers had been deployed to various parts of the country to supervise Command Agriculture (Mhlanga, 14 August 2017).

During mid-2017, soldiers were reportedly deployed to monitor the harvesting of maize produced under the scheme in an attempt to prevent some quantities being sold on the parallel market. The military personnel also went round Command Agriculture farms to ensure that farmers did not hold on to their crops (Kanambura, 22 August 2017). Nine Lieutenant-Colonels and 65 Majors from the ZNA, together with other senior ZDF officials, were dispatched countrywide to oversee the harvesting process. Among other things, they reportedly inspected the moisture content of grain and ensure that maize with a moisture content of 12.5% minimum level be harvested and delivered to the GMB (Ibid). Thus, according to Tendai Biti, a former Finance Minister, Command Agriculture was "a commandist securocratic project" (Manayiti and Mushava, 2 July 2017: 1).

In mid-2017, the Zimbabwean government was celebrating an estimated countrywide maize harvest of 1.8 million tonnes, a 300% increase from the 2016 yield of 512 000 tonnes (*Xinhua News*, 16 February 2017). By August 2017, 450 000 tonnes of maize had been delivered to the GMB as compared to only 145 000 the previous year (*African Farming*, 7 August 2017). The Commercial Farmers' Union of Zimbabwe also announced that the country had adequate food supplies for the year 2017 (Ibid). It should be noted, however, that the significant increase in the country's food reserves had little to do with the producer prices set by the GMB. In fact, it was during the 2016 agricultural season that the GMB increased the maize producer price from US$235 to US$390 per tonne (Commercial Farmers Union of Zimbabwe, 24 February 2017). During the 2017 agricultural season, when the Targeted Command Agriculture Programme was being implemented, the producer price of maize remained unchanged at US$390 per tonne (Ibid; *Zimbabwe News Online*, 23 February 2017).

It is indeed a fact that Zimbabwe's food security situation improved considerably during the 2016-2017 farming season, but the reasons for such a development are debatable. It is being argued that the significant improvement in the agricultural yield during the 2016-2017 season cannot largely be attributed to the Targeted Command Agriculture Programme, even though the scheme was implemented in a relatively less brutal manner than Operation *Maguta/ Sisuthi*. This is because the Targeted Command Agriculture initiative was fraught with numerous irregularities that severely compromised the attainment of its intended projections. Most irrigation systems where the scheme was implemented were either in an advanced state of dilapidation or dysfunctional (*Zimbabwe Standard*, 26 March 2017). In February 2016, while appealing for international donor funding and food aid, the Zimbabwean government acknowledged that the country desperately needed US$273 650 000 for emergency irrigation infrastructure rehabilitation (Government of the Republic of Zimbabwe, 2016). In March 2017, when the harvesting season had begun in many parts of the country, Chimimba David Phiri, the Head of the Food and Agricultural Organisation (FAO) in Southern Africa, acknowledged the pathetic state of Zimbabwe's irrigation infrastructure:

> The history of Zimbabwe is very interesting; there are a number of irrigation schemes that were created, but most of these schemes have gone into ruin either because of siltation over a long period of time, lack of maintenance, or irrigation equipment itself that needs to be changed (*Voice of America News*, 21 March 2017: 1).

There were also numerous reports of rampant looting of agricultural inputs by the ruling elite (*Zimbabwe Standard*, 26 March 2017). In early 2017, Professor Jonathan Moyo, the then Minister of Higher Education, revealed that US$500 million was used to plant only 153 000 hectares out of the targeted 400 000 hectares, implying that the programme achieved less than 50% of its targeted output (Institute of Public Affairs in Zimbabwe, 30 March 2017). This also meant that another US$500 million found its way "down the throats of…networked elites" (Ibid, p.1). Investigations by *The Zimbabwe Standard* (26 March 2017) also confirmed that while the target of the programme was to put 400 000 hectares under maize production, less than 200 000 hectares had been cultivated. It is in this context that in July 2017, there were allegations that the Zimbabwean government smuggled maize into the country "to cover up for the Command Agriculture flop" (*Zim Eye*, 21 July 2017: 1). There were reports that a GMB depot in Murehwa received a consignment of maize of between 50 and 70 thirty-tonne trucks from Mozambique during mid-July 2017 despite the government having banned the importation of the commodity in February (Ibid).

It, therefore, becomes apparent that the government's claim of a bumper harvest was largely based on the yields of agricultural producers from outside the Command Agriculture schemes. The good harvest from these producers can largely be attributed to above-average rainfall in most parts of the country during the 2016-2017 season (*Zimbabwe Standard*, 26 March 2017). The 2016-2017 season was the first since 1999 during which Zimbabwe experienced good rains (Latham and Marawanyika, 1 February 2017). In fact, most areas across the country received "higher than normal rainfall" during the 2016-2017 season (*Voice of America News*, 21 March 2017: 1). Mangwe District, in the historically drought-prone Matabeleland South Province, for example, had received an average rainfall of 400 millimetres midway into the 2016-2017 season, unlike the past two years during which a total of only 344 millimetres were recorded (Makawa, 19 January 2017). In February 2017, John Mangudya, the Governor of the Reserve Bank of Zimbabwe, actually acknowledged that the good rains were largely responsible for the boost in agricultural productivity which the country was experiencing (*Xinhua News*, 16 February 2017).

Conclusion

This chapter has demonstrated that militarist machinations by the state, as was the norm in Zimbabwe during Robert Mugabe's rule, frustrate the prospects of sustainable economic development in general and food security in particular. Instead, governments can create an enabling environment for economic growth through legislation, tax and duty regimes, subsidies and infrastructural developments that facilitate and spur the production and marketing of goods. Efforts by the state to uphold the rule of law and guarantee the security of people and property also contribute significantly in bringing about a conducive environment for development.

Command agricultural systems contradict business-oriented models of farming and entrepreneurship and compromise production trajectories. Governments need to integrate individual/family farming and agro-business (commercial farming) interests in their development plans. Command agriculture is a retrogressive development that failed dismally wherever it was attempted since historic times. Such statist development schemes by the Zimbabwean government, besides being futile, were a manifestation of historical ignorance which can be likened to rushing into a wilderness where others were running away from.

As Zimbabwe's agrarian tragedy has revealed, commandist agricultural programmes were initiated by politicians and largely implemented by the military. Politicians should administer the country and generate a conducive environment that incentivises and propels economic development. The military should be confined to the barracks and stick to their constitutional mandate of defending the country in times of external threats. Various sectors of the economy should be voluntarily driven productively, competitively and sustainably by small-scale and large-scale entrepreneurs with the expert advice of relevant technocrats.

References

African Farming (7 August 2017) 'Maize deliveries hit 450 000 tonnes in Zimbabwe,' Available at: www.africanfarming.net, Accessed 7 September 2017.

Alexander, J. (2003) 'Squatters, veterans and the state in Zimbabwe,' in: B. Raftopoulos, A. Hammar and S. Jensen (eds.) *Zimbabwe's unfinished business: Rethinking land, state and nation in the context of crisis*, Harare: Weaver Press, pp.83-117.

Alexander, J. and McGregor, J.A. (2001) 'Elections, land and the politics of opposition in Matabeleland,' in: *Journal of Agrarian Change*, Volume 1, Number 4, pp.510-533.

Alvarez, A. (2001) *Governments, citizens and genocide: A comparative and interdisciplinary approach*, Indiana: Indiana University Press.

Amnesty International (5 April 2004) 'Zimbabwe: Attacks on farm workers and their children must end now,' Available at: www.africafiles.org/article, Accessed 13 September 2017.

Amnesty International (October 2004) *Zimbabwe: Power and hunger - Violations of the right to food*, London: Amnesty International.

Bara, E. (2 May 2002) 'Zimbabwe's famished fields,' Available at: http://news.bbc.co.uk/2/hi/africa/1964548.stm, Accessed 15 May 2017.

Bond, P. and Manyanya, M. (2001) *Zimbabwe's plunge: Exhausted nationalism, neoliberalism and the search for social justice*, Asmara: Africa World Press.

Brinkley, J. (2011) *Cambodia's curse: A modern history of a troubled land*, New York: Public Affairs.

Cartledge, P. (2002) *The Spartans: An epic history*, London: Pan Macmillan.

Chibber, K. (26 July 2014) 'Zimbabwe's economy needs stabilising,' Available at: www.qz.com, Accessed 3 June 2015.

Chitekwe-Biti, B. (2009) 'Struggles for urban land by the Zimbabwe Homeless People's Federation,' in: *Environment and Urbanisation*, Volume 21, Number 2, pp.347–366.

Chitiyo, T.K. (29 April 2007) 'Colonial legacy of Zimbabwe's land disputes: Reconceptualising Zimbabwe's land and war veterans' debate,' Available at: www.africaresource.com, Accessed 6 October 2015.

Chronicle (1 March 2006) 'Grain imports gobble US$131 million,' Bulawayo: Zimbabwe.

Church World Service (24 July 2002) 'Zimbabwe drought,' Available at: www.churchworldservice.org, Accessed 16 May 2015.

Commercial Farmers Union of Zimbabwe (24 February 2017) 'Maize producer price unchanged,' Available at: www.cfuzim.org, Accessed 5 April 2018.

Cross, E. (4 February 2004) 'Fat cats feed on Zimbabwe's misery,' Available at: www.eddiecross.africahead.com, Accessed 28 July 2015.

Daily News (11 September 2002) 'Hunger takes toll in Zimbabwe's rural schools,' Harare: Zimbabwe, Available at: http://www.africafiles.org/article.asp?ID=562, Accessed 15 May 2017.

Democratic Kampuchea (August 1977) *Democratic Kampuchea is moving forward*, Phnom Penh: Democratic Kampuchea.

Duffy, J. (1961) *Portuguese Africa*, Cambridge: Cambridge University Press.

Dugger, C. W. (22 December 2008) 'In Zimbabwe, survival lies in scavenging,' in: *New York Times*, Available at: http://www.nytimes.com, Accessed 15 May 2017.

Duri, F. P. T. (2014) 'Linguistic innovations for survival: The case of illegal panning and smuggling of diamonds in Chiadzwa, Zimbabwe (2006-2012)' in: *Africana*, Volume 7, Number 1, pp.41-60.

Financial Gazette (26 July- 1 August 2007) 'Price blitz devastates Zimbabwe's rural economy,' Harare: Zimbabwe.

Flanagan, J. (26 May 2002) 'Starving children scavenge for berries as famine sweeps Zimbabwe,' Available at: http://www.telegraph.co.uk/news/worldnews, Accessed 15 May 2017.

Forrest, W.G. (1968) *A history of Sparta, 950-192 BC*, New York: Norton.

Freeth, B. (22 August 2016) 'Command Agriculture: The latest plan to resolve Zimbabwe's hunger problem,' Available at:

http://www.thezimbabwean.co, Accessed 21 June 2017.

Friedman, E. (1983) 'After Mao: Maoism and post-Mao China,' in: *Telos*, Volume 65, pp.23-46.

Global Security (5 June 2016) 'Stalin 1928-1933: Collectivisation,' Available at: http://www.globalsecurity.org, Accessed 21 June 2017.

Godwin, P. (August 2003) 'A land possessed,' in: *The National Geographic Magazine*, pp.100-114.

Gough, K. (1986) 'Roots of the Pol Pot regime in Kampuchea,' in: *Contemporary Marxism*, Number 12/13, pp.14-48, Available at: http://www.jstor.org/stable/29765842, Accessed: 23 June 2017.

Government of the Republic of Zimbabwe (2016) *2016-2017 Drought disaster domestic and international appeal for assistance*, Harare: Government of the Republic of Zimbabwe.

Hammar, A. and Raftopoulos, B. (2003) 'Zimbabwe's unfinished business: Rethinking land, state and nation,' in: A. Hammar, B. Raftopoulos and S. Jensen (eds.) *Zimbabwe's unfinished business: Rethinking land, state and nation in the context of crisis*, Harare: Weaver Press, pp.1-47.

History Place (1999) 'Genocide in the 20th century: Pol Pot in Cambodia, 1975-1979,' Available at: http://www.historyplace.com/worldhistory/genocide/pol-pot.htm, Accessed 21 June 2017.

Human Rights Watch (8 March 2002) 'Fast-track land reform in Zimbabwe,' Available at: www.hrw.org/reports, Accessed 14 September 2017.

Human Rights Watch (2009) *Crisis without limits: Human rights and humanitarian consequences of political repression in Zimbabwe*, New York: Human Rights Watch, Available at: www.hrw.org/report, Accessed 16 May 2017.

Hunt, P. (1997) 'Helots at the Battle of Plataea,' in: *Historia: Zeitschrift fur Alte Geschichte*, Volume 46, Number 2, pp.129-144.

Institute of Public Affairs in Zimbabwe (30 March 2017) 'Command agriculture: Descent into undisguised militarism,' Available at: https://www.theindependent.co.zw, Accessed 21 June 2017.

Isaacman, A. and Isaacman, B. (1985) *Mozambique: From colonialism to revolution, 1900-1982*, Harare: Zimbabwe Publishing House.

Jackson, K.D. (1978) 'Cambodia 1977: Gone to Pot,' in: *Asian Survey,* Volume 18, Number 1 pp.76-90, Available at: http://www.jstor.org/stable/2643186, Accessed 23 June 2017.

Kanambura, A. (22 August 2017) 'Command Agriculture: Government ropes in soldiers,' in: *The Daily News,* Harare: Zimbabwe.

Krkljes, S. (March 2017) 'Cambodian genocide,' Available at: http://worldwithoutgenocide.org, Accessed 20 June 2017.

Kueh, Y.Y. (2006) 'Mao and agriculture in China's industrialisation: Three antitheses in a 50-year perspective,' in: *The China Quarterly,* Number 187, pp.700-723, Available at: http://www.jstor.org/stable/20192660, Accessed 23 June 2017.

Kwaramba, F. (28 June 2017) 'Chiwenga after Jonathan Moyo,' in: *The Daily News,* Harare: Zimbabwe.

Latham, B. and Marawanyika, G. (1 February 2017) 'Zimbabwe farms, still reeling from drought, now battered by rain,' Available at: www.bloomberg.com/news/articles, Accessed 9 September 2017.

Long, N.V. (1988) 'Some aspects of cooperativisation in the Mekong Delta,' in: D.G. Marr and C.P. White (eds.) *Post-war Vietnam: Dilemmas in socialist development,* Ithaca: Cornell University Southeast Asia Programme, pp151-176.

Mabhena, C. (2013) 'Command Agriculture: Local knowledge and external development models in rural Zimbabwe - The case of the Makwe Irrigation Scheme,' in: *IOSR Journal of Humanities and Social Science,* Volume 12, Issue 2, pp.56-64.

MacFarquhar, R. (1983) *The origins of the cultural revolution, Volume 2, The Great Leap Forward, 1958-1960,* Royal Institute of International Affairs: Columbia University Press.

Makawa, T. (19 January 2017) 'Heavy rains and floods in Zimbabwe destroy dam and irrigation infrastructure, likely to impact two million people,' Available at: www.wvi.org/africa/article, Accessed 8 September 2017.

Mamdani, M. (2008) 'Lessons from Zimbabwe,' in: *London Review of Books,* Volume 31, Number 23, pp.17-21.

Manayiti, O. and Mushava, E. (2 July 2017) 'Command Agriculture fiasco: Zimbabwe's own version of state capture,' Available at: www.thestandard.co.zw, Accessed 8 September 2017.

Masunungure, E. (2004) 'Travails of opposition politics in Zimbabwe since independence,' in: D. Harold-Barry (ed.) *Zimbabwe: The past is the future: Rethinking land, state and nation in the context of crisis*, Harare: Weaver Press, pp.147-192.

Matonho, T. (24 November 2016) 'Land invasions hinder modernisation of Zimbabwe farms,' in: *The Newsday*, Harare: Zimbabwe.

Meldrum, A. (21 March 2003) 'Zimbabwean soldiers attack farm workers,' Available at: www.theguardian.com/world, Accessed 13 September 2017.

Meredith, M. (2002) *Mugabe: Power and plunder in Zimbabwe*, New York: Public Affairs.

Mhlanga, B. (14 August 2017) 'Army confirms aiding Command Agriculture,' in: *The Newsday*, Harare: Zimbabwe.

Moyo, S. (September 2000) 'The interaction of market and compulsory land acquisition processes with social action in Zimbabwe's land reform,' Paper presented at SAPES Trust annual colloquium, Harare.

Mudzonga, E. and Chigwada, T. (2009) *Agriculture: Future scenarios for Southern Africa: A case study of Zimbabwe's food security*, Winnipeg: International Institute for Sustainable Development.

Mugabe, R. (2001) *Inside the Third Chimurenga*, Harare: Ministry of Information and Publicity.

Mukaro, A. (28 January 2006) 'Operation *Maguta* a flop,' in: *The Zimbabwe Independent*, Harare: Zimbabwe, Available at: https://www.theindependent.co.zw, Accessed 21 June 2017.

Munslow, B. (1983) *Mozambique: The revolution and its origins*, London: Longman.

Mushita, T.A. and Mpande, R.L. (2003) 'Linking food security, relief, rehabilitation and development by civil society institutions in Southern Africa,' in: *Masvingo Workshop Report*, Germany: Diakonie Emergency Aid (DEA).

Mydans, S. (17 April 1998) 'Death of Pol Pot: Brutal dictator who forced Cambodians to killing fields, dies at 73,' Available at:

http://www.nytimes.com, Accessed 21 June 2017.

Ndlovu, Q. (30 May 2010) 'Government abandons *Maguta*,' in: *The Zimbabwe Standard*, Harare: Zimbabwe, Available at: http://www.cfuzim.org/index.php/agriculture, Accessed 24 June 2017.

Newitt, M. (1981) *Portugal in Africa: The last hundred years*, Essex: Longman.

Nicholson, P. (September 2016) 'Failed harvests in Zimbabwe caused by El Nino,' Available at: www.caritas.org, Accessed 22 May 2017.

Nsingo, E. (20 January 2009) 'Zimbabwe now a factory of poverty,' Available at: http://www.ipsnews.net, Accessed 16 May 2017.

Organisation for Economic Cooperation and Development (OECD) (2004) *African economic outlook 2003-2004: Country studies: Zimbabwe*, Paris: OECD.

Peace Pledge Union Information (PPUI) (1975) 'Cambodia 1975,' Available at: http://www.ppu.org.uk/genocide/g_cambodia.html, Accessed 20 June 2017.

Phiri, G. (27 July 2006) 'Operation *Maguta*: State-sanctioned slavery,' Available at: http://www.thezimbabwean.co, Accessed 21 June 2017.

Pilossof, R. (1 December 2010) 'The Commercial Farmers' Union of Zimbabwe (CFU) and its politics after *jambanja*,' Available at: http://solidaritypeacetrust.org/897, Accessed 21 June 2017.

Pindula (2016) 'Command Agriculture 2016,' Available at: http://www.pindula.co.zw, Accessed 22 June 2017.

Raftopoulos, B. (2003) 'The state in crisis: Authoritarian nationalism, selective citizenship and distortions of democracy in Zimbabwe,' in: A. Hammar, B. Raftopoulos and S. Jensen (eds.) *Zimbabwe's unfinished business: Rethinking land, state and nation in the context of crisis*, Harare: Weaver Press, pp.217-41.

Raymond, C. (2008) 'No responsibility and no rice: The rise and fall of agricultural collectivisation in Vietnam,' in: *Agricultural History*, Volume 82, Number 1, pp.43-61, Available at: http://www.jstor.org/stable/20454780, Accessed 23 June 2017.

Reuters Alert (20 March 2007) 'Zimbabwe says drought will worsen food shortages,' Available at: www.alertnet.org, Accessed 16 February 2017.

Richardson, C.J. (2005) 'The loss of property rights and the collapse of Zimbabwe,' in: *Cato Journal*, Volume 25, Number 3, pp.541-565.

Roberts, A. (1986) 'Portuguese Africa,' in: J.D. Fage and R. Oliver (eds.) *Cambridge History of Africa Volume 7 from 1905 to 1940*, Cambridge: Cambridge University Press.

Ruhanya, P. (9 September 2002) 'Depoliticise food aid, Catholic bishops say,' in: *The Daily News*, Harare: Zimbabwe, Available at: http://www.africafiles.org/article.asp?ID=562, Accessed 15 May 2017.

Sachikonye, L. (2003) 'The situation of commercial farm workers after land reform in Zimbabwe,' Report prepared for the Farm Community Trust of Zimbabwe, Harare: Farm Community Trust of Zimbabwe.

Schrimpf, B. and Feil, P. (2012) *Traditional food crisis coping mechanisms: A regional perspective from Southern Africa*, Stuttgart: Diakonisches Werk der EKD.

Shoko, F. (26 July 2013) 'Poll swing vote rests in Matabeleland,' Available at: https://mg.co.za/article, Accessed 5 April 2018.

Sithole, M. (10 February 2012) 'Land reform: Where did ZANU-PF go wrong?' Available at: http://www.thezimbabwean.co, Accessed 10 September 2017.

SMH (12 July 2002) 'Theft, prostitution on rise as hunger bites Zimbabwe,' Available at: www.smh.com.au, Accessed 19 May 2015.

Solidarity Peace Trust (November 2004) *No war in Zimbabwe: An account of the exodus of a nation's people*, Johannesburg: Solidarity Peace Trust.

Solidarity Peace Trust (April 2006) *Operation Taguta/Sisuthi: Command Agriculture in Zimbabwe: Its impact on rural communities in Matabeleland*, Johannesburg: Solidarity Peace Trust.

Spense, C.F. (1951) *The Portuguese colony of Mozambique*, Cape Town.

Tarisayi, E. (2009) 'Voting in despair: The economic and social context,' in: E.V. Masunungure (ed.) *Zimbabwe's 2008 elections*, Harare: Weaver Press, pp.11-24.

Thomson Reuters Foundation (18 January 2016) 'Baobab, food aid on the menu as drought bites,' Available at: www.newzimbabwe.com/NEWS, Accessed 19 May 2017.

Tran, S,T, (2016) 'Slavery: The main ingredient in an ancient Greek polis' military dominance,' Paper presented at the *Young Historians Conference*, Portland State University, 28 April 2016, Available at: www.pdxscholar.library.pdx.edu/younghistorians, Accessed 10 May 2017.

Truth Seeker (18 January 2007) 'Zimbabwe, the land of dying children,' Available at: http://www.thetruthseeker.co.uk/?p=5946, Accessed 21 June 2017.

Tsiko, S. (22 January 2017) 'Good rains bring hope,' in: *The Sunday Mail*, Harare: Zimbabwe.

United Nations (11 September 2008) 'Southern Africa: Mozambique-Zimbabwe: The commodities life line,' Available at: www.allAfrica.com, Accessed 22 April 2017.

Vickerman, A. (1986) *The fate of the peasantry: Premature transition to socialism in the Democratic Republic of Vietnam*, New Haven: Yale University Southeast Asia Studies.

Voice of America (31 December 2009) 'Zimbabwe military deploys to remove country's remaining white farmers,' Available at: www.voazimbabwe.com, Accessed 10 June 2015.

Voice of America News (21 March 2017) 'Civic group: Above normal rainfall in Zimbabwe not worth cheering,' Available at: www.voanews.com, Accessed 8 September 2017.

Volin, L. (1951). 'Soviet agricultural collectivism in peace and war,' in: *The American Economic Review*, Volume 41, Number 2, pp.465-474, Papers and Proceedings of the 63rd Annual Meeting of the American Economic Association (May 1951), Available at: http://www.jstor.org/stable/1910821, Accessed 26 June 2017.

Wedlund, S. (2008) 'Stalin and the peasantry: A study in red,' in: *Scandia*, Available at: www.scandia.hist.lu.se, Accessed 26 June 2017.

Xinhua News (16 February 2017) 'Zimbabwe forecasts maize output to triple after good rains,' Available at: www.news.xinhuanet.com/english, Accessed 8 September 2017.

Yang, D. (1996) *Calamity and reform in China: State, rural society and institutional change since the Great Leap Famine*, Stanford: Stanford University Press.

Zim Eye (21 July 2017) 'Mnangagwa smuggles maize into Zimbabwe to cover up for Command Agriculture flop,' Available at: www.zimeye.net, Accessed 7 September 2017.

Zimbabwe Human Rights NGO Forum (2010) *The land reform and property rights in Zimbabwe*, Volume 1, Harare: Zimbabwe Human Rights NGO Forum.

Zimbabwe Independent (9 January 2004) 'Four years on, land reform still marred by chaos,' Harare: Zimbabwe.

Zimbabwe Independent (18-24 November 2005a) 'Army launches Operation *Taguta*,' Harare: Zimbabwe.

Zimbabwe Independent (18-24 November 2005b) '60% government agricultural funds disappear,' Harare: Zimbabwe.

Zimbabwe Independent (13 January 2006) 'Farming for the military,' Harare: Zimbabwe.

Zimbabwe News Online (23 February 2017) 'Zimbabwe's Grain Marketing Board sets buying price for maize at 390 USD a tonne,' Available at: https://www.zimbabweonlinenews.com, Accessed 5 April 2018.

Zimbabwe Standard (12 February 2006) 'Top chefs exposed: 66 000 litres diesel for former CIO boss,' Harare: Zimbabwe.

Zimbabwe Standard (26 March 2017) 'Command Agriculture story yet to be told,' Available at: www.thestandard.co.zw, Accessed 6 September 2017.

Zimbabwe Situation (16 October 2008) 'War veterans block donation,' Available at: www.zimbabwesituation.com, Accessed 19 May 2017.

Zimbabwe Times (23 July 2008) 'Mozambique tightens screws on Zimbabwe,' Available at: www.thezimbabwetimes.com, Accessed 12 June 2015.

ZimOnline (2 October 2006) 'Zimbabwe: Agriculture minister admits food shortage,' Available at:

http://reliefweb.int/report/zimbabwe, Accessed 21 June 2017.

Chapter 15

Reproductive Health Vulnerabilities and Insecurities in Africa: Reflections on the Practices of Indigenous Family Planning Methods and the "Modern" Contraceptives in the Tshivenda Culture of Zimbabwe

Kilibone Choeni; Silibaziso Mulea & Munyaradzi Mawere

Introduction

Globalisation and westernisation have impacted negatively and positively on the lives of many people in Africa and the Global South in general. Zimbabwe and its indigenous communities have not been spared either as the aforementioned 'forces' take their toll across the continent. While many spheres of life of the Zimbabwean communities have been impacted upon, in this chapter we solely focus on the traditional methods of contraception among the Vhavenda (also known as Venda or Vhangona) people. The deployment of traditional methods of contraception in contemporary ethnic Vhavenda people remains a thorny issue, especially in the face of globalisation, westernisation, and the health political economy of the so-called modern trends of family planning that has adversely retrogressed the belief and faith in traditional Venda family planning methods by its cultural bearers. As such, it behoves one to build a narrative around this discourse of traditional methods for the non-use of traditional methods by the Vhavenda whether by design or choice as a trajectory to traditional family planning methods apathy among the Venda people as shall be revealed in this chapter.

Issues related to tradition are inexorably complex to address in their entirety in one chapter, since they usually involve histories, emotions, sociological, demographic and cultural dynamics and complexities. It is no secret among the Vhavenda that traditional family planning methods together with family planning is a private issue that cannot be debated at will because of cultural taboos that promotes secrecy and confidentiality of traditional methods of family planning. Just like copyright laws, Venda methods of family planning too belong to the custodian of that culture such that it is not everyone who gets to know about these methods without first consulting specialists who in this case are the Venda people themselves.

The Venda culture is one of the so-called minority cultures and hence, marginalised and less researched cultures in Zimbabwe. This is in spite of the fact that the Venda culture is one of the richest cultures on the land. For this reason, among others, it is important to exert concerted effort to single out and interrogate those traditions that are at the core of the Vhavenda culture. This is premptory given that the culturally diverse and historically embedded communities of Africa like the marginalised and minority Venda traditions of family planning have always been put to test and sometimes challenged by the current forces of globalisation and westernisation. In fact, the traditional methods of contraception is one such tradition that since the advent of colonialism has been subjected to criticism, subjugation and sometimes outright rejection by the state – both the colonial state and the post-colonial state (Mudede 2005). In post-colonial African states such as Zimbabwe, the subjugation and attempts to do away with traditional methods of contraception have been a result of the smearing and caricaturing of the African indigenous ways of life.

In the face of such a dispensation, many indigenous Africans have found themselves in a dilemma on the direction they should take when it comes to the issue of family planning methods. Worse still, women around the continent as elsewhere continue with their urge to control both the number of children and timing of births. This reality leads us to the gist of this research which is to ascertain the vulnerabilities and insecurities surrounding the so-called modern trends of family planning. In order to avoid tragedies and health hazards – such as cancer, high blood pressure, weight gain and sometimes prolonged infertility – brought about by the deployment of modern family planning methods such as jadel, oral contraceptive, the loop and injection, Venda traditional family planning methods become necessary.

On the other hand, the Vhavenda traditional methods of family planning have been shown to be user-friendly to both men and women as shall be revealed later in this chapter. Traditional methods such as *u vhalela maḓuvha* (the menstrual cycle rhythm methods), *u maimisa ṅwana zwa tshifhinga tshilapfu* (Protracted breastfeeding), and *u vhofha mabundu* (tying notes) will be discussed at length on their perceived advantages and supposedly shortcomings (if any). However, the dilemma casted on their way by both the modern methods of family planning and the Venda people's perpetual thirsty to continue using traditional methods of contraception which the owners believe to come without cost, cheap and readily available, hold back their family planning aspirations. In fact, modern trends of family planning methods come with a cost of travelling to the hospital or clinic, buying from a pharmacy or over the counter, and known side effects.

That said, this chapter explores indigenous contraceptives used by the Vhavenda people in Zimbabwe and other African communities. The chapter argues that the pejorative labelling and bastardisation of traditional family planning methods of the indigenous people of Africa as a result of globalisation and westernisation is not only nefarious but a crime against the people of Africa and the Vhavenda in particular. There is need for the restoration and effective use of traditional family planning methods on the premise that the practices are not only indigenous but less costly mostly safe to use and complementary to modern methods. On this note, the present chapter serves to awaken and conscientise the Venda women and other women in the African communities to resort back to their roots the Sangofa way, particularly where their cultures and traditional ways serve best.

The chapter adopts the Vhavenda culture as its case study. It was largely informed by the use of interviews with traditional healers and elderly women of the Venda culture. The study also benefitted from various sociological and anthropological perspectives on Africa. Other sources of information like the Zimbabwe National Family Planning Council and the Ministry of Health on Reproduction Health and some historical approaches like oral tradition were used. The findings of this study in general are that birth control is considered a sensitive and contentious issue which should be context-based considering the religious and traditional influences involved thereof in many African cultures such Venda, among others.

The historiographic account of the Vhavenda culture

The history of the Vhavenda people is both long and complex. It is complex because of the heterogeneous groupings such as Vhangona and Vhambedzi (who are believed to be original inhabitants of the area inhabited by the Venda people), Masingo (who are believed to originally come from Congo) and other groupings believed to have originally come from the Rift Valley (see Alliance Francaise 2007).

Today, the Vhavenda people whose culture is also known as Vhavenda are mainly found in northern South Africa and southern Zimbabwe. In both South Africa and Zimbabwe, the Vhavenda people are one of the minority groups. Their language is known as Tshivenda.

According to history, the Vhavenda though predominantly found in Zimbabwe and South Africa, have some remnants available in the Democratic Republic of Congo, where these people are believed to have originated from (Alliance Francaise 2007; Siyabona Africa 2017). As Alliance Francaise (2007) tells us, the Vhavenda were originally from either the Congo or the Great Rift Valley, migrating across the Vhembe (Limpopo) River during the Bantu expansion.

There is however another school of thought that attests that Vhavenda originated from the Mapungubwe Kingdom. According to Siyabona Africa (Ibid), the history of the Vhavenda starts from the Mapungubwe Kingdom. According to this school, historical studies reveal that king Shiriyedenga was the first King of Venda and Mapungubwe. From either 119 A.D or 800 A.D, the Mapungubwe Kingdom emerged and stretched across the Limpopo River to the Matopos in the north. The Mapungubwe Kingdom declined from 1240 and the centre of power and trade moved north to the Great Dzimbabwe Kingdom, where it was believed to have better climate conditions.

In present day Zimbabwe, the Vhavenda people are concentrated in the Beitbridge District along the Limpopo River. Their boundary stretches from Beitbridge town to Tshiloñwe, which is on the eastern side of the town, to the western side up to Zezani though there are some few Vhavenda in Mberengwa, Mwenezi and Gwanda districts. In South Africa, the Vhavenda are found on the North and West of Makhado in the Limpopo Province of South Africa (Rakhadani 2007). Their territory is totally surrounded by the Republic of South Africa (R.S.A), but in the north only a thin strip of land separate it from the Limpopo River forming its boundary with the Kruger National Park of the R.S.A magisterial district of South–East of Gazankulu. In the West, the R.S.A magisterial district of Southpansberg and Messina are its neighbours.

The reproductive health traditions and practices of the Vhavenda people

At any given time, increasing the uptake of traditional family planning medication is critical to enable women and their partners to meet their fertility goals and to reduce unmet needs for family planning. However, fears of the unknown, misconceptions or misinformation and side-effects (actual or perceived) of methods are common barriers to the adoption and contribution of traditional family contraception. The fears, misconceptions and misinformations are observable in many communities such as that of the Vhavenda of Beitbridge where according to Zimstats (2002), the total unmet need for spacing and waiting births was estimated at almost 12 %. This reflects a sizable proportion of the population that is not meeting its fertility goals. Instead, people rely on their traditional family planning methods. The main traditional methods used in the Vhavenda communities of Beitbridge include abstinence, withdrawal, rhythm (safe phases of menstrual cycle), protracted breast feeding, traditional snuffing, waist tied charms and traditional pool washings. Below, we explain some of these methods as they are used by the Vhavenda people.

351

U vhalela maḓuvha (the menstrual cycle rhythm method)

In the Venda culture, this method involves the woman counting five days after every menstrual cycle of the month to avoid falling pregnant. The five days after menstrual cycle are normally considered safe for sex as ovulation will have naturally taken place. This method usually was preferred by couples who loathed using contraceptive rites or other methods due to religious inhibitions imposed by Christianity or simply by virtue of being allergic to some traditional contraceptive medicine found in this milieu. According to Russo (2015), the rhythmic method is also known as the calendar method, it works by predicting the days in which a women is most fertile. To use this technique, a woman must chart her menstrual history for several months in order to anticipate the dates in which she is ovulating.

U mamisa ṅwana zwa tshifhinga tshilapfu (protracted breastfeeding)

The Venda people believe that breast feeding the baby for a long period of time prevents the mother from entering menstruation and thus not getting pregnant. It is believed that no matter how many sexual encounters a woman performs, as long as the baby is breastfeeding continually, the mother cannot get pregnant until then and when she stops breastfeeding (Mudede 2014). The Venda, thus, traditionally use breastfeeding as a birth control method.

U sa ṱangana lwa tshifhinga tshilapfu (partial abstinence)

The other family planning method traditionally used by the Venda people is partial abstinence. Traditionally, partial abstinence among the Venda people was physically enforced by strict separation of man and wife. At minimum, they were to sleep in separate beds, preferably in separate rooms. Normally, if there was only one bed, the husband would sleep on it and the wife sleep on a mat with her child/children. Sometimes, the woman's mother would move in for two or three years and act as a sentinel (guard) to keep watch on her daughter and son-in-law. Often, this would drive the husband away, either to go hunting or look for a job in faraway places. In other instances, the new mother herself was asked to return to her parental home and remain there throughout the nursing period. Even longer period of abstinence would be ruled in special circumstances such as the birth of *malwelavanḓa* (twins), still birth or spontaneous abortion.

Why traditional family planning methods are preferred by the Vhavenda women?

Traditional family planning methods of the Vhavenda people are a category of traditional practices. As such, they are part and parcel of Vhavenda culture which shape their lives now and in the future. These methods are handy and user-friendly not only for the elite traditionalists like grandmothers but even for the younger so-called modern generation. To gather information for this research, we interviewed traditional leaders, elderly women and women in the reproductive age group who mentioned a variety of child spacing methods. Six child spacing methods were identified along with reasons why their users preferred using them. These methods were menstrual cycle rhythm method, withdrawal system, protracted breast feeding, partial abstinence and contraceptive rites, particularly the *uṱhuṱha tshiṱaka* (Jumping over a small shrub by a woman) and *U vhoṱha mabundu* (tying notes). We discuss these in some detail in the ensuing sections.

a). U vhalela maḓuvha (the menstrual cycle rhythm method)

Many Vhavenda women, especially the old generation use the menstrual cycle rhythm method as a traditional way to help control their births. During our researches, one woman revealed how and why she use menstrual cycle rhythm method for her family planning, thus:

I am a women aged thirty years and I use the traditional family planning method of u vhalela maḓuvha (the menstrual cycle rhythm method). What I usually do is that I count five days after every menstrual cycle of the month to avoid falling pregnant. I chart my menstrual history for several months in order to anticipate the dates in which I am ovulating. Though the method is effective record keeping is careful required. This means that I have to be upbeat and up to date with the knowledge of my menstrual cycle period so as to have sex with my partner without getting pregnant, failure to follow this routine defeats my plan of the family planning technique. I prefer this method because its natural and has no side effects as it does not involve the use of herbs. What I have to do is that I follow my menstrual cycle dates religiously.

b). U mamisa ṅwana lwa tshifhinga tshilapfu (protracted breastfeeding)

Traditionally, the Venda women also use protracted breastfeeding as a method for family planning. In an interview carried out by one of the authors of this chapter with an elderly woman, Gogo Mwatsila, who used protracted breastfeeding as a family planning method during her [sexually] active days revealed thus:

u vhalela maḓuvha (the menstrual cycle rhythm method) is a very effective method because I used the method for almost the rest of my life and I have eight children who have been well spaced and spread in two year intervals. When I breastfeed the baby for a long period of time I don't experience my menstrual cycle period and thus I won't get pregnant. No matter how many sexual encounters I perform, as long as the baby is breastfeeding continually, I cannot get pregnant until then and when I stop breastfeeding. The method is very safe and reliable.

c). U ḓidzima lwa tshifhinga nyana (partial abstinence)

As was narrated by one elderly Venda woman, an eighty-five year old, Gogo Tondila, partial abstinence is also one other traditional method of family planning used by the Venda people. As reported by Gogo Tondila, Venda women usually breastfed their children for 2 to 4 years. During these 2 to 4 years, the mother and father were not allowed to be intimate. Whenever the wife was forced by her husband to be intimate, the later would be called before the Village Chief and publicly punished, for this was an abomination. During all this time, the wife and husband were normally not allowed to sleep in the same quarter. This was to avoid the temptation of intimacy. Talking from her own experience as a woman, Gogo Tondila:

I am a women aged eighty-five years and during my time of giving birth my husband and I we used this kind of family planning. Traditionally, this method of family planning would dictate that a woman could not have another pregnancy after child birth for 3 to 4 years. Famine and the threat of wars in the old days made us to be more cautious about having babies too closely together. Since there were no calendars, elders looked for certain signs of development which indicated the child was ready to be weaned. These signs included the ability of the child to walk on his own, to say a few words, and to obey simple commands.

d). Contraceptive rites

i). Ufhufha tshiṱaka (Jumping over a small shrub by a woman)

Contraceptive rites were also a common method of family planning among the Venda women. After giving birth, it is said that through the instruction of a Vhomaine (traditional healer), the mother goes to a certain shrub which the Vhomaine directed her. The mother would then jump over the shrub from either side. When the woman feels that she now wants another child she will go to the same shrub and jump on from the opposite side she jumped previously. Once she does this, the woman would be pregnant again. The problem with this method is that there is a possibility of finding the tree cut down or grown to an extent that she may not be able to jump over it. In these circumstances, the woman would not be able to conceive up until she revisits the Vhomaine for assistance.

ii). U vhofha mabundu (tying notes)

Tying notes was another traditional method of family planning commonly used by the Venda people. As narrated by the traditional healer known as Vhomaine Sengani on the 21ˢᵗ of February 2018 during our interview with her:

U vhofha mabundu involved tying a belt known as (ludede) in Tshivenda with medicine laced inside would be worn around the new mother's waist to prevent pregnancy. If the mother wants to space her children with three or four years difference it means she is going to tie three or four notes on the belt. It depends on what I would have prescribed as a Vhomaine (traditional healer).

The method appears mythical, but is said to have been very effective as a traditional family planning method. Aninyei (2008) highlights that culture includes many myths rituals and the use of herbs in attempts to regulate women's fertility. As further noted by Aninyei (Ibid), although many of these traditional methods of family planning have no harmful effects on woman's health, some however do have dangerous or counterproductive effects if instructions given by the traditional healer are not followed properly the same way modern methods of contraception operates.

In addition, the complete effectiveness of some of the traditional methods of the Venda people has remained doubtful among the Vhavenda and the world in general to some extent partly because of westernisation and also because some of the Vhavenda do not religiously follow instructions as to their proper use. The latter normally render the traditional methods of family planning useless and bound not to work.

Further, we note that understanding barriers to fertility regulation is important for periodic programming guidance in relation to the provision of traditional Venda family planning services such as tying notes. Although previous research on the Vhavenda culture (Mudede 2005) has theoretically identified negative perceptions of traditional contraception as reasons for none-use, this chapter is more practical and evidential. It sought to build evidence base for the perennial use of the Vhavenda family planning methods and deploy these to further expose the complexities surrounding family planning discourse as well as factors that may influence decisions for method choice.

In order to successfully build the evidence base for the perennial deployment of the Vhavenda family planning methods among the Vhavenda communities, this study employed various methods like in-depth interviews with key members of the target population especially men and women aged between 25 years to 50 years in the Beitbridge area. This age group was targeted as such on account of the fact that they are still in the active reproduction group. However, few group discussions (FGDS) were deployed to explore shared normative perceptions among current users and non-users of traditional methods of family planning. More interest was accorded to the personal experiences of the current users and also past users (women aged over 50) of commonly available traditional methods of family planning methods among the Vhavenda communities like abstinence, withdrawal and rhythm (safe phases of the menstrual cycle).

Family planning and the resilience of traditional methods of birth control in Vhavenda culture

The tradition of spacing births is not an alien practice to Vhavenda people. It is imprinted in its historical antecedence and narrative that long before the influx of Western ideas, the understanding of the importance of child spacing to maternal and infant health was wide spread in this culture.

Great demand for Venda traditional family planning was buoyed by the intermittent wars and famine, a common nemesis in the Vhavenda community. The Vhavenda did not want to give birth in war and famine times due to obvious reasons. The people have no gardens, seeds to plant and food to eat in times of war and famine, such that giving birth was discouraged to retard child mortality, strain on hungry breast feeding mothers and feared exponential population growth that adversely contributed to competition for the little scarce resources available (Pathfinder 1978). These are some of the reasons why the Vhavenda were highly motivated to practice family planning. According to Oso (2002), previous studies show that knowledge of traditional contraceptive methods is an important determinant of contraceptive use. Hence, a wide range of indigenous Venda traditional knowledge on family planning contraceptives is revealed and well-endowed by villagers and traditional leaders alike till today among the Vhavenda.

Despite the unavailability of "modern" contraceptives in the pre-colonial period, an array of techniques was developed to enforce taboos on fertility behaviour. Of course there is no way to document demographically the effectiveness or even the prevalence of such contraceptives in the past among the Vhavenda due to lack of documented records. Nevertheless, the fact that these procedures had their roots in deep-set ethnic traditions has indicated to many that they were not only widespread but perhaps more effective, hence their continued use. This means that the current mish-mash of broken traditions and poorly understood innovations does not in any way inhibit the survival and use of Venda family planning methods. The underlying message here is that those introducing the so-called modern family planning methods must not ignore the inherent traditions of child-spacing that capitalise on that tradition to enhance both the voluntary acceptance, appreciation, and the continual use of both traditional and modern methods of family planning.

The impact of globalisation and westernisation on the Vhavenda traditional family planning methods

Globalisation (as with westernisation) on its own brought in a lot of changes in Africa. Among its lot, is none other than Western methods of birth control like barrier methods, for example, condoms, cervical cap, hormonal methods, pill, implantable devices, permanent birth control methods and emergency contraception. Most if not all these methods have brought more harm than good to many women in the African society. In societies such as the Venda, traditional family planning methods have been caricatured as traditional, backward, mystic and pagan, yet all these are misrepresentations and misconception of some traditions and methods which worked well for their respective communities.

This part of the discourse strives to grapple with the gist of misconceptions and attitudes displayed by the Vhavenda people with regard to traditional family planning methods and as a result of the confusion brought about by the advent of globalisation. Western birth control methods certainly tore the Vhavenda family planning world into two: that which follow traditional methods of birth control and that which follow modern methods of family planning. However, Western methods seem to have triumphed over traditional methods if Zimbabwe's family planning records are anything to go by. According to UNIFEM Report (2008), Zimbabwe ranks among the top African countries that uses modern methods of family planning.

As such, since the Vhavenda live in Zimbabwe they too are represented in that ranking. Considering this fact, it is apparent therefore that, their traditional family planning methods have been overtaken by modern methods. If this situation is allowed to continue, the Vhavenda people's traditional family planning methods are bound to be blown into oblivion and eventually become extinct for generations to come. This calls for efforts to salvage and preserve them now by both family planning stakeholders like Zimbabwe National Family Planning (ZNFP) and the Vhavenda people themselves. The latter holds the honours of reviving the culture of traditional family birth control since they hold indigenous knowledge in this field.

In view of the above, it is peremptory to note that although globalisation is often mistaken as an exclusively economic phenomenon, it is obvious that, "humans on all frontiers are being forced either to shift their ideational systems radically and quickly or to live in a thought-world that no longer fit the way their world is" (Keesing and Keesing 1971: 346). Indeed, the so-called "primitive" people like the Vhavenda were not as untouched by change as they had initially been thought of. Their old age generational practices such as traditional birth control have been heavily impacted on as globalisation and in particular westernisation and capitalism continue impacting the world.

According to the Capitalists World Theory, capitalism is seen as a world of labour system that "provides the frame work for the measurement of social inequalities on world scale" (Beck 2000: 30). As such, the developing countries such as Zimbabwe have been made to believe that anything local or African (and therefore "traditional") is inferior and has to be doubted at all cost. This however, is cheap propaganda propagated by the super-rich capitalistic World countries in Europe and the Americas to maintain their 1st world capitalistic status. One way of achieving such status is through advocating the use of modern birth control in the guise of improving economic development, mortality rate and lowering the fertility rate (Mudede 2014; Fortney 1982; Haddock and Kincosto

2008). While the idea seems to be noble, we argue that demystifying, stigmatising and labelling traditional family planning methods of African people such as the Vhavenda as bad and outdated is not good either. This is done solely to force and forge a place for modern birth control methods in Africa.

Modern family planning methods have been suspected by Mudede (2014) to be a deliberate ploy by the Western countries to reduce the African populace so that it cannot become a direct threat to the West, economically, ideologically and politically owing to Africa's voluminous populations. This could be true given that countries like Nigeria, China, Singapore and Bangladesh are strong economic giants owing to their high population that provide cheap sources of abundant labour. Africa has about one billion people versus a total sum of seven billion world population (UN 2010). As urged by Malema and Mudede (2014), Africa should triple its populace to enforce its ideologies and reduce its generational gap. However, according to these aforesaid politicians-cum-academics, modern birth control methods of the West like G.E.D have cancerous side-effects to women, side-effects that are not found in traditional family birth control (Cleland *et al* 2006; Swigh *et al* 2009). Thus, one of the reasons why we argue for the revival and use of traditional methods of birth control among the Venda and other such African communities is that these methods have been in use since time immemorial without any noted major side-effects.

Delano (quoted in Hogan *et al* 2010) has observed that, traditional methods of family planning had been handed down either verbally or in writing from generation to generation as far as the Stone Age era. However, in the Venda communities, the efficacy of these methods remain poorly recognised in the face of modern trends of family planning due to several factors like religion, political interference, lack of education and lack of enlightenment and consciousness of traditional culture with regard to family planning.

Religion – Christian Influence

The influence of missionaries such as the Evangelical Lutheran Church and the Roman Catholic as an arm of modernisation, has had a mixed impact on the progress of family planning tradition in the

Venda community. Some churches such as the Lutheran are actively teaching modern contraception (Vho Luthuri, Lutumba Area, 13 September 2017). Others such as the Roman Catholics tend to see contraception as "sinful and an interference with the will of God" (Pathfinder Paper 2007). For example, at one Sermon in the Catholic Church in 2016 in Beitbridge, a Roman Catholic Pastor asked rhetorically: "Is it not a sin to control fertility? Is it not against the will of God?" Issues to do with religion demonstrate the seriousness of power that the church doctrine wields over Venda traditional family planning methods but still that does not stop the Venda men and women from using their traditional family planning methods. This is so simply because Christianity comes after tradition and culture in rural Venda communities. One particular chief, Vho Thovhele Tshitaudze, of Beitbridge East on his inauguration at Mpande village on the 14th of June 2017 emphasised the above fact by saying "Venda siyalala" (culture comes first to a muvenda).

Moreso, use of herbs and contraceptive rites as traditional birth control measures is frowned upon and discouraged by the church as heathen and pagan practices that do not work at all (Chavhunduka 2002). If one is contravening the doctrine of the church in African communities such as the Vhavenda by engaging in traditional practices of family planning, the only position one may find him or herself in is none other than excommunication from the church because some religious groupings like the Catholics arbore the use of contraceptives such as condoms and let alone traditional family planning methods of which some of them involve the use of medicinal traditional herbs that are labelled as pagan by the church. Most of the Christians who arbore the use of contraceptives believe strongly in the book of Genesis 1: 28 (King James Version) of the Bible which says people should replenish the earth and not control the reproduction of children as they are a gift from God.

Why the Vhavenda are scared to use modern birth control methods?

There are many reasons why most of the Vhavenda women are scared to use modern birth control methods and instead prefer traditional birth control methods. Some of the modern birth control methods that the Vhavhenda expressed concern on are captured in the narratives here below.

Oral contraceptive (the pill)

One Venda woman interviewed during a health talk at a Sate lite Clinic of Duvlivhadzimu on the 18th of December 2017 revealed:

> After using contraceptive pill methods of family planning for about two years, she has been trying to conceive to have her second born child but to no avail. The pill also deform my body structure as you can see I have a big body, I used to weigh 60 kgs but now I weigh 120 kgs and I am no longer attractive to my husband. This is because of the modern trends of family planning.

Another woman echoed "I also used the pill but I am experiencing a very tough time because most of the time my head will be aches continuously".

Shot/Injection

A Venda woman in a health talk group discussions held at Mashavire shops by the ministry of health personnel on 24 September 2017 revealed thus:

> *At age twenty-five I am happy because someone is doing research on these modern types of family planning. I use the injection as a method of child spacing, the problem is that I am in severe pain because most of the time I cannot get into my menstrual cycle. Then after that my stomach expands a little bit and I become shapeless. Sometimes I bleed between periods. Besides that the injection is so painful to an extent that when I think that the period of the injection has expired and I have to have another short stress of attacks me.*

Jadel

Venda women we interviewed during this research complained that when the "no plant" is inserted, it is often the case that after three years – when the plant is to be removed –, they will have gained more weight. Because of an increase on weight, many women face the challenge that when the time comes for the "no plant" to be removed, it could not be located. This causes a lot of harm – both emotional and physical – as medical doctors often try in vain to locate the no plant on one's wrist.

Recommendations

This chapter has demonstrated the continued wide use and efficacy of traditional birth control in Zimbabwe, among the Vhavenda communities and other such African communities. Despite the fact that these (traditional methods of birth control) are still suffering prerogative labelling and stigma from Western countries and a particular segment of Christian African communities, these methods have proven to very resilience and efficient. The continued use of traditional contraceptive methods has been confirmed by the respondents interviewed by the researchers and authors of this chapter, who in fact admitted and pin pointed the use and relevance of traditional family planning methods even in the advent of modern day family planning trends adopted by some women in the Vhavenda community. From this vantage point and observations made during research, we have argued in this chapter that traditional methods of birth control remain critical and sometimes even more efficient than modern family planning methods.

Given that traditional methods of birth control remain an integral part of many people in Zimbabwe (and even beyond), we recommend that the Zimbabwean government should promote and support the use of traditional methods of contraception in women healthcare, just as traditional medicine should be to modern scientific drugs. This is important considering that traditional family planning methods are safe and cost effective.

The promotion of the use of traditional family planning methods could be done and achieved by fostering education, through advocacy and campaign of the benefits of using some of the traditional methods of birth control because they save resources, time and energy given that they are tapped and resourced locally. Traditional family planners can be registered as qualified healthcare givers or experts who can competently help people in their local communities. On this note, we recommend that different religious sects and the community at large be educated on the efficacy of traditional birth control, most of which have been successfully used since time immemorial. We draw the government's attention to the fact that besides being safe, use-friendly and cheap, inadequate birth control and reproductive health skills among health organisation providers, long distance to health facilities and other cultural beliefs are some of the contributing factors that have made people to continuously use and heavily rely on traditional methods of birth control. The fact that people trust that even in the presence of modern ways of birth control, they can use traditional ones means that traditional methods of birth control are equal to and sometimes even more helpful than modern method of family planning.

Conclusion

Basing on the data harvested during this research, we conclude that different types of Vhavenda traditional family planning methods remain a mystery to be uncovered. The methods need to be meticulously researched and documented so that future generations benefit for these traditional methods of birth control, which from the research we carried out, are use-friendly, safe, cheap and effective. Failure to document these traditional family planning methods, especially in the face of globalisation and westernisation will always impact negatively on the future generations, who in no doubt would be deprived of enjoying the fruits and richness of their cultural heritage.

While the Zimbabwean government has so far taken significant strides towards the direction of researching and documenting indigenous knowledge systems – such as traditional family planning methods – through the formation of Cultural Midwifery Associations and Traditional Healers Association that issue out practicing licenses to registered traditional family planners and traditional practitioners, a lot more is still desired to be done. In fact, there is still need for documentation of traditional methods of family planning used to prevent child mortality, unwanted pregnancy, and sexual transmitted diseases in the exception of HIV.

References

Allen, R. H. (2007) The role of family planning in poverty reduction. Obstetrics and Gynaecology,

Alliance Francaise. (2007) Vhavenḓa culture, http://www.alliance.org.

Bernstein, S. and C. J. Hansen. (2006) Public Choices, Private Decisions: Sexual and Reproductive Health and the Millennium Development Goals. New York: United Nations Millennium Project.

Becker, S. and Ahmed, S. (2001) Dynamics of contraceptive use and breastfeeding during the postpartum period in Peru and Indonesia, *Population Studies,* 2001.

Blanc, Ann K. and Amy O. Tsui. (2005) "The dilemma of past success: Insiders' views on the future of the international family planning movement," Studies in Family Planning.

Bongaarts, John and Steven Sinding (2011) Population Policy in Transition in the Developing

World. Science.

Cleland, John, Stan Bernstein, Alex Ezeh, Anibal Faundes, Anna Glasier, and Jolene Innis. (2006)

"Family Planning: The unfinished agenda," The Lancet.

Delano, G. (1990) *Guide to Family Planning,* New Edition, Ibadan, Spectrum Books: Nigeria.

Gillespie, D., Ahmed, S., Tsui, A., & Radloff, S. (2007) Unwanted fertility among the poor: an inequity? *Bulletin of the World Health Organisation,* WHO.

Griffin, S. (2006) *Literature review on Sexual and Reproductive Health Rights: Universal Access to service, focusing on East and Southern Africa and South Asia,* Irvington, New York.

Hatcher, R. A. (1989) *Contraceptive Technology,* Irvington, New York.

Hensaw, S. K. and Morrow, E. (1990) *Induced Abortion: A World Review Supplement,* Alan Guttmacher Institute, New York.

May, J. F. (2012) *World Population Policies: Their Origin, Evolution and Impact*, New York:

Springer-Verlag.

World Bank. (2004) A Review of Population, Reproductive Health, and Adolescent Health &

Development in Poverty Reduction Strategies, *The Population and Reproductive Health*

Cluster Health, Nutrition and Population Central Unit, The World Bank: Washington, DC.

Siyabona Africa (2017) 'Venda African tribe', Kruger National Park: South Africa, Retrieved on the 27/03/2018 from https://www.google.co.zw/images?

www.ingramcontent.com/pod-product-compliance
Lightning Source LLC
Chambersburg PA
CBHW060022030426
42334CB00019B/2138